Fair Isle

The Archaeology of an Island Community

Fair Isle

The Archaeology of an Island Community

J R Hunter

The National Trust for Scotland

EDINBURGH: HMSO

First published 1996 by
HMSO, South Gyle Crescent, Edinburgh, EH12 9EB

British Library Cataloguing in Publication Data

A catalogue record for this book is available from the British Library

This book is published with grant assistance from

HISTORIC SCOTLAND

ISBN 0 11 495750 9

Contents

ACKNOWLEDGEMENTS

THE main archaeological survey of Fair Isle was undertaken by the author, Steve Dockrill, Alan Brooke, Nick Card, Steve Thompson and Pat Thomson, with help from Andy Addison, Sue Cotton, Gerry McDonnell, Jacqui McKinley and Val Turner. Site illustrations were drawn by Anna Chudecka and the distribution maps by Miranda Schofield.

Both the survey and the writing up were generously supported by the Russell Trust, the Shetland Amenity Trust, the Royal Commission on the Ancient and Historical Monuments of Scotland, the Society of Antiquaries of Scotland, the Department of Archaeological Sciences, Bradford University, and the owners of the island, the National Trust for Scotland.

A number of individuals provided invaluable support during the project, notably Alexander Bennett, Richard Seligman and Robin Turner from the National Trust for Scotland, Noel Fojut from Historic Scotland, Val Turner from the Shetland Amenity Trust, and pilot Edmund Bewley. The author would also like to acknowledge the encouragement and advice of Brian Smith, Julie Bond and Lyn Turner in the preparation of the text. During the programme many individuals offered advice and expertise on various topics: particular thanks are due to Mike Baillie, Jean Brown, Paul Cheetham, Anne Bloch Jorgensen, Phillip Rahtz, Valerie Thom and Diana Webster.

On the island itself, a particular debt of gratitude is owed to Pat and Neil Thomson, and to Ann Sinclair for their advice, practical help and encouragement throughout. None of this work would have been possible without the friendship, hospitality and interest of the entire island community to whom many thanks are given, and of whom many fond memories are stored.

Author's Preface

IN 1984 the writer and a small group of colleagues commenced a systematic sites and monuments survey of Fair Isle. This lasted for four seasons and was followed by a further season of small exploratory excavations in 1989. The purpose was to play some part in a long-overdue assessment of Shetland's archaeological potential and to provide a yardstick for future work. During the earlier part of the survey it became rapidly clear that the project was developing away from the straightforward sites and monuments approach that characterises most archaeological databases, and towards a broader perception of Fair Isle's development over the centuries.

True, monuments were recorded to follow from the earlier work of CST Calder in Shetland, and relict landscapes – features which Alasdair Whittle has shown to be Shetland's greatest archaeological asset – were duly surveyed and plotted. But there was far too much relevant information, not only on the ground where continuity was amply evidenced but also recorded in documents and literature, for prehistory to be given an artificial and abrupt end. Ethnographic data alone of the type collated so variously and comprehensively by Alexander Fenton provided another resource. On Fair Isle where traditions have been protected by insularity, ethnography seemed particularly apposite. Furthermore, a procession of visitors to the islands from the 17th to 19th centuries provides complementary documentation, some more vivid, some more biased than others. And so the survey expanded from one originally geared to the clinical identification of field monuments such as mounds, boundaries and cairns – the bread and butter of traditional SMRs – to embrace, *inter alia*, post-medieval settlement, animal husbandry, boat construction and water mills. In an island sufficiently remote from other landfalls, where captive economic resources have remained largely unchanged and where traditions have become moulded by a combination of insularity and necessity, any distinction between the so-called archaeology of prehistory and the so-called history of the 19th century becomes fairly arbitrary.

The result can be viewed in one of two ways, either as a contribution to the general understanding of Shetland archaeology through the ages within a North Atlantic context, or as a free-standing holistic investigation into the archaeology and history of a small settlement community over several millennia. The former provides Shetland with a wider definition of its archaeology and the latter, with no intended disrespect to Gilbert White, provides a sort of archaeological *Natural History of Selbourne.*

The book is divided into a series of chapters on a broad chronological base, but only in as much as the subject areas can be conveniently split, and a degree of overlap is inevitable. Some 750 sites were originally recorded, including post-medieval fields and military remains from the Second World War; these are all listed in detail in numerical order in an appendix at the end of the volume. The same numerical sequence is used for cross-reference purposes in the text.

On a more personal note, the experience of pulling the various threads together has been unnerving; I have entered fields of which I knew (and probably still know) very little, and have no doubt stuck out my neck in places where I would have been better advised to leave well alone. But the subject matter seemed to demand otherwise, and the more I tried to harness the various disciplines that together make it possible to understand places, populations and the passage of time, the more I realised how polarised our efforts are becoming. The need for integration and cross-reference among the disparate elements of study is over-riding; attempting this was against my better judgement, but satisfying nonetheless.

JRH
Birmingham, April 1995

INTRODUCTION

The wind and tide was contrary, the night coming on and a mist forming on top of the isle. I was seized with a strong fear, as if the Lord was going to cast us away ...

THE Reverend John Mill, from whose diary this is extracted (Goudie 1889, 11), was on route to Fair Isle on board a Dutch fishing vessel in order to carry out his peripatetic preaching duties in 1753. Mill was a hardened seafarer but on this occasion thought it prudent to discuss 'pious topics' with the boatman; he also insisted on being set down at a little used harbour rather than prolonging the voyage to the island's customary landing place. He arrived safely nonetheless and his record, in common with those of many other travellers and traders over the centuries, played a small part in moulding the oral and written traditions which surround the island's hostile geography. In clear weather Fair Isle is visible from both Orkney and Shetland, although reaching it was ironically more perilous and unpredictable than many more distant voyages of the day. By Mill's time the island had already developed a perceived remoteness and an aura of primitiveness had surrounded its inhabitants. Even the *First Statistical Account* of the later 18th century was able to draw comparison between Fair Isle and a south sea island (*OSA* XIX, 433). Unfortunately this folklore became perpetuated by early map makers who for practical reasons found the island either too small or geographically too isolated to fit on the same map as adjacent island groups: Timothy Pont's *c* 1605 map of Shetland which appears later in Blaeu's *Atlas* places Fair Isle in the page margin; Seller's 1671 *English Pilot* merely locates its position; and Kitchin's 1751 map manages to obscure it completely with the depiction of a fishing scene. Of all the early maps Mackenzie's *Orcades* (1752) alone covers it in any detail. His portrayal of the coastline is fairly accurate by early modern standards, and the landscape depicts a modicum of historically useful features including a major east-west earthen boundary that bisects the island, and even a few place-names (plate 1.1).

Travellers' descriptions and historical references of the 18th and 19th centuries abound with images of an island peripheral in a social as much as a geographical sense, where the inhabitants – the 'wild people' alluded to by a shipwrecked Armada sailor of 1588 (Ker 1920, 172) – are invariably described as 'natives'. A late 19th century source denoted them as having a look of 'savage apathy' (Vetch 1882) and Sir Walter Scott himself was tactfully euphemistic over apparent incest from his visit

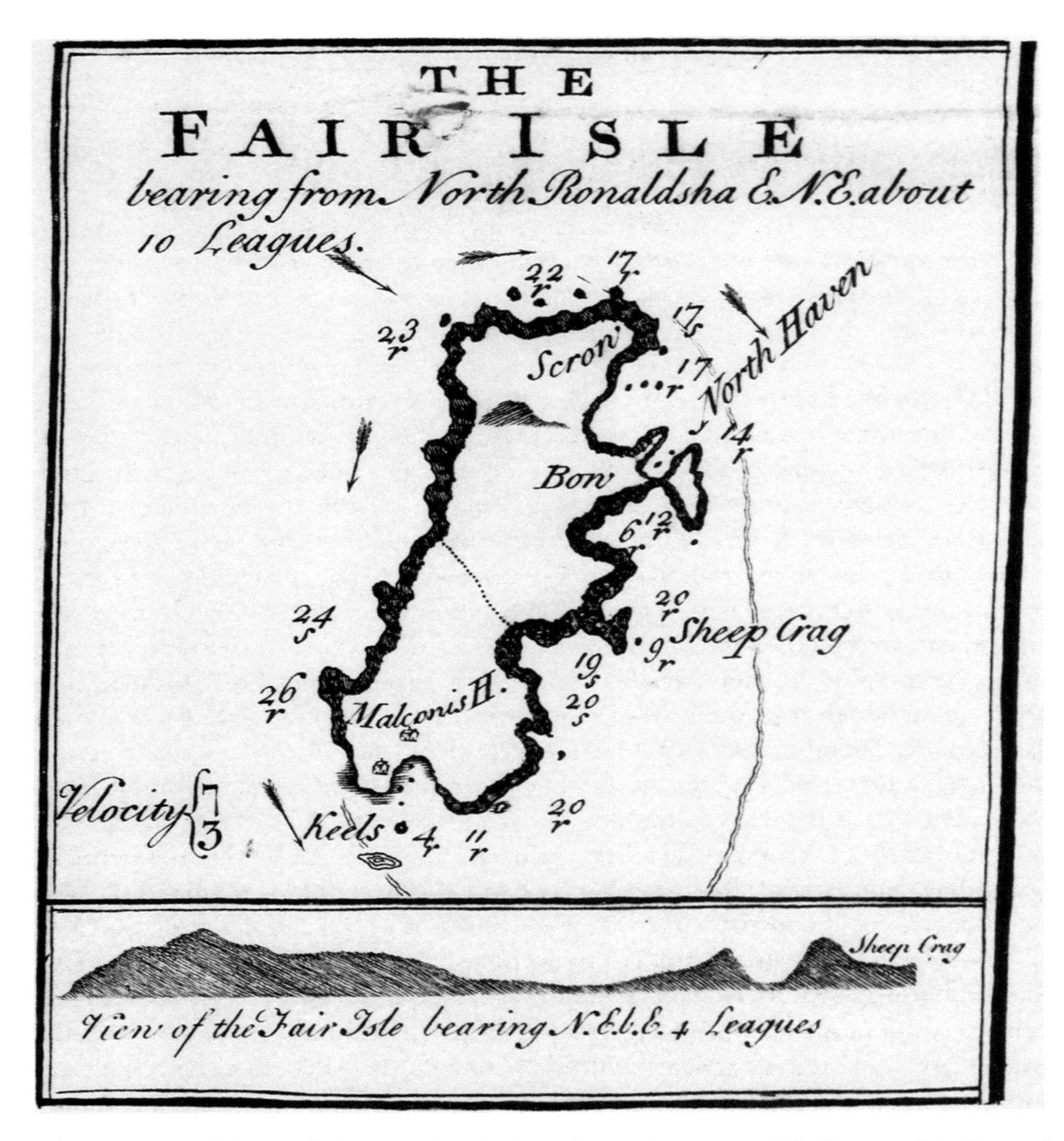

Plate 1.1 Detail of Fair Isle from Mackenzie's chart of 1752. By courtesy of the Trustees of the National Library of Scotland.

of 1814 (Laughlan 1982, 51). In contrast, another account describes the islanders as 'sober, prudent and industrious' (*OSA* XIX, 438). The colouring and bias of many of these descriptions (some are by writers who freely admit never to having landed on Fair Isle) emphasise the cultural gulf between professional classes of the south and the agrarian communities of the Scottish islands who received the attentions of their journals and memoirs. These accounts of island life, many of which have now been included in an indexed anthology (Flinn 1989), also provide a valuable record of contemporary social and economic traditions many of which are almost certainly of long standing.

On Fair Isle the retention of early traditions is easily explained in an insular economy set within barely eight square kilometres, where the natural resources of land and coastline are restricted and where exploitation is patterned according to population size and season. Continuous occupation in such an environment ensures that optimal subsistence strategies are soon identified and are retained until such time as innovation becomes either necessary or possible. Fundamental changes to these strategies occurred within the late 19th and 20th centuries as a result of mechanisation and technological advances; these took place as much in communications, trade and the availability of materials as in agriculture and fishing. It was the closest that the Northern Isles came to being 'industrialised' and marks the end of centuries of perceived rural tradition, although there is now a growing body of opinion which suggests that in a number of subsistence elements the extent of this tradition has been over-rated (eg Stoklund 1984; Morrison 1992). On Fair Isle, however, owing to the limitations of environment and location, there is a strong argument to suggest that the islanders' economic response to the 19th century landscape is likely to have been little changed from a response made 1000 or even 2000 years earlier. If this is indeed the case, then the 18th and 19th century travellers' accounts of Fair Isle might thus be seen as generating an ethnographic insight into late prehistory as much as highlighting contemporary social curiosities. This ethnographic route of approach is now quite well-trodden and has been followed in a number of other ways (eg Alcock and Alcock 1980), but is particularly suited to environments, like Fair Isle, where human survival was finely balanced.

Conservatism of subsistence tradition also fosters preservation. This manifests itself in a number of ways, for example in the retention of old buildings, routes and trackways, or in a less tangible manner in topographical names, customs and the timetabling of activities. Efficiency of method develops from hard experience and becomes suitably honed under an austere climate. Nowhere does this appear more clearly than in the seasonal cycle of the crofting year and particularly in the herding of sheep (see chapter 10). This adherence to well-tried and tested methods has a number of archaeological implications, not least in a fossilisation of the landscape and field systems, and in the retention rather than the reclamation of marginal land. Both factors are beneficial to the survival of archaeological monuments.

Archaeological monuments

In this last respect Fair Isle is of special interest despite a late 19th century observation that its only antiquity was 'a ring of loose stones 32 feet in diameter in the bottom of a hollow' (Muir 1885, 76). The island not only shows a relatively high state of preservation of field monuments but also has a critical physical location. It sits roughly equidistantly between the Orkney and Shetland groups of islands (fig 1.1), some 40 kilometres north of North Ronaldsay, its nearest Orkney neighbour, and as such holds an influential role with respect to the transmission of earlier cultural influences from one island group to the other. Perhaps more significant is the combination of its physical size and the sailing distances necessary to reach it. Fair Isle is sufficiently large to house a small but permanent population yet remote enough for that population to exercise a high degree of self-sufficiency. In archaeological terms this suggests that the island may offer a sociological unit with a clearly defined boundary inside which ancient settlement infrastructure can be confidently assumed. This archaeological concept has already been successfully explored in some detail elsewhere, notably for prehistoric communities on West Burra, Shetland (Hedges 1984), on Oronsay (Mellars 1987), and for communities from a later period on Faroe (Baldwin 1983) and St Kilda (RCAHMS 1988).

On Fair Isle the earliest settlers were almost certainly bands of Neolithic farmers whose presence is well-attested from the 4th and 3rd millennia BC in Orkney and Shetland. General opinion, based only on factors of geography, favours the colonisation of Shetland as secondary to that of Orkney, with Fair Isle used as a navigation marker or a staging post, if not settled itself, during the process of Neolithic expansion. According to excavated evidence the inhabitants of Orkney were already confident farmers in the 4th millennium BC; they were familiar with grain cultivation using stone plough shares and practised a mixed farming economy with sufficient surplus to promote craft specialisation and a degree of external trade. Their subsequent social development, based on splendidly preserved Orcadian settlement and burial sites, has been the subject of considerable focus (eg Renfrew 1979; Fraser 1983) and much can now be interpreted of their social structure and economy.

Shetland has been less well-considered, mostly because of the inferior building quality of the local geology which has tended to inhibit monumental architecture and hence bypass the attentions of interested antiquarians. However, in compensation Shetland possesses considerable areas of higher ground than Orkney. These were abandoned during the climatic deterioration of the Bronze Age when the formation of blanket peat forced the inhabitants to move to lower soils, leaving behind extensive relict landscapes composed of houses, field systems and burial cairns. Many of these landscapes now lie under peat cover, but sufficient have been identified to suggest that the Neolithic peoples who constructed them were well-organised. It seems certain that the long earthen boundaries that wind across the Shetland moorlands were the product of focused and communal effort from this primary period of settlement (Fojut 1986, 3).

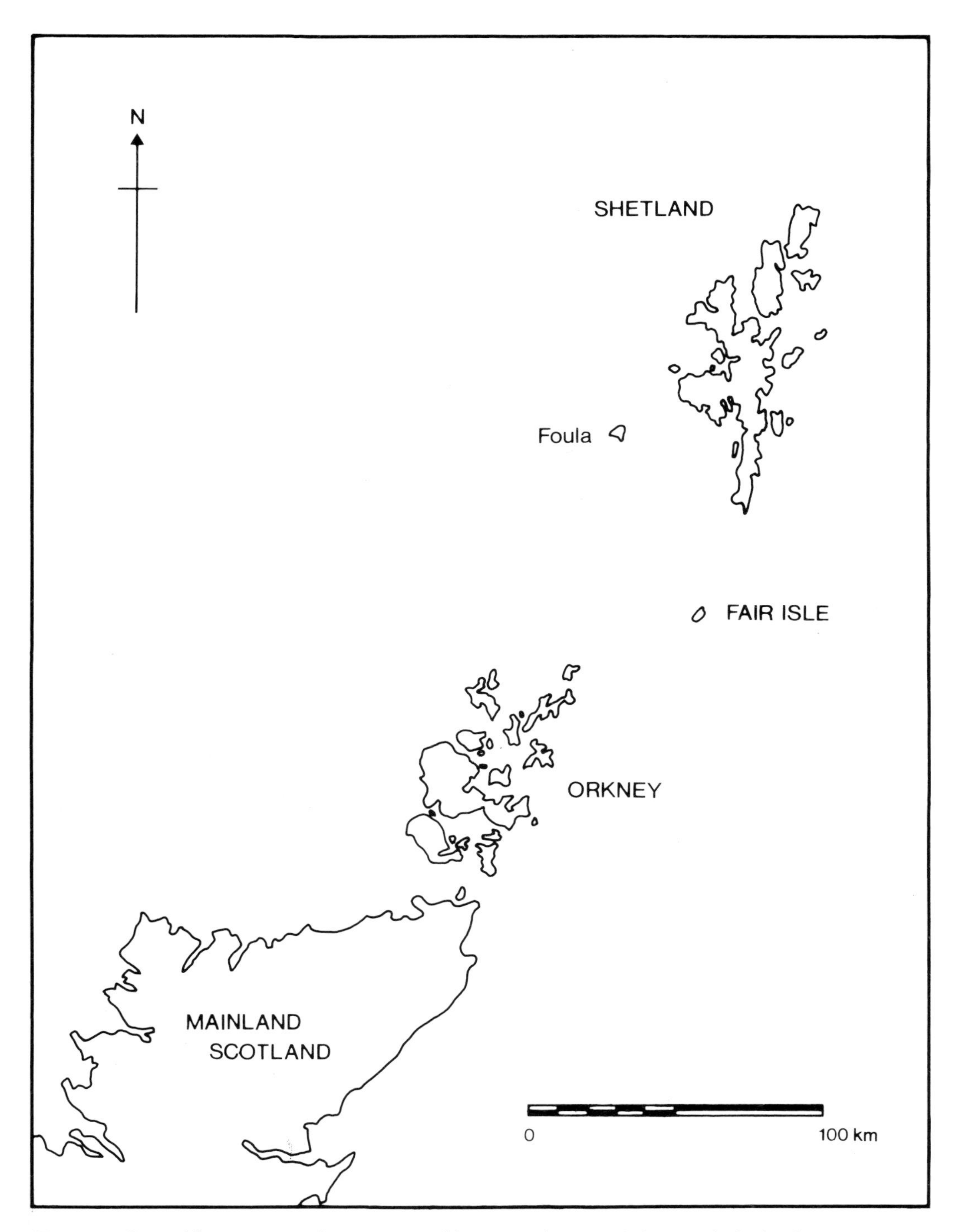

Fig 1.1 General location map showing Fair Isle's position between Orkney and Shetland.

In many respects the differing archaeological signatures of Orkney and Shetland can be seen as complementary, and Fair Isle's position is, for once, unambiguous. Its inclination lies firmly towards the geological character of Shetland where it has close prehistoric parallels in the moorland environment of West Mainland. Nowhere, either visibly or recorded, does the island exhibit the archaeological monumentality of Orkney.

Land use

In land area Fair Isle covers roughly eight square kilometres and, with the exception of the areas around the North Haven where the modern slipway has been constructed and around the former harbour at the south of the island, the coastline is mostly jagged and inaccessible. The landscape itself divides conveniently into two zones, a northern unpopulated region of moorland and a southern, comparatively lower region of arable land which contains both the modern and the historically documented earlier settlement. This division is emphasised by a stone-built wall and by an earlier earthen boundary which runs broadly parallel crossing the island from coast to coast.

The division into two zones is particularly convenient for a comparison with other parts of Shetland. The southern region of pasture and arable contains the modern crofts, crofting land and the traditional population centre of the island, while the moorland region to the north is almost entirely taken up by open grazing. With the notable exception of military stations and the Bird Observatory which developed from naval buildings in 1948, this northern sector appears to have been unpopulated in historic times. The tall drystone wall which divides the two regions follows the line of a wide earthen boundary or dyke (in northern usage the word 'dyke' describes a bank as opposed to a ditch). Known as the *feelie* dyke this straddles almost the whole girth of the island from coast to coast, and is itself of at least two phases. Analogous boundary dykes separating croft land from hill land also feature on other Shetland islands such as Foula and Papa Stour; these dykes, or the precursors on which they may have been based, appear to be of indeterminable date of origin. In the case of Fair Isle, the dyke is first recorded on Mackenzie's chart of 1752 but receives little cartographic or documentary attention thereafter. Even the Royal Commission *Inventory* (RCAHMS 1946) found it unworthy of report, and curiously so considering the dyke's stature.

The division between the two zones is not entirely definitive; some post-medieval land use appears to have spread experimentally into the eastern part of the northern region to the west of the Vaasetter headland. This development is to some extent respected by the present stone wall but not by the earthen dykes which have clearly been breached in order to extend an enclosed field system on that side of the island (see chapter 4, fig 4.1). Former rig lines belonging to this extended area are clearly visible on the survey plan of extant field systems (see chapter 10).

On Fair Isle, as with other divided landscapes in Shetland, the integrity of the archaeological resource is better preserved in the moorland sector where land reclamation, enclosures and field systems have made little impression. The dyke provides classic separation between relict landscape or groups of inter-related monuments on the moorland side, and the selective, or partial survival of individual (usually unrelated) monuments on the other side. The survival bias is pronounced according to this crude highland/lowland division, but at least both bias and expectations are simple and consistent. Nevertheless, as in all field survey the over-riding problem is still one of interpreting monuments on the sole basis of their topographical characteristics – a problem only partly resolved on Fair Isle by the occurrence of general clusters of monuments with similar, or potentially similar components, hence allowing an element of group comparison to be introduced. The effect is exampled well in a sheltered dale of the moorland zone known as the Ferny Cup (see chapter 4, fig 4.3) comprising early field boundaries, cairns, burnt mounds and house foundations; together these present an archaeological entity with a high potential for understanding early settlement infrastructure. Relict areas such as this can be compared to an excavated landscape at the Scord of Brouster which holds a similar moorland position in the West Mainland of Shetland (Whittle 1986). Comparable areas can also be interpreted elsewhere in Fair Isle, but in a less spectacular way, in Homisdale and possibly further west on Burrashield, and to the east on the Rippack.

South of the dyke the modern field and fencing system encloses all but the peripheral headlands and cliffs, and effectively blankets out most of the likely evidence for early occupation. According to census returns this sector housed a recorded peak of around 380 souls in the mid-19th century (compared to the modern arguably saturated population of around 70 inhabitants), and on that basis alone it would be surprising if anything other than minor indications of early settlement had survived. Remarkably some do, notably the class of monument known as the burnt mound (see chapter 5), but these are exceptional. However, the fencing system itself offers some modicum of consolation. Although primarily defining and sub-dividing the present crofting land, it also acts as an important indicator as to the effects of post-medieval land use on the archaeological landscape by allowing comparison between the marginal land outside the fence and the farmed land inside the fence.

Within the existing fenced grazing areas 19th century rig lines predominate although these are being slowly eroded as modern ploughing increases. Outside, earlier narrower rigs and smaller field dykes have become fossilised and survive in those few places where chance alignment of the fence has allowed them to remain undisturbed. A particularly good example lies to the east of Hoini, where the positioning of the fence line has allowed existing narrow rigs to survive beyond the fence while the same rigs inside the fence have become replaced by a later, wider version (plate 1.2; see also chapter 9). The same also applies to some other monuments: the precise positioning of the modern fence effectively governs not only the degree of monument preservation in marginal land but also, indirectly, the extent to which any conveniently situated monument outside the fence might provide quarryable material for modern shelters and walling built inside the fence. This traditional utilisation of building materials is of more than passing importance for identifying early sites on the island as well as having considerable implications for monument survival.

Plate 1.2 Photograph showing how the positioning of the fence line has preserved narrow rig lines and banking in the marginal land outside the fence (right) in contrast to the wider rig lines inside the fence (left).

Survey

An intensive sites and monuments survey was undertaken across both zones of the island between 1984-1987, and this was followed in 1989 by a season of small exploratory excavations in order to resolve a number of ambiguities that had arisen. Field survey designates only what is anomalous to a topographic or vegetational norm according to the criteria of those who carry it out, and although some cautionary safeguards can be exercised, particularly the need to work during seasons of minimum vegetational cover and low sun, interpretation is always a major factor. Furthermore, the original shapes of most sites are disguised by collapse, vegetational cover and robbing; this makes any assessment of significance, class or date speculative. Fortunately a number of monuments were quite accurately identifiable and acted as controls, usually on the basis of composition, or by morphological similarity with those outside the island. These included some earthworks, burnt mounds, house remains and, to a lesser extent, burials. Many occurred in groups. Eventually some 750 individual sites were recorded and described; these range in date from prehistory to the Second World War (the full list is included in the appendix) and are cross-referenced in the text by the site number which appears in italics.

This information subsequently provided the basis on which to interpret the landscape and settlement history of the island. It offered, for example, some potential for identifying the changing face of long-term occupation against a background of available resources, land use and external contact – three essential factors in tracking the development of Fair Isle society over the centuries.

The picture is also aided by historical evidence and documented cultural change within the broad area of the North Atlantic: Scandinavian domination from around AD 800 is attested by useful, if sporadic, reference; later Hanseatic and Scottish influences from the 15th century are relatively well-supported, particularly in their effect on social change; and later trading relationships with Scandinavia also receive comment. Much of this history is thematic and specific to matters of fishing. Above all else it serves to emphasise the importance of fish in the seas around Shetland. Most of the relevant documentation pertains to Shetland proper where the records provide a useful basis for economic and social analysis from late medieval times onwards (Smith 1977), although it remains questionable as to whether this can be accurately extrapolated to Fair Isle itself, an island both geographically and culturally peripheral. In instances of strong social and economic pressure (for example in relation to the post-medieval fishing industry) the histories of the two are largely synonymous, but links are less clear at other times. This reflects not only Fair Isle's anomalous cultural position between Orkney and Shetland but also its physical environment and its resources which enabled it, in part at least, to flourish quite independently of either island group.

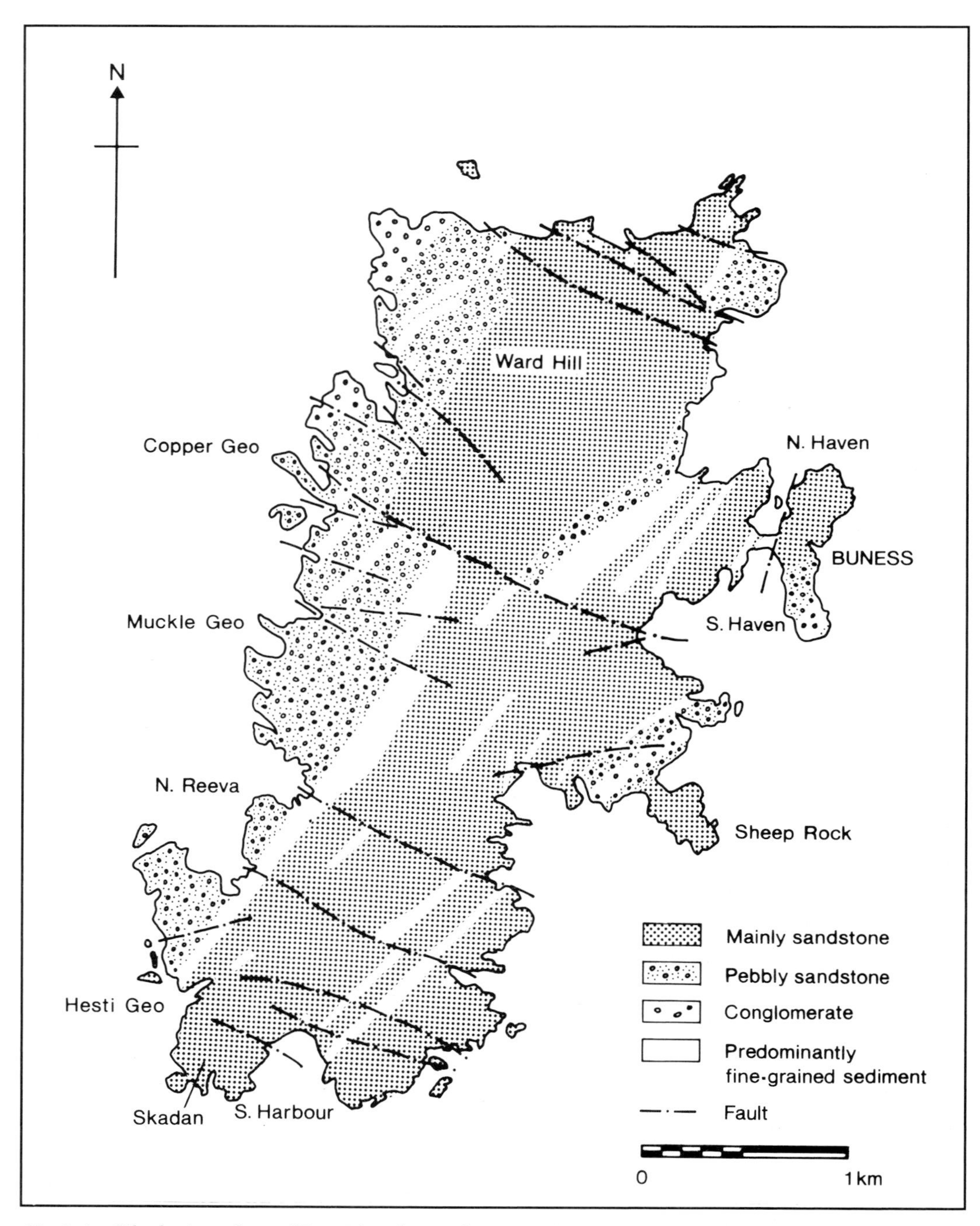

Fig 2.1 The basic geology of Fair Isle, after Mykura 1976.

2

NATURAL ENVIRONMENT

Geology

Fair Isle's location, almost exactly midway between the two island groups, reflects a compromise position between the differing elements found in both, a type of confusion manifest in its history and archaeology as well as in its geological formation. To the north lies the rugged coastline of Shetland, broken by wide voes and stippled with small islands and stacks, while to the south is Orkney with its softer landscape and coastline reflecting a different underlying geology. Shetland's geology is mainly metamorphic and varied while that of Orkney, characterised by flagged sedimentary sandstones, is ostensibly simpler and, in terms of relevance to earlier populations, of greater utility for building purposes.

Fair Isle's position within this geological environment has been explored in a series of short papers; the earliest (Heddle 1879), which also contains a useful map of the island, covers the activities of Heddle, a mineral collector 'who attacked the rocks with 28lb hammers, wedges and explosives and when possible, travelled in yachts to save time' (Berry and Johnston 1980, 257). Later papers (eg Flinn 1970; 1974; Mykura 1972) take a more considered scientific approach in the examination of the unusual red-brown glacial tills, beach formation, and igneous intrusions and mineralisation respectively. The last of these papers provides the most comprehensive coverage, the more general issues being subsequently discussed within the context of the regional geology of the area (Mykura 1976). The geological formation is of sedimentary sandstone divisible into four observable strata, including beds of mud/siltstone and conglomerate all cut by a series of faults trending roughly NW-SE (fig 2.1). Mykura suggests that the age of the beds lies between the Lower and Middle Old Red Sandstone (1976, 67) on the basis of fossil plant and fish *genera* recovered principally from the east side of the island around Buness (Chaloner 1972).

The geology contrasts sharply with the rest of Shetland with the exception of the extreme southern tip of adjacent Dunrossness which shares similarly aged sedimentary sandstones, although both lack the laminate sandstone flags which characterise the Orkney group to the south. Additionally, both are cut by dykes containing similar mineral resources. On Fair Isle dykes penetrate the coastline at the south and west and provide potential economic exploitation with the presence of veins bearing copper ore and sodic scapolite.

None of these resources occur in great quantity; even the exploitation of copper ore, historically the most important, which took place in the later 19th century, left its mark only in the form of a few place-names and some minor earthworks. Mining on a commercial scale is recorded from South Mainland as early as the end of the 18th century (Dron 1908) but the level of activity on Fair Isle seems limited by the relative inaccessibility of the deposits. Ores are known particularly from Copper Geo, around North Reeva and at Muckle Geo of Hoini, all within the steep cliffs on the east side of the island. None of these seem likely to have been exploited prior to the 19th century.

Detailed investigation of the deposits for commercial potential was not carried out until 1912 (Mykura 1972, 35) and this served to cast doubt on earlier suggestions that exploitation would be economically viable (Heddle 1879, 50). Mykura's view of the inaccessibility of surviving visible ores led him to believe that reports had produced 'an exaggerated picture' (1972, 43). Their availability may partly be a consequence of previous mining activity although no mention of exploitation is made in either of the first two statistical accounts nor in the notably early description of the islands' resources by James Kay around 1680. An early 19th century account makes a similar point citing the exploits of an eminent naturalist, Dr Fleming, who was lowered by rope from the top of a cliff, and held 'by two of the natives' in order to inspect the deposits (Hibbert 1822, 28). Scott, also interested in such matters, was 'held fast by the skirts' by two or three of the islanders, such were the dangers involved (Laughlan 1982, 52). Considering the steepness of the approaches by both land and sea it seems unlikely that all the accessible ores could have been removed even by such an early date, and thus the concept of anything other than minor exploitation in antiquity would seem unrealistic.

Other mineral resources include sodic scapolite, a semi-precious stone which occurs in sandstone sediments, found in the dykes to the south and west of the island. The stone when cleaned and polished is white, tinged with blue and usually subtranslucent (Mykura and Young 1969) but is not recorded as being exploited. Its distribution on the island (*ibid*, fig 1) is in association with the dykes although scattered scapolite veins also occur on the peninsula to the west of the South Harbour.

The relative simplicity of Fair Isle's geology to that of Shetland has considerable implications for earlier societies, notably in the availability of suitable materials not only for the manufacture of weapons, domestic tools and implements but also for building purposes for which the local stone is mostly inappropriate. By contrast Shetland's metamorphic environment offers a more varied response to primitive needs, for example the riebeckite felsite which occurs in dykes around Ronas Hill, North Mainland, lends itself to a number of tool types for which at least one quarry site has been identified (Ritchie 1968, 128-133). Steatite (soapstone) was also quarried in antiquity, notably at Cunningsburgh, South Mainland, and on Unst (Ritchie 1984), providing both stone vessels as well as temper for pottery production.

Human survival on Fair Isle in prehistoric times would necessarily require a certain level of importation, however limited, of lithic materials for basic subsistence activity. Although glacial clays may have satisfied local pottery needs and the associated flint nodules may have gone some way to fulfil other requirements, it is nevertheless difficult to envisage the island as being entirely self-sufficient. Importation, seen in later periods from both exchange and more formal trading arrangements, has to be viewed as a fundamental aspect of Fair Isle's subsistence economy even from earliest times.

Vegetation

Fair Isle's vegetational history has to some extent been moulded by post-glacial developments originating some 12,000 years ago with the retreat of ice cover, sea level being an estimated 275 feet lower than at present (Berry and Johnston 1980, 53). The rate at which the sea level rose is open to some speculation, but the presence of a diminishing landbridge between Orkney and mainland Scotland is normally accepted. According to submarine contours a shorter term landbridge leading across to Fair Isle may also have been plausible. Although the timescale of events is difficult to establish, the vegetational implications are nevertheless significant, Orkney (and possibly Fair Isle) being colonised from Scotland and therefore possessing relict populations after submergence of the landbridge, with Shetland developing its animal and plant communities in a different, wholly insular way. Orkney's geographical proximity to mainland Scotland is such as to retain a certain commonality of flora and fauna and its vegetational position, unlike that of Shetland, can be argued to be 'essentially an outlier of north Britain' (Berry and Johnston 1980, 28).

Shetland, by contrast, is seen as having a different climatic and ecological environment (eg Birse 1974; Spence 1974), previously defined at lower contours as *submontane oceanic* (Spence 1970, 23) in which the gulf stream and prevailing wind strengths both exercise powerful roles. Strong winds are a common aspect of the Shetland climate and a popular point of narrative among 18th and 19th century accounts. At Dunrossness gales periodically blew sand from the kirkyard resulting in a 'melancholy exposure' of the recent dead (Hibbert 1822, 112), while Sibbald recalls a time in the earlier 17th century when the winds 'lifted boats from the ground and broke them to bits' (Monteith 1845, 13). In the following century Gifford, caught in a Shetland gale, was blown flat to the ground and was forced 'to creep on hands and knees' (1786, *x*). Natural vegetation in this type of environment is consequently more restricted in species than further south, investigation having shown that only some 400 species of vascular plants found on Shetland could be classified as native compared to over 2200 native to the rest of Britain (Goode 1974, 50). Interest in Shetland's vegetation commences as early as 1774 with a list of flowering plants collated by George Low, with later compilations by Palmer and Scott (1969) and Berry and Johnston (1980). A list of flowering plants on Fair Isle was produced by Traill in 1906, and although this suffers from lack of habitat background for the species recorded it does nonetheless demonstrate the relative paucity of species even by Shetland standards. Almost by way of an apology Traill also noted the presence of plants which were unrecorded from either Orkney or Shetland (1906, 166), and to confuse matters further a study of algae from the intertidal zones on Fair Isle suggests that the algae affinities of the island belonged to the more northerly islands rather than with the Scottish mainland (Burrows *et al* 1954, 288).

Whichever way Fair Isle's vegetational history is seen to be inclined, whether best viewed as an adjunct to the vegetation of Orkney and North Scotland or to the insular characteristics of Shetland, the argument is largely academic. In common with both island groups its vegetation now merely reflects centuries of human influence and changes in agricultural practice in which the grazing of cattle, ponies, pigs and sheep has had a profound influence on the nature of the moorland landscape beyond the township dyke (Johnston 1974, 33). The effect has been in the reduction of hill land to a common level of acid grassland across the region as a whole, heath and scrubland having all but vanished. Relict areas nevertheless survive, O'Dell noting certain former plant communities on Foula (1939, 272) while work by Spence in the 1950s identified zones of relict landscape in Shetland, usually on small islands in freshwater lochs which had not been subjected to grazing, burning or direct human-based influence. This enabled significant differences to be observed between former plant communities and those communities now evident in comparable habitats on the modern landscape (1960, table 4).

The contrast is particularly stark with respect to the modern absence of scrub *Salix* and *Betula* species in flank and shore regions and in the greater variety of species formerly evident in plateau zones. Subsequent work by Gimingham paid greater attention to Fair Isle and examined three exposed grassland stands on the island cliffs noting *Festuca ovina*, *Armeria maritima*, *Plantago lanceolata* and *P. maritima* in all three, *Poa pratensis* in two and *Aira praecox* in one (1964, 77). He concluded that the stands were, in general, more restricted in species than those in other peripheral Scottish regions examined, dispelling any notion that Fair Isle, in view of its relative remoteness and conservatism of land husbandry, might somehow retain the vegetational integrity of an early landscape. The idea is, however, not without merit and the observed survival on Fair Isle's moorland of prostrate *Juniperus nana*, presumably the 'wild juniper' noted specifically by Tudor in the late 19th century (1883, 442), has been seen as indicative of a relative absence of drainage, fertilisers and similar modern chemicals widely used in the 20th century (Johnston 1974, 34). Juniper is also thought to have been widely exploited in Viking times both for wicker and fodder (Larsen 1991). Awareness of these fundamental vegetational changes in

Shetland is by no means a new phenomenon; Hibbert shows remarkable knowledge and insight into the former character of the landscape and the causes of its demise without the benefit of soil or pollen studies:

> *Certain kinds of small trees such as hazels, willows or birches once braced with success the cutting blasts of Shetland, while the introduction of sheep into the country, which would prevent new plants from springing up, or inundations arising from the incursions of the ocean, have probably been the conspiring causes to which their decay is attributable.* (Hibbert 1822, 428)

The best view of these changes, however, emerges with analysis of palynological data particularly where the coring has been undertaken in relation to dated archaeological activity. On Shetland this has been carried out most recently in West Mainland in relation to excavations at the Scord of Brouster on soil profiles exposed during excavation, and in relation to blanket peat formation. Analysis shows that by the time of primary Neolithic settlement the vegetation was dominated by scrub woodland of *Corylus avellena* and *Betula*, with a hill land cover of *Calluna empetrum* heath (Keith-Lucas 1986, 116). This was reduced by subsequent grazing and clearance, from which the pollen record shows that taxa indicative of pasture outweigh those indicative of arable use. A key indicator is seen to be *Plantago lanceolata*, a component normally diagnostic of grazing land whose spread may chart not only the erasure of original heathland but also the invasion of cultivated land on abandonment, a phenomenon now interpreted from archaeological evidence.

An Orkney pollen analysis undertaken in conjunction with excavations at Quanterness and Maeshowe offers a similar interpretation. Original scrubland/thicket had already vanished by the Late Neolithic and the taxa again indicate a predominance of pastoralism (Jones 1979, 22). It also seems clear that soil degeneration which occurred during this period was partly a result of man's influence on the landscape and, like the periods of abandonment noted on Shetland, had a significant impact on vegetational development. The overview, on the basis that the birch/hazel scrubland marks the climax vegetation community of post-glacial Orkney and Shetland (Jones 1979, 23), infers that Fair Isle's present vegetational cover, like that of both Orkney and Shetland, is effectively man-made and bears virtually no relation to original post-glacial plant communities or indeed to any earlier plant resources.

One possible exception concerns natural dyestuffs which tradition holds to have been of long-standing local value. Purple dye (korkeleit) could be obtained from *Lichen tartarcus* which was scraped from the rocks on the island (Tudor 1883, 439) and used for colouring wools. Other lichens and plants (unspecified) must presumably have provided additional colours, one at least being tormentil (*Potentilla erecta*) which still grows today and which in Shetland dialect form (*bark*, Stewart 1987, 200) is the presumed basis for the croft name Barkland.

The otherwise altered nature of Fair Isle's vegetation is borne out by palynological study of a column sampled from the peat beds on Ward Hill, in the north-west of the island (fig 2.1), undertaken by Charlotte Matthews as part of the recent survey project. Although the level of pollen preservation was less than desirable the data presents a fairly uniform picture (fig 2.2), the summary diagram showing Arboreal Pollen to be between 5-15%, with Shrub Pollen being generally less than 10% and Non-Arboreal Pollen accounting for between 75-95% throughout. This suggests that the landscape was formerly open in nature with very little woodland cover. The most important trees/shrubs on the diagram are birch (*Betula*), hazel (*Corylus*) and to a lesser extent alder (*Alnus*), suggesting that any woodland would have been very scrubby in nature. Small but continuous amounts of pine (*Pinus*) and the occasional grains of oak (*Quercus*), elm (*Ulnus*), ash (*Fraxinus*), willow (*Salix*) and juniper (*Juniperus*) may be explained as the result of wind action or driftwood, although the presence of juniper is of particular interest in view of Tudor's observations (above).

The most important Non-Arboreal Pollen is undoubtedly heather (*Calluna*) which, together with small but continuous amounts of grasses (Gramineae), suggest that heathland dominated the landscape. Spores of ferns (*Filicales, Polypodium*) and bracken (*Pteridium*) also occur in small amounts, although the large peak in sample 13 is best seen as a freak occurrence caused by a pollen cluster falling on the sample location (M Atherden pers comm). The presence of sedges (Cyperaceae), probably cottongrass, may indicate a fairly damp environment; their increase in the upper part of the diagram might reflect changing climatic conditions, possibly the climatic deterioration from around 500 BC previously interpreted from palynological data in Orkney by Jones (1979, 23). Pastoral activity is supported by the presence of ribwort plantain (*Plantago lanceolata*) and the sorrels and docks (*Rumex*), although the latter is concentrated in the middle and upper portions of the diagram. Occasional grains of goosefoot (Chenopodiaceae) and daisies (Compositae), also in the middle of the diagram, provide the only evidence for possible arable farming, but the absence of cereal grains or specific arable weeds is noteworthy.

There is a good correlation between this Fair Isle diagram and the upper parts of diagrams from Orkney and Shetland cited above subsequent to the main clearance phases of birch and hazel woodland. The Fair Isle column belongs to the expansion of heather heathland, the lower boundary of which, by analogy with the Scord of Brouster data, can be calculated at around 1500 BC. It points to a landscape dominated by heathland on the higher ground, grasses and sedges in the lower damp areas, and birch, hazel and alder scrub in the more sheltered spots. Pastoralism predominated with the possibility of some arable activity, suggesting an economy little different from that of today.

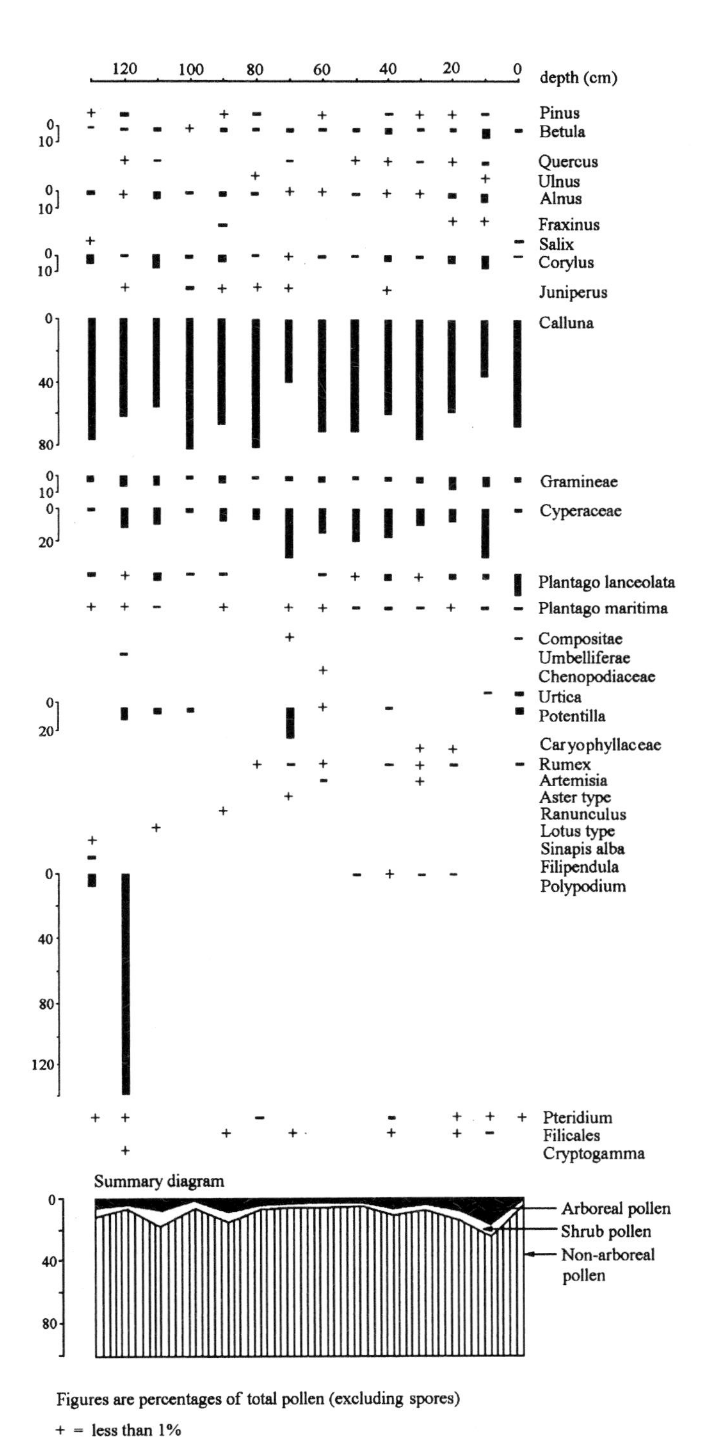

Fig 2.2 Pollen diagram of Fair Isle from column extracted from peat deposits on Ward Hill.

Although the face of the modern landscape is largely irrelevant to the study of early occupation, one significant aspect of its evolution is both applicable and traceable in subsistence economies – namely peat, probably the single most valuable resource available to man in the Northern Isles. In a predominantly treeless environment fuel supplies were devised using a certain degree of resourcefulness (eg turf, seaweed, dung) and peat production was no exception, its recovery and treatment (not to mention the specialist implements required) representing the continuation of long-standing traditions which have since been comprehensively documented (eg Fenton 1978, 210-238). The scale and duration of exploitation throughout the islands is such that the topography of parts of the landscape in late prehistoric times might appear markedly different from its modern equivalent.

As a natural product blanket peat is normally considered to have formed in the Northern Isles within the 2nd millennium BC, a period roughly coinciding with the Early Bronze Age. Both natural and human factors are seen as being causal with climatic change, a rising water table and clearance representing the main elements of formation (Moore 1975). In historic times its value as a commodity is unquestionable, as witness the name *Torf* Einar – one of the early Earls whose name results from his apparent innovative use of peat as a fuel. Later sources additionally relate how the inhabitants of North Ronaldsay, Orkney were obliged to collect their peats from Eday some 14 miles away, while on Shetland the peat supply for the Out Skerries involved regular passage to Whalsay. One visitor to Lerwick in the mid-19th century described meeting 'droves of women proceeding on their never-ceasing journey to the mosses in the hills for peat, with their cussies or straw baskets on their backs, and knitting eagerly with both their hands' (Wilson 1842). It was, however, an activity local to those areas where peat was cheaply available and the techniques of cutting and storing actively pursued. Peat burning therefore receives mention, almost in the manner of a curio, in the description of Fair Isle by a Spanish sailor in 1588 who was clearly unfamiliar with its properties and who described the fuel as something that the islanders took out of the ground (Ker 1920, 172).

The Fair Isle peats were fairly easily obtained, the main formations occurring at the north end of the island within the higher moorland beyond Ward Hill where, as part of the scattald, the peat deposits along with turf (also a possible fuel source), seaweed, grazing rights and minerals were held as common resources. The date of the first use of peat on the island is unknown but, by analogy with peat ash recovered from archaeological hearths elsewhere in Orkney and Shetland belonging to Iron Age and Viking period contexts, a similar period would seem reasonable. However, unlike most other areas the Fair Isle deposits seem not to have been threatened by overuse, despite an estimated 40 cartloads per year for each of the 19 holdings recorded as late as 1940 (O'Dell 1940, 291).

Animals and fish

Although the Fair Isle peats were local, their carriage nevertheless required a relatively lengthy and undeniably hilly journey to the settlement land at the south of the island from the moors at the north. Traditionally this was undertaken using ponies, although later oxen were used, and it is no doubt a reflection of English society and sensibility that most of the visitors' descriptions of Shetland peat cutting dwell in greater detail on the ponies and their apparent suffering than on the peat cutting itself. One notable exception was Christian Pløyen, Governor of Faroe, whose visit to Shetland in 1839 prompted him to remark that he had thought it impossible to manage the peat moss more wastefully than in Faroe, but having visited Shetland his opinion was 'quite changed' (1894, 20).

The records pertain mostly to parts of Mainland Shetland but the consensus of opinion nevertheless points to the miserable lot of the animals, and to the fact that they were allowed to run wild even in the winter without maintenance from the owners, and might even be obliged to live on seaweed (Brand 1701, 117). One late 19th century visitor to Fair Isle described them as being 'in a pitiable condition' and often being blown over into the sea (Reid 1869, 51). Exceptionally the animals were not employed in drudgery work in Walls and Sandness according to the *First Statistical Account* (*OSA* XIX, 517). This was at a time when horses could 'hardly be got for money, being scarce and dear' according to the diary of the Reverend John Mill (Goudie 1889, 11) although by the mid-19th century most crofters possessed their own stock. The treatment of ponies (shelties) is best reflected by Hibbert whose description seems fairly typical:

> *The sheltie is left to feed on the hills during the whole of the year; and in the most inclement weather of winter is never admitted within the warm walls of a stable being frequently compelled to subsist on the driftware that is left by the ebb. On my arrival in Shetland, early in Spring, I found these animals in such a half-starved state, owing to their scanty supply of winter feed, that the growth of the summer herbage was necessary before they had so sufficiently recovered their strength as to bear a rider over the moors of the country.* (Hibbert 1822, 421)

In origin the characteristic short, sturdy breed may have developed from the same stock as the Norwegian horse (Berry and Johnston 1980, 138), although horses also appear on the earlier symbol stones of Shetland and a breed of similar stature was identified among the Late Bronze Age material from Jarlshof (Platt 1956, 212). The breed is not necessarily to be seen as resulting from a new emphasis on horses introduced by Viking colonists, indeed the species from Viking deposits at Jarlshof appears to be greater in stature than the modern sheltie (Platt 1956, 214) – an observation also evident from the contemporary assemblage at Pool, Sanday, Orkney, excavated under more stringent conditions of recovery (Bond forthcoming). Cross-breeding with horses from the Armada vessels seems unlikely, especially on Fair Isle if there is any truth in Kay's late 17th century observation that the horses were eaten as a result of the food shortage brought about by stranded Spanish sailors (Bruce 1908).

The breed was ideally suited to the carriage of loads along steep or narrow tracks and on Fair Isle ponies were again utilised during the Second World War for the carriage of military supplies to the station on the crest of Ward Hill. Hibbert, citing Shirreff's observations, relates how they were kept solely for the purpose of carrying home the peats (1822, 124). Around 70 such animals were temporarily enclosed on the island in 1804, probably in the area around Skadan and the aptly named Hesti Geo, representing approximately four or five ponies per household, arguably an unnecessary number if used solely for the seasonal carriage of peats, especially bearing in mind the proportion of the island's vegetational resources required for their survival. While they may have facilitated the exploitation of the island's peat from Norse times onwards, they are almost certain to have played a major part in the degeneration of the moorland landscape where they were allowed to roam and graze for most of the year.

Fair Isle's most obvious and historically important natural resource was the sea, and the later history of the island is inextricably tied in with boats, fish and maritime-based activity (see chapters 3 and 10). On an island of this size in such a relatively remote location the potential of marine resources can hardly have been overlooked by early settlers. The primary attraction must however have been the fertility of the land rather than the riches of the sea, partly because landfall is only accessible by (modern) boat in all but a few locations around an otherwise ruggedly inhospitable coastline, and partly because the archaeological record (such as it is) for the Northern Isles fails to demonstrate the exploitation of deeper sea resources until comparatively late in the settlement sequence.

For the former, there are three acceptable harbours, the North and South Havens created around the formation of a tombolo between the main part of the island and Buness, and the South Harbour at the southern end of the island – location of the 'pitiful skiffs' alluded to in the *First Statistical Account* (*OSA* XIX, 437). The North Haven is now used as the main harbour and, with a latterly constructed slipway, will presumably remain as such. The South Harbour, by contrast, was a traditional harbouring point for the local boats and certainly the most convenient in relation to the known settlement foci. It is, however, disadvantaged by rocky approaches, particularly for larger boats although the placing of an adjacent *bod* built specifically for a 17th century Hamburg merchant by the laird (Bruce 1908, 55) suggests that this was not necessarily a deterrent. More than one account points to the popularity of the location as a regular stopping point for boats on route to Shetland from Orkney.

As far as the archaeological record is concerned the nearest major excavated site at Jarlshof shows evidence of fishes that were presumably caught from boats rather than land line from the later part of the first millennium BC (Platt 1956, 213). This is supported at a number of other sites, notably in the later Iron Age from Orkney, for example in the Birsay area where much archaeological research has been concentrated. The nature of the marine economy appears to shift in the 10th and 11th centuries AD when, partly due to Norse influences, deeper sea fishing was employed, as evidenced from remains of species recovered from a number of settlements including Jarlshof (Platt 1956, 214) and the Birsay sites (Wheeler 1977; Seller 1986, 215; Rackham, Bramwell *et al* 1989, 101). Species normally considered to be diagnostic of deeper waters are those of the gadoid group (particularly ling, hake and torsk) although certain problems arise concerning the likelihood of seasonal inshore movement. Artefactual support for this trend occurs at Underhoull, Unst – a site, like Jarlshof, adjacent to prolific fishing grounds – where the recovery of unusually heavy line sinkers suggests deeper sea fishing and where the use of nets has also been inferred (Small 1966, 241).

Prior to the Bronze Age little is known. At least part of the problem concerns difficulties associated with the physical recovery of small fish bones, particularly in acid soils, not to mention difficulties in interpreting the precise role of fish bone in archaeological contexts. For the first of these, fine sieving and recovery techniques are relatively recent advances and many earlier excavations of Neolithic and Early Bronze Age sites therefore present a picture biased in favour of larger fish bones recovered using only the naked eye. As far as archaeological contexts are concerned, difficulties arise in evaluating the presence of fish bones as being part of a human diet as opposed to being the consequence of animal and bird prey (eg otter), particularly in cases where the context is funereal and a likely animal habitat. There are also significant problems in the understanding of survival biases (Jones 1991). The substantial deposits of shell middens that proliferate in some early settlements at least demonstrate that Neolithic society exploited some of the coastal resources available, and more recent investigations using sieving have since promoted the feasibility of fishing from boats in Neolithic Orkney, at Quanterness (Wheeler 1979) and Birsay Bay (Rackham, Bramwell *et al* 1989, 101).

The trend towards offshore resources in the later period is normally seen as being a consequence of introducing Norse fishing methods into the Northern Isles (Berry and Johnston 1980, 94) and while there is undoubtedly some truth in this, there are also other factors at play. Climate and population pressures were both especially relevant themes at this time and the move towards a greater dependence on fishing as, for example, might be inferred from the 'overwhelming' reliance on marine resources interpreted at the Norse site of Freswick (Morris and Rackham 1992, 98) may reflect pressures more fundamental to society than the relatively simple imposition of Norse culture. In addition, increased controls on fish bone recovery continue to demonstrate that although the emerging data strongly identifies offshore fishing, it does so on the basis of a likely trend already operative before Norse times (eg Rackham, Allison *et al* 1989, 257) and hinted at throughout prehistory. Many of the problems concerning marine resources have been of the archaeologist's own making and the interpretation of a Norse-founded trend, based largely on a maritime reputation, is perhaps not entirely acceptable.

Fair Isle no doubt conforms to the same marine trends evident elsewhere in both Orkney and Shetland with the possible exception of the proportion of diet represented by fish. Even in Norse times fish seems to have constituted only a small part of the archaeologically recorded diet despite the fact that all the excavated sites in Orkney and Shetland are coastal (eg Rowley-Conwy 1983, 109). Given its insularity Fair Isle might be expected to show a greater proportion of fish in the diet and, in view of the boat travel necessary to reach it, a greater tradition of localised fishing throughout prehistory.

Problems also arise over the appearance of the field mouse *Apodemus sylvaticus*, whose interpreted Norwegian origins and subsequent spread in the Atlantic and Scottish islands is portrayed on the basis of the 'founder effect' theory of genetic evolution (Berry and Johnston 1980, fig 19). Its ultimate appearance on both Foula and Fair Isle is conveniently ascribed to 'chance colonisation from a viking ship' (Berry 1974, 154), although in fairness it should be added that this field mouse and the house mouse (*Mus musculus muralis*) pose special difficulties of interpretation on small insular locations (Berry and Tricker 1969). Other species where Norse influences might be seen to operate include the Shetland horse (above), the gannet, whose temporary disappearance has sometimes been attributed to Norse hunting (Berry and Johnston 1980, 131), and the characteristic breed of Shetland sheep which shows certain affinities with the primitive feral Soay species found on St Kilda, notably in the horns and in the moulting and colours of the fleece (Berry and Johnston 1980, 139).

As far as the sheep are concerned this relationship is possibly coincidental; the Shetland breed is indigenous and its modern characteristics may stem from apparent inbreeding in the 18th century when the flocks were allowed to roam wild. Hibbert, for example, observed that sheep were 'almost to be regarded as in a state of nature, since they range at large over the skathalds during the whole of the year' (1822, 436), while a generation earlier the *First Statistical Account* for Aithsting and Sandsting reported that the number of sheep 'cannot be properly acertained as they go at freedom on the hills; and some of them are so wild as only to be caught by dogs' (*OSA* XIX, 338).

Archaeological deposits in both Orkney and Shetland show sheep/goat remains to dominate the faunal assemblages even from Neolithic times, yet despite the weight of material there is no evidence to indicate that the primitive Soay breed evolved in Shetland. On the contrary, there is evidence from a number of sites to suggest that it did not, for example at Jarlshof the Late Bronze Age levels contained remains of sheep similar to the long-horned Soay together with those of a more slender stock (Platt 1956, 212) while those of the Viking levels appeared to contain a mixture of both types (Platt 1956, 214). At Buckquoy on Orkney the Late Iron Age sheep were 'small by modern standards, slightly larger than the Soay' (Noddle 1977, 207) but by the final Viking phase the stock was virtually indistinguishable from the Soay type – a development which Noddle ascribes to a process of selection caused by the pressures and environment to which the breed was subjected during those centuries (1977, 208). The Fair Isle sheep, therefore, if formerly derived from Shetland stock, belong to an evolution entirely separate to that of the Soay on St Kilda, although following a largely parallel process of selection for which the Norseman can only be partly held responsible.

According to most animal bone assemblages from the Northern Isles sheep were a major resource factor providing wool and milk (and ultimately meat) from prehistory onwards, and understandably so considering the vegetation available. The Fair Isle position was probably little different and sheep have historically constituted a major part of the economy. Their importance in this respect can be measured from the utilisation of every patch of grazing land however small, remote or inaccessible around the island's edge. Sibbald's memorable description of Sheep Rock (see chapter 10; Monteith 1845, 50), although a 17th century account, not only emphasises this but also attests to the richness of the grazing. Sheep have thus played an important part in Fair Isle's economy, particularly in the 19th century, almost to the extent that within modern culture the island and the animal are synonymous. There is perhaps some truth too that the name of the island derives from ON *faar-ey* meaning 'island of sheep' (see chapter 8).

Birds

One undoubted by-product of Fair Isle's insular location is its bird population which presumably offered important subsistence potential in earlier times. Shetland, including Fair Isle, occupies a significant stepping-stone along the migration tracks of birds on route across the North Atlantic, the nature and timing of the passage being vulnerable to changes in temperature and prevailing wind but normally occurring around March/April and September/October in modern times. Fair Isle's present ornithological importance lies in metering both the timing and species content of these movements, which for earlier populations would have acted as a bonus and welcome food source in the natural cycle of annual subsistence events. However, it would seem, given the inferred climatic changes during the last 5000 years, that these movements would be both unpredictable in volume and unreliable in timing. They cannot be accurately designated as specific factors in the settling of the island.

Breeding colonies on the other hand are a different proposition although, according to modern breeding figures, the differences between breeding species among the individual island groups in the North Atlantic is remarkable. The picture shows a generally diminishing number of species according to latitude (Berry and Johnston 1980, table 14) although other factors have also been identified, particularly with regard to the gannet and fulmar population (Serjeantson 1988). Identification of breeding species in earlier periods is difficult to assess, stability being influenced not only by climatic fluctuations but also by man's persisting impact on the environment and inadvertent destruction of habitats in open fields and level ground surfaces.

Like that of fish, the archaeological interpretation of bird remains in settlement deposits causes a number of difficulties but shows great potential for further investigation. Bourne and Dixon point out on the basis of evidence from Jarlshof (1974, 131) that birds, and especially seabirds, constituted a major element in the diet of early Shetland populations; this has been confirmed by a recent analysis of material from coastal sites carried out using modern recovery and sampling techniques (Serjeantson 1988). The data suggests that seafowl were a reliable resource throughout antiquity in the Northern Isles, so much so that domestic fowl only appear to become common relatively late, in the Viking period (*ibid*, 212).

There are, however, a number of problems of interpretation, for example with the Late Neolithic material from Quanterness where a preponderance of very small bird species might be argued to be the product of owl or otter activity as opposed to human diet (Bramwell 1979). A similar problem arose in Birsay Bay where the Middle Bronze Age assemblage was partly explained as lying adjacent to 'an eating perch for a falcon' although some of the larger species recovered, including the gannet, were seen as being more directly the product of man's appetite (Rackham, Bramwell *et al* 1989, 107). The gannet itself, and indeed the (now extinct) great auk both feature strongly in the archaeological record, and this might be seen as a reflection of their relatively large body size and food value rather than of their ubiquity (Serjeantson 1988, 213f).

While the breeding species may have altered over the years it is nevertheless clear that on Fair Isle the resource was a valuable one, not perhaps as much in food terms as for feathers which could be exchanged or traded out of the island for items not otherwise obtainable internally. Birds probably only constituted part of the diet, Hibbert recording in the early 19th century that the islanders consumed 'mostly milk, fish, wild-fowl, and wild-fowl eggs which they take from among the precipices by climbing or going down the rocks by the assistance of a rope' (1822, 124). Ironically, this inaccessibility may have resulted from human impact on the landscape causing the nesting grounds to retreat from immediate human reach. Some of the cliffs, stacks and inlets contain Scandinavian bird-name elements (eg *Fugla* or *Maava*), which not only suggest the importance of the nesting locations but also give some measure of the extent of the fowling tradition.

Bird assemblages from recent Viking period excavations in the Northern Isles now attest to the importance of seafowl in the subsistence economy, not simply as a seasonal resource but as an all year round activity. At Buckquoy, analysis of the species recovered indicated the presence of birds known to be visitors during different seasons; moreover, these were identified from moorland, meadow, shore and open sea habitats (Bramwell 1977, 209), suggesting a wide-ranging hunting and fowling environment which had been utilised at a serious rather than at a casual level.

Tales of fowling bravado and accidents on the cliffs of Fair Isle and elsewhere are relatively common (eg Drosier 1830). Scott himself records one such event involving a boy who fell to his death while taking young seafowl from their nests shortly before his arrival on the island in 1814:

> *About a fortnight before we arrived a fine boy of fourteen had dropped from the cliff, while in the prosecution of this amusement, into a roaring surf by which he was instantly swallowed up. The unfortunate mother was labouring at the peat moss at a little distance. These accidents do not, however, strike terror into the survivors – they regard the death of an individual engaged in these desperate exploits, as we do the fate of a brave relation who falls in battle, when the honour of his death furnishes a balm to our sorrow. It therefore requires all the tacksman's authority to prevent a practice so pregnant with danger. Like all other precarious and dangerous employments, the occupation of the crags-men renders them unwilling to labour at employments of a more steady description.* (Laughlan 1982, 53)

An account by Kay written around 1680 further emphasises the apparent frequency of these tragedies; his simple description of the island includes important information regarding the value of feathers, not to mention young falcons which had a high reputation far beyond Fair Isle itself. In the 17th century the King's falconer often visited Shetland to collect young peregrines; the hawks were considered by some to be among the best in Britain (Brand 1701, 128). Kay's description of the island is one which underlines the importance of this natural resource:

> *It may seem needless to tell that there are no Forrests, Woods, nor Parks here. Here are no Lochs, no Rivers, no Trees, no Broom, no Whins, no Partridge nor Moor Fowl. But here are great multitudes of Sea Fowls which are not a little beneficial to the Islanders by reason of their feathers, which is a chief commodity of the place. But truly they buy them dear, always with the hazard, sometimes with the loss of their lives: for these fowls nestling in very high Rocks*

> *more than 100 fathoms deep from the surface of the earth, they go down on ropes to catch them: where it comes to pass that instead of catching the prey, they sometimes catch a slip whereby they are either crushed on the rocks or drowned in the sea. Here likewise is an excellent Falcon, which nestles and hatches in this place, whose young ones are taken with the same difficulty and hazard that ye Sea Fowls before spoken of.* (Bruce 1908, 55)

Whether earlier populations used these resources is another matter. The present seabird population of fulmars, skuas, puffins, kittiwakes and cormorants will not all have been present; in fact even in Scott's time neither the fulmar nor the great skua, two of the main species evident today, were likely to have been inhabitants (Bourne and Dixon 1974, 131). Some insight into the variety of former species comes with the records of 19th century ornithologists, although their methods often leave something to be desired. One such ornithologist was Robert Dunn, author of *The ornithologist's guide to the Islands of Orkney and Shetland* (1837), whose equipment on a visit to Osnafirth included a shotgun and no less than 140 pounds of shot. In any event, early exploitation of seabirds may have depended on edibility, either as an acquired taste or as a consequence of desperate hunger. Eggs and feathers were perhaps a more acceptable alternative. Whatever the early diets may have been they seem unlikely to have been much better than the fare experienced by Tudor who, even by 19th century standards, experienced some discomfort and offered his own advice to the unwary traveller:

> *Here a word of caution. No one should land on any of these islands, where there is a chance of being storm-stayed for several days, or it might be, though rarely in ordinary summers, weeks, without a pocket enema, as alteration in diet, and what not, are apt to bring on violent constipation, which purgatives seem at times to increase instead of dispersing. One or two lives might have been saved here, and in Foula, had this simple means of relief been within reach.* (Tudor 1883, 430)

3

THE SEA

Geography and landfall

In view of Fair Isle's size, relative isolation and subsistence needs, a traditional importance given to boats, to fishing, and to things of a general maritime nature is predictable. Colonists who were able to weather the passage across the Pentland Firth from mainland Scotland to Orkney would not have been unduly reluctant or incapable of crossing further to Fair Isle, and ultimately to Shetland. In good weather Orkney and Shetland are mutually visible; even from the relatively low hills of Sanday, Orkney, the cliffs of Sumburgh Head and Foula are both clear, with Fair Isle looming large in the middle ground. This alignment was also the basis of the beacon system set up by Earl Paul in late Norse times; it enabled a chain of fires to be lit southwards from Sumburgh to Fair Isle, to North Ronaldsay, and so onwards to Sanday and the south, thus providing a rapid if superficial level of communication (Pálsson and Edwards 1978, Ch 67).

Boats themselves, although rare in the archaeological record, were essential not only for primary migration and colonisation, but also for much of the daily subsistence and communication which followed. For any island economy which sought to look beyond the simple basics of self-sufficiency the availability of boats and the ability to navigate them was critical. Evidence for trading networks within the Northern Isles can be traced back to the Bronze Age when steatite (which outcrops in Shetland but not in Orkney), either in vessel or in ground down form for pottery temper, was brought to Orkney (Buttler 1989, 194). The extent to which Fair Isle played a part in this or similar systems is unknown, but the presence of relict landscapes (see chapter 4) together with a likely Bronze Age burial containing a steatite urn (*744*) suggests that the island may have been more than a mere navigational aid. The distribution of steatite and its implied trade, particularly in the Viking period (Buttler 1991), suggests that the waters between Orkney and Shetland were crossed with plausible regularity from the Bronze Age onwards. This has implications for transportation of goods and cultural contact, as well as for other types of exchange not apparent in the archaeological record.

There is no evidence to suggest that traffic was anything other than localised at this period; more distant communication, for example from Ireland and Britain, is only evidenced from the later Iron Age where the nature of contact is confused rather than aided by the spread of Christian missions. Subsequently, Norse movement between Scandinavia and Ireland undoubtedly brought Fair Isle to the frequent (and

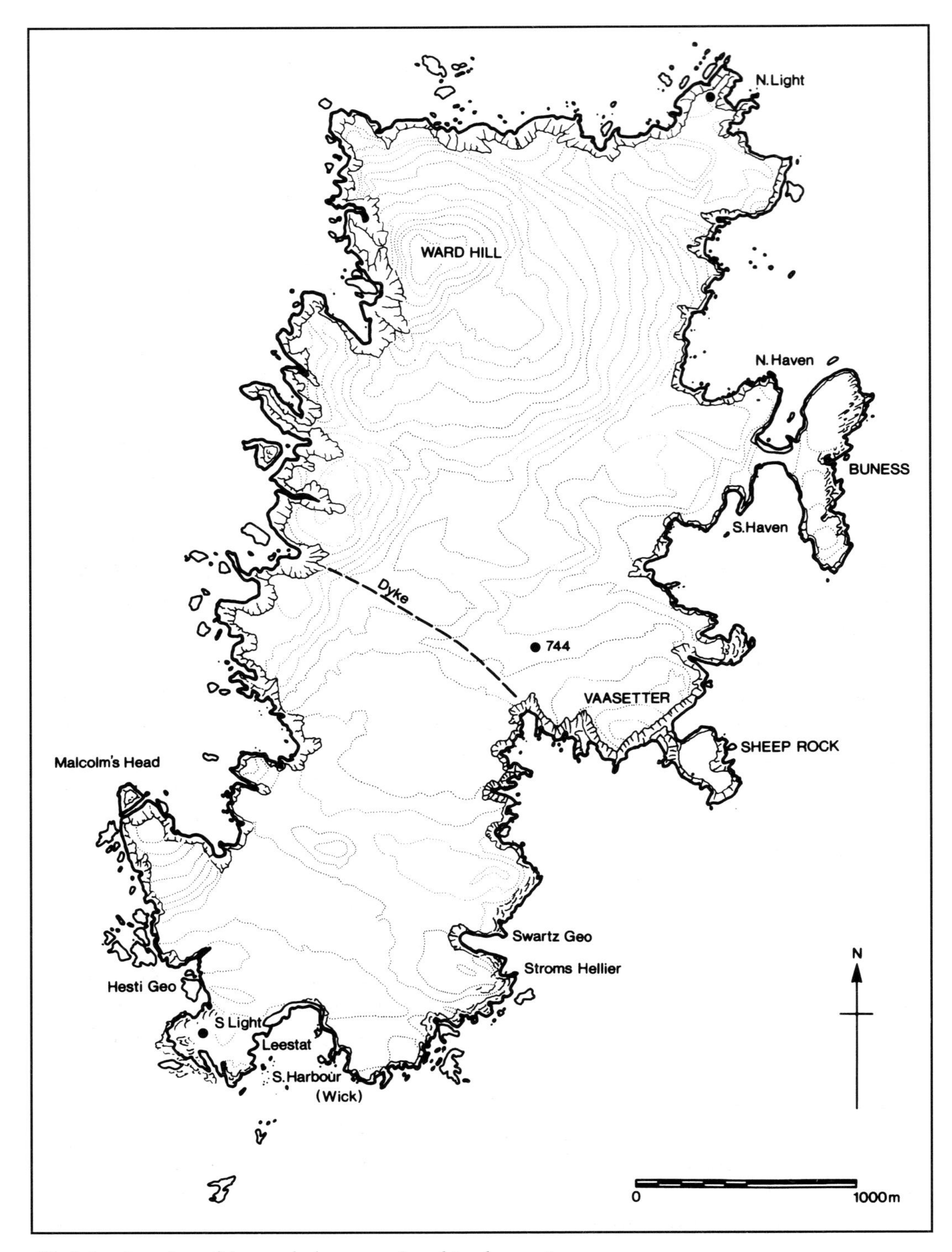

Fig 3.1 Location of sites and places mentioned in chapter 3.

possibly unwelcome) attention of migrants, traders and other travellers. Furthermore, on the basis of what is currently known of Norse seamanship, the island is almost certain to have been used as a sailing marker.

Within this framework of North Atlantic movement Fair Isle, despite its nodal position, had a relatively late cartographic debut, but so for that matter did Shetland itself which is first depicted in the later Middle Ages. By then much of the known coastal detail around the Northern Isles could probably be attributed to the movement of Hansa traders (O'Dell 1939, 230), and by the end of the 16th century navigational information was being published by the Dutch. There is some evidence too that regular transport schedules were in operation around the islands (Osler 1983, 26). Timothy Pont's map of Shetland followed less than a generation later and arguably ranks as the first 'accurate' map of Shetland, although hardly of Fair Isle which is crammed into the map's elaborate border. Much the same can be said for Sibbald's 1711 depiction (published by Monteith), itself little improved on van Keulen's distorted view of 'Faierhil' on a Dutch map of 1695. Mackenzie's chart of 1752 (plate 1.1), although schematic and with little internal detail, at least provides a relatively reliable outline and can probably be hailed as the earliest representation of the island proper using base lines and triangulation (Smith 1987). Detail, however, is first seen on George Thomas' 1839 chart which is generally hailed as the first 'scientific' map of the island (see chapter 9, plate 9.1) and is frequently reproduced in any discussion on Fair Isle's history (eg Heddle 1879; Waterson and Jones 1981).

In all periods archaeological evidence to both north and south of Fair Isle shows an economy in which fish was an important, if not a key component. Although there is some problem regarding bias in the archaeological record (see chapter 2), fish remains are ubiquitous in excavated deposits in the Northern Isles and must be seen as reflecting an activity which was both feasible and commonplace. In the events which are recorded in the *Orkneyinga Saga*, it was possible for Uni and his men to disguise themselves successfully as fishermen on Fair Isle (Pálsson and Edwards 1978, Ch 69); indeed, the earlier trick played on Dagfinn Hlodvisson, the Fair Isle beacon keeper, was one which required warships to be confused with fishing boats (see chapter 8). Later, Earl Rognvald went out rowing disguised as a fisherman and subsequently shared out his catch with the poor (*ibid*, Ch 85). These passages attest to the common occurrence of fishermen and fishing in the Fair Isle waters by the 12th century.

Elsewhere the presence of boats is by implication; it is, for example, possible to interpret a pronounced shift towards the utilisation of deeper sea resources during the Viking period on the basis of both excavated fish bone data (eg Wheeler 1977, 214) and artefactual evidence (eg Small 1966, 241). It is unclear, however, whether this reflects a saturation of terrestrial resources at this time, or simply the development of subsistence variation.

Fair Isle's settlement evolved within a maritime context in which the sea was a fundamental feature of existence. So too was climate; the combination of North Atlantic waters, fogs, rapid tidal flows, sudden squalls and the strength of prevailing winds had the effect of generating traditions of boat building, seamanship and local practice with pronounced regional characteristics. These differences are already crystallised in the accounts and descriptions written in the 18th and 19th centuries and attest to time-honoured customs, as well as to superstition. It is also clear that the respective maritime traditions of Orkney and Shetland, characterised by differences in environment and the nature of fishing itself, are divergent. Fair Isle's maritime personality appears not to have reflected the traditions of either island group, although the south of Mainland Shetland comes closest; the island's geographical position, its trading needs and its cultural connections provided the basis for a separate development.

The island's isolated position, remote but ironically within sight of main shipping lanes from medieval times onwards, has been the basis of much of its reputation and myth. Tudor's description of the island as being a 'conspicuous example of matter in the wrong place' (1883, 431) is one such report. Others, including a late 19th century Teutonic poem which portrays the island as an insect detached from its swarm, convey a similar, if less appropriate, impression (Jensen 1881, 12). Much comment from this period borders at worst on melodrama, at best on romanticism; both derive their origins partly from the island's name and partly from the rugged and foreboding outline seen on approach. That the same poem should describe the inhabitants as 'men forgotten by the world, strange to the age' is the product of a combination of literary convention and local legend which contemporary accounts do much to perpetuate. One traveller in 1832, a medical student on board the steamer *Magnus Troil*, caught in the mist between Fair Isle and Sumburgh provides proof enough. The passage is worth quoting in full:

> *... on a sudden, as I was leaning over the bow, two yawls full of strange looking mortals, broke through the mist, pulled astern of the ship without hailing, and disappeared in the driving fog. They were Shetland fisherman, the first I had ever seen, and I shall never forget the impression their strange garb made upon me. Dressed in their skin coats and breeches, with their nether limbs cased in high boots, they rather resembled the pictures we have seen of some of the Esquimaux tribes, ... the long fair hair of the Shetlanders, escaping in coils down upon their shoulders from beneath their large pendant caps of variegated worsted certainly gave them a more picturesque appearance than the inhabitants of a still more northern clime. These boats, extremely sharp at both ends with an extraordinary spring fore and aft, were not the least curiosity about them, and the rapid glance I caught of the whole as they burst suddenly*

through the fog, and were as quickly re-invested in its heavy canopy, imparted an air of romance exceedingly in accordance with my feelings of enterprise ... (Charlton 1832)

Seen from a distance, particularly in bad weather, Fair Isle's coastline is indisputably both ominous and inhospitable. The north and west approaches are huge and jagged, with Ward Hill and the western cliffs running almost sheer for 200-300 feet. Sheep Rock and the Vaasetter cliffs are equally foreboding to the east, to the extent that visitors were known to become 'giddy and sick' simply by watching the islanders manoeuvring sheep on the surface (Laughlan 1982, 50). Scott, whose observations tend to suffer from cynicism rather than exaggeration, wrote of 'hideous chasms' (*ibid*) while the diary of Miss Janet Schaw of Edinburgh, a less experienced traveller on route to the West Indies, recorded the approach as 'one continued chain of perpendicular rugged rocks' (Schaw 1939, 38).

Within this perimeter, however, two more sheltered regions have almost certainly provided accessibility and haven from the earliest days of settlement. At the south, the bay still referred to as the South Harbour is particularly suited to small boats and offers one of the few stretches of low shoreline on the island. Its main advantage, that of shelter from both easterlies and westerlies, is probably reflected in the local name *Leestat* at the north-east side. Some earlier sources (including Thomas' map of 1839) refer to the area as the *Wick* (ON *vík*, bay), a name often associated with shelter and landing. It was no doubt in this area that the 'pitiful skiffs' referred to in the *First Statistical Account* (*OSA* XIX, 437) are to be found, conveniently located adjacent to the present and historically documented settlement on the southern slopes. The bay still possesses the clear remains of no fewer than four sets of boat nausts, two of these lie at the north or north-east and two at the west or north-west (see chapter 10).

Approaches to the island in that quarter possessed the added benefit of convenience for boats travelling to or from Orkney, but the disadvantage of being dangerous to those unfamiliar with the jagged rocks which punctured the approaches. It was also unsuited to large boats, being 'a creek for barks, but no commodious harbour' (Sibbald 1711, 35), whereas James Kay, peripatetic minister to the island in the later 17th and earlier 18th centuries and no stranger himself to discomfort and danger in crossing from Dunrossness, described the access as being 'full of rocks' (Bruce 1908, 49). One of his successors, the Rev. John Mill, dispatched in a small boat from a Dutch fishing vessel a few miles north of the island in 1753, had already had enough of the crossing before reaching the south end:

The wind and tide was contrary, the night coming on and a mist forming on the top of the isle. I was seized with a strong fear, as if the Lord was going to cast us away which made me entertain constant discourse with the boatman

> *on pious subjects; and growing cold, I desired them to put me ashore at the north harbour which lay nearest.* (Goudie 1889, 11)

It says much for the stamina of Mill, as well as for the vagaries of weather, that his final visit to the island (at the age of 83) was made in 1793 in an open boat from Dunrossness. The north harbour to which he alluded in his diary 40 years earlier was provided by the natural formation of a sand tombolo across to Buness at the north-east part of the island. Although providing modern anchorage it was clearly less favourable in earlier times; in the 16th century Buchanan described it as 'affording a safe harbour for small vessels' (1827, 61). Kay noted it as being suitable for small boats in the summer but unacceptable during the winter (Bruce 1908, 49), presumably in view of the difficulties posed there by a north wind. This was also observed by Fotheringhame in a report on the island in 1804. Low, who managed to gather much information about the island without actually being able to land, identified a 60 ton limit on vessels that could safely land there (1774, 195). His information, which includes knowledge of channels and winds around the island harbour, seems well-founded and derives from a visit by James Robertson who visited the island around 1771 (Hibbert 1822, 124).

At Buness the harbourage contains two elements, a north and south, separated by the sand tombolo. The south of these, infrequently used today, is unmentioned in any of the earlier reports, the north being identifiable either topographically or by inference. Nor is there any record of the rate of the tombolo formation, the presence of which may have had implications not only for the suitability of landing in earlier periods, but also for the efficacy of an adjacent promontory form (see chapter 7). The absence of naust remains in either north or south part of the area would tend to support a lack of confidence in permanent boat stationing in that general area. One of the problems may have been the dangers from a north-east wind, for which reason the boats might be 'attached to rocks by means of rings' (*OSA* XIX, 435).

By the time of the *Second Statistical Account* all the boats on the island were recorded as lying on the south side of the island 'in a creek' which was also remembered as providing shelter for cod fishing vessels from the mainland (*NSA* 1845, 96). Muir, whose superficial ramblings on the island in 1885 are perhaps less creditable, described the south end as being 'the ordinary landing place' (1885, 75) inferring, by implication, that the north end was less popular. His comment probably copies the description 'usual landing place' on Thomas' chart. Thomas additionally denotes Hesti Geo at the south-west side of the island as a 'landing place with off shore wind', but this is not to be recounted elsewhere. Part of the popularity of the south end must have derived from the proximity of settlement and the convenience of being able to boat quickly on occasions of emergency or at the sight of passing vessels with whom trade was both frequent and profitable. Flags could also be hoisted on these and other occasions, for example at the time of Scott's departure from the island on August 10th 1814, a sign which his ego took to indicate a 'distinguished mark of honour' (Laughlan 1982, 54). A device for this, a tall wooden flagpole some 8m in length, pivoted near the base, is still in position on a natural mound at the south end (*18*).

This populated part of the island was obviously known to Scott who rowed in a small boat from the anchored Lighthouse Yacht, noting that the north harbour featured only 'seafowls and seals' whereas the south end offered 'land and breakfast' (Laughlan 1982, 50). Janet Schaw's diary on the other hand, written by one less familiar with rural Scottish ways, gives a particularly vivid account of the scene that greeted her:

> *I have been the more particular as to this island, as I do not recollect ever to have read any description of it, or indeed even heard of it, till the Captain advised me to trust to it for Sea-Stock, as an inducement to us to go north about, which, however, at that time, we refused to do. He assured me, we would get poultry of all kinds extremely cheap, also eggs, fine dried fish and the best Cabbages in the world. By the time we came on deck, he had hung out his flag and was plying off and on in the offing. The Sea was at that time running high, and it had become to blow pretty fresh. I felt myself pretty uneasy for the boats, which, they told us, were extremely small. The signal was not out above a quarter of an hour, when we observed the shore full of people of both sexes, who were scrambling amongst the rocks, when presently they seemed to part, as if by consent, the one half making towards the town, while the other half descended to the bason I formerly mentioned; and we soon saw them distinctly launch a number of boats, and put out on this rough Sea, a sight which greatly increased my anxiety. But as they came nearer, I was much pleased with the lightness with which they bounded over the waves ...* (Schaw 1939, 39)

Janet Schaw was fortunate that on that occasion both the weather and the sea allowed meeting and exchange to take place. Low was less lucky. He passed by twice, each time anticipating being able to land, but was thwarted on each occasion. His description of the southbound voyage as being 'a most troublesome passage' (1774, 195) was almost certainly an understatement. George Griffin, a priest, also made two fruitless attempts to reach the island in 1841. Letters written to his mentor, Bishop James Kyle, not only emphasise the real logistical problems of moving around the Northern Isles at that time, but also (one suspects) to yarns spun entirely for the benefit of a young cleric already ill at ease with travelling to remote rural parts. His missive of July 18th is especially transparent:

> *I have my doubts that if I am once landed on the Fair Isle (which may require more than one attempt, as often the boats cannot land) it may be months before*

> *I get off, as there is a tremendous surf surrounding the Island and the native boats are scarce sea worthy being as I hear no longer than the breadth of a dining table.* (Dilworth 1988, 121)

Nor was Scott's passage to the island entirely without its moments of drama. The Lighthouse Yacht was driven into the Sumburgh roost, all the landsmen on board being 'sicker than sick' and Scott himself making a rare admittance of discomfort:

> *This is the only time that I have felt more than temporary inconvenience, but this morning I have headache and nausea; these are trifles and in a well-found vessel, with a good pilot, we have none of that mixture of danger which gives dignity to the traveller. But he must have a stouter heart than mine who can contemplate without horror the situation of a vessel of an inferior description caught among these headlands and reefs of rocks, in the long and dark winter nights of these regions. Accordingly, wrecks are frequent ...* (Laughlan 1982, 49)

There are many tales of delay and hardship as a result of poor weather; these served to enhance, if not exaggerate, the island's reputation for inaccessibility. One such case occurred in 1892 when, according to the *Shetland Times* of February 13th, 'the people of Lerwick were startled to hear that in Fair Isle the people had almost been starving and had been without communication with the mainland for 62 days'. A subsequent edition (March 5th) contained a letter from William Manson, a commercial manager on the island, who denounced the tale as 'scandalous falsehood' spoken by 'loose babblers'.

Wrecks

The difficulties posed by local waters and sudden changes in weather, particularly fogs and strong winds, inevitably heightened the factors of danger which accompanied any movement around or between the Northern Isles. Fair Isle, lying across the north-west/south-east stream of currents between the Atlantic and the North Sea, is especially treacherous. Small compensation lies in the richness of plankton and fish shoals which are produced by the same marine effects. Manned light stations at the north and south points of the island were constructed in 1892 to a design by the Stevensons, although these had been preceded briefly by a rocket system from a building still visible near the turf dyke. These stations also included foghorns, one of which suffered from problems of overheating after prolonged use causing sudden failure. A letter of complaint in the *Shetland Times* on September 9th 1983 reported this to be a 'frequent occurrence'. The history of the lighthouses has been outlined by Thom (1989, 19f) and is not discussed further here.

Accounts of maritime tragedies in the area are numerous and galling (Morrison 1981), and the dates of more recent examples have been used by O'Dell to chart the direction and duration of shipping movements around those waters from the 17th century (1939, fig 5). His compilations identify the start and eventual extinction of the 17th century Greenland whaling industry, the developing Irish sea routes, the opening up of the Americas, and the commencement of trade through Archangel (*Arkhangelsk*) in the late 18th century. They suggest too that the majority of ships on route to the East Indies or the Americas passed Sumburgh Head; those bound for Archangel probably used Fair Isle as a beacon. More importantly perhaps in terms of the dynamics of maritime movement and the nationalist influences involved, the data portrays the Dutch as being dominant from around 1600 to the Napoleonic wars (1939, fig 6). On the basis of the shipping picture produced in which Fair Isle appears nodal, it is perhaps not surprising that a map of wrecks localised around the island (plate 3.1) should show such great variety and number. It emphasises again the seeming incongruity between Fair Isle's geographical remoteness and the density of its bypassing population.

The wrecks and disasters are by no means all foreign. Any community with a heavy reliance on the sea encounters its own share of trauma; the smaller the community the greater is the impact of tragedy at both personal and economic levels. A minister in Mainland Shetland recorded the effects of one such tragedy which befell open boats far out at sea from his parish at Delting:

> *When weather overtakes during the night, the poor are forced to desert their lines and make for the shore – some never make it. The present minister remembers two boats being lost in one night, by which accident 10 widows and 53 fatherless children were left.* (*OSA* XIX, 404)

On Fair Isle itself, where by the later 19th century the use of the sea and fishing was more intensive, almost every family might have a boat at sea simultaneously, the vulnerability being enormous. Several major disasters are recorded: Mill recalls one around 1779, when 'four homes had been ruined, the heads thereof were drowned carrying into the isle supplies for their families' (Goudie 1889, 57), and another occurred in 1897 when a sudden gale caught boats that were out bartering. This latter event was sufficiently tragic to merit headline space in the *Shetland Times* of September 4th in that year as an 'Appalling Disaster' even by Shetland standards. The subsequent issue of September 11th carried a fuller story including an eye-witness account of events of the island. This followed an appeal for the sufferers and was written under the somewhat insipid banner of 'An Interesting Account' by a Mr Cruikshanks, a telegraph linesman, who with his colleague Mr McHugh, a telegraph engineer, had been on the island when the disaster took place. The account, which illustrates a significant aspect of the island's subsistence economy and of its social organisation, is worth citing in full:

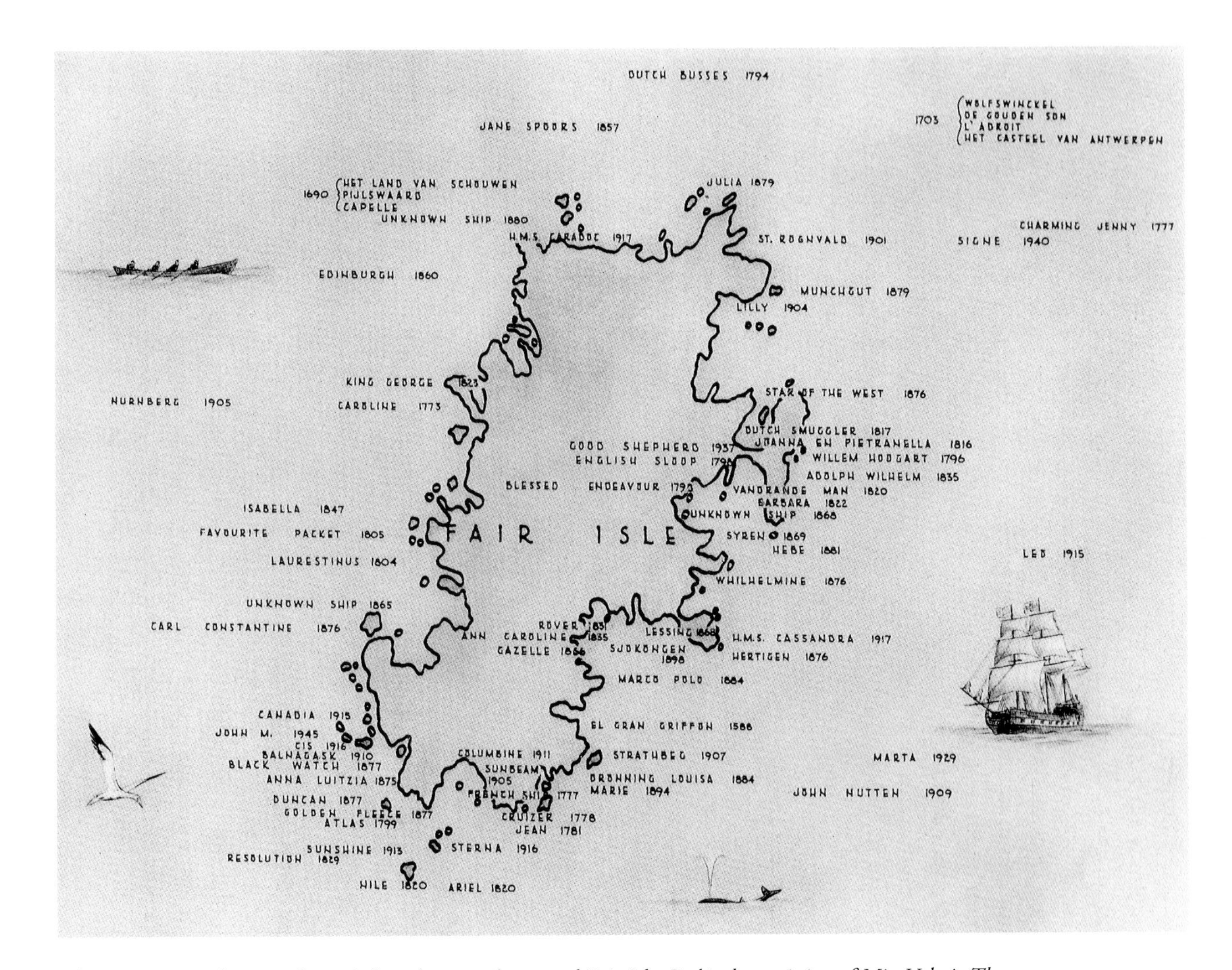

Plate 3.1 Distribution of recorded modern wrecks around Fair Isle. By kind permission of Miss Valerie Thom.

Mr Cruikshanks stated that they were landed on Fair Isle on Thursday morning last by the Northern Lighthouse steamer Pole Star. When the Pole Star was landing her passengers there were five ships off the island sailing to the eastward, and two hours afterwards, when they got ashore, fifteen ships were to be seen. It has been a long custom of the islanders to board passing vessels to barter vegetables, hosiery, etc., with them in exchange for money or provisions; and on this occasion four boats set out for this purpose. The weather at the time was fine, but in the course of the day it began to blow very hard from the north-east. The boats had all got on board ships, some of which were as far away as twelve miles to the south-east of the island. Late in the afternoon the first boat came ashore, but it was well on in the night before the second boat regained the isle. They reported that they had seen the missing boat[s] still making for the eastward. They had come up to one vessel, which, however, did not take them on board, and they had then proceeded for another, which was some distance further to the eastward. By this time fear prevailed amongst the relatives of the two boats still at sea. The whole population of the isle crowded down to the post office, which is at the south end of the island, where some distressful scenes took place. During the whole night watch was kept, not a single individual going to sleep. Next morning, about six o'clock, a dark speck was sighted on the horizon far to the eastward. When it was definitely made out, a relief boat was immediately launched, and set out with eight of a crew. When they came to the boat a tragic event happened. The boat had contained six men and a boy. The boy and two of the men were lying dead in the boat, and four men were feebly pulling. One of them looked round, saw the relief boat coming, and immediately fell back dead. The previous exertion and the sudden joy that relief had come at last had apparently been too much for the poor fellow. The other three men were very much exhausted, and all had to be assisted out of the boat on reaching the landing place. The story they told was a sad one. They stated that on the previous evening, about nine o'clock, they and the missing boat were in at the lighthouse at the south end of the isle – so close, indeed, were they that had it been calm they could have hailed the lighthouse; but the tide turned and took them away to the eastward again. The boy and the two men had expired shortly before that. They lost sight of the second boat about nine o'clock at night, and when they were rescued they were under the belief that this boat had reached the isle. Needless to say, the scene when the dead bodies of the four men were carried ashore was of the most heartrending description. Regarding the fate of the missing boat, which contained other four men, not the slightest hope is entertained. It was at first hoped that the men might have got on board one of the passing vessels, but this hope was abandoned when it was learned that the two boats had been in

> *company at nine o'clock on the previous night. By that time, of course, all vessels would have been many miles to seaward. There was no ballast in the boat, so that she would probably not have sunk. As to the cause of the men succumbing so quickly, the survivors seem to say that it must have been through fright and the tremendous exertion the men made when they realised that the gale was on them, and that they might have a difficulty in reaching the island. None of the men were over fifty, and the night, though cold, was not so bad as to cause death through exposure. The disaster leaves the island in a state of desolation. There were only thirty-four families on Fair Isle, and there being much intermarriage, nearly all are related. The number of dependents, so far as ascertained, is thirty-four. Some forty people have left Fair Isle lately in consequence of the poor prospects of making a livelihood there through the small prices for fish and the scanty rations from crops.*
>
> *The steamship Pole Star has returned to Stromness without finding any trace of the missing boat. All hope has now been abandoned. (Shetland Times* 1897, September 11th, 5)

The columns of the same newspaper subsequently became the focus of an appeal for the disaster dependants. The fund's progress was monitored weekly until the end of November that year – an unprecedented duration for a tragedy of that type.

Reliance on the sea could also be vulnerable to other dangers; Brand recorded how two-thirds of the island's population had been lost by the smallpox with the result that there was not a sufficient number of men left to manage the boats (1701, 123).

Other stories abound throughout the Northern Isles, but the episode which is most recounted and which is particular to Fair Isle is the wreck of the *El Gran Grifon*, flagship of the Spanish Armada's supply squadron, which sank off the south-east of the island in 1588. The event belongs to a general context of Armada events in the Northern Isles (Anderson 1988), but the relevance here, apart from the instance of the wreck itself and the excavation subsequently undertaken (Martin 1972; 1975), lies in the diary entries made by an anonymous survivor of the crew (translated in Ker 1920) and by other contemporary accounts. These provide the earliest description of the island and its inhabitants, although it is unfortunate that many subsequent accounts (some of which may originate from James Melville, Minister of Anstruther in Fife through where the surviving Armada sailors passed on route home) became corrupted and exaggerated during later transmission. The records of Sibbald (edited by Monteith) and Hibbert, on which Tudor and others relied, contain vivid but unlikely tales of Spanish sailors becoming weakened by hunger and pushed over the cliffs by the islanders, while others were given shelter in fish skeos which had been previously rigged to collapse on those inside (Hibbert 1822, 92). Tudor for one identified discrepancies in this derived narrative; his further observation of Melville's sermons against 'Papists and Spainyarts' does much to direct the blame for the corruption (1883, 434).

The *El Gran Grifon*, along with three other Armada ships, had become detached from the main fleet in the North Atlantic during their enforced return to Spain. Encountering bad weather, already overloaded with sailors rescued from one of the other ships, the *Barca de Amburg* which had since sunk, and structurally damaged from the affray in the English Channel, the ship had scant hope of reaching Spain intact. The vessel, which was little more than a glorified Baltic hulk, was suitably armed with 38 guns (Martin 1972, 59), but had been originally designed for transport not for warfare. In a successful attempt to avoid being flooded by on-coming seas, the commander Juan Gomez de Medina (frequently confused in many accounts with the Armada commander, the Duke of Medina Sidonia) had no option other than to allow the vessel to be carried as the autumn gales dictated. Heavy seas were almost matched by another danger – that of enforced landing within islands which, according to the hulk's pilot, were 'Scottish, and inhabited by savage people' (*gente salvaje*). A more correct translation of *salvaje* is probably wild or, given the nature of the prevailing religious climate, heathen. At least a part of the crew would almost certainly have derived from the ship's original port of Rostock and the waters around the Northern Isles will have been familiar to them. Ultimately, on September 28th, after considerable distress the patched-up vessel was driven ashore on Fair Isle; here the narrator makes the curious comment that 'anything was better than drinking salt water' – presumably a reflection of the pilot's superstition.

There is, however, some ambiguity regarding the nature of the arrival at Fair Isle in that the anonymous account makes no mention of being wrecked. Martin's interpretation of the evidence (1975, 146) suggests that the ship probably rode out the storm during the night of September 27th (the island was reached at sunset that day) before making an attempt to run ashore at a suitable place early the next morning. Swartz Geo, an inlet with a sloping pebble beach, was almost certainly chosen, but the exercise may have been thwarted by the strong current which crosses the mouth of the inlet and which may have dragged the *El Gran Grifon* into the reefs of the adjacent Stroms Hellier (plate 3.2; *520*) where her remains were eventually found. Most of the crew and soldiers on board, together numbering nearly 300, despite being exhausted and suffering from many weeks of malnutrition, reached the safety of the cliff top. By the time that conditions were suitable for transport off the island some 6 weeks later, almost 50 of this number had perished from hunger. Their remains are reputed to be those exposed in a mass grave at the south end of the island in the early part of this century.

According to written sources occasional plundering of the wreck took place, including the intended use of a one-man submarine in the early 18th century, a machine which Martin describes as 'an ingenious but terrifying contraption' (1975,

Plate 3.2 The overhanging geo of Stroms Hellier in which El Gran Grifon *was wrecked. Copyright Colin Martin.*

160). Mention also appears in the *First Statistical Account* which congratulates Captain Roe from England who, in 1740, was 'fortunate enough to raise two brass guns' (*OSA* XIX, 435). Their whereabouts are unknown. The site itself was identified by Martin in Stroms Hellier, a narrow rocky inlet at the south-east of the island, where the scattered remains of a shipwreck were recorded by underwater survey and excavation (Martin 1972, fig 2). The hull had not survived, but its general location was interpreted from the recovery of heavier artefacts, typically bronze and cast-iron guns, shot and lead ingots. Study of the armaments points towards a defensive function for the ship – a function fully in keeping with its documented role as a supply carrier.

4

Earthworks and Field Systems

Major earthworks

Some of the most visible but least researched monuments in the Northern Isles take the form of linear earthworks and banks which fulfilled a variety of functions from prehistoric times through to the present day. In marginal areas they have the advantage of changing little over time other than by reuse and erosion, but otherwise present problems in securing dates of origin. Fair Isle, like most other parts of the Northern Isles, contains examples of various types (fig 4.1) with the majority lying in marginal land. By far the largest is the *feelie* dyke itself (*226*), shown on Mackenzie's chart of 1752, with a maximum width of about 8m, a surviving height of some 2m and an original length of over one kilometre running across the island from Gunnawark to Haswalls (plate 4.1). A similar monument (*225*), not shown on Mackenzie's chart and therefore arguably later, survives only in part but has an adjacent western point of origin and runs in a south-east direction before being flattened into the landscape by ploughing which took place in living memory. This more southerly boundary, which is depicted on Thomas' 19th century map (1839), appears to be aligned towards a major burnt mound but has become eroded to a point at which it is no longer possible to assess the chronological relationship between mound and boundary (see chapter 9, plate 9.1).

It is perhaps significant that the two dykes bear the names North Gunnawark and South Gunnawark respectively at their western origins. *Wark* is presumably the indicator of 'work' or 'monument', usually taken to imply a feature of some antiquity, and the need to differentiate might be taken as implying a degree of contemporaneity. A third possible example (*211*), almost completely eroded and visible only with a low sun over a distance of some 80m at the east side of the island, is less easy to understand. Its alignment appears to be unrelated to the others, suggesting a radically different division of the landscape. Its width, which is consistently of about 5m, makes alternative interpretation difficult.

As far as can be seen, the two main upstanding monuments show an upper construction of turf and earth, suggesting that their original size would have been more formidable than the present slumped appearance appears. Neither is associated with a ditch from which the constructional material might have been derived; presumably the bulk was transported from the hill land at the north where scouring of the turf would be unevidenced today. Their construction, however, was an exercise requiring planning and organisation, and was presumably for communal benefit. On

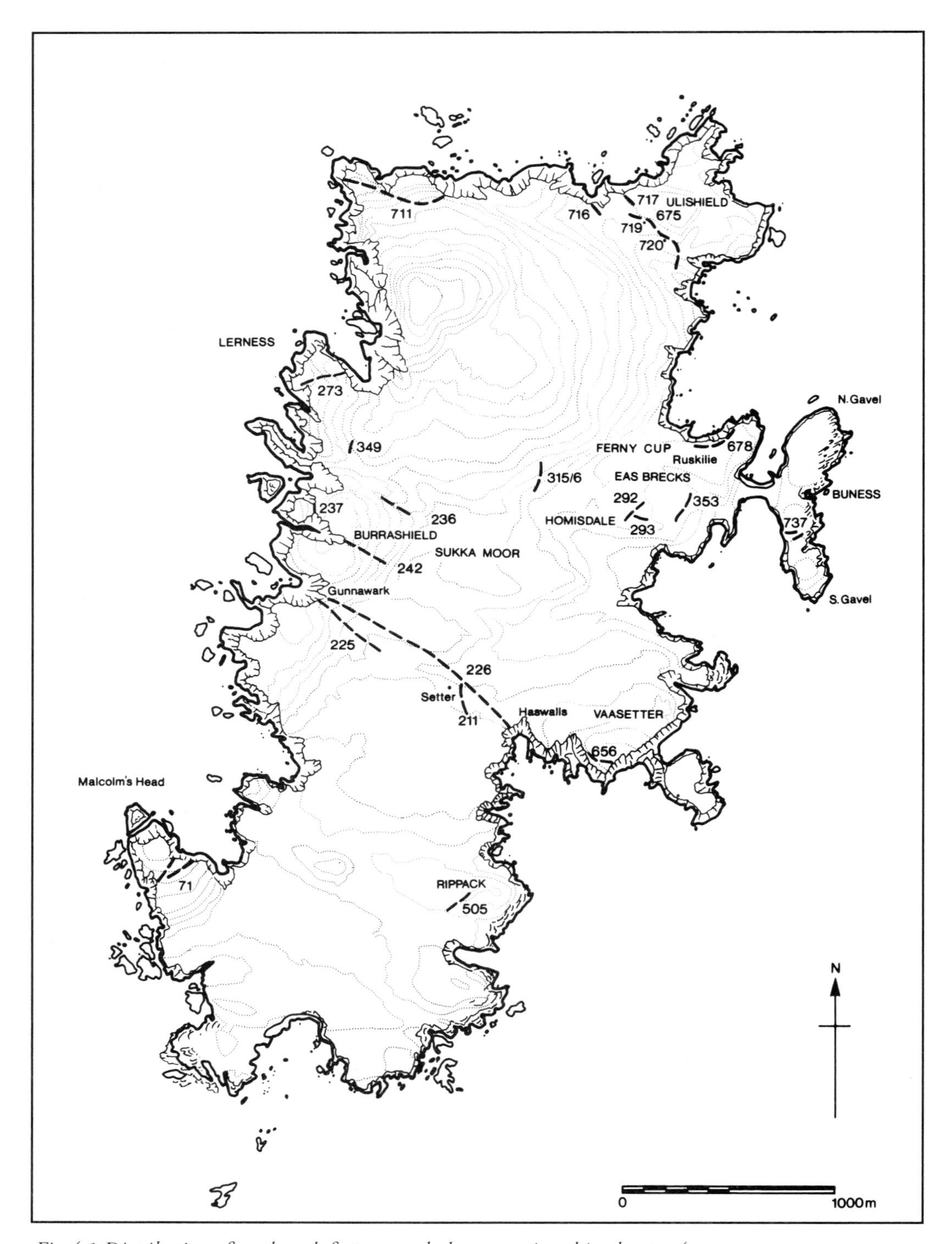

Fig 4.1 Distribution of earthwork features and places mentioned in chapter 4.

Plate 4.1 The western origin of the feelie *dyke (226) and the later stone wall which runs parallel. A further earthen dyke (225) can be seen on the left.*

Fair Isle, as on other islands where similarly massive dykes survive, the monument serves to separate the common land (scattald) from the townlands, but whether this is a deliberate division for land use purposes, or derived from some earlier function, similar for example to the 'treb dyke' where the interpretation is normally viewed as territorial (eg Lamb 1980a, 9 and 21f), remains open to question. The latter explanation is preferred by Fenton who sees such monuments reused in a more modern context, possibly as *pickie* dykes which may already have existed in the later Iron Age (1978, 13). On Fair Isle the *feelie* dyke is cut by the modern road and shows a composition at that point which may be interpreted as having stone footings, or at least a substantial stone component in the lower part of the matrix – a characteristic which Fenton considers relatively early.

Post-medieval agricultural traditions in Shetland necessitated this fundamental division of land use, but there is a suspicion that the location of the dyke on Fair Isle may have been originally dictated by an existing boundary. The current stone wall has to be seen as the latest in a series of linear monuments whose functions may have differed, but all shared commonality of position across the narrowest part of the island. Mackenzie's chart of 1752 at least serves as a *terminus ante quem* for the *feelie* dyke's date of origin.

Smaller earthworks

Elsewhere on the island smaller boundary features constructed in a different manner and using different materials clearly served other functions, not all of which are apparent from the evidence available. A number of low examples, typically constructed of earth, turf and stone, occur within or around the margins of townland to the south where they might be interpreted as representing relict sections of dyke separating the infields and outfields of individual tunships; a few of these may be related to local field names. This general group is discussed below (chapter 9) in relation to post-medieval settlement.

However, many other smaller boundaries appear to delineate individual headlands, groups of headlands or peninsulas. Here the construction is of markedly different character, seemingly formed by the setting of large stones at intervals across the landscape followed by the infilling of intermediate spaces with earth, turf and smaller stones. The most impressive lengths still visible lie in the barren moorland sector where one of the largest (*675*) isolates the entire north-east corner of the island, roughly following the line of the Burn of Wirrvie for 300m but on a higher contour. It survives as a winding line of irregularly positioned large stones set like dragon's teeth (plate 4.2), some almost 1m tall, partly submerged by a pool at the western end and eroded at the east, where its collapsed form is still visible in the cliff section. A small amount of overburden makes it consistently visible to a width of about 1.5m. Two sub-circular earthworks lie along its route; these were originally interpreted as settlement sites, but investigation has since caused them to be reconsidered as burial monuments (*719*; *720*, chapter 6) linked together as part of an overall boundary system.

Plate 4.2 Boundary (675) at Ulishield showing surviving 'dragon teeth' set stones.

A section cut through the earthwork (fig 4.2) showed that the individual large stones had been set into grey silty clay subsoil and that subsequent peat development had effectively subsumed the bulk of these foundations, including the smaller support stones. Assuming the section to be representative, it would indicate that a substantial part of the original visible monument now lies buried below the peat cover.

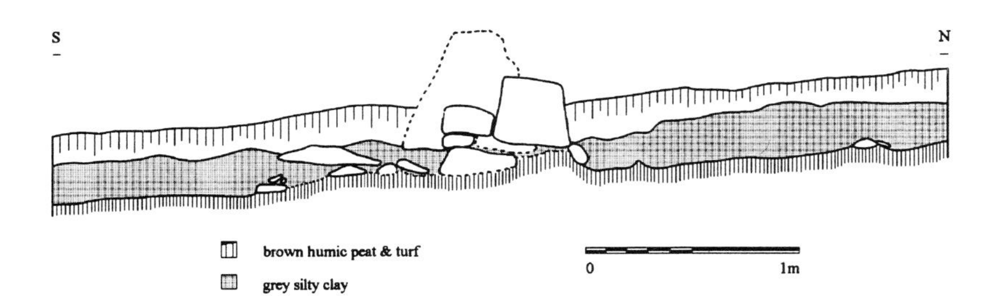

Fig 4.2 Section through boundary feature 675.

Although the original layout of the boundary appears to isolate the main headland, it seems possible that a later(?) modification also drew in (or separated off) the headland immediately adjacent to the south. This was carried out by the construction of an earthwork some 100m long with its junction some 50m from the cliff at the east, running down to terminate at the burn in the base of the valley. The construction seems to have relied less on large set stones and more on an earth and stone matrix, suggesting a different phase of construction. The fact that it survives substantially better than the earthwork from which it appears to spring might indicate a more modern date of origin. It also strengthens a suspicion that the nature and extent of the land enclosed appears to have been significantly more important than the contours of the landscape on which it was built.

In common with a number of other boundaries on the island the main length may have had precursors; two partial boundary lengths were identified at the west end of the monument, one (*717*) lying slightly to the north-east and running parallel for about 60m, and the other (*716*) lying to the south-west where it runs parallel for a similar distance before turning to terminate at the burn. Both were constructed by the same method, although the former appears to have been subjected to a greater depth of peat formation and is therefore possibly earlier. The latter (*716*) causes a further problem of interpretation; its use of the burn as a terminal corresponds to a similar situation at the eastern end of the main earthwork (*675*). This might suggest that the earthworks were concerned not so much with annexing the headland as with providing an irregular enclosure bounded by earthworks to the north and the east (*675*), to the west by cliffs and to the south by the burn. Local names either on the headland itself or in the immediate vicinity offer little indication as to how these apparently divided parts of the landscape might have been used. The general area is known as Ulishield, the landscape providing suitable higher pasture as the second element suggests.

At the north-west of the island an earthwork of similar construction, and the longest of its type on Fair Isle (*711*), stretches for almost 500m in an area where the headlands are neither prominent nor well-defined. Its course follows a gently curving line from what appears to be an arbitrary point on the west cliffs to an equally arbitrary point on the north cliffs. The area enclosed has no natural definition and the course of the earthwork appears to ignore any help that the natural topography might offer, sweeping in an uncomfortable arc across a steep hillside. It currently survives to a width of about 2m, intermittently visible, and with a maximum height of around 0.5m. One point of interest lies in a stone-sided feature some 2m square interpreted as being an integral part of the construction located towards its western end. The local name *Sheena Wheeda* ('white rig') seems to be applied to the enclosed area, although it also seems to have been extended to include certain coastal features.

On the west side of the moorland zone two smaller but more specific headland areas are annexed by similar earthworks types. The larger of these (*273*) winds for over 200m from cliff to cliff isolating the headland of Lerness while the smaller (*237*), identified for around 50m, defines the isthmus across to a stack west of Burrashield.

A further boundary (*71*), but of different construction, lies on Malcolm's Head, a steep headland at the south-west of the island, and location of a Napoleonic Tower as well as a modern coastguard's hut. A partially exposed section shows that the south-east side consists of a line of single large stones against which a matrix of turf and earth was heaped from the north-west and then consolidated. The earthwork takes the shortest distance (some 100m) between two opposing inlets in the cliff, effectively defining a natural promontory. It also exhibits a curious adjunct on the north-east side; this is of less substantial construction and runs for about 70m to a point along the cliff edge. It is difficult to see whether this was designed to increase the area enclosed (assuming it to be later), or alternatively to hinder access (animal or human) to that part of the promontory. The apparent need to define or annex promontories in this way is unlikely to be unique to Fair Isle; detailed fieldwork elsewhere in Shetland will no doubt serve to show the phenomenon to be more widely distributed. On Fair Isle at least it must be said to be extraordinarily persistent, even in the smallest location. On Buness, for example, the South Gavel appears to have been annexed by an earthwork based on large set stones located across a natural constriction (*737*).

Not all boundaries of this type possess termini that are both coastal; two (*236*; *242*, some 60m and 240m long respectively) run roughly parallel across Burrashield some 300m apart. Both appear to have a point of origin in the western cliffs, each passing along a natural gully to terminate down in the plateau of Sukka Moor, one terminal being marked by a low mound, possibly a burial. They provide a man-made emphasis to a land division already defined by natural features. A possibly related boundary lies inland to the north (*349*), identifiable for only some 20m but perhaps belonging to a larger system of land division of which these boundaries survive as fragments. One (*242*) may originally have been associated with a headland boundary (*237*) of similar construction; as such the three sites may represent a specific landfast enclosure. Within this defined area, apart from a number of military monuments located on the high ground, post-medieval crub bases predominate on the lower slopes (see chapter 7), among which a small number of cairns and burnt mounds are evident.

An equally remote landfast enclosure might be interpreted on the east of the island at Eas Brecks by three extant lengths of irregularly set stones (*292*; *293*; *353*), together totalling some 380m in length. The individual stones, the largest measuring approximately 0.5m in height, although lacking any earth and turf cover, were not initially recognisable as a linear feature until a number of sockets were also discovered. This particular part of the moorland has been subject to a reclamation project in recent years and the loss of several of the stones and overburden may be explained accordingly. The position of the individual stones (and empty sockets) showed no regularity in their spacing, and this tends to conform to the construction of other stone-based boundaries on the island. It is conceivable that these alignments may represent the surviving parts of an enclosure which formerly covered much of this low but barren hillside, embracing an area of some 2.6 hectares. It is of added interest that one of the earthfast stones exhibits a possible cup mark, and that the general area is defined as being the find location for a flint core, now held in the Shetland Museum (Acc. no. ARC 65750).

At the most obvious level of interpretation the isolation of individual headlands or peripheral parts of the island might be seen as representing the most efficient method of creating enclosures for livestock, although presumably some form of stockading may also have been necessary at its top. In locations where marginal land is almost entirely surrounded by cliffs or water, a simple earthen or stone-based boundary across the narrowest point of land access is an economic and convenient method of security. While this might explain a number of the well-defined headlands discussed above, it is not an entirely satisfactory interpretation for every example identified, particularly those where the likely area of enclosure appears to ignore either naturally defined termini or topographical features.

None of these earthworks have a surviving local name which might support an enclosure theory, nor are any noted, even in passing, in the verbose and often pedantic descriptions of the 18th or 19th centuries. The visitors who provided these descriptions in the most part restricted their visits to the populated south part of the island, but the earthworks receive no mention in either of the *Statistical Accounts*, perhaps suggesting that they played no part in the economic life of the island at that time. The modern organisation of the sheep *crue* – the annual gathering and shearing of the common hill sheep beyond the dyke – is based on a traditional system of man movement and sheep driving along the hills and moors, yet none of the annexed areas noted here play any part whatsoever in this process. The method of shepherding employed (see chapter 10), based on topography, terrain and local knowledge, is the product of generations of experience; the fact that these monuments are not currently used as part of the modern *crue* suggests that they belong to a different, earlier process altogether.

Conversely, it may be no coincidence that local names such as *Hestaness* and *Buness* contain animal elements (horse and cattle respectively), suggesting not only enclosures but also a relatively early date of use. Neither, unfortunately, currently show any sign of extant boundaries, although some support comes from a record in the *Second Statistical Account* which describes how the Buness headland was 'fenced off with a high stone dyke across its isthmus' (*NSA* XV, 95). Stone-built dykes would appear to be a later, but not altogether unrelated issue; in fact there are a number of examples on the island where an existing earthen (field) boundary has been surmounted by a later stone version. The question here, however, is not so much the nature of the boundary as its function, and whether the creation of a natural headland enclosure is altogether a suitable or safe place to retain animals, especially given the precipitous cliffs which surround most of the sites, not to mention the strength of prevailing winds.

The converse argument might therefore be applicable, namely that the earthworks were constructed in order to keep animals *away* from the more dangerous edges – also a dubious solution given both the extent of the cliffs still unprotected and the loss of valuable grazing land. Nevertheless, it might be noted that a low, stone-built dyke (*656*, the *Pony Dyke*) located for about 150m above the south-west face of Vaasetter is locally recorded as being used to prevent horses from falling over the edge. Loss of grazing land here would be minimal. The slope is particularly insidious as well as steep, and a boundary at this point but not elsewhere on Vaasetter is understandable.

Less easy to understand, however, is the location of the final earthwork of this type to be discussed (*678*). This lies on the north-facing cliff at Ruskilie to the west of Buness, where it closely follows the cliff line for a distance of some 200m. The construction appears to be stone based like those noted above, and about 2m wide, but there are no obvious termini – the relationship is with the cliff edge, sections of which have collapsed destroying parts of the earthwork in the process. Erosion has almost certainly placed the monument nearer to the sea than at the time of construction, but the form and nature of any associated enclosed land to the north remains open to speculation. The name Ruskilie may be compared to *Russikil* in Papa Stour (Stewart 1987, 117) from *Hross*, a horse, and *gil*, a ravine or narrow valley, although this seems not altogether topographically appropriate.

Field systems

An additional class of earthworks can be identified on lower lying land below the 70m contour line, away from the coast, and in apparent association with other archaeological monuments. A complex of these occurs as part of the best preserved area of relict landscape on the island, in the Ferny Cup – a sheltered dale in the eastern moorland (fig 4.3). The linear features appear to consist of both field dykes and lynchets, the former representing internal field divisions and the latter demonstrating the terracing effect of land use in this sloping area. There is no visible evidence for any outer boundary or dyke which would have defined the cultivated area as a whole, although the need for this may have been partly negated at the north where the hillside rises almost precipitously from the valley bottom. The surviving landscape only covers some 1.7 hectares, the landfall being such that its original extent is unlikely to have been much larger, despite the presence of a modern road cutting across the north-east end.

From a constructional point of view the field dykes differ significantly from the earthworks already discussed; earthfast stones are not visually apparent and in those places where erosion permits inspection, the matrix appears to be of earth, turf and small stones. The survey plan was drawn up during early spring, a particularly suitable time for low vegetational cover, but even then some of the dykes were indistinct and several became wholly unidentifiable during the summer months. A number were only observable for distances of 10m or less, whereas others measured over 50m and, in the case of one of the lynchets, over 100m. It seems possible that some of these dykes may have incorporated small clearance cairns, such was the unevenness of their width, and this would accord with known excavated examples elsewhere in Shetland (below) where the dykes themselves might be viewed as performing a combined division and clearance function. The nature and dimensions of the fields to which they relate are not clear from the surviving evidence, those at the south-west end point to more than one period of division – a concept also suggested by the relatively high density of monuments in the immediate vicinity. These include cairns, small enclosures, burnt mounds and the remains of at least two houses (*333* and *342*).

An excavated transect across a positive lynchet adjacent to one of these structures (*333*) demonstrates the comparative thickness of the buried soils at this point (around 0.5m) compared to those in the negative lynchet below (fig 4.4). This latter

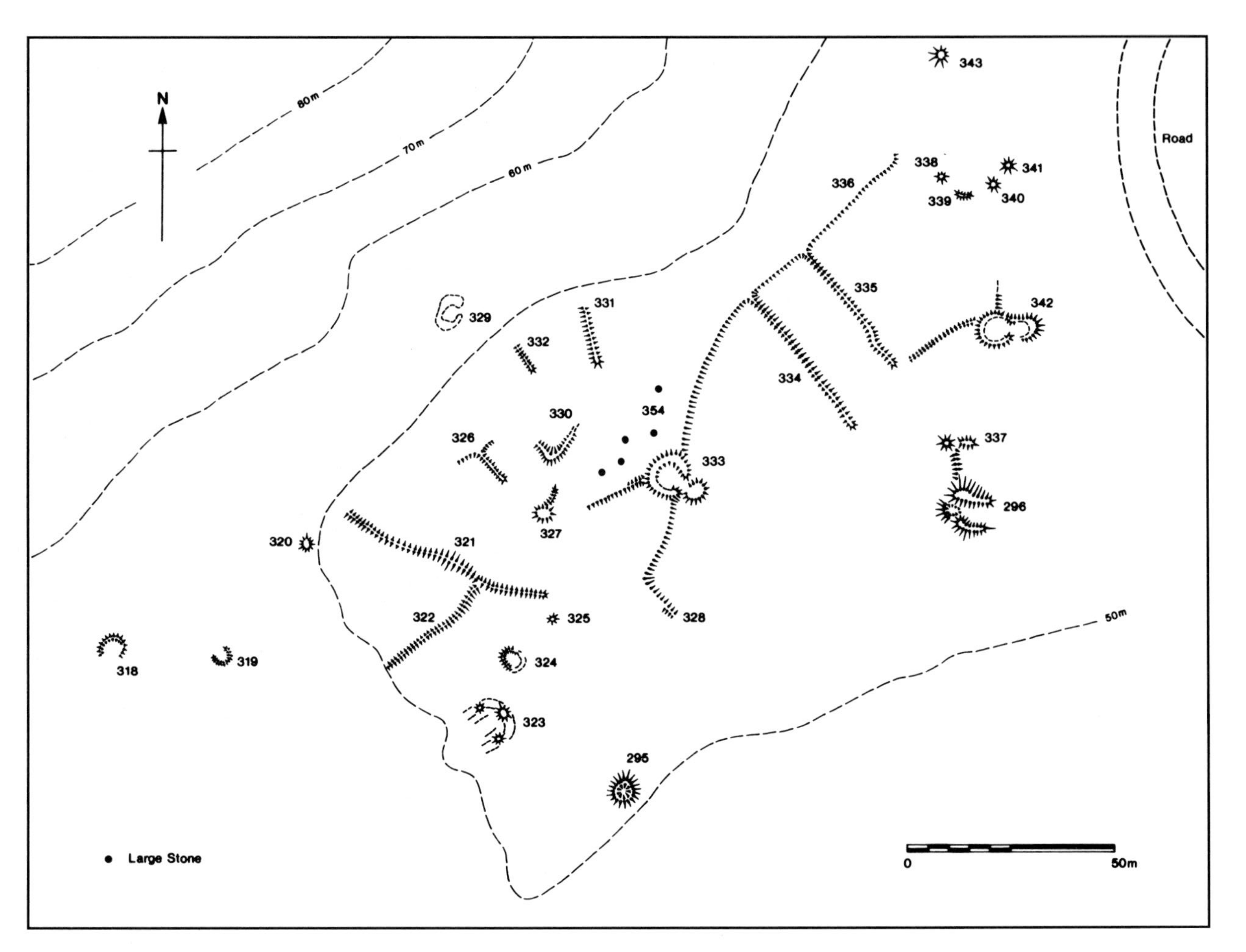

Fig 4.3 Plan of monuments in the Ferny Cup area.

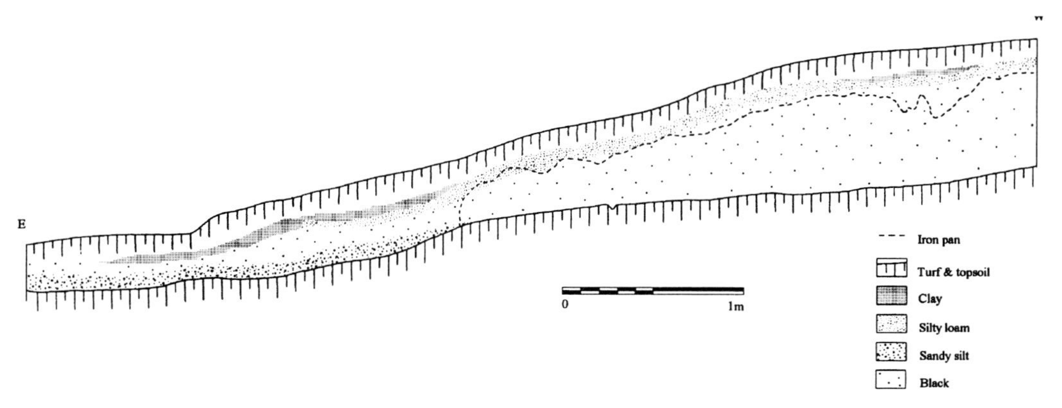

Fig 4.4 Section through lynchet in the Ferny Cup.

narrow profile was identified elsewhere by augering, cores being taken at 5m intervals over a distance of 100m along the eastern projection of the transect. Magnetic susceptibility samples taken in a vertical column from the transect section showed that these buried soils offered enhanced susceptibility appropriate to an anthropogenic origin, an interpretation supported by the presence of ard marks cut into the natural clay subsoils at the deeper end of the profile. Manured cultivation was supported from the results of micromorphological analysis, probably using seaweed (Chrystall 1994). The section additionally showed the presence of iron panning, presumably formed by leaching of the upper soils.

Reference to the prehistoric landscape at the Scord of Brouster (Whittle 1986, fig 4) may give a broad idea as to how the original field system at the Ferny Cup may have been devised, the landscape being brought into use by clearance and tilling, with the subsequent inner land division reflecting the location of associated structures. One of Whittle's main concerns lay in the determination of a relative chronology for the individual components of this system, an exercise made more complex in the Ferny Cup both by the lower level of preservation and by the range of monuments in the vicinity. The two landscapes also exhibit a further major difference, namely the location of the houses in relation to the respective field systems. At Brouster the buildings lay within the fields themselves, whereas in the Ferny Cup both of the interpreted houses appear to represent part of the dyke structure and take an almost nodal position in the organisation of the boundaries. This may perhaps reflect a shortage of cultivable land at the time forcing settlement sites into positions which minimised the loss of this valuable commodity. If this is the case, as indeed the need to cultivate such small areas as the Ferny Cup suggests, it says much for the likely density of prehistoric settlement in the more fertile south part of the island and hence much for the enormity of the archaeological loss that has taken place there.

Elsewhere in the moorland zone other examples of similar field dykes, probably of equal antiquity, survive only in fragmentary form. On higher ground to the south-west of the Ferny Cup two short lengths of curving boundary (*315* and *316*), at 30m and 20m in length respectively, may represent surviving traces of a comparable field system, the former possibly representing a lynchet. Compositionally they appear consistent with those already discussed and lie at the head of Homisdale, a sheltered area topographically analogous to the Ferny Cup, in which peat formation appears to have buried most other traces of the early landscape. Although the maximum peat depth in Homisdale is little more than 0.5m, its smoothing effect on the landscape is significant. Nevertheless, ditch clearance and re-cutting has since enabled part of this buried landscape to be identified (fig 4.5). One of the features severed by the ditch has the surface appearance of a line of irregularly spaced stones traceable for almost 40m across the slope of the dale (*299* and *300*). However, the buried profile, seen from ditch cutting, indicated a deeper, stone-based feature with a definable earth and turf matrix suggesting a field dyke. Similar examples of sporadic stone alignments in the vicinity might therefore be interpreted accordingly at the north-west end of the dale (*312* and *313*), and also at the south-west (*304*). Above the ground, the importance of the area can be inferred from the survival of burnt mounds, cairns and other possible features with which these surviving lengths of dyke may have been associated.

Field boundaries also enabled a further area of probable early settlement to be identified. This lay to the south-east of the island in a sheltered part of the Rippack – a gradually rising promontory beyond the fenced area. The remains here consist of at least six separate lengths of boundary or dyke, the composition of which appears to be consistently of earth, turf and small stones. Surviving lengths vary between 8-80m, but all lie between 1.5-2m in width and in a definable area covering some 1.7 hectares below the 50m contour. In places where erosion or rabbit activity has allowed the matrix to be studied, the basal element shows a high content of small stones, again pointing towards primary land clearance. This is supported by the character of the largest example (*505*) whose length is punctuated by low cairns interpreted as belonging to clearance. At the north-east it terminates at the largest cairn in the group. The relative positions of these monuments suggest that they may belong to more than one phase of land use, although the respective layouts of these phases, not to mention the extent to which other monuments in the immediate vicinity may be related (eg amorphous mounds and possible foundations), is unclear.

Interpretation

Interpretation of these various linear features would benefit considerably from some knowledge of their likely age – an exercise almost impossible to conduct from survey alone. Nor is there much in the way of existing research in Shetland on which to base

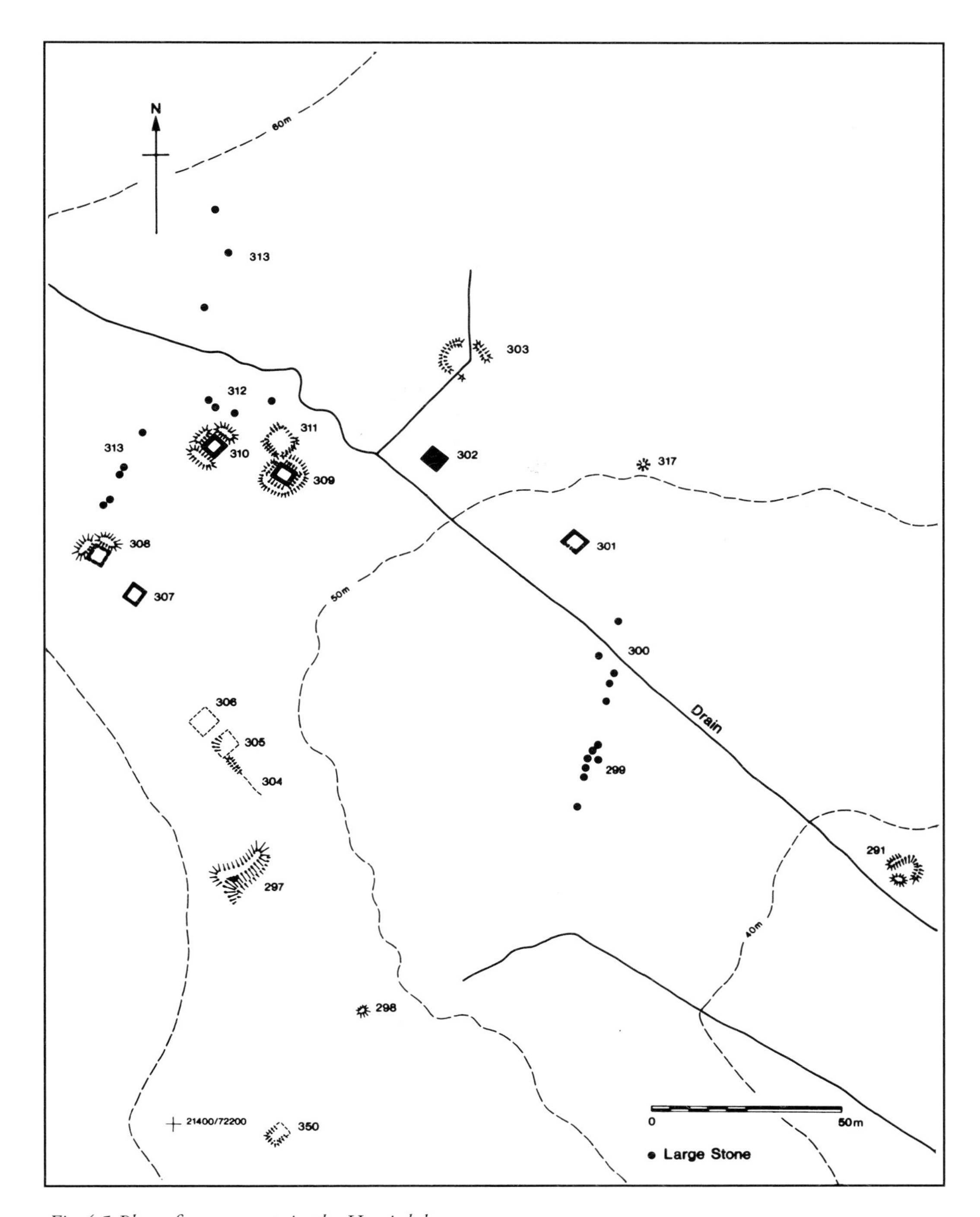

Fig 4.5 Plan of monuments in the Homisdale area.

a comparative study. Fojut's fieldwork shows that dykes and walling are characteristic features of the ancient landscape throughout Shetland; he suggests that the larger monuments may have territorial implications (1986, 8). A similar interpretation has since been suggested for West Burra Isle where a detailed sites and monuments survey points to a boundary system, defined by 'lines of earthfast stones' (Hedges 1984, 53), apparently dividing the island into six units. These monuments, like those noted by Fojut, tend to run across high or marginal land, often incorporating prominent natural features or existing monuments (usually cairns) into the route. The most detailed work, however, relates to linear systems in the West Mainland where Whittle has identified a series of stone banks up to 800m in length, which he interprets as a gridded but unfinished pattern of land demarcation (1986, 55).

Smaller boundaries, usually interpreted as field dykes, have perhaps received more attention in view of their proximity to settlement sites. Hamilton, for example, investigated enclosures at Jarlshof in relation to Bronze Age and Late Iron Age occupation (1956, 25). He inferred the enclosing of an adjacent promontory in both these phases and, on the basis of contextually related structures, ascribed its function to stockholding. It is an interesting reflection of traditional land use that these two boundaries, although separated by five feet of sand and some 15 centuries (according to Hamilton), follow roughly the same course. Constructionally the earlier form is recorded as 'drystone walling' (*ibid*); the later form is not described.

At Tougs, Burra Isle, Hedges was able to make a constructional distinction between boundary or perimeter dykes (ie those which separate hill and cultivated land) and field dykes (ie those which sub-divide the cultivated areas). The former, which appeared as 'straggling, and frequently interrupted, lines of large boulders' (Hedges 1986, 9), was seen in section to consist of a matrix of large stones with small stones and overburden, while the latter was composed of small field stones in a matrix of light brown soil (*ibid*, fig 5). This reflects Fojut's view that the smaller dykes functioned partly as field divisions and partly as types of linear clearance cairn (1986, 7), a view later confirmed by excavation at the Scord of Brouster (Whittle 1986, 140). Here, investigation was specifically directed towards understanding the construction, sequence and chronology of field systems, including lynchets, which lay in association with houses. Whittle was able to identify a basic constructional design – the monuments survived to a width of some 2-3m, were under 1m high, and were composed of both larger and smaller stones (*ibid*, 45). This was slightly modified by exploratory excavation which suggested that some of the dykes were multi-phase and that large stones, as used in the upland boundaries, may also have been an important part of the matrix (*ibid*, 46, also fig 41). As on Fair Isle, lengths of these dykes lay wholly or partly hidden below peat formation. Whittle's work emphasises the value of excavation in harness with field survey in such cases.

Few sites and monuments surveys have considered boundary features in any depth, but the overview tends to point towards a general model of classification which might be applied to the Fair Isle examples. At the lowest level of interpretation the sites here can be classified within a broad constructional typology as belonging to one of three variants which may have either functional or chronological implications:

1. 'Monumental' turf and earth construction with a possible stone base
2. Set stones with earth and turf infill
3. Earth, turf and loose stones

On Fair Isle the first type is represented by major boundaries which may have divided the island into (at least) two parts. The most substantial survivor of the sequence is the *feelie* dyke whose dimensions surpass those of all other linear monuments on the island, in places being as wide as 8m and surviving to a height of some 2m. It merits the status 'monumental' and might be seen as the product of communal effort. It appears to serve a specialist function and has parallels on other islands in Shetland as a major landscape divider. These dykes usually occur at specific topographical locations, and in each case the matrix is predominantly of turf in order to facilitate a height appropriate for either the exclusion of animals or some form of visual territorial impact. Similar monuments outside Shetland, identified in Orkney and more recently in England from aerial photography, are tentatively ascribed to the Bronze Age. The Shetland variety is post-medieval in use, but not necessarily post-medieval in origin.

The second type, which contains the majority of coastal earthworks discussed here, mostly appears to define headlands, groups of headlands, or possible hilltop enclosures. The earthworks are of smaller stature, around 1.5m wide and with a base of sporadically placed earthfast stones. The type seems to reflect a constructional method characteristic of more minor boundary features where substantial width and height were unnecessary. Earthworks of this type are unlikely to be stockproof (Fojut 1986, 7) and in order to act as animal enclosures some form of superstructure such as palisades or fencing is almost certain to have been required. Unlike monuments of type 1, these are not locationally specific; their constructional technique is unvaried irrespective of apparent function or location, even in those places where the accessible geology would allow alternative methods of building (eg the South Gavel). They appear in inland as well as coastal contexts and, in view of the consistency of their appearance under different circumstances, they may have a chronological implication. The fact that two of these earthworks (*675* and *236*) appear to conjoin likely burial sites argues in favour of a prehistoric rather than medieval method of land division.

The third group contains earthworks of similar surviving dimensions but whose location usually lies within sheltered dales away from the coast. They show an apparent association with other archaeological remains where they constitute elements of relict landscapes. The composition is typically of earth, turf and small stones but without any evidence for a skeleton of large earthfast stones. They appear to represent field divisions integral to settlement sites where they have useful parallels at the Scord of Brouster dating from around the turn of the third and second millennia BC (Whittle 1986, 146), rather than the more isolated winding boundaries of type 2. They too represent 'early' monuments although the chronological relationship between types 2 and 3 is unclear. Both types 2 and 3 may be considered to have been constructed by individuals or small groups of individuals.

This classification excludes only one example, on Malcolm's Head (*71*), where an earth and turf matrix has been applied to a line of laid stones. It might be argued that the proximity of bedrock to the grass surface on this scoured headland prevented stones from being embedded in the manner of type 2 to which the locations of the termini conform. If nothing else, this particular example emphasises the problems of trying to presuppose an *a priori* classification where none may exist. Nevertheless, the three earthwork groups provide a broad chronological model; they offer a suitable springboard for a more detailed analysis of the island's prehistory.

5

Burnt Mounds

ONE of the main monument types identifiable on Fair Isle is the burnt mound, so called on the basis of a characteristic composition of small burnt stones and a kidney- or crescent-shaped mound outline. Even in surviving form, usually turf-covered, burnt mounds represent distinctive landscape features and have now been recognised in many parts of Scotland, Ireland and western England. They appear to result from a method of heating water by quenching fire-heated stones in an earthfast tank, the spent stones eventually accumulating in the form of mounds. The tanks themselves, usually constructed of stone or timber, have been identified from excavation on a number of sites, usually located between the 'horns' of the crescent. In fact the crescent shape might be interpreted as the discard pattern of the spent material. In Ireland pioneering excavation and experimental work by O'Kelly (1954) has led to the now widely held interpretation that the process was essentially for cooking, although debate continues to as to whether the sites are of permanent or of 'hunting' status. A subsequent interpretation, less widely held, sees these sites as representing a type of sauna (Barfield and Hodder 1987). While they may undoubtedly have fulfilled a dual function – this receives some support from Irish evidence (O'Drisceóil 1988) – it is the opinion here that the primary process for which they were constructed was for cooking.

According to antiquarian records, field monuments of this type have long been recognised as ancient landscape features in the Northern Isles, although it was not until the 1960s before any connection with Irish type sites was made (Calder 1963, 78). Only recently, however, have questions regarding their social and economic significance been posed, largely stemming from the results of detailed sites and monuments survey which has tended to show a distribution considerably more widespread than hitherto supposed. Lamb's systematic survey showed over 20 likely sites on Sanday, Orkney (Lamb 1980a, nos 32-52) and 16 from neighbouring Stronsay (Lamb 1984, nos 99-114); both are surprisingly high figures bearing in mind the extent of modern agriculture and the relative sparsity of marginal land. This density has recently been reflected in other parts of Scotland, particularly in the south-west (RCAHMS 1987), as the result of more detailed landscape study. In Ireland the burnt mound, or *fulachta fiadh*, is now seen as the most common prehistoric type site with over 4000 examples being identified (Buckley 1990, 9).

Detailed work elsewhere in the region, notably by Parry on West Burra, Shetland, has attempted to identify the burnt mound as a specific component of relict landscapes (Hedges 1984, 47), whereas at Tofts Ness, Sanday it has been implied that the burnt mound may have offered a more specialised function (Hunter and Dockrill 1990, 66). Elsewhere in Orkney, work by Hedges at the sites of Liddle and Beaquoy has shown the presence of structures associated with the tanks themselves (1975), although similar features have not been replicated to the same level on other sites. It has, however, led to a review of features within other monuments, particularly brochs, where stone tanks and burnt materials might now be seen in a different light (Barber 1990a, 92).

Distribution

During the field survey of Fair Isle some 28 burnt mounds or possible remains of burnt mounds were identified. The greater majority of these were unequivocal, usually defined by their crescent shape; those which offered slight doubt were confirmed by a strong response from magnetometry. However, four mounds remain open to doubt (*65*; *178*; *179* and *216*); these may have been caused by flattening and spreading, the result being a relatively minor topographical feature with an ambiguous magnetic response. All four have been excluded from the distribution map (fig 5.1). Included on the map, however, is an example noted in the Royal Commission's *Inventory* (1946, no. 1201) which has since been ploughed out (*428*). This particular monument was remembered locally and the loss of other similar mounds (whether recorded or not by the Royal Commission) is also likely to have been noticed by a small crofting community familiar with its environment. None have been reported and this suggests that the preservation of burnt mounds has been generally secure during the last two or three generations – a time of specific threat from changes in land management and developing agricultural technology.

In view of these changes it is perhaps surprising that the picture of distribution is not confined entirely to the moorland aspect of the island. Of the 24 sites plotted, slightly more than half lie where their survival might be anticipated whereas the others are recorded in areas of pasture, many having survived in the face of intensive post-medieval occupation and land use. Other monuments, even boundaries, appear not to have shared a similar level of preservation in that part of the island. Although ploughing, minor robbing and even the construction of the Funniquoy mill system have all presented a demonstrable degree of threat, the indications are that the illustrated distribution of burnt mounds might be viewed as a reasonable reflection of their original distribution in prehistory.

A major factor in their survival is almost certainly physical stature, although composition is also important. Mounds of stone are difficult and time-consuming to shift and, unlike many other features, pose little in the way of a hazard to formal agriculture. Even on an island such as Fair Isle where building stone is at a premium, burnt mounds are effectively valueless owing to the small, fractured nature of their

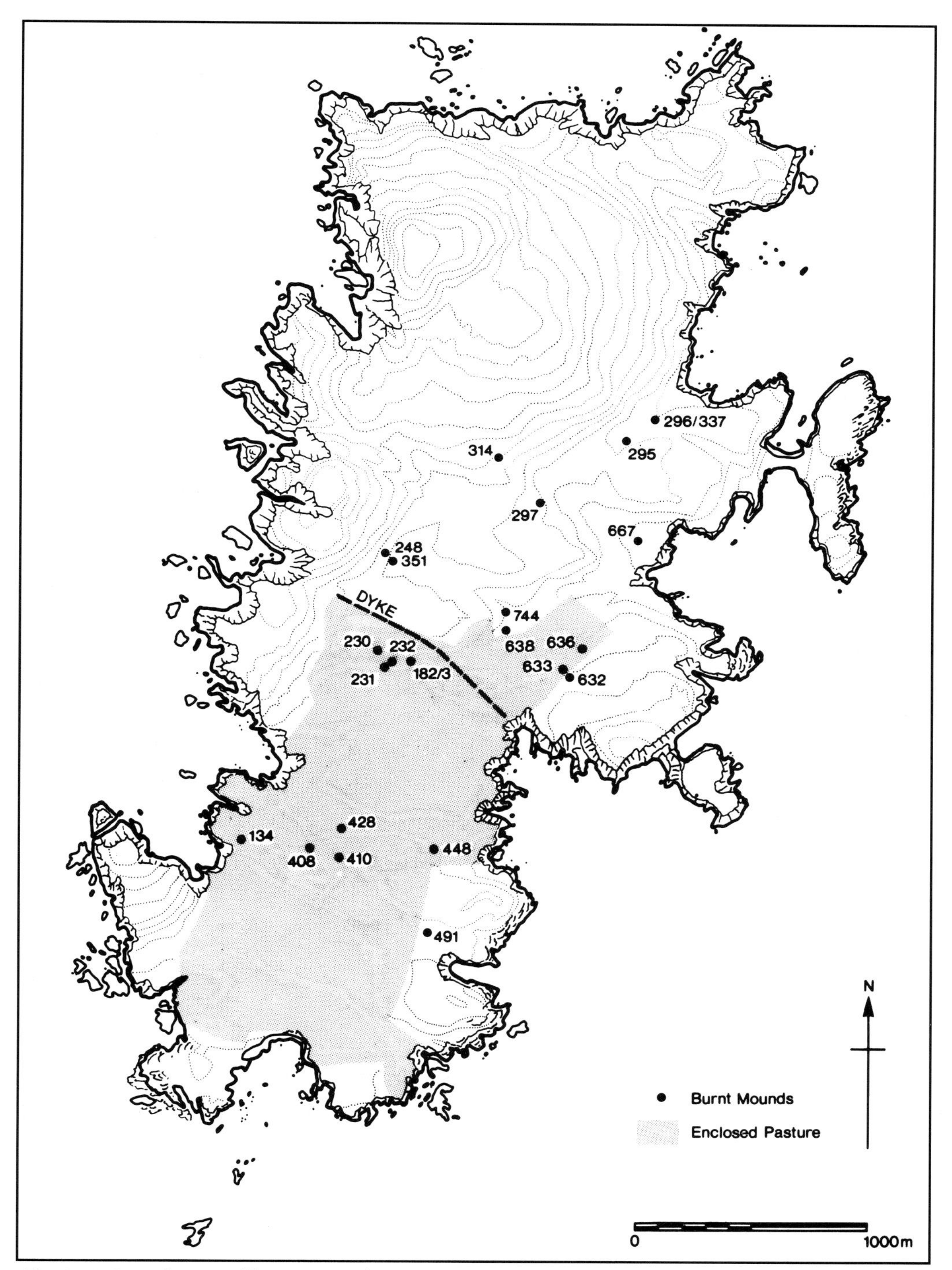

Fig 5.1 Distribution of burnt mound sites in relation to enclosed pasture.

stone composition; robbing is not therefore a major threat, although it has clearly occurred. Some mounds may even be continuously supplemented as clearance cairns but their underlying character is nevertheless distinguishable from burial or settlement mounds on the basis of geophysical properties (Hunter and Dockrill 1990). It might be added, too, that the retention of burnt mounds as landscape features in Fair Isle, even in cultivated areas, is also due in no small part to the concern for their preservation by the present and recent island population.

The Fair Isle mounds differ widely in recorded stature and form, although a proportion appear to conform to the customary crescent shape, presumably reflecting either an original discard pattern, minor robbing or a combination of both. The most substantial example (*231*, RCAHMS 1946, no. 1196) covers an area of approximately 30 x 20m and, with a height of over 3m, is probably the largest example of the monument type in Shetland (fig 5.2). It is unfortunate, to say the least, that it should have been bisected by a modern cable/pipe trench. Another example (*744*, RCAHMS 1946, no. 1195), damaged during road construction in the later 19th century, is recorded as having contained possible cremations which may relate to secondary activity (see chapter 6). Some have suffered from plough damage (*182* and *183*), and others from the intrusion of water coursing (*134* and *667*). The remainder were ostensibly unaffected by major erosion and vary in ground area

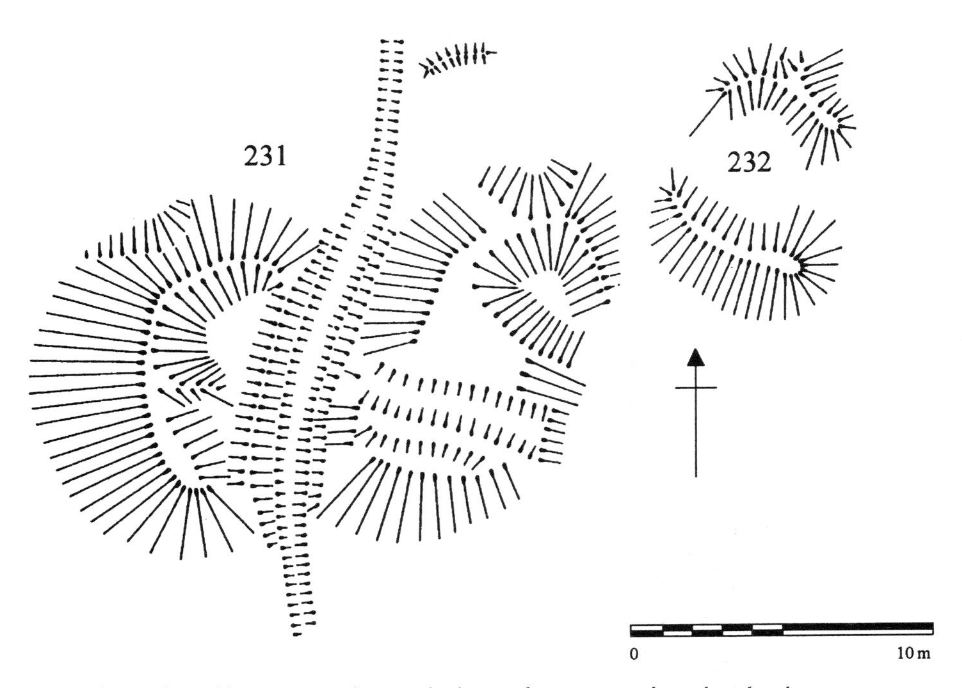

Fig 5.2 Hachure plan of burnt mound 231, the largest burnt mound on the island.

between *c* 8 x 5m (*633*) and *c* 19 x 13m (*232*) with a surviving height usually within the range of 1-1.5m.

Associations

Although some burnt mounds gave the impression of being fairly isolated, others could clearly be associated with centres already postulated from the analysis of earthworks lying within moorland or marginal landscapes (see chapter 4, and below). In contrast, however, those lying within the cultivated southern part of the island lacked any such association with other standing monuments. This distinction is so clear cut that it can only reflect the fundamental differences in modern land use between the two zones. It further emphasises the phenomenon of differential preservation which appears to favour the burnt mound in areas of cultivation.

An immediate overview suggests that the burnt mounds might be used with some confidence as an indicator of early settlement locations. They appear to be good archaeological survivors; their distribution is considered to have endured major agricultural change and, in those places where the landscape is marginal (and hence preserved), associated archaeological features are also evident. This in itself suggests that burnt mounds are component (and permanent) rather than detached monuments. By definition, therefore, any burnt mound lying in isolation on Fair Isle might be interpreted as the sole surviving component of an original site complex. Moreover, the apparent integrity of their distribution is a further important factor in their favour; on an island as small as Fair Isle their locations might be viewed as a confident indication of the totality of settlement during the period in which burnt mounds accumulated and were used.

A provisional classification of burnt mound types has been attempted by Barber (1990b) in an effort to explain how the differing manifestations of tanks and burnt material, from the simple *fulachta* at one extreme to the more complex evidence from structural remains at the other, might be explained within the context of a common process. His four types are seen as representing 'arbitrarily-selected points on a continuum' (*ibid*, 99) in which mounds or groups of mounds lying in association with other monuments occupy the central part of the spectrum. In general the Fair Isle mounds conform to this picture of linkage, even although the evidence for associated monuments is not always as strong as might be desired (below).

In any event it would be difficult to explain the burnt mounds on Fair Isle as being anything other than component elements of a larger settlement infrastructure. It is not realistic to consider them (even the few which apparently stand in isolation) as belonging to Barber's class 1 – the 'hunting' *fulachta*, traditional hunting stations where the kill was cooked and consumed before the huntsmen returned home. On an island as small as Fair Isle this interpretation lacks credibility. Equally unlikely is a notion indirectly developed from dendrochronological studies, namely that burnt mounds may reflect the cooking places of semi-nomadic populations obliged by climatic factors to move from place to place. Although the hypothesis is possibly justifiable on the basis of a correlation between some burnt mound dates and dust emission from volcanic activity at Hekla, Iceland, it is an untenable scenario on Fair Isle where size alone makes the concept of a continuous 'post-holocaust' movement of peoples quite ridiculous.

Rather must the burnt mounds on Fair Isle be seen as part of the infrastructure of prehistoric settlement, the full nature of which is far from clear; in the Ferny Cup, for example (fig 4.3), three burnt mounds (*295*; *296* and *337*) are located at the very edge of a relict landscape composed of house remains, field systems and cairns. It is interesting to note that one hypothesis currently under consideration elsewhere sees burnt mounds as 'servicing' monuments of some other type, from which they are set apart (Russell-White 1990, 89). This might certainly be viewed as the case here in the Ferny Cup, as well as elsewhere, for example on the Rippack where a burnt mound (*491*) lies peripherally to a likely early field system, at Burrashield where two others (*248* and *351*) lie at the edge of an earthwork and associated structural features, and at Homisdale where a further example (*297*) occupies a similar position in relation to an earthwork and probable house sites. Less apparent, although undoubtedly in the vicinity of early boundaries, is a burnt mound (*314*) situated on the valley slopes south of the Ferny Cup.

There is no way of telling by field survey alone whether this apparent detachment is a consequence of differential survival, chronology or a deliberate contemporary siting. A useful comparison in this respect is offered by Parry's West Burra survey (Hedges 1984) which identified no fewer than 16 burnt mounds on an island with less than half the surface area of Fair Isle. The majority appeared to be associated, either individually or in small groups, with other monument types (*ibid*, fig 2). With only one exception, at the site of Tougs (subsequently excavated by Hedges), all these examples lay at the edge of the monument group which in each case had a house as the focus. Contemporaneity between burnt mound and structure(s) is implicit. The exceptional site was caused by the insertion of an additional structure between a field wall and the mound itself. However, in its primary state the mound was interpreted as being contemporary with an adjacent oval house (Hedges 1986, 27) and, like the other examples on the island, adopted a position at the edge of the nucleus. By analogy, therefore, in the instances so far identified on Fair Isle the mounds might be interpreted as belonging to, but lying at the fringe of, settlement units.

Three other burnt mound sites on Fair Isle (*410*; *448* and *638*) might be also be included, although in each case the associated remains are less clear, nor are boundary features evident as a component element. One (*410*) occupies a position adjacent to monuments which may be interpreted as burials (below) whereas the other two have spatial associations with later monuments; in one instance (*448*) these are stone shelters and short lengths of foundation with walling, and in the other (*638*), banking and low mounds, two of which appear to contain stonework. Reuse of stone is well-attested on Fair Isle and invariably occurs in the vicinity of discovery, the presence of later stone monuments on the landscape often acting as pointers to the siting of earlier remains. This topic is discussed more fully below (see chapter 7).

The remaining burnt mounds have no visually associated features, either ancient or modern, and all stand within fields of recently or formerly cultivated arable land. These unexceptionally lie within the enclosed part of the island although three (*632*; *633* and *636*) occupy positions to the north-east on land reclaimed during relatively modern times. Two (*408* and *428*), both now removed, are located in the central part of the croftlands where cultivation has probably been at its most intensive, while the remaining examples (*182*; *183*; *230*; *231* and *232*) also lie within heavily worked land adjacent to Pund. Two of this last group (*182* and *183*) have all but been ploughed out, but the others are substantial. Any assumed structures lying in association may have been robbed for the construction of Pund croft and its dyking. Ploughing has since rendered the field surface smooth, even to the extent that one of the great *feelie* dykes that crossed the land at this point has been totally obliterated. This is particularly unfortunate as the ploughing also destroyed any relationship that may have existed between the dyke and the burnt mound complex.

As far as can be seen the final two burnt mounds recorded on the island also stand in isolation rather than as part of a group of mounds. One (*744*) is recorded from documentary evidence only and was destroyed during road construction, while the other (*667*) appears to have been heavily affected by excavation work undertaken during the construction of the water milling system. Nevertheless, even excluding these last two examples, a maximum total of 11 early settlement complexes might be conjectured, of which at least four can be viewed with a high degree of confidence, and a further five with reasonable justification (see fig 6.1).

Dating and duration

Given the likely identification of settlement foci, there still remains the problem of assessing the date and duration of occupation – factors which are indeterminable from field survey alone. Part of the problem lies in the dating of associated monuments, particularly the house remains, and this issue is pursued below. However, as far as the burnt mounds themselves are concerned research elsewhere in Scotland has shown a wide range of (radiocarbon) dates, particularly from the Bronze Age, but also from the Iron Age and Christian era (Barber 1990b, table 4), giving rise to the concept of a common tradition and hence allowing the creation of Barber's model. In Ireland, Brindley and Lanting have undertaken a comprehensive dating programme restricting the sampling to wooden tanks (1990) and have shown the distribution to lie almost entirely within a Bronze Age context. It remains questionable as to whether the wooden tanks are a Bronze Age phenomenon or whether the age distribution is otherwise greater. The common factor throughout appears to be an absence of dates within the Neolithic period.

Dating of these monuments poses a number of problems and these have been outlined by Baillie (1990), but a further issue concerns the duration of the mound formation and the likely amounts of stone generated by heating the water. The extent to which stone might be reused is an additional complicating factor. Where research of this nature has been carried out (eg Russell-White 1990; Barber 1990b) it seems clear that the mounds related to settlement (ie those of the Fair Isle type) may have been of relatively short duration. This has emerged not only from experimental work, which has shown that a small mound might easily have been created by sporadic 'ceremonial' use over a relatively long period, but also from those sites which have multiple radiocarbon dates. Barber has pointed out that these multiple dates appear to show little difference between one date and the next within the samples from a single mound (1990b, 101). Given the precision of radiocarbon dating, it could be argued that mound formation took place over the course of a few generations at the very most. This might be used to explain the clustering of burnt mounds, as they appear on Fair Isle and in other places, as being a reflection of successive rather than of contemporary activities.

Exactly why the mounds should be replaced is a matter for speculation; it cannot have been a problem caused by the availability of stones for heating on the basis that the sites are normally adjacent. Encroachment of the waste stones around the tank, the need for more space, or lifespan of the tank are all possible causes. The problem on Fair Isle may have been quite local, and possibly due to the tank itself in that that the available geology is unsuited to the provision of slabs for tank construction. Alternative materials of a less permanent type may have been required, for example compressed layers of turf and stone were used on the island in relatively recent times to provide watertight banking for the mill reservoirs. Timber is a possible alternative material but may have been too precious a commodity to use in such circumstances. It is interesting to note that the Shetland *Inventory* records the presence of a 'cist-like structure and stone implements' at a burnt mound (*491*) on the Rippack (RCAHMS 1946, no. 1197), although the nature of this 'cist' is unqualified.

Investigation

It was to examine the tank problem and to provide further information as to the character of the Fair Isle mounds that an exploratory excavation was undertaken during the summer of 1989. Work was restricted to a single mound (*633*), an irregular example measuring approximately 8 x 5m, which bore sufficient traces of a crescentic form to indicate where the tank might have been located. In terms of size and surviving height (*c* 1m) it was at the smaller end of the scale represented by the

Fair Isle group, but larger than many known from elsewhere, for example from Kebister, Shetland, where several mounds were recorded with diameters of around 2m (Lowe 1990). It lay below Vaasetter, adjacent to a similar burnt mound (*632*) within an area of enclosed land which had been reclaimed involving levelling as well as ditch and dyke construction. No other monuments were recorded in the immediate vicinity.

A major part of the exercise was concerned with geophysical survey which was carried out by taking measurements with a fluxgate gradiometer at 1m intervals across an area measuring 20 x 20m; this area included the visual topographical limits of the mound itself. The resulting plot (fig 5.3) clearly illustrates the extent of the burnt stone on the basis of its strong positive magnetic response against the surrounding background. It shows a pronounced crescent-shaped pattern of stone distribution, slightly different to that observed topographically. The negative areas, mainly to the north of the positive anomalies, represent a magnetic phenomenon associated with these positive anomalies rather than indicating separate features.

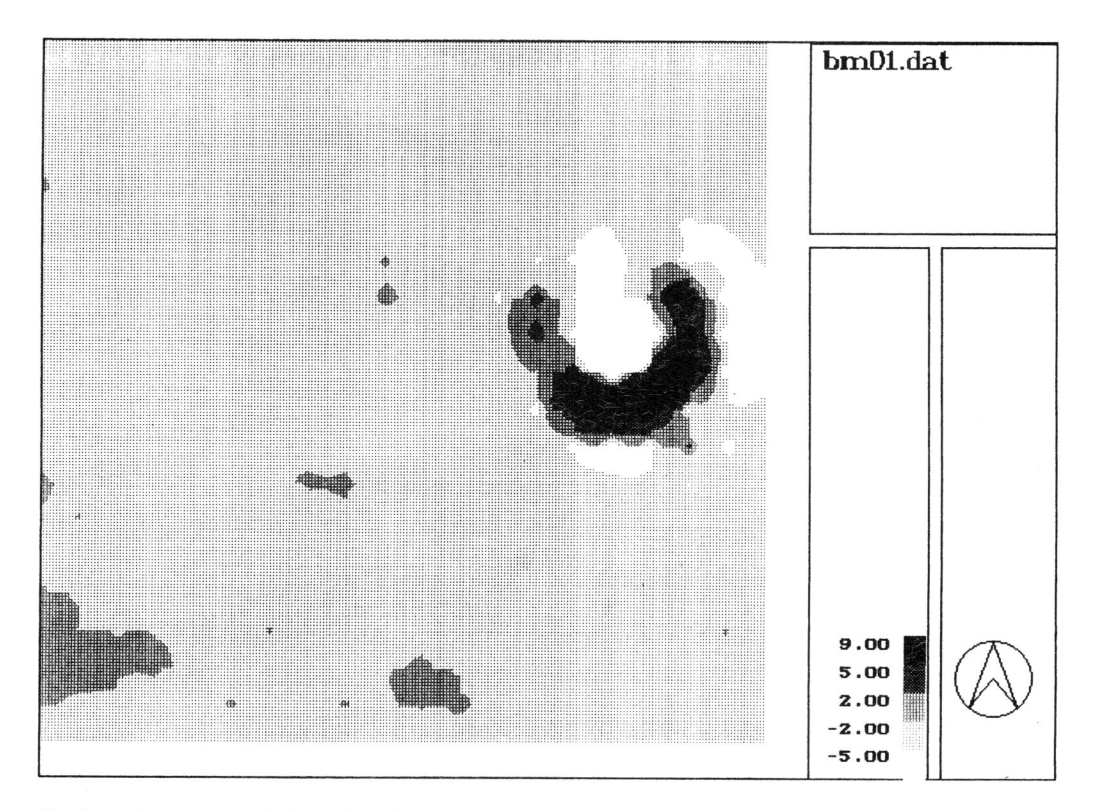

Fig 5.3 Burnt mound 633. Plot of magnetometer survey showing crescent-like anomaly caused by burnt stone.

However, an area of negative response approximately 2m wide between the 'horns' of the mound might also be caused by the likely location of the tank or pit itself. It is worth recording, in addition, that the magnetic survey identified no other anomalies which might be construed as being structural within the area covered.

On the basis of this evidence a narrow L-shaped trench was opened in order to test the magnetic data by including coverage of both 'horns' and the inferred position of the tank. Excavation was undertaken in a manner designed to minimise damage to the monument against future investigation or display, while at the same time attempting to resolve specific issues. Simple removal of the peaty turf and cleaning of the area satisfied the first of these issues, namely that the true distribution of the burnt stone had been identified by the magnetometer survey. Further cleaning and removal of sub-surface accumulations subsequently revealed the outline of the tank area, again confirming the survey results.

This central part of the monument was seen to be poorly drained and the turf had merged into a black waterlogged peaty silt. At approximately 0.3m below the ground surface this was replaced by the infill of a tank or pit some 2m in diameter. The fill was composed of angular rubble in a clay silt matrix and was subsequently quarter-sectioned; this is illustrated together with the site plan in figure 5.4. Excavation demonstrated that the profile of the tank area was rounded in nature and that there was no evidence for flagged sides or for any surviving form of lining other than small patches of clay. It was, in effect, a pit approximately 2m wide at the top narrowing to approximately 0.4m at the bottom, and with a maximum depth of around 0.9m. Stones comprised some 60% of the fill; these were proportionally larger than those forming the burnt mound and may possibly represent the last firing, or a stock of stones set aside for firing.

The irregularity of the sides and rounded profile suggested that no inner fixture had been utilised, nor were any postholes or other securing features evident in the cut surfaces. A clay lining cannot be discounted, although no *in situ* evidence was found, but the friable and relatively non-porous nature of the bedrock through which the pit had been cut suggested that water could have been contained quite naturally for a suitable period of time.

The presence of slippage and minor collapse would, however, have been inevitable; cleaning out would also have been difficult. The excavated fill – a mixture of silting and stone – may indicate that this was the very reason for its eventual demise, although the upper contents seemed to represent infill of a more deliberate character. The construction was generally crude, but this may reflect the nature of the bedrock more than anything else. In contrast to much that has been suggested above, the arrangement would appear to lack a certain design for permanency or, perhaps more accurately, regular use. Without further excavation on other Fair Isle sites it is not possible to indicate whether these characteristics are typical of the other island

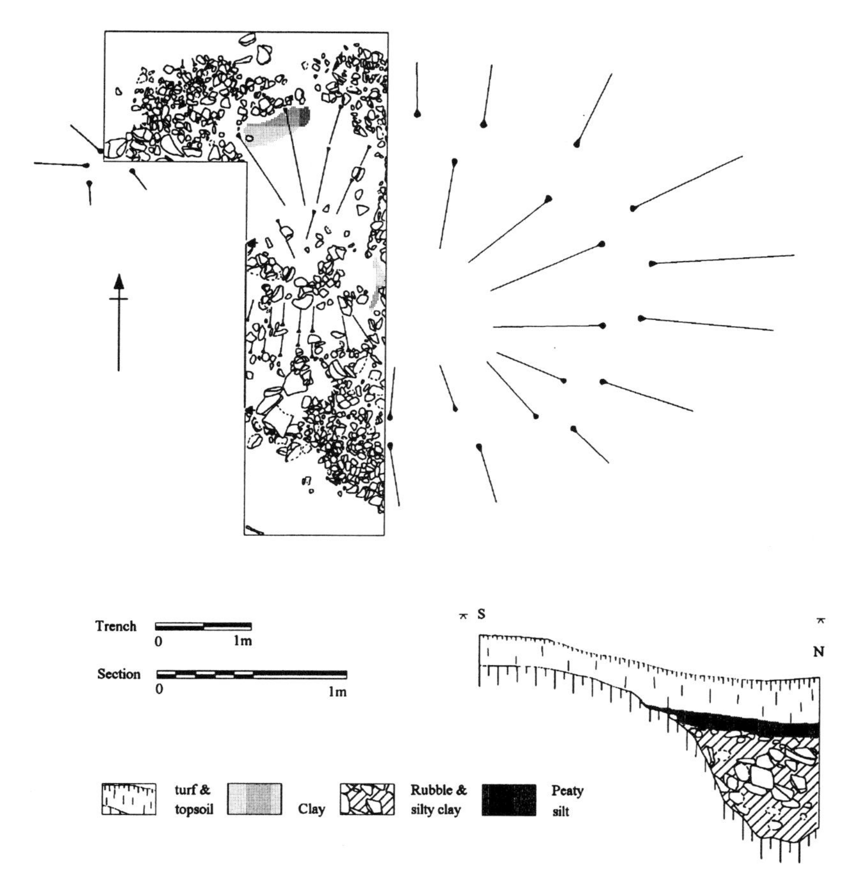

Fig 5.4 Burnt mound 633. Detail of survey, excavation and section.

mounds, but on the basis of this single example it can be argued that at least the smaller mounds may not have been intended to be used frequently. Accordingly, this gives increased plausibility to their locations at the fringes of settlement nuclei.

On the face of it the same can perhaps not be said for the massive mound near Pund (*231*) where other factors might be seen to be at play, but on closer scrutiny (and despite the ravages of the intrusive pipe trench) it is possible to interpret from the earthworks survey (fig 5.2) a series of discrete units forming the basis of the whole. If this is indeed the case, the mound can be viewed as a series of successive monuments forming a similar pattern to that interpreted elsewhere on the island. The implication for further analysis of larger monuments of this type becomes self-evident.

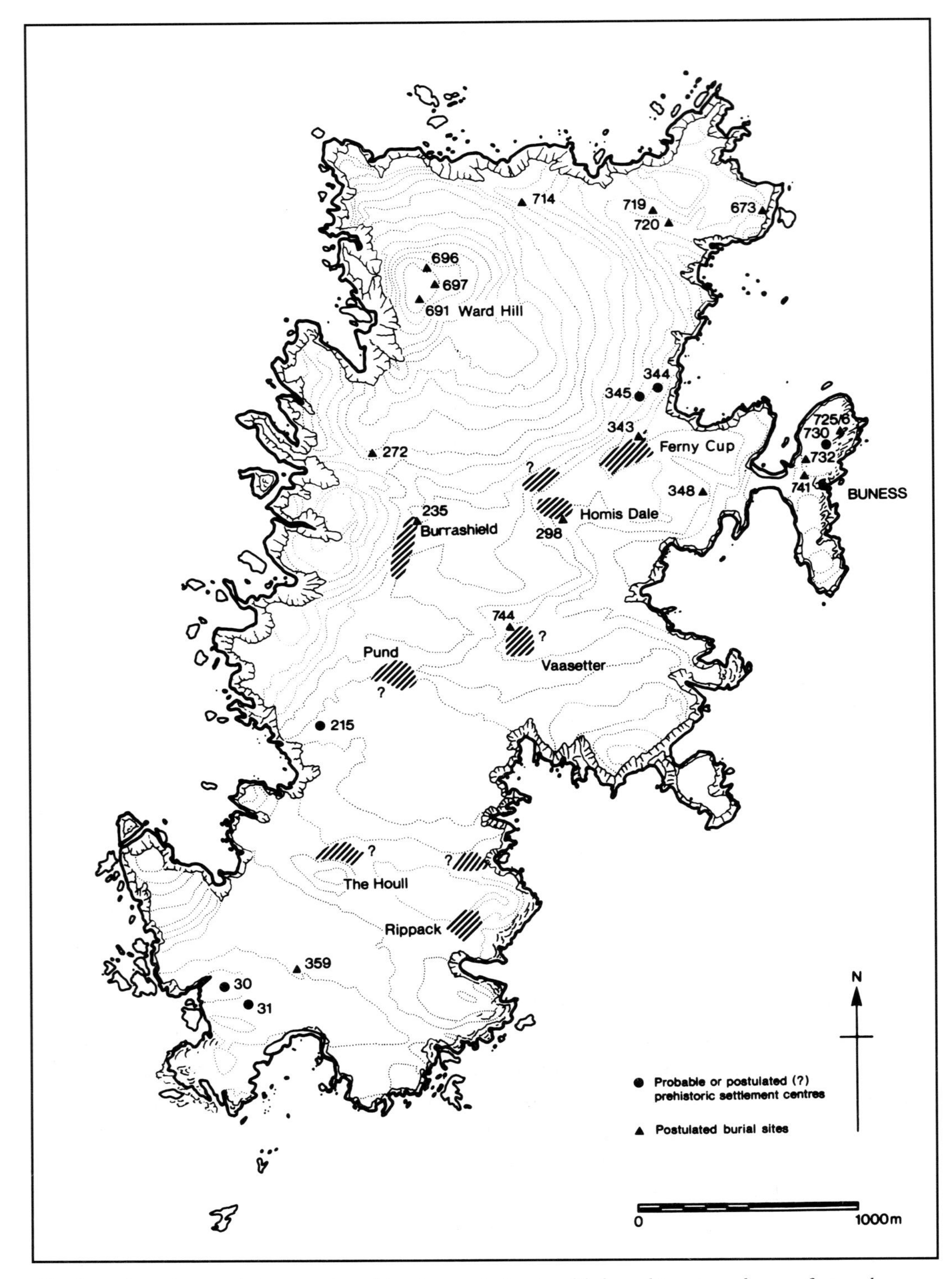

Fig 6.1 Locations and sites mentioned in chapter 6 showing likely prehistoric settlement foci and burials.

6

Houses and Burials

Houses

A relationship between burnt mounds and houses has been postulated by Hedges (1986, 27), but the issue has not been explored in any depth and awaits more detailed investigation of the houses themselves. In the meantime, the traditional approach to houses has been one based on morphology, typically 'oval' or 'round', the history of which has been well-reviewed by Hedges in a general discussion of 'oval houses' in Shetland (1986, 21-25) and also by Whittle (1986, 138-140). The study of prehistoric domestic sites in the Northern Isles is relatively modern and less shrouded in the misunderstandings of antiquarianism than might otherwise have been expected. Its pioneer, CST Calder, undertook large scale survey and excavation work in the early post-war years and his findings, although now substantially outmoded in terms of their interpretation (but not in the value of their primary data), still rank as the single most important yardstick for the study (eg 1962 and 1963).

The Ferny Cup

The concern here is mainly with two particular sites recorded during the survey (*333* and *342*, fig 6.2), in fact with the only incontrovertibly prehistoric houses on the island. Both lie within the Ferny Cup area and represent elements of a small tract of relict landscape which also includes field systems and lynchets, cairns and three burnt mounds (fig 4.3). Both houses appear to be integral to a common system of land organisation and use, and are therefore seen as being contemporary. In each case the house appears to act as part of a planned boundary design, one (*333*) for example being nodal to three land use divisions. A similar arrangement, but on a larger scale, has been identified by Whittle (1986) at the Scord of Brouster.

Both houses at the Ferny Cup appear to conform to a similar format composed of two conjoined sub-circular or penannular units: a larger unit with an internal diameter of approximately 6m; and a smaller unit measuring approximately 3m internally. The nature of the junction between the two arcs is unclear in each case, but the overall effect is of a figure-of-eight or keyhole shape. One (*333*) has a narrow constriction between the two units. In fact the smaller part is particularly difficult to interpret as a result of erosion. The walling thickness of both sites varies considerably, but this seems more due to collapse of the rough stone and turf matrix or to differential turf cover than to any original or evolved structural factor. A maximum

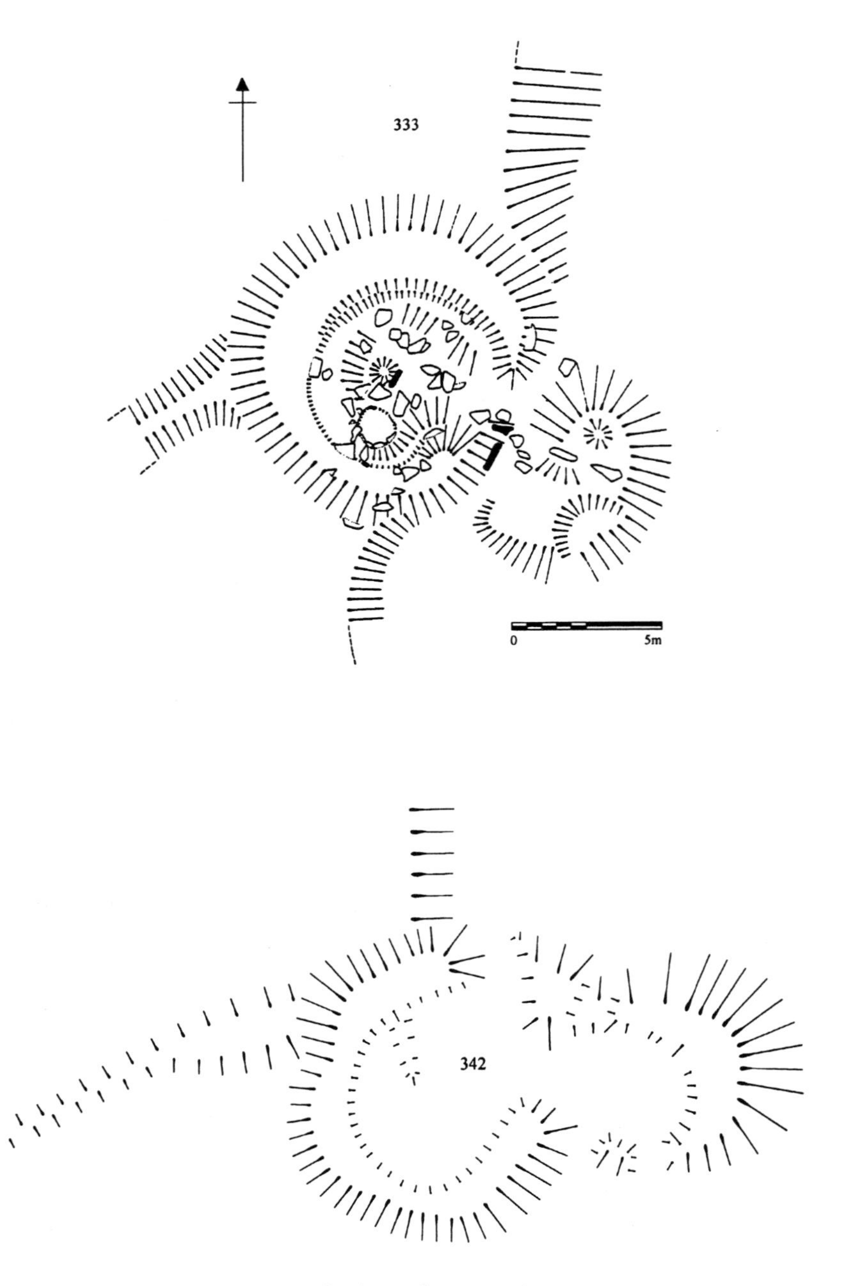

Fig 6.2 Hachure plans of houses 333 and 342 in the Ferny Cup.

wall core thickness of approximately 1.5m seems consistent for each structure, and this allows in each case for a maximum external dimension of around 14m.

The more central of the two houses (*333*) still stands to a height of approximately 1m; investigation has shown the presence of internal revetting, a stone-sided pit and a number of large stones in the interior, presumably representing internal arrangements. The junction with the smaller unit at the south-east is flanked by upright stones and leads across a rough stone passageway to an area which appears to contain a high proportion of midden and burnt material in its composition. The overall state of preservation can only be described as exceptional.

The other house (*342*), lying some 90m to the north-east, is slightly less well-preserved by comparison, and less regular in its formation. With the exception of a narrow turf-covered feature at the north-west side it lacks any obvious evidence of internal features, although rabbit activity indicates the presence of some stonework. Its walling survives to the slightly lower height of around 0.7m. Unlike the other house (*333*) which appears to stand at the core of the relict landscape it lies at the fringe of the complex; presumably this is a reflection of landscape erosion, in particular the constructional effects of a modern road and embankment adjacent to the east.

The consistency of the wall thickness in both instances appears to contrast with the walling of those houses identified by Calder where irregularity of thickness between 1-3m was commonplace. Part of this was almost certainly a reflection of geological factors in that neither suitable coursing nor orthostatic stones were readily available, but other underlying influences may also have been at play, possibly with chronological implications. This inconsistency of wall width, together with a pronounced absence of an outer face, appears to characterise a number of buildings, including the Late Bronze Age/Early Iron Age house at Mavis Grind, Shetland (Cracknell and Smith 1983), a building at Sumburgh (Lamb 1985, fig 6), and an example more recently published at Tougs, Burra Isle (Hedges 1986), dated to the Bronze Age. On all three sites the wall width appears to conform to no predetermined structural design and, in one case at least (Mavis Grind), the variation in thickness might be explained as being the result of later buttressing. However, on each site the internal organisation appears to have been more formally prepared with inner facings, bays and plinth arrangements.

Mavis Grind, however, appears to represent a single-celled sub-circular structure, slightly larger than the Fair Isle examples, with an internal diameter of approximately 7m. By contrast the Tougs house and the Sumburgh house, in common with many other examples on Burra Isle, were of twin-celled design, and in that respect provide direct parallels for the Fair Isle houses. The larger unit of the Tougs building had an internal diameter of 4.8m and the smaller unit, connected by a short passageway, a diameter of 2.5m. Remarkably, at least seven other structures on Burra Isle share a similar layout, but unusually (in so far as Calder's classification is concerned) they appear to show walling which, like the Fair Isle examples, is of consistent rather than of variable thickness. Hedges was first to identify this fundamental difference in classification (1984) and further interpreted the smaller of the two units in each case as being an 'annexe' (*ibid*, 47). It is interesting that his observations should continue to point out that this 'annexe' was located at the eastern end of each of the buildings – a feature shared with the two Fair Isle houses, and which may have climatic or even ritual implications.

The Burra Isle houses with the greatest similarity to those on Fair Isle, in terms of both morphology and dimension, are those at Bight of the Sandy Geos (Hedges 1984, fig 3), at Minn (*ibid*, fig 4) and at Southerhouse (*ibid*, fig 7). House 3 at Minn, which has the greatest proportion of wall surviving, exhibits a figure-of-eight shape and in all respects is the closest parallel to those on Fair Isle. The commonality continues in that House 1 at Southerhouse also acts as the nucleus for a boundary/lynchet system. Clearly there is an established tradition or evolution into which the Fair Isle houses can be set. In this respect it is interesting that there should be less similarity between the Fair Isle houses and those identified at the Scord of Brouster by Whittle (1986). Geology alone is unlikely to be the only reason for this, in that the buildings recorded by Whittle conformed to the single-celled type with formal inner face but with a thick undefined outer walling. These factors, taken together with a noticeable absence of associated structural features (including burnt mounds), suggests that they belong to a different phase of this broad settlement evolution.

Whittle's dates from carefully selected excavated contexts place the Brouster structures within the Neolithic/Early Bronze Age, and therefore provide a potentially important control on structures of this design and attested organisational arrangement. The absence of burnt mounds with Neolithic dates has already been observed above, and on this further basis it would seem reasonable to assume that structures of the figure-of-eight form of the Fair Isle and Burra Isle type, ostensibly associated with burnt mounds, belong to the Bronze Age – a concept supported by the dates from Hedges' excavation at Tougs. As far as Burra Isle is concerned the issue is further complicated by the presence of (?)later round houses. However, the distribution of all monument types suggests an implicit spatial relationship between the figure-of-eight houses and the burnt mounds – a relationship to which the round house is apparently both peripheral and irrelevant.

Hedges' subsequent suggestion of a settlement model for Burra Isle, based on the clustering of dated sites around the Neolithic/Early Bronze Age period (1986, 24f), although limited in its geographical application, is also worthy of consideration on Fair Isle. He argues that some of the best arable land in Shetland occurs at relatively high altitudes and that these areas would have been first to become abandoned during periods of climatic deterioration. Most of the relict landscapes surviving today belong to this category and many are therefore relatively early in the settlement sequence. In less marginal areas, however, the impact would have been comparatively less but those areas would also have endured later, continuous processes of settlement involving a systematic destruction of earlier remains. The effect identifies a bias towards the survival of Neolithic/Early Bronze Age monuments in the higher altitudes and places a premium on the preservation of later Bronze Age and Iron Age remains at lower altitudes.

On Fair Isle it provides a satisfactory model for the interpretation of differential survival, although the intensive demands of an adjacent population may have been less pronounced at any of the three sites of Brouster, Mavis Grind and Tougs than on Fair Isle itself where the reuse of building materials, for example as shelters or planticrues, has been actively pursued. Structural survival in the higher margins of Fair Isle has been strictly limited accordingly. Even in the Ferny Cup where the two prehistoric houses are still visible there are also a small number of stone-built post-medieval features (eg *323* and *329*) whose composition is almost certainly derived from a pre-existing structural source. The valley also contains a small number of low, sub-circular or sub-rectangular enclosures (eg *318*; *319* and *324*) with a maximum internal length of 4-5m. These appear to be of earth and turf composition and their integrity within the prehistoric landscape is open to some doubt.

Homisdale

Elsewhere on Fair Isle traces of other early structures are few and ambiguous, even within the higher altitude zone denoted arbitrarily by the hill dyke. Most promising is the general area of Homisdale slightly to the south-west of the Ferny Cup (fig 4.5) where a similar topographic and sheltered environment exists, and where buried earthworks are also evidenced. Here a degree of peat formation and the fairly extensive use of planticrues have served to create a visible focus at the north-west head of the valley, whereas lower down the valley evidence from stream and ditch cuttings suggests an early, buried landscape. This is to some extent supported by the presence of a large burnt mound (*297*) located at the valley side and by a further feature, possibly structural (*291*), lying opposite. This takes the form of a sub-circular bank composed of earth and stone approximately 2m wide and standing in places to a height of over 1m. Its overall diameter is around 9m and rabbit activity in the centre indicated the existence of a significant degree of stonework. In certain respects it compares favourably with the central house in the Ferny Cup (*333*), although it lacks the 'annexe' or smaller unit which appears to characterise other buildings here and on Burra Isle. There is, however, a structural ambiguity at the open (south) end which may reflect a subsequent development; the monument otherwise provides reasonable evidence for a further early structure on the island.

At the north-east of Homisdale a less satisfactory monument (*303*) lies near the head of the valley. This takes a similar form but, on the basis of evidence from a ditch cutting which bisects it, does not appear to have a stone component. A relatively large part of its circuit appears to be open and, although it holds a commanding topographical position, it is not convincingly early. There are a number of similar monuments elsewhere on the island, and they offer an uncomfortable reminder as to the limitations of field survey. Two of these (*344* and *345*) stand as low sub-circular earthen enclosures on the high ground north of Eas Brecks with external diameters of 7m and 5m respectively. Both show some evidence of minor internal stonework and both appear to have entrances. In association with one (*345*) is a probable line of earthfast stones. Two further examples lie between the Ferny Cup and Homisdale (*318* and *319*; fig 4.3); again these are of similar sub-circular form and size, but apparently without utilising constructional stone.

Apart from a few boundary features discussed above in chapter 4, the remaining monuments in the Homisdale area take the form of planticrues; nine of these survive in various states of preservation, some with external banking which give the impression of earlier structures lying below. This phenomenon was first pointed out by Calder who identified a planticrue overlying a prehistoric building (from which it had presumably been quarried) at Isleburgh, Northmaven (1963, 71). Excavation here across the banking of one of the planticrues (*308*) failed to realise any similar evidence (see chapter 7). Nevertheless, the occurrence of this planticrue concentration suggests the presence of an earlier favourable stone source in the immediate vicinity for which boundaries, a burnt mound and a likely structure are the surviving elements.

At the same end of the valley as the planticrues, but further to the north-west and on higher ground, lie two more ambiguous boundary features (*315* and *316*; fig 4.1) and an adjacent burnt mound (*314*). These may constitute other components of this same early landscape, although their geographical separation would tend to point towards an additional discrete unit of settlement. No structural forms were identifiable in the immediate vicinity but the topographical changes caused by the peat formation on the relatively higher slopes has been considerable.

Burrashield

A similar problem is posed by the remains on the lower slopes of Burrashield where post-medieval activity has been equally prevalent, although in this case in the presence of a series of small rectangular foundations measuring typically 5 x 3m. Situated along the hill contour below the 80m line over 20 such foundations were recorded (fig 6.3). A few of these were of stone construction (eg *257* and *260*), while some others utilised either facing stones or earthfast corner stones within a predominantly turf and earth matrix (eg *259*; *266* and *268*). Although a number of

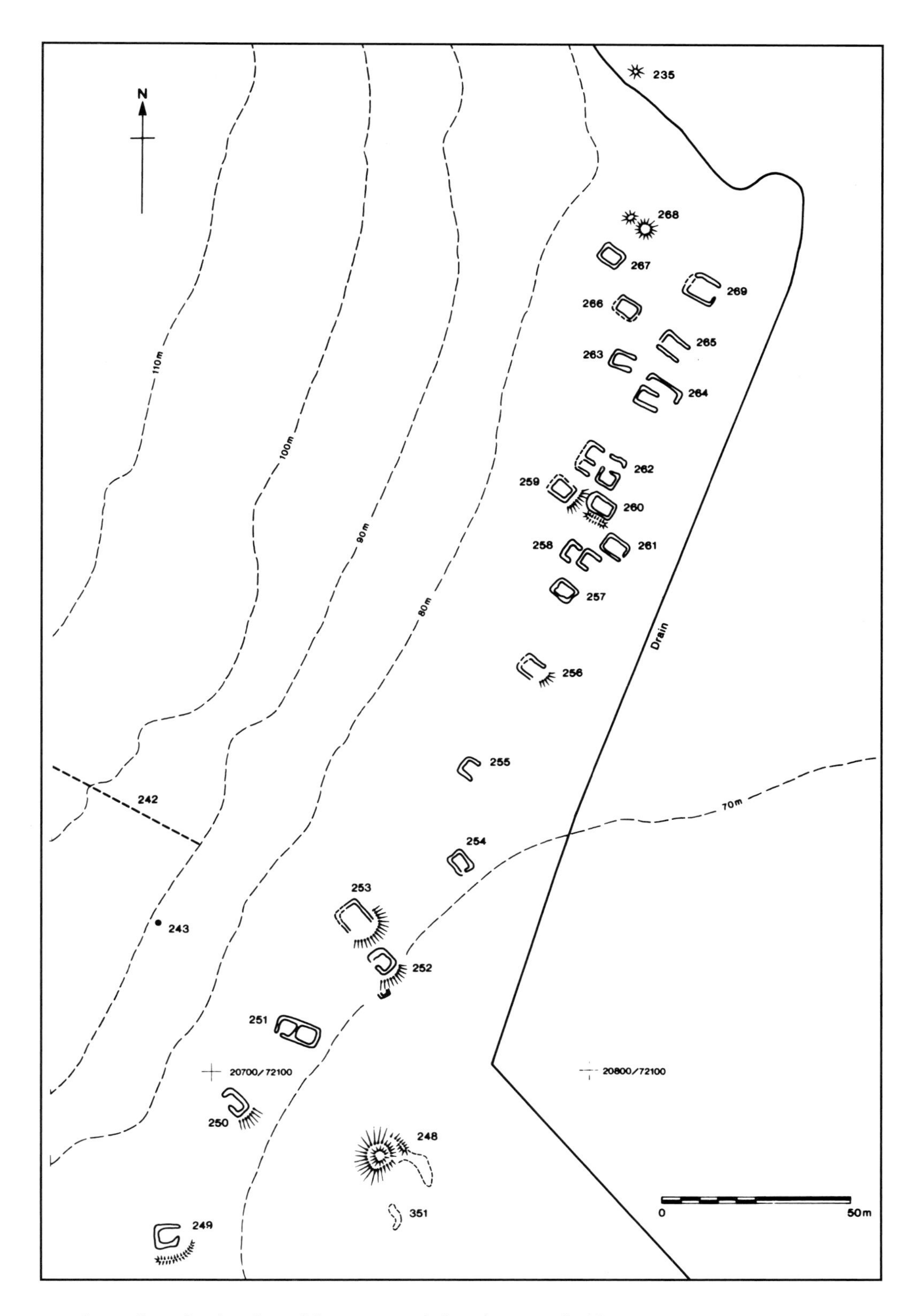

Fig 6.3 Plan of archaeological features recorded in the Burrashield area.

small quarry workings are identifiable in the vicinity they are inconveniently located and it seems more probable that the stone was derived from existing structural sources. This argument is strengthened by the presence of burnt mounds (*248* and *351*), two parallel boundary features running directly up the hillside apparently acting as a land division (see chapter 4 above), and a small cairn (*235*) against which the northerly boundary terminates. Furthermore, the design of several of the 'modern' foundations exhibits features which are not necessarily explicable in terms of modern usage, for example terracing and the need for outer banking (eg *249* and *260*). On the other hand, it has to be added that exploratory excavation on one of these sites (*257*) failed to recover any evidence of earlier features or occupation.

The Rippack

The record is only marginally better on the lower slopes of the Rippack on the east side of the island, where an area of marginal land provides an interesting contrast within the predominantly cultivated southern zone. Here a complex of field boundaries, cairns and later structures in the form of planticrues and small enclosures provides the nucleus of a likely settlement location. A substantial burnt mound (*491*) sits at its fringe (fig 5.1). A further burnt mound (*448*), lying some 300m to the north of the Rippack within a more cultivated part of the landscape, stands adjacent to a series of planticrues, lengths of walling and later foundations. A series of ambiguous features including mounds and boundaries, aspects of which are argued to belong to post-medieval 'tunship' occupation (see chapter 9), lie nearby and may in themselves be of early origin. The same degree of ambiguity surrounds the vicinity of a further burnt mound (*638*) which lies within an area heavily disturbed by mill activity along the Burn of Gilsetter below Vaasetter. Some of the adjacent landscape features are undoubtedly the upcast from mill channels but others, notably two mounds (*641*; *643*), appear to contain more than casual stone fill. Both are approximately 7m across and one (*641*) is the findspot for a piece of worked steatite according to Ordnance Survey records.

These, therefore, constitute the areas on Fair Isle where early prehistoric settlement, taken on the basis of burnt mound distribution (seen here in terms of Bronze Age occupation), can be located with varying degrees of confidence (fig 6.1). The examples in the Ferny Cup and in Homisdale respectively are unequivocal, with a possible additional complex at the west end of the latter. On Burrashield and the Rippack the evidence is less forthcoming but both are prime sheltered locations on the lower slopes. Less satisfactory is the evidence north of the Rippack, but the degree of post-medieval activity in what is now marginal land and the general ambiguity of the landscape features is strongly in its favour as an early site. The Gilsetter area, too, is attractive for the same reasons. The other burnt mound indicators lie within areas of more intensive cultivation and modern activity: the three groups located adjacent to the ruins of Pund, below Vaasetter, and around the Houll respectively are clustered on more favourable land where interpreted settlement may have been not only of longer duration but also more vulnerable to the intensity of later activity. Only at the Houll are there obvious associated early features and these are more likely to be of a burial rather than a settlement nature (below).

There are, inevitably, possible structural features elsewhere on the island which do not lie in proximity to burnt mounds but whose general character is open to the widest range of interpretation which field survey tends to generate. Within the enclosed southern part of the island where a low level of survival might be anticipated, possible structural outlines (eg *30* and *31*) are almost certainly vestiges of later settlement and can be more appropriately associated with post-medieval land use (below chapter 10). However, outside the enclosed area in the south part of Burrashield and located adjacent to the modern fence line a low, irregular mound approximately 6m in diameter (*215*) is probably of earlier origin. It contains a series of orthostats and appears to be associated with a length of banking. Its preservation is to some extent fortunate, given the line of the fence, although much of its bulk may have been removed for the construction of a sheep shelter which lies a few metres away in the enclosed field. A small exploratory excavation positioned between the monument and the sheep shelter indicated that stonework or rubble associated with the monument extended well beyond its topographical limits. An early date for the monument was supported by the recovery of a few fragments of coarse abraded pottery from within the stone deposits.

A final example may lie on Buness, where an irregular mound with an approximate diameter of 8m appears to contain a large proportion of stone within its composition (*730*). The monument is confusing; its centre appears to have become filled with angular tumble, and a length of banking extending to the east may be associated. Unlike any of the other structural remains interpreted from the island it is unique in having Ordnance Survey documentation.

Burials

The nature of prehistoric burials in Shetland is as much a reflection of the limitations of geology as anything else. The differences between Orkney and Shetland can be argued to be less due to ritual or belief than to the character of the constructional materials to hand, although there are exceptions, notably the heel-shaped cairn. Orkney is geologically more fortunate in having natural laminar sandstone ideally suited to the construction of chambered tombs, passages, corbelling, stalls and alcoves. By contrast, much of Shetland offers only irregular boulders of various sizes. Building techniques which have been developed in Shetland, whether for houses or burial monuments, reflect the crudity of the materials available rather than the skills of the people who used them. Fair Isle is geologically inclined towards Shetland and it is with types there that analogy must be made.

Credit for first identifying the extent and diversity of Shetland's early burials must once again be given to Calder whose efforts, culminating in his article of 1963, produced a total of over 230 individual monuments of simple cairn or chambered cairn type. Additionally, he was the first to note the similarity of layout between certain chambered interiors and that of domestic houses (1963, 40). His distribution list, however, produced no examples of burial on Fair Isle, but neither did the Royal Commission *Inventory* (1946) on which it was based and on which his 1963 paper served as an update. The mention of burial in the Commission's volume is restricted to a single reference, a burnt mound (*744*) which was destroyed during road construction in the 19th century and which is recorded as containing cremations of likely Bronze Age character (RCAHMS 1946, no. 1195). Anderson's subsequent description of this recovery merits inclusion in full:

> *In 1874 a small burial mound, about 8 feet in diameter and 2½ feet high, was removed in the course of the construction of a road between the North and South Havens in Fair Isle lying midway between Orkney and Shetland. In the mound there was found a large, oval-shaped, rudely formed and unornamented urn of baked clay. Although imperfect it measures upwards of 12 inches in height. Beside it there was a smaller urn of steatite, also oval in shape, but much more neatly formed. It measures 5½ inches in its longer diameter, and almost 5 inches in its shorter diameter across the mouth, and stands 4 inches high. Under the rim is a bevelled band, giving it something of an ornamental character. Close by this mound, in a flat space, there were found at intervals a number of flat stones, from 6 to 12 inches under the surface, and below each stone there was observed what is described as a 'a carefully-rounded hole, about 6 inches deep by about 10 inches broad, very smooth on the inside, and lined with about an inch thick of a soft, black, adhesive substance resembling a mixture of peat moss and clay, and containing in the bottom a whitish substance resembling bone ash'. These phenomena thus imperfectly observed indicate in all probability a small cemetery of urns set in the ground, with stone covers, and having no mounds heaped over them.* (Anderson 1883, 73 and fig 57)

Anderson presumably referred to construction of the road to the South Harbour, not to the South Haven; a consensus of opinion places the likely location of this mound slightly south-west of the mill complex.

Calder's activities were concentrated on the main islands of Shetland. The absence of recorded sites on Fair Isle is more likely to reflect the lack of his attention rather than the absence of sites themselves. Nevertheless, it has to be said that no dominant burial monuments are readily apparent on the island and that the *Inventory*, for all its shortcomings, provides a reasonably comprehensive corpus of the larger archaeological features. Even the leisurely attentions of 18th and 19th century middle-class visitors from the south, who might normally be relied upon to make archaeologically useful observations, produce little information. However, a list of items collected over the years from Fair Isle and published in the Society of Antiquaries of Scotland's *Proceedings* for 1883 contains evidence for a possible burial at Gillie on the west side of the island. Within a cist described as approximately 3-4 feet long and 1½ feet wide were recovered a stone cup and a large broken steatite urn; two abraded pounding stones were found outside.

As Parry has shown (Hedges 1984), there is no substitute for detailed fieldwork and this is readily apparent from his results at West Burra which identified a number of hitherto unrecorded burial cairns. It is interesting that Parry should also echo an idea expressed by ME Hedges which postulated a relationship between types of burial cairn and burnt mounds; this originally emerged from excavation work at the Orkney site of Quoyscottie (Hedges 1977, 144) but has not otherwise been pursued. Part of the problem lies in distinguishing between burial cairns and other types of cairn on the basis of superficial survey evidence, although the number of cairns on Fair Isle is probably too small to make this a worthwhile exercise. To some extent the absence of burial monuments, more particularly cairn fields, is surprising on an island within which all activities (including burial) must, by the nature of insularity and distance, have been contained. Unless the excarnation of human remains or even their dispatch to the sea is considered to have been commonplace, it might be expected that some small part(s) of the island might be put aside for their ritual disposal. The phenomenon, however, is not uniquely prehistoric; a similar problem applies to Christian burials through into the post-medieval period (see chapter 11).

The evidence, such as it is from field survey with limited support from excavation, shows a picture of diverse information much of which is ambiguous. A number of possible sites lie within areas already identified as being of archaeological interest – in the Ferny Cup and the Rippack, although in both instances the cairns could equally occupy a clearance or boundary function. Many, for example, conform to the general small size of cairn (typically with a base diameter of *c* 2m) identified at West Burra by Parry (Hedges 1984, 49), although others are considerably greater. None, however, exhibit the kerbing or formality of the larger examples noted by Calder, or even the isolated example excavated at the Scord of Brouster (Whittle 1986, fig 34). Of the seven cairns recorded in the Ferny Cup all but one are most satisfactorily explained as resulting from clearance; in fact a group of four probably constitute the basis of a boundary feature at the north-west edge of the complex. The exception (*343*) is larger than the others with a diameter of approximately 5.5m and a surviving height of around 0.6m; it lies adjacent to this group, located further up the valley slope where a convenient sheep route has eroded a track through the interior revealing stonework and a likely orthostat. The monument is difficult to interpret but seems to lack the solidity of house remains. In as far as can be seen, it lies outwith the relict field system. A mound of similar proportions (*348*) lies on Eas Brecks above Homisdale adjacent to a boundary system formed by an alignment of large stones. Its composition also appears to be of earth and turf with some stones and also seems too insubstantial to be of dwelling origin. A burial function is plausible for both.

In the Rippack area four small cairns constitute the backbone of a possible field system (*505*; fig 4.1) and three others, also between 2-3m in diameter, can be interpreted similarly. At Burrashield, a single cairn, also around 3m in diameter (*235*; fig 6.3), appears to mark the terminal of a long boundary and presumably acts in the same way. In Homisdale, however, the only cairn evident (*298*) appears to lie remote from the interpreted centre of settlement and adjacent to a burnt mound. It is one of the two examples on the island that might support a theory proposed by Parry that some burial monuments may have been built using material quarried from burnt mounds (Hedges 1984, 49). The other lies immediately east of the Houll in the southern part of the island where two mounds, each around 5-6m in diameter (*412* and *413*), also stand close to a burnt mound. Neither monument appears to be sufficiently large or appropriately stone-based to represent structural remains. In none of these instances, however, can a burial function be interpreted with any confidence from field survey alone, nor can any date be postulated. Only in one instance where a similarly sized mound (*359*), located more centrally to cultivation, is visibly cut by rig lines can any *terminus ante quem* be given for the date of its formation, and only then in the vaguest of terms. Nor for that matter can any of the small mounds or cairns lying elsewhere in the island offer greater scope for interpretation; in nearly all cases they either lie at the edge of modern field boundaries, mark tracks in the moorland, or lie within exasperatingly indeterminable spreads of stone, scree or other rubble, for example on Buness or within the military debris of Ward Hill.

On Buness the extent of strewn stone from both coastal and human effects is a major confusing factor for any landscape study. This is unfortunate as the headland occupies a prominent, almost romantic position with considerable archaeological potential; it was, as Muir rather naively observed 'a rather sweet spot, and would form a delightful house to one making Fair Isle his occasional retreat' (1885, 252). One likely burial monument stands out simply through size and position (below) but other contenders are less easy to distinguish. Three possibilities include the base of a kerbed cairn with a diameter of some 5m (*732*), a smaller cist-like feature, also with possible kerbing (*741*), and a small stone setting which appears to form the base for a later cairn (*725*). Other cairns in the area appear to be either of more modern origin or less easily divisible from the presence of walling, ruined enclosures and rubble from quarrying. Kerbed cairns, or to be more precise regularly formed cairns with side stones, also appear in a clearance capacity; three examples, all broadly rectangular, were recorded at field edges in the southern part of the island.

In the vicinity of Ward Hill, the highest point on the island, the difficulty in interpreting (or finding) the monuments stems from a modern military desire to occupy prominent or vantage positions on the landscape – positions which offered similar advantages in prehistoric times. At least three (unproven) potential burial sites can be cited. One, a likely cairn some 6m in diameter (*691*) underlies the concrete rubble of the radar station on the apex of the hill, and another lies on the lower slopes slightly to the north (*696*). This now takes the form of a dug-out feature with a diameter of around 7m, although the origins appear to be that of a cairn. The third example may have been a cist, approximately 2 x 1m, with slabbed stones surviving down the two long sides (*697*). In all instances the original function can only be identified by excavation.

There are, however, some larger monuments which invite discussion, notably two apparent house forms (*719* and *720*), which were observed as representing components of an earthwork (*675*) at the far north-east end of the island. One (*719*) was identified as a mound some 13.5m in diameter with likely peripheral banking (fig 4.1). The interior appeared to consist of heaped tumble, partially turf-covered with a possible entrance and alcove. The other (*720*) was more amorphous, slightly smaller, but also appeared to contain heaped tumble. Both were interpreted as 'houses' in the sense of domestic structures, and were seen as analogous to similar structures in the Ferny Cup and at Brouster which also acted as focal points of linear earthworks. However, exploratory excavation at one (*719*), undertaken in order to expose the basic outline of the structure, indicated that the monument was of a very different character. The investigation was undertaken in a manner designed to minimise damage and consisted of little more than turf removal and cleaning, although some excavation of superficial debris was also carried out in order to clarify the emerging features.

The outcome was the presence of a cairn constructed of irregularly sized stones with a single central chamber (fig 6.4). Only the main part of the monument was exposed, but this suggested that the cairn measured some 10m across and, on the basis of evidence from the southern part of the trench, may have been square, or at least straight-sided. No formal kerbing was identified at these edges although the presence of some large earthfast stones (stippled on plan) may represent the rudiments of a primary design. Internally the main chamber was interpreted as lying north-west/south-east and measuring approximately 6 x 2m. The north-east edge was formally faced but appeared to give access to an additional but smaller chamber measuring approximately 1.1 x 1.6m set at right-angles. This was faced less effectively. The terminal of the main chamber had been more carefully constructed,

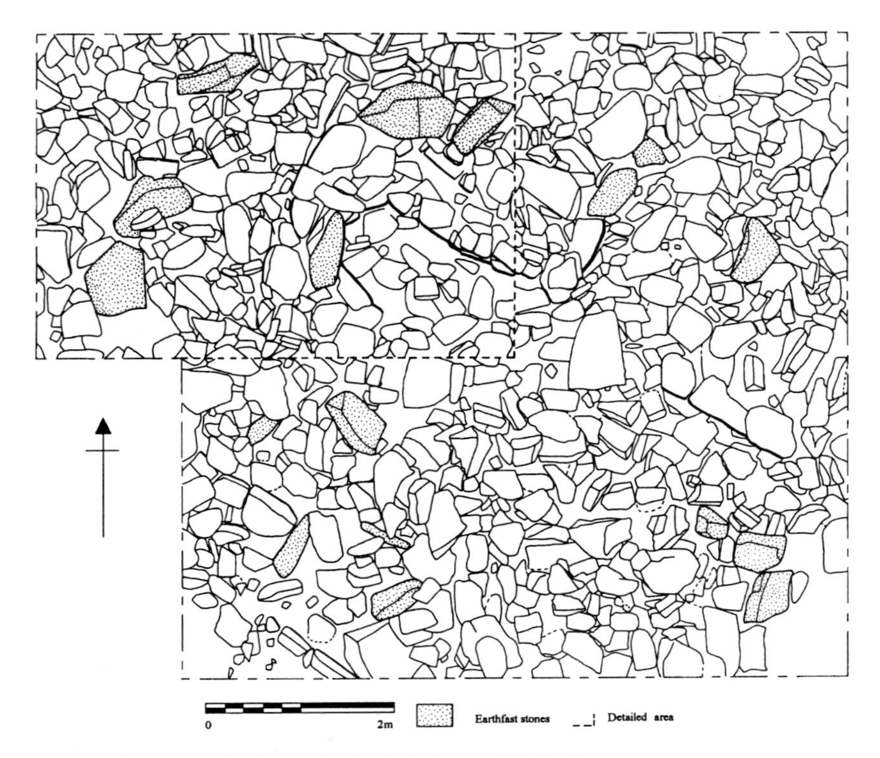

Fig 6.4 Exposed stonework of putative burial 719 at Ulishield.

possibly with double-faced walling and gave the impression that some form of shelving may have been featured. The south-west wall was the most difficult to interpret; facings were almost non-existent and this was further confused by a possible secondary cist which may have been constructed from the outside. The main chamber itself appeared to lead directly out at the south-east where the passage had been 'blocked' by two large earthfast stones.

No human remains, cremated or otherwise, were recovered, but nor for that matter were any vestiges of domestic occupation, even traces of midden, pottery or other general debris. Although investigation had been relatively superficial, the total absence of any anthropogenic material which might have indicated a shieling or other similar structure, together with the internal layout of the monument, points towards a burial. The overall design, even seen from the evidence of this superficial investigation, compares favourably with many of the simpler forms of burial cairn recorded by Calder on Mainland Shetland. The other site (*720*), lying some 80m away to the south-east along the same earthwork, was not investigated but, by analogy, would seem to be of similar function. Both sites give the impression of having been quarried for usable materials, and possibly also for plunder.

An additional large burial cairn might also be interpreted on Buness where a mound measuring approximately 13 x 10m (*726*, plate 6.1) holds a prominent landscape position on the North Gavel. A strong local tradition of burial surrounds the headland but the monument appears in the Ordnance Survey records as 'unclassified'. The central area appears to be kerbed by substantial stones; these define a sub-rectangular area some 6.5 x 5.5m which contains tumble lying across two turf-covered, hollow areas. Accordingly the core would appear to have been entered, but the kerb is otherwise undisturbed. The monument has all the character of a burial cairn although the kerbing arrangement has a secondary appearance to it.

Plate 6.1 Burial monument 726 on the North Gavel, from the SE.

On the western cliffs of the island, sheltering within the slopes of Lerness, are the remains of a stone-built feature (*272*, plate 6.2) which may also represent an early burial monument. It survives as the skeleton of a stone-built structure *c* 7 x 3.5m internally. In its original form it might be viewed as being heel-shaped with maximum internal dimensions of *c* 4 x 3.5m with a construction of substantial orthostats typically 0.8m high. In the better surviving parts these show a double-faced walling construction approximately 1m wide; in the less well-preserved areas the walling exists only as a spread of rubble and tumble. A secondary phase might be identified as a south-west projection of the existing form which involved a straightening of the north-west wall to produce a shape which was broadly rectangular. The monument is unremarkably located: it lies at the side of a barren, weather-scarred gully near the crest of the hill in a position which is secluded rather than prominent. Its main feature is the magnitude and shape of the orthostats which are much more in the Orkney style than those seen elsewhere on the island.

Plate 6.2 Burial monument 272 on Lerness, from the N.

These remains clearly impressed the Ordnance Survey and were duly recorded as an antiquity, although it has to be said that a degree of doubt must surround this interpretation. There is, for example, no surrounding cairn or even major traces of one, although construction of a burial chamber against a hillside could partly obviate this need. The main points in its favour are the impressive nature of the earthfast stones and the heel-shape of the primary layout which is well-paralleled among the prehistoric burial cairns of Shetland. It is possible that an original burial cairn may have been reused as a shelter rather than as a planticrue in more modern times, particularly during military activity; this may account for at least some of its enigmatic character.

The final two potential burial sites both lie within the extreme north-east part of the island; in fact taken together with the two large cairns (*719* and *720*) they might be said to point towards an area in which burial might have been more particularly dedicated. Both appear to represent small cist burials which have generally survived later modification, although not disturbance. In part this is due to their remoteness and to their unobtrusive positioning within the topography. One (*673*), a low mound barely more than 5m in diameter, lies below a slope at the top of a cliff and is unobservable from any other point on the island. It appears to contain two roughly parallel cist-like depressions, each approximately 1 x 0.6m, one having orthostats at its two short ends and the other with a single orthostat at one long side. The other example (*714*) lies on more open ground to the west and is slightly larger, measuring approximately 2 x 1.5m. Its edges are defined on three sides by bedded, kerb-like stones, although the unevenness of its appearance suggests that later disturbance has occurred.

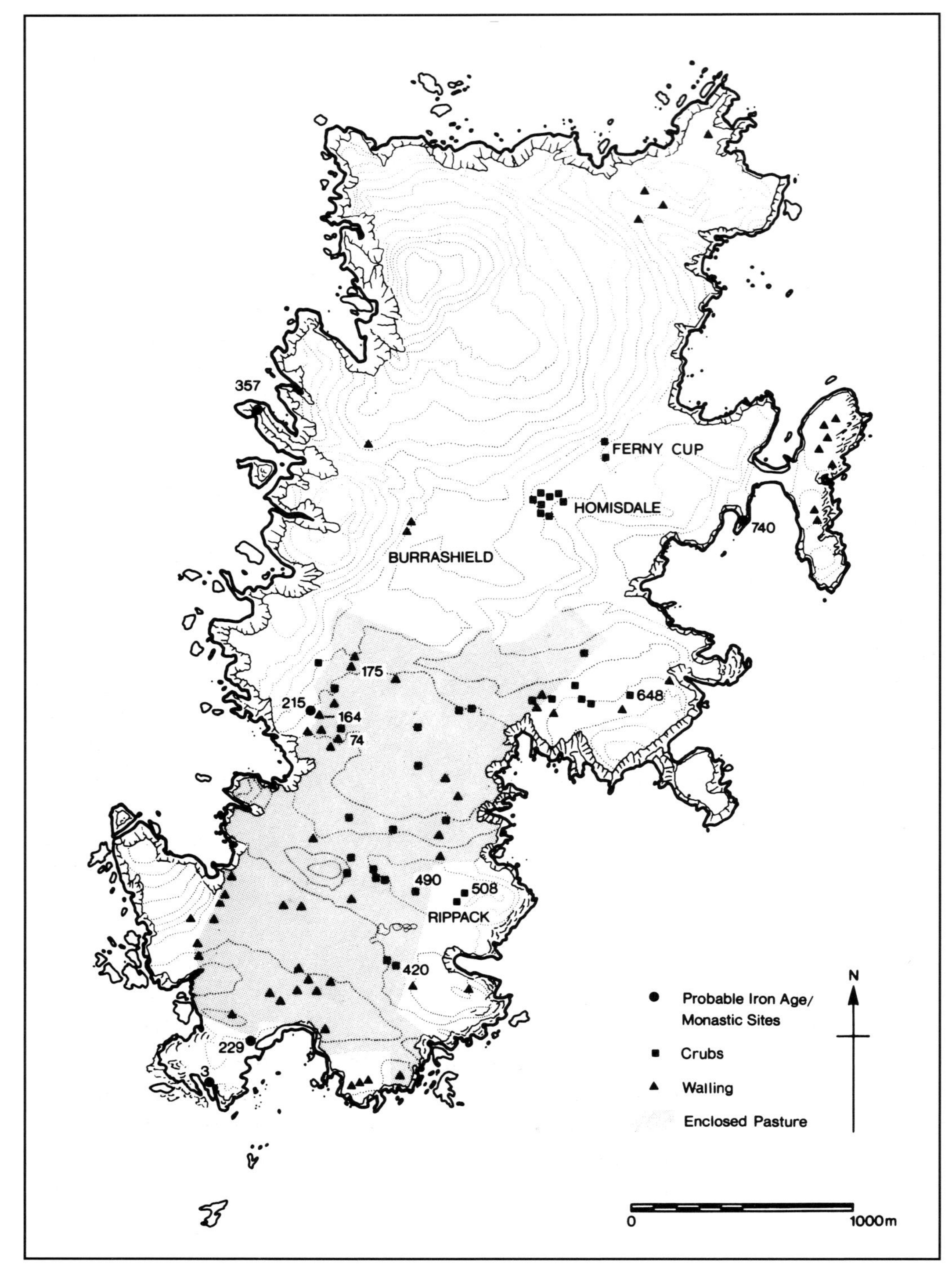

Fig 7.1 Locations and sites mentioned in chapter 7 showing probable Iron Age sites, crubs, walling and enclosed pasture.

7

From Iron Age to Viking: Landscape Analysis

The Iron Age landscape

The effects of climatic change during the Bronze Age which forced settlement to move to the lower slopes also constrained its later development within those same contours. The upper slopes became marginalised, fossilising the Neolithic and Bronze Age landscapes, while the lower usable soils met increasing demand from Iron Age times through to the present day. This movement to lower soils also coincided with a discernible shift towards territoriality, also identified throughout the rest of Iron Age Europe. In the Northern Isles many of the structural remains from the middle of the first millennium BC show a tendency towards clustering, notably to the focus of a broch, as society became more nucleated for defensive purposes. However, successive periods of occupation, often in the same favoured place to minimise loss of good soils, make the interpretation of individual phases of settlement by field survey extremely difficult. While some monuments of the Iron Age such as brochs or promontory forts are, by virtue of stature or character, well-defined, others are almost impossible to recognise physically, let alone interpret as specific period sites. It is not an issue unique to Fair Isle; anyone conversant with the archaeological landscape of the Northern Isles will also be familiar with the frustration that accompanies its analysis, in particular the period from the Iron Age through to later Norse times.

The problem of landscape interpretation has been considered in some detail in an examination of the extent to which the economic systems of late prehistory might have persisted into the post-medieval period and might therefore be recognised on the post-medieval landscape (Hunter 1991). The exercise is appropriate to Fair Isle and to the Northern Isles generally in view of the wealth of written accounts produced by visitors to the islands in the 18th and 19th centuries; these provide a theoretical starting point in reviewing the landscape of earlier times. Excavation is also now beginning to identify a high level of consistency in the economic records among sites which cover this broad period, even though the individual sites themselves usually fail to reflect settlement continuity over the longer term.

Those excavated sites which show the longest duration of occupation or use also tend to show hiatuses at similar points in the settlement record. There is, for example, a group of monuments on Orkney at Howe, Pierowall, Quanterness and also at Pool, which appear to point towards a utilisation of Neolithic burial sites during the Iron Age after a lengthy period of desertion – a phenomenon which might be interpreted as reflecting shifts in both social change and land use. A chronological overview of occupation in the Northern Isles taken from other, non-synchronous sites tends to confirm this view of consistent patterning, but with breaks in settlement continuity in the early 2nd millennium BC, in the pre-broch period and in the period following later Norse settlement in the 12th and 13th centuries AD.

There are a number of reasons as to why this patterning should appear, not least of which is the bias in Iron Age studies towards broch sites as a result of their size, landscape dominance and the attention afforded to them by antiquarians. Despite this dedicated academic focus they are still not fully understood (eg Hedges 1985; Armit 1990) and their role within the infrastructure of Iron Age society, which most scholars now agree contained a greater degree of territorial organisation than in earlier times, is still open to debate. No obvious broch sites have been identified on Fair Isle, but in any event the local geology is largely unsuitable for their construction. An Iron Age landscape free from brochs in north Scotland is difficult to accept under the present state of knowledge, but it is equally difficult to imagine an island offering so much fertile land lying unoccupied for a period of over a millennium before the first Viking settlers made their mark. Iron Age organisation on Fair Isle may have been less defined than some academics might wish to accept, but the fact that the island boasts at least one promontory fort (*740*) says something for a modicum of internal organisation. The mere existence of this promontory fort, located at one of the few landing places on the island, is proof enough of the fact that insularity alone cannot be cited as a reason for security or alienation from a structured Iron Age society elsewhere in the Northern Isles.

A useful comparison can again be made with the island of West Burra where the close proximity of other islands is such as to somewhat diminish the effect of insularity, and where the local building stone is equally bad. There, too, no brochs were identified from field survey, but Hedges interpreted Iron Age occupation on the basis of a small number of 'round' structures with a distribution which appears to be discrete from earlier 'oval' houses (1984, 51). A similar arrangement might be interpreted for Fair Isle on the fertile southern part of the island; certainly one structure lying on the margins (*215*, see chapter 6) would come into this category. This change in house form seems a reasonable working guide for landscape studies; it receives much of its integrity from Hamilton's work at Jarlshof where one structural complex shows a neat stratigraphic sequence from oval to round (1956, 18-39).

Post-broch studies offer even greater difficulties of landscape interpretation, if only because the duration of the broch effect and its impact on settlement has still to be fully determined. It is, however, becoming clear that some nucleated sites of the 5th century AD onwards did not possess a broch as their social or architectural basis and therefore that other lines of evolution beyond that of the broch itself must be considered (Hunter 1990). That such sites appear to be in a minority might also be ascribed to methodological bias as much as a *de facto* distribution. Archaeological evidence for post-broch settlement in Orkney and Shetland, particularly of dispersed type, is remarkably difficult to pinpoint and has tended to provide one of the several enigmatic areas of so-called Pictish studies. Pictish culture in the Northern Isles is definable less by settlement remains, of which few are known (eg Ritchie 1985), as by objects and typology – characteristic metalwork, designs, painted pebbles, and symbol stones. This is normally the stuff of excavations; places like Fair Isle and much of Shetland therefore remain blank areas of Pictish distribution simply by default. It may, however, be more profitable to pinpoint Pictish settlement by working backwards from subsequent Viking sites. Excavation elsewhere suggests that settlement locations which were important to the Picts were, it seems, also important to the Vikings. This may be partly for political reasons and partly for the need to retain settlement sites close to the best, but limited soils on the lower slopes – a phenomenon which argues for consistency of general location irrespective of cultural change.

It is all the more frustrating that this Late Iron Age society existed in a proto-historic period in which early Christianity also made its mark. The identification, for example, of monastic sites which characterise the early spread of Christianity in the north and west, is itself an issue of concern in these regions (see chapter 11), and provides an ironic but fitting end to a millennium fraught with difficulties of interpretation.

The Landberg promontory fort

The only incontrovertible Iron Age site, the Landberg promontory fort (*740*), lies on the east side of the island adjacent to the South Haven and survives as a flat grass-covered tongue of land over 40m long but no more than 12m across at its widest point (plate 7.1 and fig 7.2). The cliff faces are almost sheer for 25m down to the sea and the scale of erosion is severe. The position is fortuitously strategic in that it commands views over the approaches to the North and South Havens, is easily accessible, but is also easily defendable once access has been achieved. Although the land area enclosed is relatively small and might shelter no more than a few families, the approach is proportionally small and well-protected. Access is gained by a narrow trackway leading through a series of ramparts across a natural rift from the north. This site, currently the only scheduled monument on the island, receives mention, albeit cursory, in the Royal Commission *Inventory* of 1946 (no. 1194) based on fieldwork carried out in 1930, and has since been the subject of more detailed investigation by Lamb within the wider context of Iron Age promontory forts in the Northern Isles (1980b, 43-49). Lamb's survey plan (from a site visit in 1970) additionally provides a useful control against which to measure the rate of subsequent erosion (*ibid*, fig 14).

Plate 7.1 The Landberg promontory fort, from the NW.

The promontory plateau itself is more elevated than the landward approach which slopes gently up from sea level, the distinction being exaggerated by a revetted bank on the landward edge of the promontory and by a deliberate deepening of the natural rift between the two. Outer protection is afforded by three ramparts, each now barely more than 1m high created from turf and bedrock upcast scooped from between the rampart bases to form shallow intermediate ditches. Access through the ramparts appears to have been specifically designed to facilitate a straight line of visibility from the brow of the promontory, in fact two of the ramparts are edged with large earthfast stones at the east side of the track in order to emphasise the entrance line. This follows a raised track across the rift before leading directly through a passage in the main rampart on the promontory.

Although three ramparts lie to the east of the track on the landward side and are identifiable for about 13m, only two are evident to the west, each about 6m long. The most northerly example is absent – a fact for which erosion is unlikely to be responsible. Lamb identifies these defences as 'dump' ramparts, a description which reflects their mixed composition and relatively low height. Both characteristics are essentially a product of the local bedrock which is difficult to dig into. Lamb

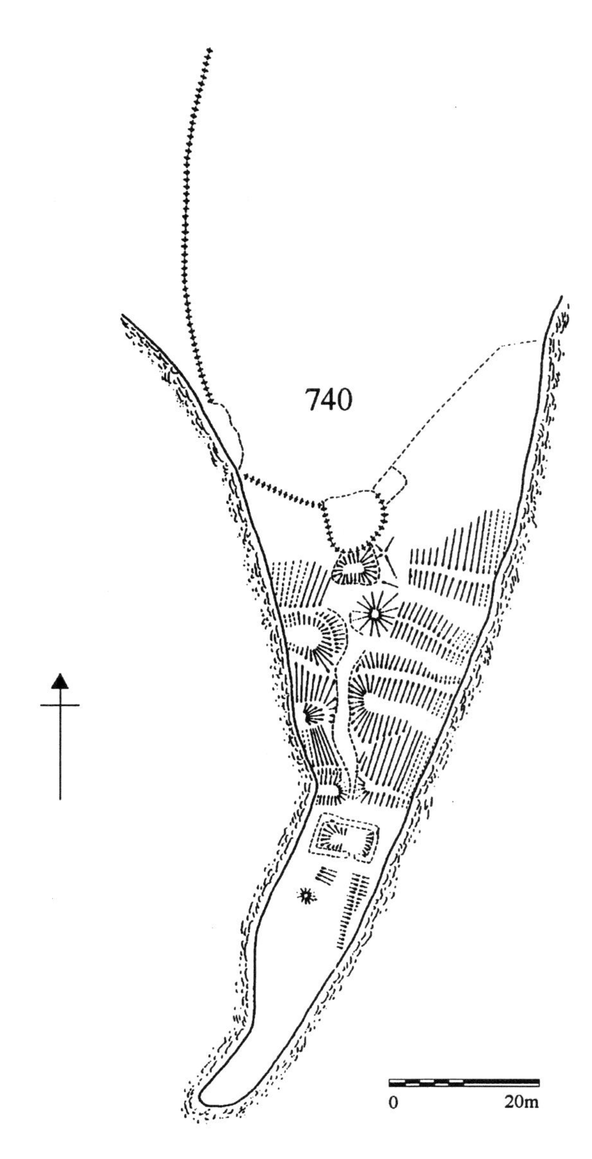

Fig 7.2 Plan of the Landberg promontory fort 740.

interprets their surviving height as being little different from that of the original construction and draws a useful analogy with a similar promontory site at Hog Island Sound, Mainland Shetland. The two sites have similar topographies and almost identical low multivallate defences which might be seen, given the difficulty of excavating the local bedrock, as being an appropriate method of obstructing or slowing down attackers who were simultaneously bombarded from the more elevated safety of the promontory (Lamb 1980b, 50).

On the promontory itself wind erosion and rabbits have played havoc with the surviving archaeological remains. On the southern part of the tongue the 'string of shallow depressions' observed by Lamb during fieldwork in 1970 and interpreted as possible hut sites (1980b,80) are now barely evident; even the main rampart facing the landward side is difficult to distinguish from the turf and tussock-covered erosion. Directly behind it, however, the remains of a rectangular structure approximately 9 x 5m externally lying across the promontory is still visible; the collapsed walling is approximately 1m wide and survives to a height of some 0.6m, although the large facing blocks and core of loose stones visible during Lamb's fieldwork are no longer evident. The structure does not appear to be of the blockhouse type and is probably secondary; coarse pottery and some later medieval material has been recovered from the vicinity, particularly from the north-east corner of the promontory where rabbit activity has generated amounts of midden. Probing in that quarter suggests that these deposits are up to 1m in depth. Within the structure itself and on the north-west side the depth is little more than 0.5m, and on the southern part of the promontory no deposits appear to have survived at all.

North of the outer ramparts on the slope leading up to the promontory the landfall is broken by a low embankment located in a broad arc across the approach. This earthwork, which appears to be composed of earth and turf barely more than 0.4m in height, is more apparent on the western side where it circles round to the north than on the eastern side where it terminates at the cliff edge. It survives for a total distance of some 100m and narrows into a small sub-circular enclosure some 8m in diameter just below the outermost rampart. This enclosure is almost certainly some form of animal fold, presumably for sheep, into which the animals could be channelled using both the shape of the earthwork and the topography of the promontory approach as a funnelling device. The construction seems later than that of the promontory fortifications. It is, however, significant that none of the other headland earthworks already noted (see chapter 4) exhibit this type of penning arrangement, a factor which goes some way to support an alternative hypothesis for their use.

Monasteries

A number of early monastic sites in the Northern Isles have been identified by Lamb (1973) on the basis of groups of structural foundations on promontory positions, usually located behind an earthwork or *vallum monasterii* on the landward side. Several examples are postulated elsewhere in Shetland, notably the Birrier of West Sandwick, Yell and the Kame of Isbister, Northamavine (*ibid*, 77), but although Fair Isle possesses a small number of headland earthworks appropriate to a monastic function, none have been verified by excavation.

Monastic settlements in the north, assuming derivation from Irish or at least Columban origins in the 7th century AD, appear to have taken one of two forms: either the eremitic insular type whereby one or two monks would seek some remote outpost such as a rock stack on which to build a simple cell, or, alternatively, a larger type of settlement. This latter type in some instances may have reached almost urban proportions with cells, workshops and farm buildings focused around a central chapel. Their locations, although also remote, appear to have been selected within convenient distance of a lay population necessary for both the supply of certain subsistence needs and as a focus for Christian mission. A population of appropriate size is unlikely to have been resident on Fair Isle, nor is it likely that the subsistence resources of the island could have supplied a monastic community in addition to its own population. It is more probable, however, that Fair Isle was better suited to eremitic monasticism, traces of which are more difficult to identify and for which the *vallum monasterii* was not necessarily a component.

The northern and western parts of the island are topographically more suited to this type of stack or promontory location, but only one site fulfils even the most basic requirements. The site, at Burrista (*357*) in the north-west of the island, consists of an eroding promontory, access to which can now only be made across a precipitous narrow track (plate 7.2). The surviving land area contains at least two small

Plate 7.2 The possible monastic site at Burrista (357) on the west side of the island.

enclosures, possibly structural, and two low grass-covered mounds. Problems of access and safety were such that detailed survey was not possible. No earthwork was evident across the landward side, but the scale of erosion has been such that any 'vallum' might easily have been lost. Nor were there any traces of a more substantial rampart system which might indicate a fortified enclosure of a type similar to the Landberg promontory. In any event the location, high up in the moorland, is both remote and awkward to reach and far better suited to a monastic function. If there is any early Christian establishment on Fair Isle, Burrista must at least be a contender.

Another potential candidate is a low earthwork (*229*) identified for 40m against the site of the (now demolished) church at the south end of the island (see chapter 11, figs 11.3 and 11.4). Although only 0.3m high, this was identified curving in an arc to the north and west of the present graveyard and reaffirmed by geophysical survey. The antiquity of this site is unknown, but a recent salvage excavation on the cliff face below the graveyard has produced coarse pottery together with mammal material dated to the 7th or 8th centuries AD (radiocarbon reference: AA-11696, N

Fojut, pers comm). The location is uncharacteristic for an early monastery, being low-lying and topographically undefined, although it might be remembered that part of the function of the vallum itself was to provide definition – a physical barrier between respective secular and ecclesiastical worlds.

A less likely candidate also lies at the south of the island (*3*) on a low promontory overlooking the rocky coastline, but in no way holding a remote or inhospitable location. A thin tongue of land has been annexed by a narrow earthwork barely 15m long across the narrowest point. This earthwork, almost 0.2m high, seems to have been constructed without the need for large stones and was devised in a relatively complex curved manner despite the flatness of the topography. The headland otherwise bears no traces of activity or building.

The Viking landscape

Scandinavian culture is usually cited as being the basis for post-medieval economic and social traditions in the Northern Isles, with linguistic and ethnographic evidence being held up as proof. It is ironic that settlement archaeology appears not to reflect the same level of continuity in a physical structural sense and that the sites which have been the focus of excavation attention have tended to show occupation of relatively short-term duration. Jarlshof is an exception, but elsewhere, at Underhoull (Small 1966), on Orkney at Buckquoy (Ritchie 1977) and at Birsay (Hunter 1986), the evidence suggests that settlement shift occurred at fairly regular intervals and that the presence of *lacunae* in the settlement record is almost predictable. Multi-period sites such as Pool, Orkney (Hunter *et al* forthcoming) serve only to emphasise that such divisions exist. In the case of Pool the latest excavated remains belong to the Norse period within the 12th or 13th centuries; the subsequent medieval deposits presumably lie elsewhere, possibly beneath nearby (but now abandoned) 18th and 19th century ruined dwellings and farm buildings. It is a gap in the settlement chain which is remarkably difficult to fill throughout the Northern Isles. The period between the 13th and 18th centuries contains few physical links; those which have been identified, such as The Biggins, Papa Stour (Crawford 1985; 1991), Sandwick (Bigelow 1985) or Tuquoy, Orkney (Owen 1993), are themselves short-term.

As far as landscape study of this later period is concerned the potential is for understanding the more general issues of settlement expansion, rather than for identifying specific locations – a factor which presumably mirrors the processes of land-taking, and which might be evidenced in place-name analysis (eg Marwick 1952). The phenomenon should cause few problems on an island as small as Fair Isle, where nucleation is evident in as much as the derived modern settlement is spatially documented from townships of the 18th century. It is, therefore, in those general areas of later settlement that the greatest potential for identifying earlier settlements might lie.

For reasons which are predictable, even if they are not understood, the occurrence of a 'control' site which might show settlement continuity in a single place from the Iron Age through to the post-medieval period is an unrealistic concept. Those excavations which show the longest span of settlement also appear to confirm the lack of continuity; this has been emphasised by two excavations on the island of Sanday, Orkney, at Pool and Tofts Ness, where the settlement gaps in one site were filled by occupation in the other, and *vice versa*; together the two covered a broad period between the 4th millennium BC and the 13th century AD. Although the approach methodologies and local landscapes differed somewhat, both sites occurred on the same small island, had access to the same resources and shared a common technological development. It is of particular relevance here that the environmental record on Sanday shows a common subsistence economy; the overview suggests that limitations of climate and land utility may have fostered a process of maximising local resources and developing traditions at a relatively early stage in the evolution of each site.

Of particular relevance, however, is the extent to which the developed economy on Sanday was largely unaffected by a major cultural change – namely the Norse colonisation. It is quite clear that the same basic type of economy followed in the Iron Age was being continued in the Norse, and that although some minor differences were evident, the change of cultural dominance appears to have been largely irrelevant taken over the longer term (Hunter 1991, 191f). It seems probable that the landscape and its resources were sufficiently inflexible to changes of cultural management and this points towards continuity of traditions, certainly from the Iron Age through to pre-industrial modern times. Settlement in the Northern Isles during this period involved a process of adaptation to pre-established and proven methods. The more closely the period is examined from a settlement standpoint, the harder it becomes to treat it as anything other than a single era in which the subsistence economics appear to remain constant and in which landscape change is largely unevidenced. It is, in a sense, a period of prehistory through to the 17th or 18th century.

This degree of assumed continuity is the most plausible reason why the archaeological evidence is so unforthcoming. Hedges' predictive model for the survival of settlement remains acts as a useful working guide in this respect (1986, 24f); it explains why many sites from these later periods, lying on the lower, better ground, were often replaced *in situ*, ultimately by modern settlement, even although much of their local evolution leaves no traces on the present landscape. A similar argument, but using different evidence, was also explored by Smith in a comparison between Iron Age spheres of influence and Norse land use as interpreted from 17th century scattalds (1984, 106). This type of data emphasises, too, the potential of taking modern settlement as a starting point and tracing it backwards in time – an exercise carried out with some success by Baldwin on both Faroe (1983) and Foula (1984). The potential on Fair Isle is somewhat less, partly because the early field or land boundary systems on which Baldwin based his landscape analysis have barely survived, and partly because the related study of place-names has never been formally attempted. The latter has, as a starting point, the collection of local (mostly unwritten) names on the island including those of topographical features and fields, drawn together by the late Peter Davis of the Observatory staff, but the former is a fact of field survey life and is irredeemable. With this unpromising start other, complementary, avenues of approach have to be adopted.

Walling and planticrues (crubs)

Apart from current settlements, there are additional pointers to archaeological sites in the southern part of the island where modern occupation within the enclosed land is assumed to have blanked out all traces of earlier occupation and land use. Of particular interest, for example, are a large number of short lengths of walling, usually distinct from field boundaries and therefore unlikely to be the relicts of field dykes, which take an ostensibly random position within the field system and which appear anomalous on an otherwise grazed or cultivated landscape. There are over 60 of these spread across the island (fig 7.1), roughly half of which lie within the enclosed area. Normally described and used as sheep shelters, these are also common in other parts of Shetland where the landscape is equally dedicated to an economy based predominantly on sheep. In origin they are probably late landscape features; Baldwin identifies them as the *buils*, the places where sheep could gather for shelter from the prevailing wind during severe winter weather and where they could be fed hay (1978, 115). He observed that they appear, as on Fair Isle, in a variety of forms and sizes, T-, S- or Y-shaped, or even as single lengths, but that they occurred predominantly on the scattald. In this respect Fair Isle differs from the norm in that the majority lie within the enclosed crofting area on the better land – a distribution of particular interest in that it reflects the locations of available stone in a part of the island where major landscape changes have occurred.

These units of walling on Fair Isle take on a variety of shapes, sometimes a simple straight line, but more often an L-shape, T-shape or even an H- or Y-shape, rarely more than 10-15m in maximum length (plate 7.3). Normally uncoursed, and without true facings, they probably reflect the difficulties of acquiring suitable building material. Many of the wall bases (particularly at the ends) are constructed of large hewn stones with smaller rubble built into the upper regions. It is more feasible to assume that they represent the utilisation of an existing stone resource on an island where useful building stone is notoriously hard to acquire. Each length of walling may identify the approximate vicinity of an earlier monument and therefore act as a general guide to previous settlement locations. The nature and date of these

Plate 7.3 Examples of sheep shelters or similar walling within the enclosed pasture.

are unknown; they may identify post-medieval structural remains as much as those of earlier periods, but it is interesting to note that their distribution also includes some specific areas of attested early settlement. It is perhaps predictable that they show a strong concentration on Buness, a headland of ambiguous landscape features where monuments are difficult to define but where supplies of stone from both quarries and monuments themselves are in abundance.

The fact that few of these *buils* appear to be located adjacent to modern or historically documented settlement suggests that some process of discontinuity in the settlement record has occurred or, more likely, that the modern distribution of dwellings represents the surviving elements of an earlier, larger distribution, on the assumption that the walling lengths have an archaeological basis. Testing of the hypothesis by exploratory excavation was undertaken on three separate sites within the enclosed area, in each case the excavation being limited to the opening of a narrow trench adjacent and at right angles to a length of standing walling (*74*; *164* and *175*). On two of these sites removal of the turf and immediate topsoil revealed stonework or rubble which clearly pre-dated the upstanding structure; in one (*175*) the excavation continued to natural without trace of any archaeological features. This limited experiment tends to suggest that the seemingly random distribution of walling lengths within the enclosed fields might be used as a tentative guide to earlier activity.

The interpretation of walling lengths is to some extent paralleled by the distribution of planticrues on the island (fig 7.1). These small square or sub-rectangular stone-built enclosures, typically 4 x 5m and sometimes standing to a height of around 1.5m, are characteristic landscape features throughout Shetland and provide growth environments which are both wind-proof and animal-proof for young plants. Each tends to exhibit uncoursed, unfaced rubble walling with substantial stones set along the base, particularly at the corners. Like that of the walling, their distribution appears obtuse and appears to lack an obvious spatial relationship or association with other landscape features, including those associated with modern settlement. It is difficult to believe that they are locationally specific, although there is a tendency for them to occur in sheltered rather than exposed places and, like the walling, they might be argued to reflect a pattern of pre-existing structural remains. Scott appears to have noticed their unusual landscape distribution although he ascribes it, as he did to all matters native which he failed to understand, to general lack of local organisation:

> *An odd custom prevails:- any person, without exception (if I understand rightly), who wishes to raise a few kail, fixes upon any spot he pleases, encloses it with a dry stone wall, uses it as a kailyard till he works out the soil, then deserts it and makes another. Some dozen of these little enclosures, about twenty or thirty feet square, are in sight at once. They are called planty-cruives; and the Zetlanders are so far from reckoning this an invasion, or a favour on the part of the proprietor, that their most exaggerated description of an avaricious person is one who would refuse liberty for a planty-cruive; or to infer the greatest contempt of another, they will say they would not hold a planty-cruive of him. It is needless to notice how much this licence must interfere with cultivation.* (Laughlan 1982, 28)

There are some 37 examples on the island, in varying states of survival ranging from a skeletal outline of surface stones to a few extant functioning versions. Over 20 lie inside the enclosed area while outside there is a specific concentration in

Homisdale (plate 7.4, see also fig 4.5), in a region of interpreted early settlement which also includes a burnt mound and a possible house. One of these planticrues is still in use and stands to a height of around 1.5m (*307*) while the others survive only at foundation level, one being levelled and painted white to function as an aircraft

Plate 7.4 Planticrues exhibiting outer banking in the Homisdale area.

landing aid (*302*). The likelihood of reused stone in their construction was observed by Williamson during one of his visits to the island in the early 1960s; his acute, and from our point of view extremely useful, understanding of the changing landscape led him to comment on a pair of 'portal' stones which appeared to belong to a larger stone alignment in Homisdale (1965, 26). These stones are no longer extant and Williamson's description is their only record. He noted, in his observant way, that much of the complex had 'obviously been built into the local planticrubs ...' (*ibid*).

There are also two probable examples in the Ferny Cup (fig 4.3), the main identifiable tract of relict landscape on the island; one of these lies in a sheltered gully to the north-west of the valley and shares general dimensions with crub forms as well as exhibiting substantial stones at foundation level (*329*). Despite the obvious local romance of the site (where fern growth provides the overall name for the valley) it would be difficult to ascribe the remains to anything other than a former planticrue, although the nature of the stone construction suggests the robbing of an earlier building in the valley bottom.

More detailed examination of several of the planticrues indicates that the existing enclosure shape was a secondary modification of an existing form. A number exhibit obvious rebuildings, butted joints, blockings or other features indicative of structural alteration. Those which appear to be modifications of earlier versions include an example with a rounded corner on the Rippack (*508*), one with an unusual angular form within the cultivated area (*420*), a foundation which also contains a massive flat-topped stone on Vaasetter (*648*), and a version with overlapping corners near the present kirk (*490*). Diversity of this order would tend to suggest that the planticrue was not always the primary function. The kirk area itself contains four stone-based examples and at least 14 turf forms (fig 7.3); it represents a somewhat ambiguous landscape state in that the vegetation is that of moorland and has not been cultivated within living memory, even though the land is enclosed. Being moorland it might be expected to exhibit a certain level of relict archaeological landscape, but this is restricted entirely to the stone- and turf-based planticrues noted above. The absence of earlier monument types in the kirk area, particularly boundaries, tends to suggest that whatever structures provided material or locational inspiration for these planticrues seem unlikely to be of very early date.

One of the planticrues near the kirk (*490*) demonstrates a further characteristic, namely a type of outer banking which is identifiable around several other planticrues

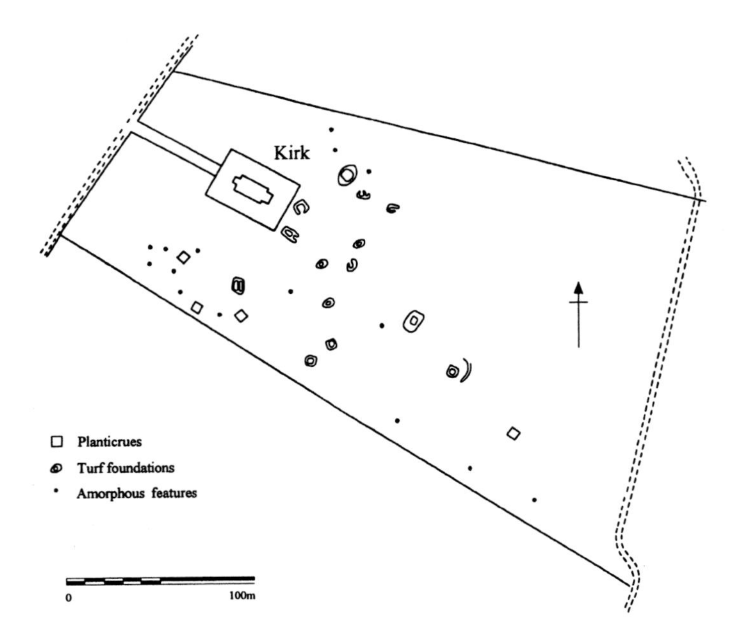

Fig 7.3 Distribution of planticrues around the present kirk.

on the island. The feature is particularly emphatic near the kirk where the green of the turf banking contrasts sharply with the local heather cover. However, the best examples lie in Homisdale where a concentrated group of planticrues appear to be surrounded, either totally or partially, by a low grassy bank which presumably represents the accumulation of organic deposits and soil removed from the interior. It is, however, conceivable that they might equally represent the remains of a pre-existing stone structure, the stone of which was robbed in order to create the planticrue itself – a phenomenon previously identified by Calder elsewhere in Shetland (1963, 71). However, this latter possibility was only partly borne out by excavation in the three specific locations which were examined.

On one site in Homisdale a section was placed across a planticrue base and its surrounding bank (*308*), but this only served to indicate the richness and homogeneity of the interior deposits in comparison to the less rich, more varied profile on the exterior. The section (fig 7.4) illustrates the nature of the external deposits which can presumably be explained as reflecting outcast materials. It suggests, too, that at least part of the external surface may have been cleared away at the time of the planticrue construction. Internally the deposits appeared to have been well-cultivated, again down to a cleared surface, although at least three humic layers were evident. The walling itself, seen in section, was double-faced (a quality not readily apparent from its surface survival) and approximately 0.6m wide. The finds recovered throughout the investigation consisted entirely of modern debris, and there was no evidence of earlier archaeological features. Eight planticrues lie in this narrow valley together with a number of earlier monuments including a sub-peat dyke (fig 4.5), and while on the face value of this single trench there appears to be no direct relationship between the planticrue and earlier remains, the likelihood of clearance shown in section may not preclude such a relationship from having taken place.

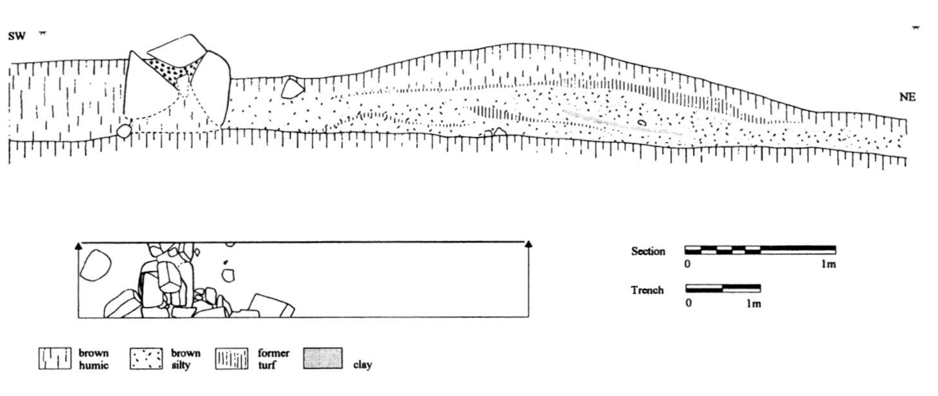

Fig 7.4 Section through planticrue 308 on Homisdale.

In another investigation, a similar trench was used to section an unusual planticrue (*323*) in the Ferny Cup area which was thought to be of special interest in view of possible secondary activity. The planticrue survived in the shape of a partial enclosure with an internal diameter of approximately 7m, although the south-west part was indistinct. The composition of the enclosure showed a construction of earth, turf and stones although without the formality and substance of walling identified among the few early structures recorded. The interior, however, contained two roughly parallel stone lines forming a rectangle approximately 5 x 4m. This was a single course high and appeared to represent a roughly faced foundation, presumably for the planticrue. Unfortunately the depth of the surviving soil profile was barely more than a few centimetres and the sectioning of the monument failed to produce any stratigraphic information, although it did yield a single sherd of coarse pottery. The overview, however, points towards reuse of the site – an interpretation based on the composition of the enclosure which was clearly different to the outcast and organic nature of the banking around the Homisdale planticrue.

The third investigation took place on Burrashield where a section was placed across the walling of a stone foundation, presumed to be of planticrue origin (*257*, fig 6.3). The foundation was rectangular, approximately 5.5 x 4m internally with walling represented by an alignment of earthfast stones, the largest of which were located at the corners. Again the depth of surviving stratigraphy was minimal, although the section demonstrated that the original walling was probably of double-faced construction. Other than a possible modern drain line no archaeological features were recorded.

The evidence from all three investigations does little to offer positive support for the interpretation of planticrue location: only in one instance is the theory of reuse tenable; in the other two the provision of a stone resource in the general vicinity rather than in the immediate location is open to further questioning.

There are few other pointers that might be used to indicate where this Iron Age and later settlement might be located. The better land in the south part of the island was almost certainly occupied as offering the better agricultural soils, the higher land to the north being of secondary value and, since the assumed climatic deterioration of the Bronze Age, was marginal. It is interesting to note that the locations of walling lengths and planticrues north of the *feelie* dyke lie unexceptionally in association with groups of early monuments, or at least with monuments of mooted early date determined either on the basis of monument type or on clustering. There is no evidence north of the dyke, for example, of these stone features lying outwith this early distribution. This strengthens the argument that later monuments were located on the lower, better soils thus making the distribution of these stone features south of the dyke of particular significance.

8

Viking and Norse Settlement

By the time of the later Iron Age and Viking period the written word, although often misleading, provides an additional level of evidence. The first documentary record of any note for Fair Isle comes with the *Saga* sources which, given the interval of time between the events which took place and the date of writing, are less than satisfactory even if they are interesting. Predictably, the main source is the *Orkneyinga Saga*, although *Njal's Saga* also contains mention of the island more in a locational capacity. Fair Isle was the dwelling place of David the White with whom Kari spent the winter (Magnusson and Pálsson 1960, Ch 154); the reference at least shows that Fair Isle was permanently settled by the Norse in the 11th century and, more practically, that the habit of not voyaging during the winter months was still sensibly retained. The *Orkneyinga Saga* is more explicit and provides the stage for at least some of the drama in the feuding between Earl Paul and Earl Rognvald in the 12th century.

Two main episodes are narrated, both revolving around the beacon system established by Paul which used Fair Isle as a signalling point to North Ronaldsay in the south. In the first episode Dagfinn Hlodvisson, a farmer on Fair Isle, was placed in charge of the beacon and had the responsibility for lighting it in the event of Rognvald's ships being sighted sailing from Shetland (Pálsson and Edwards 1978, Ch 67). Rognvald, by allowing his ships to lie off South Mainland in sight of Fair Isle, and by a cunning process of raising the sails little by little to give the impression of approaching the island, tricked Hlodvisson into lighting the beacon. This resulted in the lighting of beacons throughout the Orkneys, in the scrambling of Earl Paul's men and in the intended annoyance and disruption to all concerned – disruption which culminated in fighting among the beacon keepers.

In the second but connected episode Uni, one of Rognvald's retainers, arrived on Fair Isle with three men purporting to be his sons (Pálsson and Edwards 1978, Ch 69). He took a house there, he and his sons becoming an accepted part of the island community, ultimately to gain the confidence of the new beacon keeper, a man called Eirik. Having achieved this, and by successfully pouring water on the beacon to prevent it from being ignited, he allowed Rognvald to sail from Shetland to Orkney unobserved. The passage contains some useful implicit information. It suggests that the island appears to have been well-populated at that time, and that fishing, an activity ostensibly carried out by Uni's 'sons', seems to have been an accepted part of local life. Furthermore, the fact that the 'sons' were unrecognised may indicate a

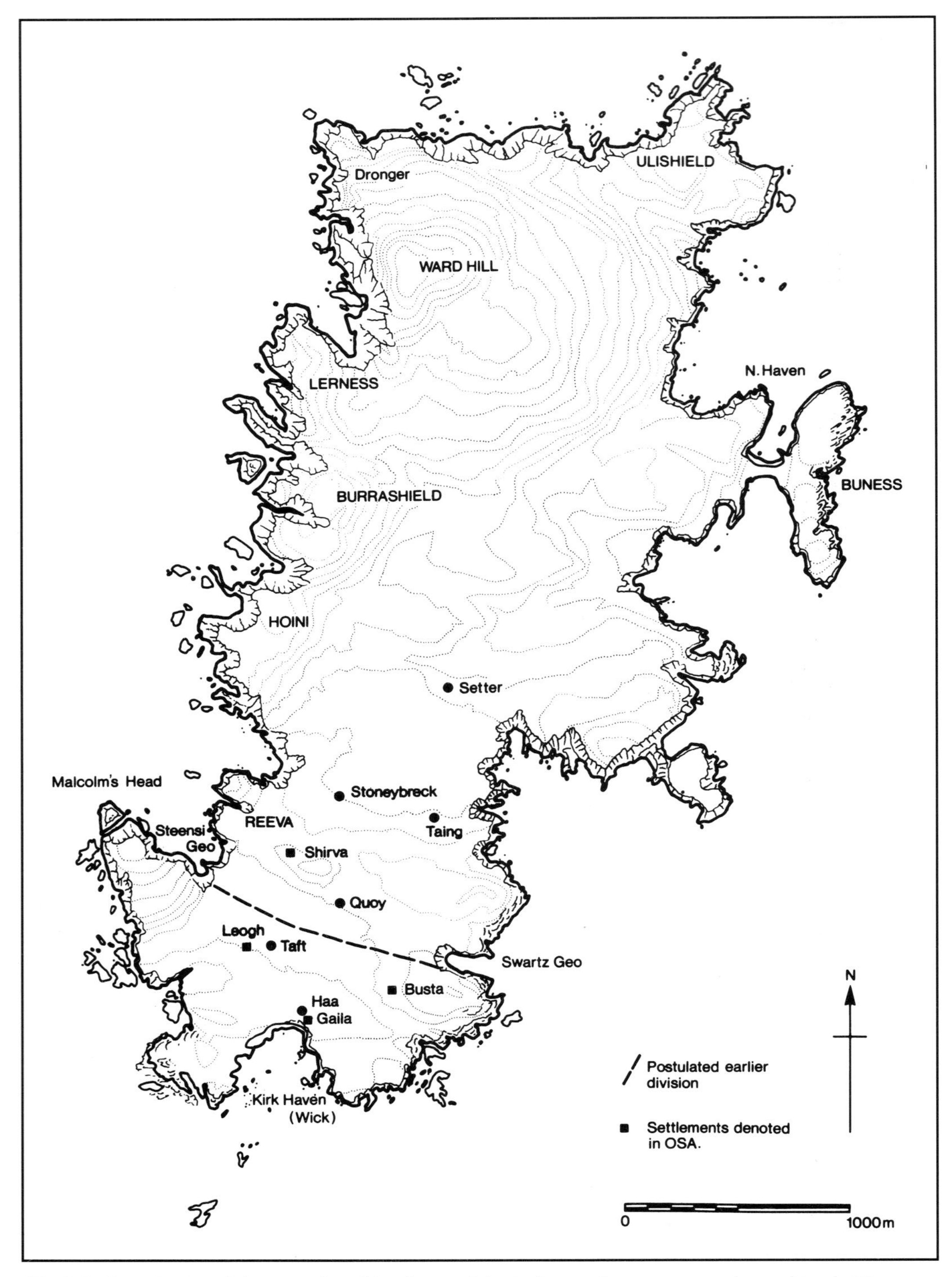

Fig 8.1 Locations and sites mentioned in chapter 8 including settlement centres denoted in the First Statistical Account.

degree of political and social separation between Fair Isle and Mainland Shetland (Smith 1988, 34).

The high place on which this beacon is reputed to have been built is almost certainly above the western cliffs on Ward Hill, the tallest point on the island at around 220m above sea level. Further south, Malcolm's Head is the site of the modern coastguard lookout, but is approximately half the height and has only an obscured view of Shetland. Furthermore, Ward Hill belongs to a group of high points in the Northern Isles bearing the element *Ward* or *Wart* (Clouston 1932) derived from ON *varða* (beacon or cairn). The occurrence of these names throughout Shetland was noticed in the early 17th century by Sibbald who, in one instance, commented on the presence of 'a heap of Turfs and Piets' (Monteith 1845, 33), although it is not clear whether these were beacons for signalling or for possible lighthouse purposes. At least two earlier visitors to Fair Isle claim to have knowledge of remains on the summit, one describing 'ruins of the guard house where, centuries ago, the lonely watchman spent many a weary night, ready to kindle his signal fire at the approach of a hostile sail, as when King Harold's warships were seen nearing Hjaltland's shores' (Reid 1869, 50). Reid's description of the island appears in the aptly titled *Art Rambles in Shetland* and is, to say the least, schematic; he may have confused Ward Hill (often cloud-covered) with Malcolm's Head to the south on which the ruins of a stone-built Napoleonic watch tower (*72*) still stand. However, the other source is more reputable. In 1814 Scott's party spent the day sight-seeing on the island. Scott himself went to examine the reputed copper deposits while two of his colleagues took it upon themselves to inspect 'the remains of a danish lighthouse upon a distant hill called, as usual, the Ward or ward-hill'. Their remaining colleague stayed back to ensure that the dinner was being cooked properly (Laughlan 1982, 52). Given that the events recounted in the *Orkneyinga Saga* did in fact take place in all or in part, Ward Hill is the most likely spot. Beacons have been lit there in more recent times, but it has to be added that the apex is laboriously hard and time-consuming to reach, that to retain dry material there for any length of time would be extremely difficult in such a damp environment, and that the concept of carrying up water, even part of the way, to soak the material is almost a non-starter. The summit is currently spread with a thick cover of military rubble from the Second World War (see chapter 13). Traces of any purpose-built station that might have made beacon-keeping feasible will have been long destroyed. For all that, however, the story is a good one.

The beacon was also used during the Diamond Jubilee of Queen Victoria in 1897, the public celebrations for which involved the lighting of 52 bonfires throughout the Shetland islands. All 52 sites were listed in the *Shetland Times* (June 26th 1897, 4), 18 still retaining the 'wart' element or its equivalent. The Fair Isle fire was denoted as being on 'The Wart'. However, despite recorded good weather 'much endeavour was made with glasses to try and locate the fire on Fair Isle [from Mainland Shetland], but although one of the lighthouses was observable, the bonfire could not be made out' (*ibid*).

The *Saga* references to Fair Isle are relatively late in the overall scheme of Norse settlement and colonisation in the Northern Isles. Most scholars would now agree that settlement started around AD 800 although its nature and density is still subject to debate. Before then, in the later 8th century, Fair Isle was almost certainly known to Norse sailors as a navigational marker in the journey from Western Norway to Ireland. This route saw the gradual occupation of the Northern and Western Isles as part of a wider process of exploration by the Norse which ultimately embraced Faroe, Iceland and Greenland. A period of climatic warming did much to support subsistence economies in the north-west of the new environment, but this was a less critical feature of subsistence in the Northern Isles where the exploitable resources were better able to withstand adverse climate or growth factors. Temperature effect modelling has shown Shetland's greater overall viability in this respect in comparison to other areas (McGovern *et al* 1988).

The passage from Norway to the Northern Isles was not a difficult one in the summer months; the Shetland Isles (*Hjaltland*) straggled conveniently for over 110km longitudinally and could be reached with a modicum of navigational skills, without perhaps being out of sight of land for little more than a day (Crawford 1987, 13). Fair Isle's tall, austere landmass was more readily identifiable and is likely to have been a significant stepping stone for boats travelling in either direction along the leg between Orkney and Shetland. It seems likely that the island, in common with much of the rest of Orkney, Shetland and even parts of the Western Isles, was subject to sporadic contact during the summer months. This level of contact may have involved trade or plunder, or both, but is not of a type which leaves much in the way of archaeological trace. Such contact would also have brought word of the fertile landscapes back to Scandinavia resulting in an inevitable colonisation from a homeland where prime land was already at a premium.

More permanent settlement undoubtedly followed in the early 9th century but archaeological dating methods are not sufficiently well-tuned to make the case unambiguously. Early 9th century settlement therefore stands as a matter of high probability rather than proven fact; it depends also on the ease with which land could be taken, and on the extent to which the existing inhabitants might be prepared to share or become subdued. This is a particular point of concern to which much research has been addressed in Orkney.

Relevant *Saga* sources are either written too late to be credible, or are otherwise unconcerned with minor issues of primary colonisation peripheral to the more major thrust of dynastic business. The consensus of *Saga* opinion suggests that much of the landscape was empty, for example *Egil's Saga* (Pálsson and Edwards 1976, Ch 4), what little habitation there was being occupied by peoples who, according to the *Historia Norvegiae*, lived in underground dwellings (Anderson 1922, 330). Both these points have now been successfully corrected by excavation work undertaken during the last two decades. Research has identified the presence of a Late Iron Age or Pictish society throughout the islands and has, through the excavation of settlement sites, interpreted a period of interface – of cultural assimilation or co-operation – between native and incoming Norseman. Sites on Orkney such as Buckquoy (Ritchie 1977) or Birsay (Hunter 1986) point towards the integration of the two different cultures, although it has to be emphasised that other opinions still insist upon total native subjugation at the hands of Norse incomers. In Shetland, where detailed archaeological investigation of this period is awaited, the problems are still unresolved. Evidence from the excavations at Jarlshof, for example, shows little in the way of an existing, or surviving, native influence; alternatively, the St Ninian's Isle treasure – a deposition of native silver bowls and objects dated to the 9th century (Wilson 1973, 147) – is often cited as proof of a more confrontational period of cultural change. However, by the later years of the 9th century the creation of the Earldom of Orkney had formalised Norse sovereignty throughout the Northern Isles. Norse superiority appears to have been complete and by the time of the 12th century, the time at which the events on Fair Isle supposedly occurred, Norse domination was unquestionable.

The strength of Norse culture in the Northern Isles is difficult to understate: it lies at the root of many current traditions, especially those concerned with exploitation of the land and the sea; it plays a significant part in the modern dialect, notably in Shetland; and wholly dominates the place-name vocabulary of both island groups. This surviving Scandinavian-based culture is the relic of a tradition stemming from the period of colonisation, although history sees it weaken somewhat from the 15th century (Smith 1990). Influences from Scotland, not to mention the economic power of German trade, subsequently provided means for change. However, even by the beginning of the 18th century Scandinavian influence was still persisting, albeit at a lower level, and carried with it not only key elements of an early subsistence economy in agriculture and fishing, but also a valuable ethnographic record.

It is a frustrating irony of research into the Viking and Norse worlds that this welter of ethnographic and linguistic data has yet to be reflected archaeologically. The number of proven, let alone excavated, Norse sites in the Northern Isles is remarkably few (despite the preponderance of place-names), the number of burial sites can almost be counted on the fingers of two hands (eg Crawford 1987, fig 31), and the understanding of settlement infrastructure and organisation continues to lie wide open to speculation (eg Steinnes 1959). Archaeological research directions are partly to blame, and these have since been redefined in an important review paper (Bigelow

1992). Shetland, for example, has received much less attention than Orkney, but even the detailed survey undertaken on Fair Isle failed to identify any evidence whatsoever, other than place-names, of Viking remains. The closest evidence geographically (apart from Jarlshof) lies in two hoards dated to around the 11th century and deposited in the South Mainland (Graham-Campbell 1976, 116; 1993, 176f); one, at Quendale, contained fragments of 'ring-money' and uncoined silver while the other, in Dunrossness, contained pieces of an arm-ring together with further fragments of 'ring-money'.

An early aspect of Norse influence in the Northern Isles possibly stems from navigation rather than physical contact in the naming of basic or directional seascape features such as islands or headlands (*-ey* and *-ness* respectively). Fair Isle's earliest recorded form *Friðarey*, usually translated as 'island of peace' or 'island of tranquillity' derived from ON *friðr*, (eg Stewart 1965, 248), probably stems from this period. The name may seem inappropriate, given the wildness of the local weather, seas and currents; more plausible is a derivation of *Farey* (ON *faar-ey*), with the same root as Faroe, meaning 'island of sheep'. A third, more recent suggestion (Thom 1989, 3) is that the current name may have derived from 'Fire Island' reflecting the status of the beacon. In earlier cartographic and documentary sources the island tends to occur with the definite article and in this respect is unusual. 'The Fire Island' would make sense in identifying the island's very specific function, although it is unlikely to have been a primary name form.

Norse influence, therefore, may have been exercised on the landscape without Norse feet ever having been set on dry land. A similar case has been made by Fellows-Jensen (1984, 149) who argues that navigation rather than the dubious process of 'ness-taking' was the behind many of the headland names in the area. The argument is perhaps best advanced by examples in the Western Isles where Norse headland names occur among a predominance of Gaelic topographical names. Fair Isle, however, does not conform to this pattern; almost all its topographical names are either Norse or Norse-derived and there is no way of distinguishing which of the visible coastal features may have been referred to first. Many are clearly of secondary origin (eg Malcolm's Head), others possess elements indicative of land use, for example Ulishield or Burrashield (ON *skjoldr*, shieling), or animal names such as Buness (ON *bu*, livestock); those of the *geos* (inlets or creeks) are even more specific – but a few are ambiguous such as Lerness (ON *leir*, clay), Dronger (ON *drongr*, pointed rock), Hoini (ON *honni*, crag) or Reeva (ON *rifa*, cleft), and might possibly represent those primary names which reflect the island's physical characteristics in the early years of passing boats. There is, additionally, the complication that fishing traditions have since tended to apply a separate, unwritten toponomy to land-based navigational features – a toponomy which for reasons of superstition was deliberately distinguished from that used whilst on land.

In view of passing traffic, it would be surprising if the island had not become a focus for settlement in the 9th century. It would be surprising, too, if the fertile lands at the south of the island were not already under Pictish plough or at least under the control of a small community based on that side of the island. Landing could be safely carried out at only two places (see chapter 3), the option at the North Haven being too far away from the fertile slopes, leaving that at the south of the island (Kirk Haven) as the most suitable and likely point of approach. The name 'Wick' (ON *vík*, bay) applied to this landing suggests that this was the predominant harbour.

Research into Scandinavian settlement in the Northern Isles has produced a predictive model for where settlement is most likely to have been focused, the basis being a set of simple criteria which encapsulate the main requirements of a subsistence economy set within a North Atlantic environment. The fundamentals are well-established; they require sea access, a safe bay, level ground for a farmstead, and adjacent well-drained arable land and suitable pasture. Small's superimposition of the model onto the Shetland landscape emphasises the strictly limited locations available (1968a, fig 1). Fair Isle's failure to feature in this analysis was not, one suspects, because the island was in any way unsuited to permanent settlement, but because the sea access fell short of that deemed optimum in Mainland Shetland. The remaining factors are otherwise adequately satisfied in the south part of the island where primary Scandinavian settlement might be predicted within reasonable distance of the bay at Kirk Haven and with access to the best arable land, or to land which was already under cultivation.

It has to be assumed, too, that each of Small's suitable locations had the potential for housing more than a few isolated farmstead units. On the basis of what is known of Norse farming, critical factors for land saturation would seem to have been the area available for grazing as much as the amount of land suitable for cultivation. Groupings of units tended to lie adjacent to the best arable land and, by the time of documentary records in the 16th century, many emerged into township units with fiscal implications. The system reflects a Norwegian solution to a situation in which the best land was always in short supply. In Shetland this is seen most clearly at Jarlshof where Hamilton's excavations demonstrate how a single 9th century farmstead evolved into a nucleated multiple-farmstead complex by the early Middle Ages (1956).

This evolved system may be reflected in later centuries; in Fair Isle the documentary record of the late 18th century *First Statistical Account* refers to the island's houses as being:

> *confusedly thrown together as chance, whim, or conveniency directed, into four clumps or towns, under the fine sounding names of Shewah, Lioh, Bustah, and Gelah (sic). These four little towns, as they are called, contain the inhabitants,*

> *of which there are 32 families, about 7 persons in each; 106 males, and 114 females; in all, 220. (OSA* XIX, 436)

The number of houses is unspecified. Of the four only Gaila is not recorded on the modern map, but appears on Thomas' map as 'Geila'. By the time of the *Second Statistical Account*, towards the middle of the 19th century, these 'towns or hamlets' had been increased to six by the inclusion of 'Seutter' and 'Taing' with a total population of 232 souls living in 35 houses (*NSA* XV, 95f). On the basis of one family per house, which seems to be the inference of both accounts, a crude calculation suggests that each township consisted of between five to seven houses with a local population of around 40-55 individuals in each group. The point here is not to evaluate the implications of the population size (for which see chapter 9; plate 9.1) as much as the evolution of the nucleation. Are we to believe, for example, that 'Seutter' and 'Taing' were purely creations of the 19th century, or is it more likely that they represent the rebuilding of ruined farmsteads? Both appear on Thomas' map of 1839 but each is depicted as an individual building, not as a cluster. It is interesting too that the anonymous Armada account of 1588 refers to only 17 houses (see Martin 1975, 148), approximately half the number of the *First Statistical Account* some two centuries later, but makes no mention of any nucleation or clustering.

A nucleated system of this nature undoubtedly had sociological implications, ultimately reinforced by the legalities of taxation, but was in part originally rooted in the need for co-operative measures within the tight confines of the farming calendar. This is especially pertinent on Fair Isle where the combination of insularity and limited resources still necessitates a high degree of communal effort. The nature of the Norse agricultural cycle to which this was directed has been expounded on many occasions (eg Small 1968b, 7f), and points to a spring manuring, ploughing and rotational sowing (oats, barley and bere) of the infields adjacent to the farmstead. In May the lambing sheep were brought down into the folds, egg collecting took place and the summer grazing was organised. Depending on the number of animals it may have been necessary to utilise even the smallest, most inaccessible patch of grazing land. The use of Sheep Rock is a case in point, although it is unclear exactly when this became physically detached from the main landmass. Haymaking started in late summer, the amount depending on the level of outwintering; the grain harvest followed, probably well into September. The rounding up of the sheep would have been an important communal activity, and its method of operation may have been little changed on Fair Isle since Norse times (see chapter 10). Fishing, the other major part of the subsistence economy, which became more significant as population pressure mounted on limited terrestrial resources, was also seasonal and may have required a similar level of collaboration.

Cant (1984, 173) has pointed to the 'vigorous communal quality' of this type of settlement system as being one of the fundamental controlling factors within Shetland society of the early Middle Ages. To the south, Orkney, although colonised within the same period, was controlled more specifically as an appendage of Norway by virtue of the Earls, while to the north lay the very different republican atmosphere of Iceland. Cant saw Shetland, together with Faroe, as a type of 'buffer zone' between these two contemporary political extremes. Within this environment Fair Isle belonged firmly with Shetland.

Place-names and settlement

The spread and relative chronology of Scandinavian settlement, particularly in Orkney, has been much clarified by the study of place-names. The Northern Isles are especially suited to this approach, not simply because the preponderance of names are Scandinavian or Scandinavian-derived, but because they relate to both settlement sites and to components of the man-made environment such as fields, as well as to natural features. There is a potential infrastructure to be interpreted. Marwick's model of Norse settlement evolution based on the evidence of farm names (1952) continues to provide the platform for this type of study; his work underlies most modern discussion of settlement toponomy in the Northern Isles (eg Nicolaisen 1976; MacGregor 1986; Crawford 1987, fig 50). There is general agreement that within local settlement processes certain habitative names are of chronological significance – that some names are diagnostic of primary colonisation and that others belong to later periods of occupation. The interpretation is based on comparative studies of place-name elements common to both the Northern Isles and to the Scandinavian homeland, and is also skat-based according to medieval rentals. There is, additionally, a confusing element involving status.

The inferred settlement process identifies the *-by* suffix as being indicative of primary occupation (ie possibly of the *landnámsmen*) in a sequence in which *-land*, *-garðr* and *-bólstaðr* elements follow, with *-quoy* (*kví*) and *-setr* reflecting the later phase of settlement, sometimes in marginal areas when all the best land had been taken over. The chronology is relative and localised, although some scholars have been prepared to postulate absolute values for part of the process; Nicolaisen, for example (1976, 85-6) considered that most of the *-land*, *-garðr* and *-bólstaðr* stage occurred prior to the end of the 9th century, and that *-quoy* generally post-dates 900 AD. A number of qualifications have to be made to a highly simplified scheme: *-skaill* names, for example (of which there are none on Fair Isle), are also probably early but have a strong status connotation (Marwick 1952, 238-40) while *-setr*, a later element, has continued to pose problems of acceptable interpretation (eg Fellows-Jensen 1984, 162). On Fair Isle the 'setter' farm site, if original, is probably uncontroversial.

It lies adjacent to the hill dyke and therefore might be argued to reflect a later sequence of settlement evolution, possibly with a pastoral connotation, whereas the 'quoy' site occurs more centrally and is harder to evaluate by the same model. A number of other problems have also been observed: plotting of second level names in Shetland show that even by the secondary stage in the colonisation process not all the better land had been taken over, and that there was a clear separation between broch sites (with good land) and Norse settlements (Small 1982, 246). However, on an island the size of Fair Isle where all the available land was strictly limited the same situation is unlikely to have applied. Nevertheless, Small's work emphasises that land quality and value is only one of the relevant factors to be taken into account. Further complexities have also emerged from a comparison between place-names in Shetland and Faroe; some names common in Shetland are essentially absent in Faroe (MacGregor 1986, 85). The use of parallel modelling therefore must become questionable.

The surviving farm names on Fair Isle provide little in the way of a classic data set for place-name analysis (fig 8.1). A few (Busta, Quoy and Setter) might be interpreted within an overall settlement sequence, but many of the others are of non-diagnostic type or are simply topographical, for example Stoneybreck (ON *brekka*, slope), Shirva (ON *skirva*, rocky ground), Leogh (ON *loekr*, boggy ground, flat ?, or with a possible Gaelic root), or of more modern origins. The very nature of some of these descriptions points to the fact that these were not sited on the better land and are therefore unlikely to be primary. Nor is there any way of knowing whether some of the potentially diagnostic forms (eg Setter and Quoy) are relatively modern introductions to which traditional names were applied, or whether the sites themselves were reused. Setter, for example, is specified in the *Second Statistical Account*, but not in its predecessor half a century earlier. Quoy appears in neither document, nor is it depicted on Thomas' map of 1839. A few *-by* (ON *býr*) names are recorded but are not extant and occur only on Davis' name map, for example Hoolaby (farm by the hill) below Leogh, Greenaby (pasture farm) and Kennaby (farm below the hill), both adjacent to Busta. Their descriptive nature points towards distinguishing elements and therefore places them late in any overall sequence. Marwick, using parallels in Orkney (1952, 243-4), has also pointed out that such *-by* names often survive merely as names applied to fields or even small districts.

If these names are dismissed from the reckoning for the time being the earliest parts of the model are represented by a single farm name, Busta, located at the eastern side of the southern part of the island. The derivation is almost certainly from ON *bólstaðr* or *bustaðr* (also evolving as Bouster or Bister), meaning a portion or lot, and therefore tends to be indicative of a secondary process of land division. In Shetland this process is also identifiable from the presence of cardinal elements in some of the forms (Waugh 1991, 18). Analysis of similar names in Shetland (MacGregor 1986,

94) appears to point towards land quality where the surrounding fields were all part of the name implication. Marwick's understanding of Orkney examples led him to believe that they occupied fairly central positions and that they were 'relatively early settlements, not fragmentary or residual areas which could be utilised at a later period' (1952, 233). Both interpretations can be satisfied; the soils are some of the best and the present location lies at the eastern margins of the arable land. Spatially, this points to a primary settlement focus towards the centre of the island, possibly in the vicinity of *The Haa* below the hill, a location conveniently near the bay and harbourage. However, within that general area of focus, evidence from neither farm nor field names give any suggestion of early Norse settlement. Slightly to the north the name Taft (ON *toft*, house site) is one which is often thought to possess some association with antiquities, and adjacent to the south-east is Gaila (ON *geil*, fenced area?), the only one of the four 'towns' noted in the *First Statistical Account* to lie within this central zone. It can be no coincidence that Gaila is variously described as the 'main' or 'largest' village in later accounts (see chapter 9) inferring earlier status.

A further interesting, but speculative factor lies in the form of a modern landscape feature, a stone dyke which runs from Swartz Geo on the east coast to Steensi Geo at the west, and which bisects the whole island at the south end. Other than the *feelie* dyke further north this is the only total division of the island. The area divided off includes Busta at the east, Leogh at the west and the area of *The Haa* and Gaila in the centre. Marginal (hill) land occurs at each side, and partly beyond the dyke line to the north. It is perhaps relevant, too, that the surviving post-medieval rig lines show differences in alignment either side of this dyke (see chapter 9, fig 9.7) therefore suggesting that the division, although perhaps not the stonework, is of some antiquity. The area contained also includes a number of field names with the *-deel* suffix (ON *deild*, strip or patch of ground), such as Whilladeel and Moosideels in the central part, and Innerdeel and Outradeel south of Busta. Near Leogh, names such as Buggarts or Whilligert (ON *garðr*, enclosed area) and Whinnerwalls (ON *vinja*, pasture) contain elements which may be considered early (Jakobsen 1936, 45 and 116). Some similar names, Steensdeels and Muggideels, occur just beyond this division near Shirva but by far the majority are contained to the south of the dyke. Also included are a number of *-rig* names (eg Sham Rigs, South Rigs, and particularly Toon Rigs) which attest to intensity of later cultivation in this particular area.

The overview suggests that land use south of this dyke was both older and historically more intensive than land use to the north. The diagnostic place-names occur in a concentration which is hard to ignore and which suitably reflects both the best land and proximity to the best harbourage. It might also satisfactorily explain the location of Quoy, a name late in the sequence – if indeed it belongs to Norse settlement – slightly to the north of the dyke. Similar, but by no means identical settlement concentrations have been observed on other small islands, notably on

Foula where both uncorrupted field names and tangible field units had survived from relatively early (Baldwin 1984), and on Papa Stour where Crawford points to a large central farm surrounded by satellite settlements (1984, 45; 1991). Absence of a primary name element on Fair Isle might perhaps be explained by processes of continuous use, intensity of settlement and sub-division of fields in a historically central place. Such processes may have assisted in, or even brought about, levels of toponomic change. There is, as a final matter of interest and support, a certain coincidence in the location of the island's highest status post-medieval dwelling, *The Haa*, holding the same central position.

Identification of likely Norse sites on Fair Isle is probably best seen as a process of calculated speculation in which place-names can provide an initial pointer. The model is one which can only be tested by excavation, a method thwarted in the Northern Isles by the likelihood of continuous localised site occupation from Norse times through to the present day. This is a factor likely to be even more pronounced in small insular environments, like Fair Isle, where the land resource is limited. There is a case, too, on Fair Isle to argue for complete loss of any primary farmstead given the intensity of subsequent change and cultivation to the likely core of settlement. Field survey encountered no structural remains on the island other than those illustrated below (chapter 9), which were interpreted as belonging to the post-medieval period. Nevertheless, it has to be added that in a largely unchanged tradition, there is a strong dimensional similarity between these foundations and those of earlier Scandinavian type.

Buildings of the Viking and subsequent Norse period are to some extent of predictable type and layout; those so far excavated in the Northern Isles have shown a construction of low stone walling, sometimes with a turf component, supporting a timber braced roofing system covered with turf or heather. Dimensions vary with interpreted function, but the later Norse longhouse form, with separate inner chambers for inhabitants and cattle respectively, is perhaps best seen at Jarlshof up to a length of around 45m (Hamilton 1956, fig 72), although these tend to be the result of extension down the long axis of earlier, shorter versions with separate byres. The Brough of Birsay, Orkney, shows a broader range of types and sizes (Hunter 1986, 106) but there the settlement is likely to be atypical. Elsewhere in Orkney, at Westness (Kaland 1973; 1993), at Buckquoy (Ritchie 1977), and at Pool (Hunter *et al* forthcoming), the settlement sites are of the individual farmstead type and conform to the same general picture of sub-rectangular buildings often with bench arrangements around a focal hearth. In Caithness, the site of Freswick also shows some evidence of nucleation (Batey 1982; 1987) and in Shetland, the one other early site excavated, at Underhoull, Unst (Small 1966), demonstrates that the same basic house plan was adopted irrespective of the quality of the local building stone. The use of timber, a rare commodity in the Northern Isles, is evidenced as support posts in some examples, but until later is otherwise restricted to indigenous scrub material, for example willow, which may have been used in roofing frameworks.

Finally, some mention should be made of relevant architectural characteristics, for which there are field survey implications, in the later periods of Norse colonisation. Initial research, for example, now suggests that structural expansion may have occurred latitudinally rather than down the long axis (eg Bigelow 1987, figs 4-5), although insufficient investigation has been undertaken to show whether this is a widespread phenomenon. During this later period it also seems that timber may have been used more as a building material; excavations at The Biggins, Papa Stour have identified the extensive use of timber in the early Middle Ages (Crawford 1991, 40f) and some farm names, for example those based on ON *stofa*, are thought to have been architecturally distinctive. On Faroe, an equally treeless environment, Thorsteinsson (1976, 19) has noted a heavy reliance on timber within the structure of later buildings, some being almost totally timber-built, a practice he ascribed to a combination of driftwood and importation. These traditions may have been of long standing (Smith 1980). Hibbert recounts how in Shetland in the 19th century 'the most ancient houses which belonged to the wealthier udallers were composed of wood; and that planks were cut out in Norway of such a shape, as that they might form, when joined, proper habitations' (1822, 414).

Hibbert's observations point to the continuation of what may be viewed as a long established tradition of importing building timbers, a tradition also encapsulated in an unhappy episode in *Njal's Saga* (Magnusson and Pálsson 1960, Ch 159). Flosi, an old man, decided to venture out of Iceland to get himself some house timber from Norway. On returning he stubbornly ignored well-meaning advice and sailed too late in the year. He was never seen again. But for his stubbornness, the extent of this tradition may never have been known.

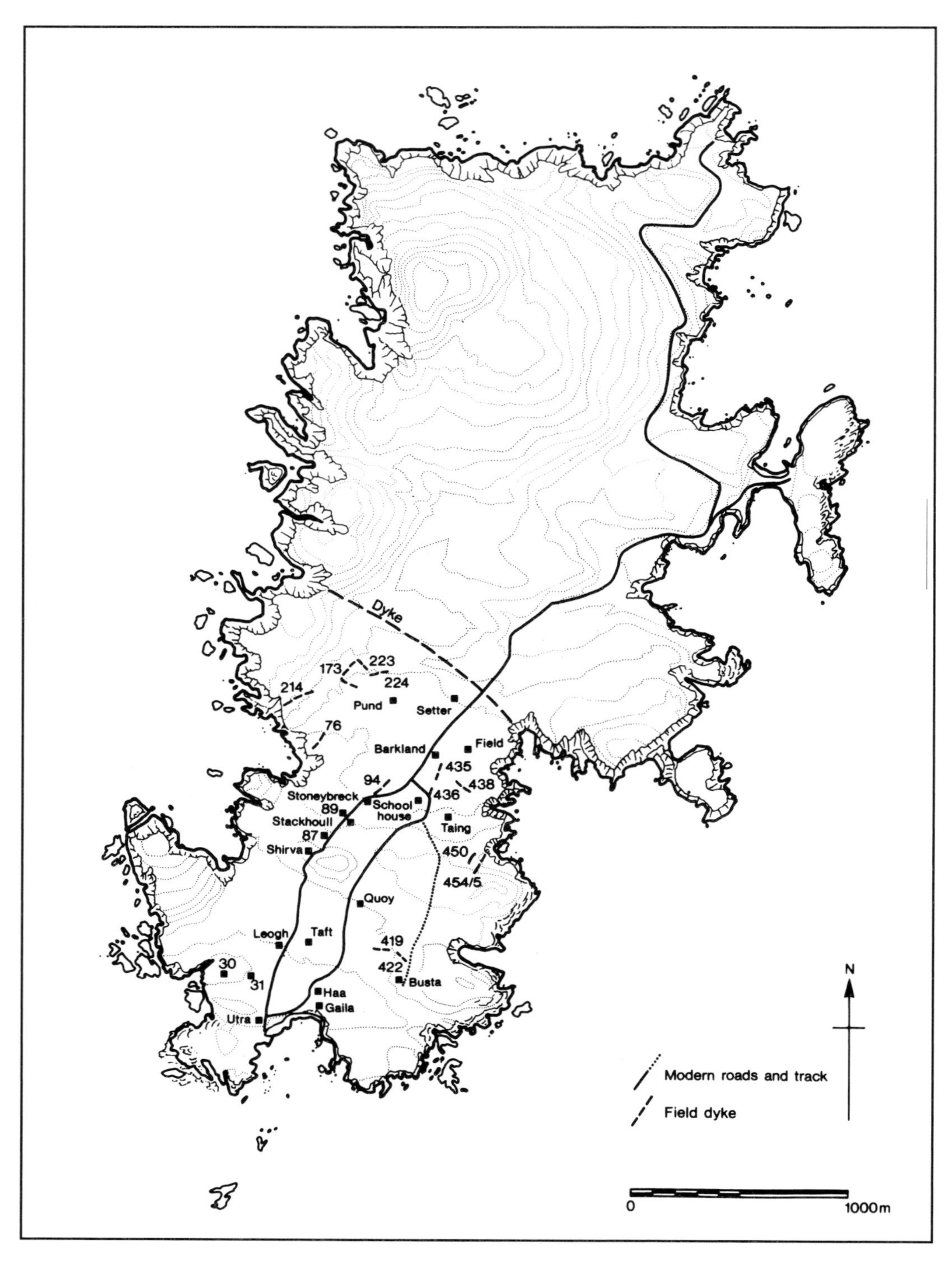

Fig 9.1 Locations and sites mentioned in chapter 9 including modern roads and tracks.

9

LATER SETTLEMENT

BY the end of the 18th century the subsistence economy and social evolution of the late medieval period become more clearly expressed in historical documentation. Until that time the island receives little more than cursory attention, often with ambiguous credibility, by passing visitors and by both national and local historians. The nature of occupation is only vaguely documented, invariably using population as a base descriptive criterion; settlement, economy and the organisation of space – elements to which archaeological and historical research are normally directed – are rarely discussed in any detail. Fair Isle was, after all, of difficult access, located in a place which was neither geographically important nor commercially significant. Its relative remoteness had ensured an apparent conservatism in its traditions, but later, when the era of 19th century travelling was at its height, that same remoteness and tradition also caused Fair Isle to emerge with an unfortunate curiosity status – an island somehow fossilised in a changing world.

The wider historical context is little more supportive, Shetland as a whole being subject to a 19th century romantic ideology which took a heightened interest in all things Scandinavian. The date of 1469 – the year when Shetland was passed into Scottish sovereignty – became erroneously seen as heralding the abrupt and lamentable end of a wholly dominating Norse era, 'the ruin of the native race' as Goudie perceived it (1887, 237). This over-emphasis of things Scandinavian in Shetland affairs and a misconception of subsequent Scottish and foreign influences has been well-aired by Smith (eg 1977; 1990). However, during the 16th and 17th centuries Norwegian influences diminished: the Hanseatic merchants plied directly with Shetland bypassing the Norwegian middlemen; trade with Norway continued in a more minor way, notably with timber for houses and boats; and udal laws and land rights became gradually lost. Equally, Scottish influences became stronger, although even at their height neither Norwegian nor Scottish influences could ever be said to have dominated landholding, trade or social affairs on Shetland to the extent that the islands might be viewed as an obvious sovereign appendage. Shetland retained an individual identity throughout, its personality being moulded by geography, climate and the fundamentals of its necessary subsistence economy. This same theme is echoed continually.

On the ground these broad political variables occurred as changes in land ownership, land use and economic fortune to which the Shetland farmer or fisherman was both unwitting pawn and victim. For several centuries the

Shetlanders' problem of oppression was 'a problem of human nature, unaffected by mere changes in personnel' (Smith 1990, 29). Before the 15th century Shetland was effectively governed from a distance. Absentee Norwegian landlords collected taxes via locally based representatives (fouds) and the Shetlanders, together with their developed social structure, were left largely undisturbed. This, as the 19th century saw it, was the 'golden age' of Shetland society, but one which became progressively eroded with the movement of the Hanseatic merchants into Shetland and with increased financial interest by Norwegian landlords. During the 16th century commercially minded Scottish entrepreneurs (the Scottish lairds) moved in to embark on a process of disordered land-buying in the quest to acquire capital and maximise rent potential from tenants, a process which resulted in the break-up of surviving medieval estates and land holdings, and the structure which underlay them. Mismanagement, lack of an understanding of viable subsistence economics, and the inevitable factors of bad harvests and famine combined ultimately to produce bankruptcy.

By the beginning of the 18th century lands were being bought up by more careful owners (the merchant lairds). In the absence of Hanseatic traders who had now been banned since the Act of Union in 1707, these lairds perceived an unhindered potential for the fishing industry. To such an extent did fishing dominate the Shetland economy that it entered into the rental agreements between tenant and merchant laird (Smith 1992), often with dire sociological implications. The lairds received their fish and in return provided certain necessities for the tenants, thus inducing potential debt and ensuring dependency. Furthermore, in a move to maximise returns the lairds began to break down land holdings in order to provide possessions for increasing numbers of fishermen and therefore, by implication, created further thinning of land resources among local populations (Smith 1992). This tied system continued through towards the end of the 19th century, stimulated by either cod or herring, and occasionally strangled by famine, disaster, disease or poverty. The tenant often became a victim; much of the documentation that survives points to a Shetland population which was both inhibited and vulnerable until the Crofters Act towards the end of the 19th century provided an element of change.

The Crofting Commissioners eventually visited Shetland in 1892 and spent several days on Fair Isle hearing cases in the Wesleyan Chapel and inspecting crofts. The event was reported in some detail in the *Shetland Times* (September 10th) and was an occasion which, not surprisingly, was recorded as causing 'unusual interest'. Also present was the laird of the day, John Bruce of Sumburgh, who considered his own stewardship to have been beneficial:

> *The proceedings commenced by a long statement by Mr Bruce of his dealing with the island since it came into his possession in 1866. The people were in a*

> *very primitive state, and in great poverty. He believed it required a strong paternal Government to keep it right and, he set about in that direction by building a store where provisions were always kept, so that there had been no case of destitution since. A school was built, a library started, work provided as much as possible, and cultivation put on a better footing. He met with opposition at first, but as the people began to find the advantages of the improvements opposition died away, and the present results of his management were very satisfactory.* (*Shetland Times* September 10th 1892)

His claims were not disputed by the islanders, who wished to be considered under the terms of the Act as crofters rather than be bound by the leases held by Bruce. A compromise was reached whereby the islanders became crofters and Bruce's regulations for peat and turf-cutting and future division of the scattald were agreed. The outcome on fair rents, later published in the *Shetland Times* for November 19th, was to make a total rent reduction on the island of approximately 23%.

But on March 6th 1897, a banner heading in the *Shetland Times*, 'Probable exodus from Fair Isle', epitomised the persistent vulnerability of a system which relied heavily on external economics. It announced that the proprietor of Fair Isle 'has written to his tenants there that he intends forthwith to discontinue his fishing operations on the isle ...'. In economic terms the reasoning was self-evident: 'at one time they [the islanders] received as much as three shillings for each hundred weight ... about five years ago the price had fallen to two shillings. This year it is to be only half of that ...' (March 6th 1897, 3). The implications of this were apparent even to the newspaper correspondent who continued by pointing out that 'its failure [the fishing] means the failure of that small community'.

Population

The earliest, albeit vague, population report of any detail belongs to the Armada account of 1588 which identifies 17 houses on the island (Ker 1920, 172). This number is largely supported by James' description in the early 17th century – the first recorded description of Shetland in English – which records some 16 households. The sourcing is unclear but James' additional reference to problems with the scald or leprosy 'and therefore out of Orkney and Shetland they who are also infested are sent into the Fair Isle' (MacGillivray 1953, 51) does not occur in the Armada account and therefore suggests an alternative origin. Of other early texts, Kay's 1680 account is especially noteworthy in giving a more broadly based description not only of population, but also of land use:

> *This Isle is indifferently fertile, so far as it is manured, yielding greater increase than any land in Zetland: but the cultivated ground is but little, lying*

altogether in the South end of the Isle: the rest they reserve for pasturage and fuel, though the most part of the Isle might be made good corn land. Their grass here is very short, but very fat, as appears by the more than ordinary fatness of their milk and butter. There is no grain here but Oats and Beer whereof they seldom want as much as serves themselves. (Bruce 1908, 55)

By the middle of the 18th century there is good evidence to show that the inhabitants of Fair Isle had been experiencing hard times in the Quendale Estate under the laird Robert Sinclair. Administration papers analysed by Ballantyne (1993) show that debts amassed by the islanders had reached the figure of £4823 scots by the end of 1764, the annual rent of £830 including elements for poultry money, feather money, bere, lamb and wool. Earlier valuation of the estate for sale purposes (it was eventually sold to James Stewart of Brough in 1766) provides a useful record of individual situations, settlement names and rentals from the mid-1700s. Many of the individuals are on record as considering their holdings to have been overrated; the report additionally notes the phenomenon of coastal erosion, poor fishing and a child begging in the island. Only three settlements are listed, at Leogh (24 merks), at Shirva (48 merks), and one which combined Gaila and Busta (24 merks). At least some of these centres may have their early roots in Norse times (see chapter 8) and, assuming a typical pattern of evolution, they may also represent the foci for the 17 'hovels' witnessed in the Armada account.

The earliest maps are not particularly helpful: Mackenzie's chart of 1752 shows only two buildings, both at the extreme south of the island roughly in the locations of Gaila and either the fish store or the present site of Utra (Melville House) which is unrecorded in the *First Statistical Account.* It is of some interest that, within the terms of Mackenzie's conventions, these buildings are each defined as 'a farmhouse' as distinct from 'a church' or 'a remarkable gentleman's house', neither of which are portrayed elsewhere on the island. Another map attributed to Mackenzie, probably from around 1750, is curiously different, showing no fewer than eight houses which appear to surround a smaller feature in the centre. A further building, set slightly to the north, appears to be of a different style altogether. Given the overall form of the island in comparison to Mackenzie's 1752 version, it is difficult to give the illustration much credibility. Its intention is presumably merely to depict the presence of habitation; van Keulen's 1695 map which depicts several vague buildings serves a similar general purpose.

By the time of the *First Statistical Account* of the late 18th century the island sported a population of 220 (*OSA* XIX, 436). No new settlement locations appear to have been added to those already recorded. The *Account* identifies the same four names and describes them as houses 'which are confusedly thrown together as chance, whim or conveniency directed, into four clumps or towns under the fine-sounding names of Shewah, Lioh, Bustah and Gelah [sic]. These four little towns as they are called, contain the inhabitants, of which there are 32 families' (*OSA* XIX, 436). Each tunship will have held, on average, eight families in roughly as many buildings. The concept of the tunship or 'town' was unprecedented to most visitors in Shetland and is invariably the subject of comment. Hibbert's crude explanation is one of several which endeavour to explain its intricacies to the unwary traveller; the text pertains to Unst, but is universally applicable.

> *The nature of a Shetland town may afford a curious subject for antiquarian speculation. It is possible, that among many Scandinavian and Saxon nations of Europe, where land was originally allodial, a solitary inclosure, within which was built no more than one habitation, was styled a Town; but along with the introduction of feudality small solitary possessors would be more rare, and as the name of Town would include not only the mansion not only occupied by the lord, but the cottages of his dependents, it would thus be in time associated with a large collection of dwellings. It is, therefore only in thinly inhabited districts, or in countyries unfeudalised until a very recent period, that the original meaning of the word would stand a chance of being retained. Thus, at the present day, if a Shetlander incloses land from the scathold, and surrounds it with a fence, it is still called a Town; and when a stranger is directed to repair to the town before him, he may be surprised to descry that it consists of a single inclosed habitation.* (Hibbert 1822, 414)

In 1771, some 20 years prior to the *First Statistical Account*, James Robertson visited the island and noted somewhat fewer inhabitants, around 170 (cited in Hibbert 1822, 124). This suggests that the four tunships had expanded internally rather than new tunships being established. He also gave an account of the same economic simplicity echoed in both earlier and later sources:

> *The men were employed in catching fish, which they salt and sell to their landlord. The women knit stockings, or spin lint and woolen yarn. The natives speak the English with a Norse accent. Their food is mostly milk, fish, wild-fowl, and wild-fowl eggs, which they take from among the precipices, by climbing, or going down the rocks by the assistance of a rope.* (Hibbert 1822, 124)

The Rev. John Mill, minister of Dunrossness in whose jurisdiction Fair Isle lay, kept a diary of his visits to the island throughout his period of ministry during the last half of the 18th century. His observations provide a major commentary of the period, particularly with respect to population, religious activity and education (see chapter 11). In editing the diary Gilbert Goudie gathered background material and collated much of Mill's information, including data on the island's school register.

Figures collated by Goudie (1889, 201f) and taken through to 1838, covering roughly the period of the two *Accounts*, show an approximate threefold increase in the number of pupils of both genders. The greatest changes lie within the two decades from about 1810 to 1830, the implications immediately pointing to a massive adult over-population by the middle of the 19th century. Perhaps more ominously, the same figures show approximately two male births for every female birth taken over the same period. Even by the time of Scott's visit in 1814 the writing may already have been on the wall. Scott identified some 30 households totalling around 250 inhabitants living in 'miserable huts', the number of people on the island being too great to be maintained in bread which had to be brought in from Mainland Shetland (Laughlan 1982, 28). Despite this Scott was told that few ever left the island, although three had been pressed for the navy and five or six were currently on board the whalers (*ibid*, 51).

Lack of emigration was also observed by Fotheringhame, whose job it was to evaluate the island's resources (which also included the inhabitants) for estate purposes in 1804. His tally of 230 individuals (119 males and 111 females) is undoubtedly accurate, although some question surrounds his observation that the population 'has been nearly doubled within these last 30 years'. The *Second Statistical Account* of 1845 shows a generally consistent figure of 35 households and 232 individuals (*NSA* XV, 96), although this appears to belie the increase suggested by the school register. The loss of numbers during this period may be explained at least in part by minor migrations to Orkney in the 1830s.

By the mid-19th century a greater level of data becomes available; it has been possible, for example, to investigate general trends in population patterning across the whole of the Northern Isles (Fenton 1978, 157f) with interesting implications for Fair Isle. Rough calculations on population figures derived mostly from statistical account sources demonstrate an average population density per household in Shetland of approximately 6.6 persons, slightly higher than in Orkney, around that time. At least part of this figure can be attributed to population expansion prior to the first *Account* when many of the houses may have been occupied by two units, one containing the father and his family, the other his eldest son and family (*ibid*, 158). Ultimately this may have led to an increase in the number of dwellings and outsets; on Fair Isle the effects of this necessitated breaching the *feelie* dyke at the eastern side of the island and extending the cultivated land northwards into the margins (fig 9.7). Problems with outsets are well-attested elsewhere in Shetland and noted with mixed blessings in the *First Statistical Account* for Delting. There, as well as being seen as an improvement 'in order to find a settlement for the young men to marry', it was considered doubtful as to 'how far these outsets or new inclosures have been for the good of the island' (*OSA* XIX, 411). The available data for Fair Isle suggests that a major part of the population increase which gave rise to the need for outsets may have already occurred by the time of the first *Account*, with only a minimal increase during the following half century leading through to the second *Account.* Figures for the period between the two indicate a household population density in the order of 6.6-6.8 persons, slightly higher than Fenton's figures for Shetland generally.

Prior to the *First Statistical Account* the records are scant rather than unreliable, but if a middle household density per unit figure of 6.7 were to be extrapolated, it would suggest an island population of about 115 persons for the 17 houses of the Elizabethan (Armada) period. This compares with double that figure during Fotheringhame's survey of 1804, rising to a census peak of some 380 around 1861 with an increased household density. The figures depict (table 1) a gradual population rise and fall, identified at 10 year intervals, reaching a peak in 1861. The level of change is over 50% in each direction and is also effectively mirrored in the number of occupied households. There appears to be no major gender imbalance throughout the period covered.

Year	Units	Males	Females	Total	Per Unit
1841	35	119	113	232	6.6
1851	40	129	150	279	6.9
1861	53	190	190	380	7.2
1871	38	107	119	226	5.9
1881	31	108	106	214	6.9
1891	30 (34)	100 (126)	89 (97)	189 (223)	6.3 (6.6)

Table 1. *Summary totals from census returns, and figures for average population per unit. Figures in parenthesis represent temporary increase of population boosted by lighthouse construction at the time of the 1891 census.*

Analysis of the census figures highlights some interesting factors, notably the phenomenon of multiple families living within the same 'town' complex. In 1841 the main centres of population were still those noted in the *First Statistical Account*, at Shirva (82 individuals in 15 families), Lough (50 individuals in 8 families), Busta (50 individuals in 5 families) and Gaila (32 individuals in 8 families), but with new individual units, presumably outsets, at Taing and Setter, as well as a new unit known as Schoolhouse. Thomas' map of 1839, only a few years earlier (plate 9.1), shows a similar distribution, as well as locating Setter and Taing towards the hill land in typical characteristic outset position. Such cartographic licence as was permitted shows individual house units at each of the named tunships. The absolute numbers of these units is inaccurate but the relative depictions are correct. Both Setter and Taing are each shown as a single dwelling unit. The arrangements of the units, depicted in neat blocks at all but Gaila, may be equally significant given Gaila's arguably special status in the settlement patterning of the island. According to the

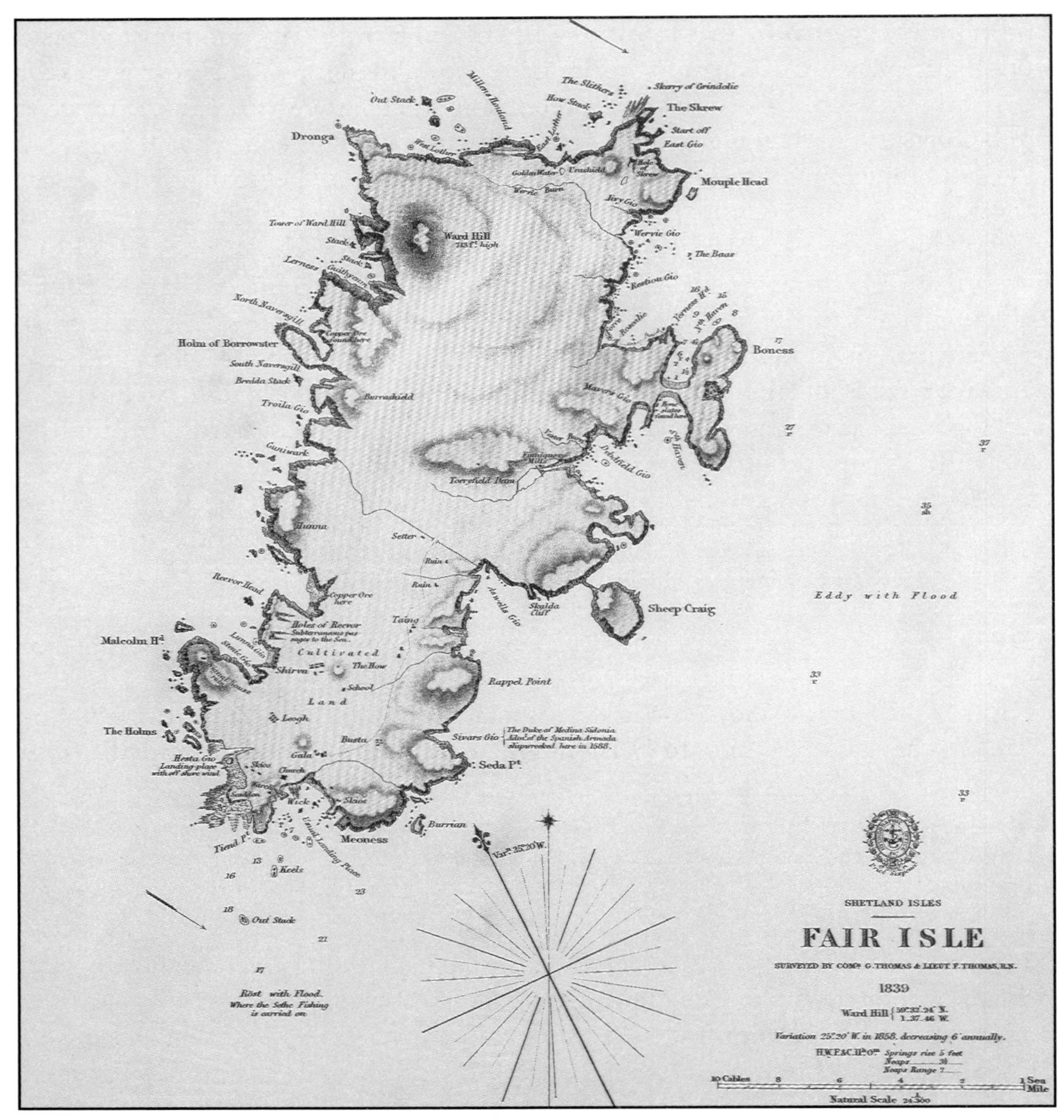

Plate 9.1 Thomas' map of 1839 showing settlement patterning at the south of the island, and also the oddly shaped feelie *dyke. By courtesy of the Trustees of the National Library of Scotland.*

census the head of each household was a 'fisherman', with the exception of the teacher at Schoolhouse. Four of the families, including two at Busta, consisted of ten or more individuals.

By 1851 the island population had increased by about one fifth and the census return is more detailed with respect to individual houses within each complex, as well as to their occupants. No longer is occupation confined to the head of the household, but also to dependants; it covers work such as knitting, hosiery and housekeeping. Also listed are farm labourers, scholars (ie school children), a beachman and peat boys and girls. Later returns include a blacksmith, a midwife, spinsters, servants, a dressmaker and a 'teacher of English, Writing, Arithmetic'. The last of these, James Cheyne, had six of his own children in his school in 1861, with two more under school age.

The 1851 census is significant in that it names individual dwellings within the main complexes and denotes, presumably for locational purposes, the presence of a west road. An east road appears for similar purposes in the 1861 return. Both these returns illustrate the continued expansion of the population to a recorded maximum of 53 units in 1861. Many of the 'new' dwelling names merely contain descriptive elements of existing names (eg Netherlough, Mid Lough, Upper Lough) while others appear for the first time. These include some names which still survive (eg Stackhoull, Stoneybreck, Taft, Field, Quoy and Pund), together with others which are no longer extant (eg Shadler and Dale). There is no way of knowing whether any of these 'new' names are in fact existing names which have eluded record and which may designate earlier settlement names, or whether they represent a new nomenclature devised in order to provide necessary habitation definition for census purposes.

By 1871 the return shows the island population to be in decline, partly aided by the effects of mass migration to Canada. The number of households was reduced to 38 and the population to 226. By 1881 this had declined still further, although in both returns the population figures still point to the same four main centres on the island. These are not entirely recognisable by name, but can be ascertained by a process of identifying those units which originally belonged to each complex before the breaking down of the units for census purposes in 1851. By 1891 the population had fallen below 200; approximately 30 units are identifiable and most of these can be readily associated with modern crofts or known foundations. The remainder are represented by two or more units in the same location, for example at Busta, Gaila, or Shirva where the population density still appears to have been concentrated, although it was somewhat less than 20 years earlier. The population figures and number of dwellings for 1891 are clouded by the presence of temporary lighthouse workers on the island. Their number included stonemasons, a carpenter, a plasterer and quarrymen. Also on the island at that time, and presumably associated, were a contractor's time-keeper and an inspector of public works. At Melville House (Utra), where the factor had lived in 1881, was the registrar who had lodging with him a clerk and a grocer. A spirit merchant is also recorded as living at Pund.

Although the general population trends can be identified, it also seems clear that Fair Isle, being a relatively small island, was particularly vulnerable to sudden and dramatic population movement. This was indeed the case as recorded by Mill in his

1799 visit when he observed a decrease in the population, that 'four families were ruined, their houses lying desolate' as a result of a boating tragedy (Goudie 1889, 57). At the beginning of the same century Brand noted only 10 or 12 families, blaming the 'smallpox' for decimating some two-thirds of the inhabitants (1701, 127), although there is some doubt as to whether the reference is to Foula, not Fair Isle (Baldwin 1984, 62). Later, in the 1860s, over 130 Fair Isle inhabitants left the island in one day to start a life in New Brunswick, an exercise partly motivated by the laird's managerial needs (Knox 1985, 171), and one for which the mid-19th century redistribution of land (planking) and associated changes in the settlement patterning was almost certainly a factor.

These changes in population almost certainly had an effect on the island's subsistence dynamics. Even at the relatively low population level in 1881 there appears to have been some food shortage. Tudor's account, for example, which also includes the available arable acreage per croft, pointed out that although an industrious tenant could grow sufficient bere and oats for his family's needs, it was still necessary to import 'meal for half a year's consumption' (1883, 438). This also begs the question as to how greater levels of population may have survived. Tudor's comment reiterates Scott's observation of importing food some 70 years earlier, and also Fotheringhame's similar comment that half the bread had to be provided by the proprietor. Later, in 1841, George Griffin was warned that Fair Isle's population was decreasing through food shortage (Dilworth 1988, 120). His information no doubt contained an element of scaremongering to which he was particularly susceptible, but which contained an element of truth nonetheless. By the 20th century population decline had been massive, and in the 1940s the population was less than half the number recorded in the *Second Statistical Account*. Ironically, a contemporary land use survey showed an island economy which at face value had changed little from that described by both Kay or Robertson two and a half centuries earlier (O'Dell 1940). Meanwhile, St Kilda had been evacuated.

Settlement

The nucleation of settlement indicated by 18th and 19th century records is not immediately apparent on the modern landscape, although some extant outbuildings may once have served as dwellings in their own right in a cycle of reuse and change of function to which rural buildings in the Northern Isles seem particularly susceptible. Of the four tunships recorded in the *First Statistical Account* Gaila is no longer extant, Leogh has developed into two parts (upper and lower), while both Shirva and Busta still stand in the same evolved location. Only at Shirva are foundation remains of earlier buildings still visible as minor earthworks to any great extent. These lie bisected by the modern tarmac road which winds around the west side of the Houll. The original trackway which the road replaced (the 'west road' of the 1851 census) took a more direct route across the hill and gave access to the Shirva tunship on its western side. Roads and trackways tend not to feature on the early maps; Mackenzie's chart shows no examples and Thomas' map of 1839 depicts a single route leading from Gaila, via Busta, up the east side of the island to the hill dyke suggesting that a western route, which presumably existed to provide access to Shirva, was of secondary importance.

At least two buildings (fig 9.2) are discernible on the west side of the modern road within the existing area of Shirva. Remains of others, as well as parts of those recorded, are likely to have been obscured by more recent levelling and building. One (*84*) measuring some 13.5 x 3.5m shows an interior divided into three roughly equal units, with a small adjunct, or possibly part of another structure, lying adjacent to the south-west. The other building (*83*) is somewhat larger at approximately 20 x 5m but its internal arrangement is unclear from surface survey. Again, a smaller structure appears to lie in association. The whole area around these two units contains a

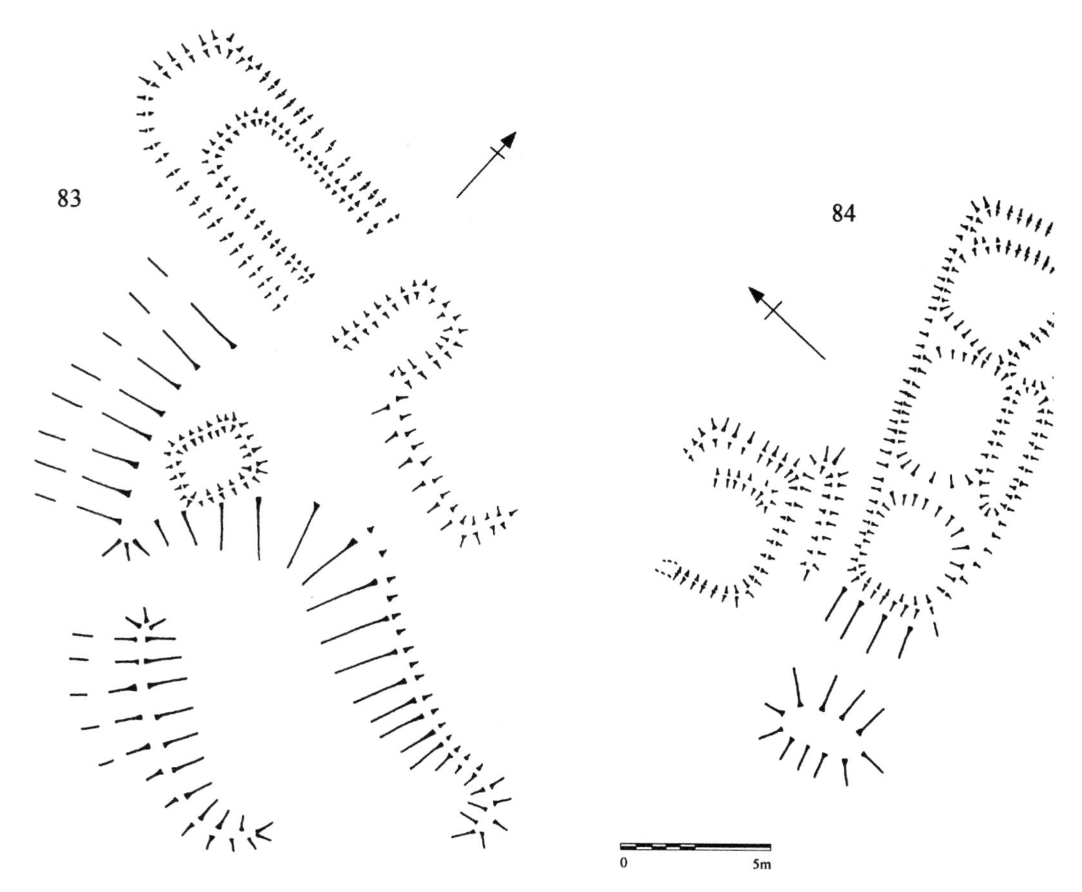

Fig 9.2 Plan of structural foundations at Shirva (sites 83 and 84) to the west of the modern road.

number of uninterpretable surface undulations and features. On the eastern side of the modern road at least six more buildings were recorded (*431*, fig 9.3), including one example with part-standing walling. These survived in a thin strip of land between the new road and the former trackway at the east. Only one of these (*f*) contained three internal divisions and measured some 15 x 4.5m with a possible smaller adjunct (*g*) lying in association. The other two fully identifiable forms (*a* and *d*) were somewhat shorter at 10 x 4.5m and 11 x 4m respectively and were each sub-divided internally into two parts. The remaining three (*b*, *c* and *e*) had all been partially destroyed by the new roadway.

Even at this superficial level of survey it becomes possible to identify at least eight buildings, excluding the present standing forms, which represent the Shirva tunship. While it is difficult, even using excavation, to ascribe function to the individual units, those with internal divisions almost certainly represent habitations, or part habitations. It is, however, not possible to determine how many of these were standing, were in dwelling use, or were ascribed different agricultural functions, at any one given time.

Elsewhere on the island other foundation remains provide further evidence of the documented distribution of settlement. At the south end a complex structural foundation (*407*, fig 9.4) almost certainly represents a part of the Gaila tunship

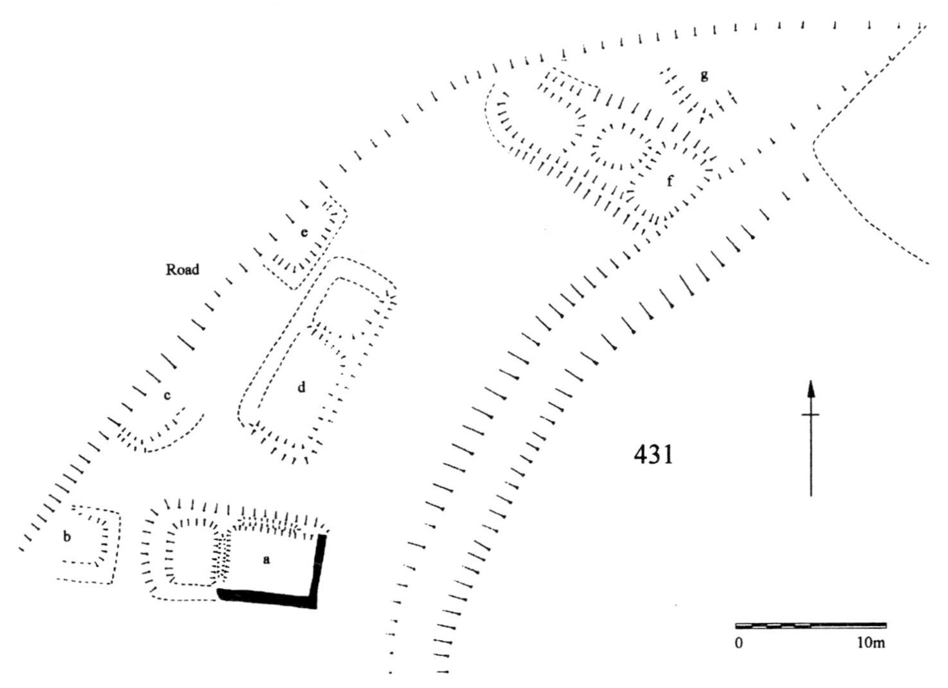

Fig 9.3 Plan of structural foundations at Shirva (site 431) to the east of the modern road.

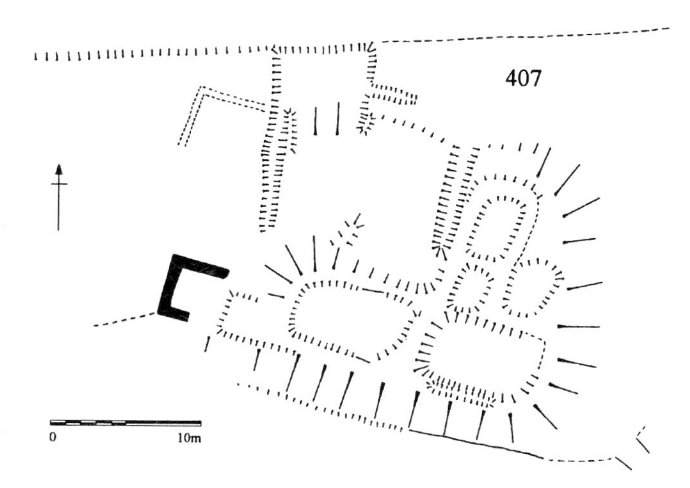

Fig 9.4 Plan of structural foundations (site 407) in the vicinity of the 'Geila' field name.

according to field name evidence. The site is of interest not only in view of its postulated early origins (see chapter 8), but also because of its unusual configuration which appears to point towards the development of a single focus rather than a situation where separate buildings evolved within a general area, as for example at Shirva. Morphologically it has much in common with structural development in Shetland within the Middle Ages as noted by Bigelow (1987). The plan also shows part-standing walling and other earthwork features in the general vicinity. It is also of some interest that the 1871 census return should refer to it as the 'Hall of Geila' – a description repeated by a visitor in 1865 who also noted specifically the presence of two floors (Muir 1885, 75). There is possible confusion here with *The Haa*, the residence of the laird's factor which lies a short distance away, where Scott dined as guest of the tacksman in 1814 and which still stands as a two-floored house. Both Gaila and *The Haa* possess a very distinctive status connotation. It is perhaps no coincidence that while Robert Sinclair was laird in the mid-18th century his contact should be a merchant living at Gaila who conducted business on his behalf throughout the island (Ballantyne 1993, 15).

No similar structural features were recorded at the remaining two sites alluded to in the *First Statistical Account*, Busta and Leogh, but well-defined foundations survive at Taing (*444* and *445*, fig 9.5), mentioned in the *Second Statistical Account*, and at Taft (*375*, fig 9.5), a site recorded later that century. The Taft site is the largest of the foundations recorded and stands at approximately 25 x 5m with three, or possibly four, internal divisions. At Taing the structures are relatively narrow; one (*444*) measures some 10 x 2.5m with two internal elements and a sub-circular corn drier, and sits within a definable rectangular yard or enclosure now bisected by a part-standing

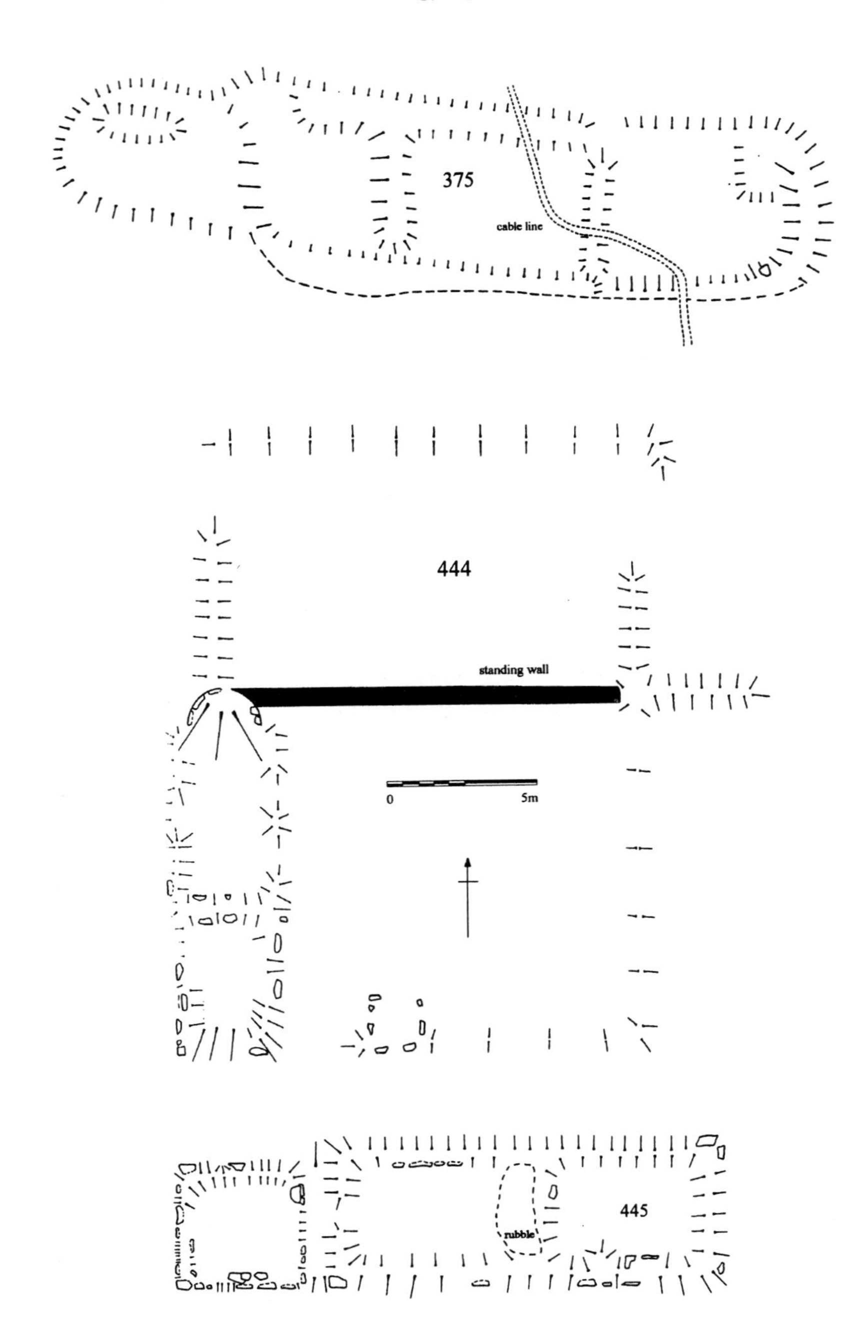

Fig 9.5 Plans of structural foundations (sites 375, 444 and 445).

wall. The other (*445*), slightly larger at approximately 11 x 3m, is also divided into two elements but appears to have a separate square structure added to one end.

Evidence of earlier settlement and land use is not entirely represented by structural foundations. There are, for example, a small number of earthworks, typically low, linear features, which appear to represent the only surviving remains of earlier post-medieval land use systems. These relict field boundaries survive north of Stoneybreck (*94*) and adjacent to Pund (*173*, *223* and *224*) and presumably reflect their respective infields. In the case of Pund this takes the form of three sides of a crude rectangle over a total distance of approximately 300m (fig 9.7). This has survived to a height of almost 1m in places and, on the western side, still retains a thin strip of the contemporary field surface containing narrow cultivation lines.

However, neither these field boundaries nor the structural remains appeared to conform entirely to the tunship patterning indicated by the two statistical accounts. North of Shirva, and partly cut by the modern road, the remains of a large structure measuring some 24 x 5m (*87*) appears to lie in isolation from the main Shirva nucleus in a field known as Kirkalees within an area of reputed early ecclesiastical activity. The three internal divisions (fig 9.6) point to a domestic function, reinforced by a likely sub-circular corn drier at one end. Slightly further to the north a relatively small foundation some 12 x 5m (*89*) might be viewed as part of a Stackhool complex, although it now lies on the other side of the road to the modern unit. Elsewhere, however, south of (lower) Leogh structural remains (*31*) were recorded in a field known as Hoolaby, a name with a strong habitative connotation and mentioned as a dwelling in the 1851 census return. These remains took the form of a partitioned building measuring some 15 x 7.5m with further possible remains lying adjacent (fig 9.6). Some distance away to the west, but equally remote from known population centres, less well-defined earthworks (*30*) may also indicate structural foundations. Both sets may represent dwellings either of the population peak post-dating the second *Account*, or conversely of earlier periods, pre-dating the late 18th century records. No other clearly defined foundations were identified during the survey; even the two sites denoted under the category of 'ruin' on Thomas' map, located at the east side of the island, failed to exhibit any physical trace, although they could conceivably be identified with the sites of modern Field and Barkland.

The presence of some of these standing structures, away from the traditional tunship centres, supports the view of a wider distribution of settlement resulting from the population increases of the mid-19th century. The remains at Hoolaby are a particular case in point, to which can be added a small number of sites, all in outset or remoter locations, where surface features point towards relict survival of activity, although not necessarily settlement itself. These tend to be represented by small dykes which presumably represent localised areas of enclosed land which have partly survived later agricultural changes.

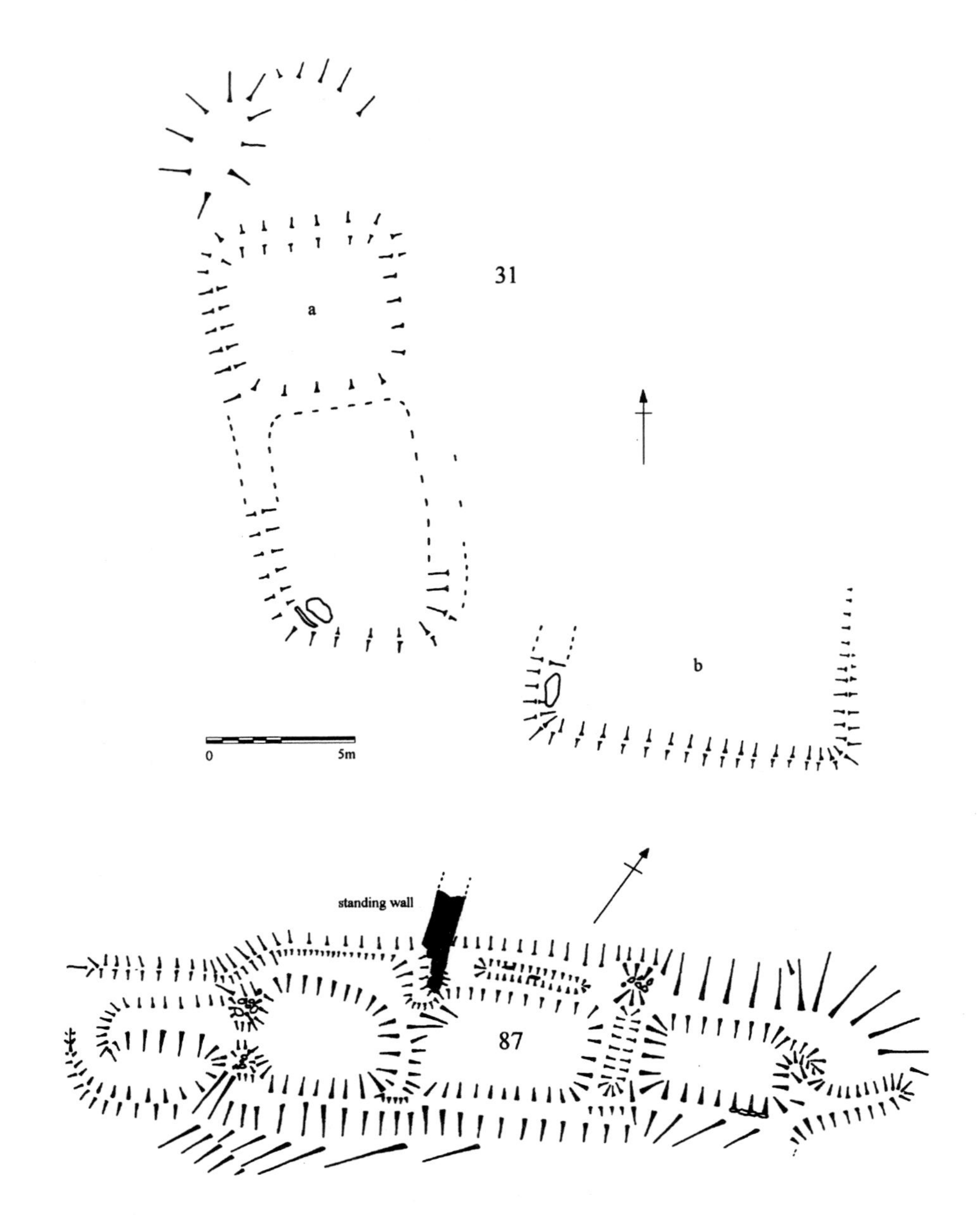

Fig 9.6 Plan of structural foundations (sites 31 and 87).

A few of these bear field names containing the *-toon* element which tends to confirm location within a dyked area and with a settlement connotation. One, a low, curved field boundary containing projecting stones (*76*) survives for some 45m in a field known as *Taftitoon*, possibly running northwards into a field with the name *Maidgestoon*. Both fields lie at the north-west edge of the cultivated area. Further to the north-west, in current marginal land, another low boundary was identified for approximately 120m (*214*); this lay in an area denoted as *Swirritoon*. Another example occurs in a field called *Greenaby*, a name with habitative potential recorded in the 1861 census return. This lies adjacent to Busta where likely enclosure foundations were recorded (*419* and *422*). In at least two other locations on the eastern flank of the island no field name appears to have survived: one complex (*435*, *436* and *438*) may ostensibly pertain to earlier land use focused around Barkland and Field; but another (*450*, *454* and *455*) appears to belong to a (lost?) settlement unit on the eastern edge of the island. The boundaries appear not to be associated with attested prehistoric occupation in that area (see chapter 6), although such occupation may have offered attractive constructional materials. The overview, therefore, suggests a slightly wider distribution of settlement than the later documentation might suggest, but with regrettably little indication of relative chronology. Scope for this has been possible elsewhere (for example on Foula) but only on the basis of a high level of preservation of the infields and associated dykes (Baldwin 1984).

Modern agricultural changes to the south part of Fair Isle have effectively wiped away all traces of the 17th-19th century landscape (fig 9.7). The few remaining patches of relict infield boundaries survive as the only evidence of a network of field units and arrangements which littered the southern slopes. Not only would this have presented a vastly different spectacle to that of the modern landscape, but it may also have been an unexpected sight to the traveller from the south unaccustomed to this type of seemingly disorganised use of space. Sibbald commented briefly on this curious northern phenomenon in 1711 (Monteith 1845, 14). Many of the later writers on Shetland are more descriptive, but unfortunately appear to amalgamate other earthwork features of different dates including hill dykes and possibly some prehistoric remains. Hibbert, for example, noted that most habitations were surrounded by crude dykes; these sometimes enclosed one cottage but sometimes united many which were distant from each other, their overriding characteristic being one of 'great irregularity' (1822, 116). On visiting Unst he described the dykes as 'winding in every direction in the most zig-zag manner. One dike may include thirty or forty towns, and every farmer is obliged to repair a certain extent of his fence...; but so imperfect are these enclosures, which consist of turf or stone, that, by the incursions of sheep, horses, and swine, they are thrown down every year.' Scott, partly for this reason, and always quick to spot a shortcoming in local husbandry methods, referred to turf dykes as 'useless' (Laughlan 1982, 38).

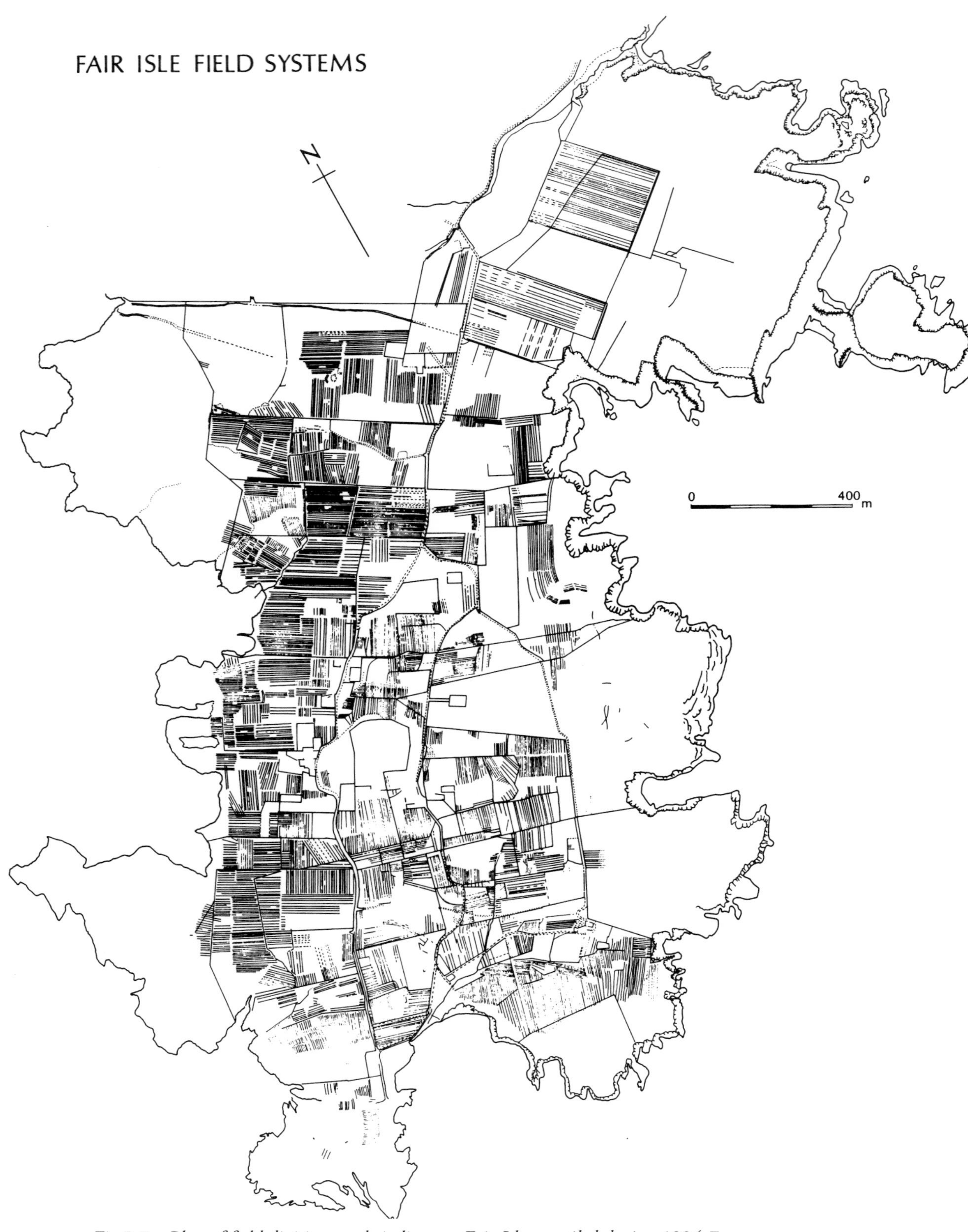

Fig 9.7 Plan of field divisions and rig lines on Fair Isle compiled during 1984-7.

Dykes rarely feature within the statistical accounts, presumably because they were such a common part of every local landscape; in fact only the *Second Statistical Account* mentions the hill dyke on Fair Isle – the 'fence of feal' which shut in the cultivated land and protected it from sheep (*NSA* XV, 95). No mention is made in the *First Statistical Account* even although, according to Mackenzie's map, the hill dyke had already been constructed by the mid-18th century. There is, however, reference to the amount of arable land, some 75 acres in all, which was divided among the inhabitants 'in small and nearly equal parcels' (*OSA* XIX, 437). The method of division is undefined and it appears to pre-empt a more major period of enclosing throughout Shetland in the 19th century. Before that time the earthworks may have been limited to hill dykes and prehistoric remains, many of which may have been retained in a secondary capacity, but by the end of the 19th century most arable land on Shetland was both enclosed and divided (Knox 1985, 148f).

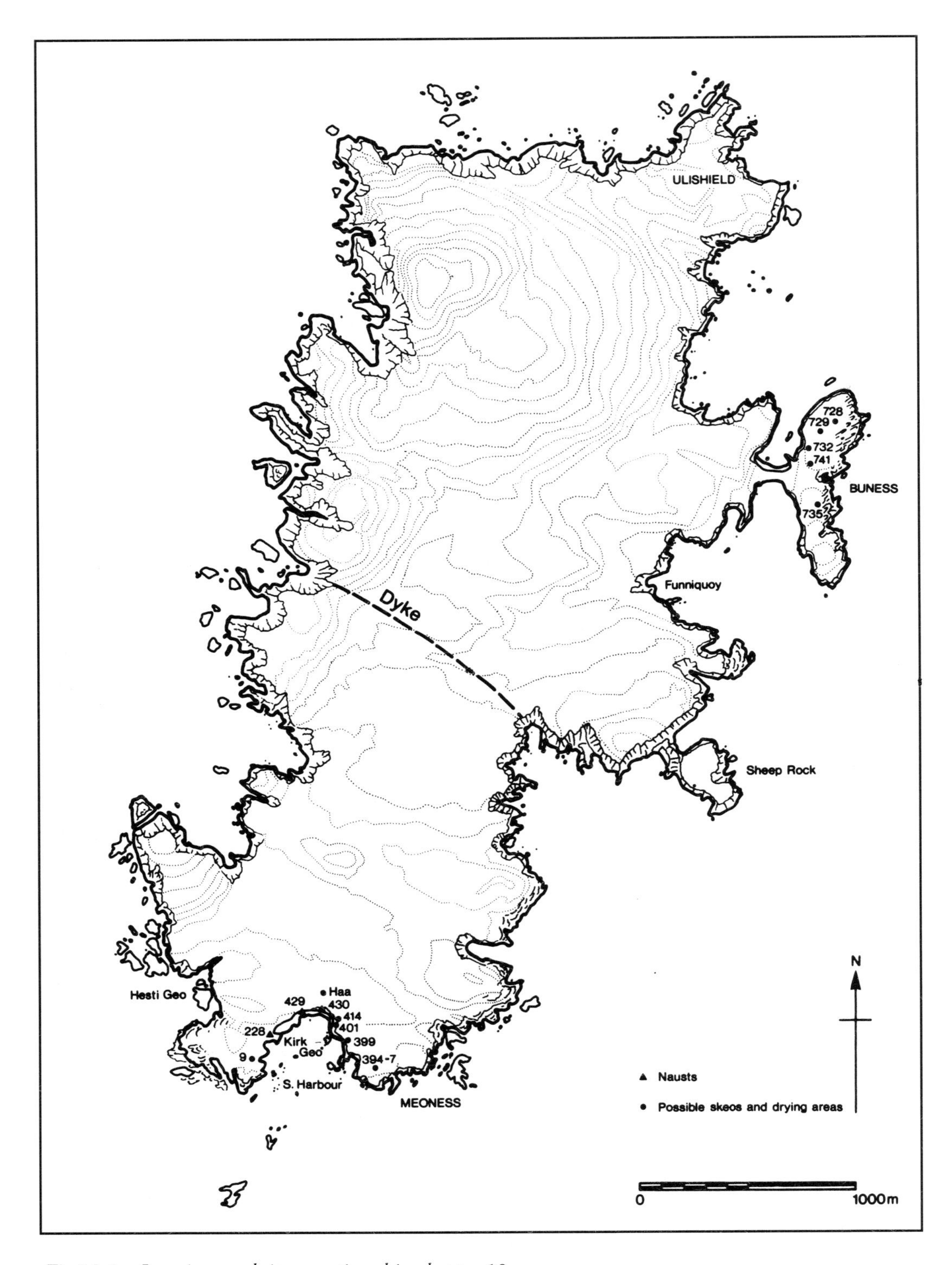

Fig 10.1 Locations and sites mentioned in chapter 10.

Post-Medieval Economy

Land use

As previously highlighted, all Fair Isle's cultivated land lay at the south part of the island, separated from the hill land to the north by the *feelie* dyke. Although this division is unspecified in the Armada account, it was certainly apparent by the end of the 17th century when Kay makes distinction between 'cultivated land' and land 'reserved for pasturage and fuel' (Bruce 1908, 55). Mackenzie's map of 1752 is quite emphatic in making the distinction: not only is the dyke depicted from coast to coast (with a convention showing it to be of turf), but the land on either side is coded by water colours – brown to the north indicates heathland, and pale green to the south indicates 'grass or cornfield'. By the 1790s the pasture is described as being home to '400 sheep, whose wool and mutton are equally excellent, and also nearly 200 black cattle, besides some goats, which have been lately imported, and horses, which, for domestic purposes, they bring from Shetland' (*OSA* XIX, 437). Scott's distinction between the north and south parts of the island is implicit rather than stated; he notes that 'the plain upon which the hamlets are situated bears excellent barley, oats and potatoes' but that the rest of the island was 'beautiful pasture – excepting to the eastward, where there is a moss, equally essential to the comfort of the inhabitants since it supplies them with peats for fuel ...' (Laughlan 1982, 50).

This area of common grazing, or scattald, offered other uses, as Scott observed. The inhabitants also enjoyed rights of peat cutting (for which the horses were exclusively used) as well as for turf. Peat, the burning of which was seen as an act of some strangeness in the Armada account (Ker 1920, 172), was the only fuel other than driftwood available on the island, although some turf may also have been used. Peat cutting had been a basic necessity of life throughout Shetland since Norse times, and was probably carried out in a relatively uncontrolled fashion although with a high degree of traditional methodology and expertise (eg Fenton 1978, 217-39). Unusually, one visitor to the Shetlands in 1839, Christian Pløyen, an ambassador from Faroe, was highly critical of the way in which the exercise was conducted.

> *I had thought it was impossible to manage peat moors more wastefully than in Faroe, but my opinion is quite changed now that I have been in Shetland; the Shetlanders outdo the Faroese in this respect; they lay waste the green sward, which is cut off before the peats are cast, and no trace is left behind. Nothing remains but the black, naked surface.* (Pløyen 1894, 20)

Turf, or more strictly its removal, was a contentious local matter on which much energy was expended both on Fair Isle and elsewhere. Turf was a common and easily obtainable material which could be used as a substitute for, or in conjunction with, building stone, or for dyke construction. A number of planticrue bases were of turf foundation, partly created by the stripping of turf in the growing area, but it also seems that turf could be used in a more major structural capacity. One early 19th century traveller to Shetland found himself sleeping with three sheep on the floor of a barn 'which with walls and roof were all of turf or peat' (Bowes 1976). The use of turf and peat in walling has a number of valuable ethnographic parallels in Norway but is less usually recorded in the Northern Isles, although some seasonal structures are known from Fetlar (Fenton 1978, 233-6). Hibbert cites its occurrence in a non-load-bearing capacity as an internal division between parts of a house, observing that 'in most of the Shetland habitations, a partition of turf runs across the room which is occasionally carried up to the height of the house, being intended as well for the purpose of storing up victuals as for a separate dormitory' (1822, 115).

In the matter of turf cutting on Fair Isle, Fotheringhame's audit of 1804 took the predictable viewpoint of an estate manager:

> *The inhabitants all reside in the south end of the island. Their houses are likewise covered with turf from the want of straw for thatching. Formerly it would seem they had been prohibited by the proprietor from digging this turf within the hill dyke, that is in the south division of the island where the arable land and grass ground is situated. And of late the surface of this part of the island has been cut up in the most shameful manner, not only for roofing their houses but also for peats ...* (Fotheringhame 1804)

In most parts of Shetland, *pones* (thinly cut turves) were a common roofing material, often with regional variation in style of use. Fenton's study identifies those used on Fair Isle as being strips typically 5.5 ft x 1.25 ft, cut thin and 'rolled up like wallpaper' (1978, 176). Hibbert describes two types of dominant roofing in the early 19th century, *flaas* (compact vegetable layers, consisting of the short fibres of mossy or heathy roots closely interwoven with each other), or *pones*, thinly cut swards of earth on the surface of which grew a short grass. *Pones*, he observed, always had a grass covering and were used exclusively for roofing, but never in dyke construction. *Flaas* were taken from the surface of dry moss land by tearing rather than by cutting (1822, 114); when laid double on a roof they were considered to be impervious to rain.

It was partly to alleviate the landscape and grazing problems associated with the removal of turf for *pones* that Fotheringhame recommended the introduction of slate in 1804, initially for the roofing of the warehouse and the main dwelling house (*The Haa*). It seemed to him a waste that a substantial part of the island's surface was annually destroyed in order to cover these roofs, especially since the final product was 'neither wind or water tight'. Nor is this the only report of turf roofing being unsatisfactory. One Methodist minister staying in Shetland in 1824 had the misfortune to encounter a heavy shower and wrote how the rain 'penetrated the roof and ran down the inside of the walls so that when I arose I could scarcely find a dry place to set my foot' (Raby 1824).

The southern part of Fair Isle provided the inhabitants with whatever produce could be grown in the harsh North Atlantic environment. A consensus of historical and literary accounts point to a subsistence economy in which bere and oats dominated the cultivated crops; these were supplemented by fish and wild-fowl among others, and continued into the 20th century as a part of the staple diet. Scott, on visiting Fair Isle in 1814, had already experienced the agricultural systems of Mainland Shetland at first hand. He observed that the inhabitants directed their attentions between fishing and cultivation and were less interested and less conscientious in the latter than was desirable. Spades were used in preference to the plough which he found 'beyond description awkward' (Laughlan 1982, 28). Unusually, the same criticisms were not levelled at Fair Isle where he recorded the rotation of barley, oats and potatoes and the nature of the runrig system on the island, although he commented specifically on the preference of the spade over the plough (*ibid*, 51).

The many materials and items not available naturally on the island had to be imported from elsewhere, or managed without. One well-attested method was by trade with other islands or with passing ships (below) by which means local produce, including woollens, feathers, chickens, fish or surplus crops, could be exchanged for the necessary hardware, or simply for 'luxury' items which were otherwise unobtainable. The method was also one which effectively bypassed any market controls imposed by the proprietor. Scott noted 'worsted stockings, nightcaps and other similar trifles' being knitted by the island's women. It appears this offshore trade had been much interrupted by the war with America. In addition, a thriving trade between Orkney and Shetland already existed by the end of the 17th century (Brand 1701, 179) and is almost certain to have provided Fair Isle with trading connections in both directions.

Alternatively, in a process already well-established by Scott's time, goods, particularly hardware, were necessarily brought in as part of an agreed rental arrangement with the proprietor. The relationship between proprietor and islanders was an important one. The proprietor, via his factor, acted as both buyer of the island's goods and as supplier of necessary materials and tools, the island being too small to foster anything in the way of specialised craftsmanship. In the early 19th century, for example, the proprietor provided the islanders with appropriate materials for their work. In return the islanders sold him fish, oil, feathers and linen for cash, and the cash was then used to pay rent. The arrangement was not only open to great abuse on the proprietor's part, but also made the islanders both dependent on, and vulnerable to, the benevolence and enlightenment of their proprietor. Fotheringhame describes one such typical arrangement:

> *There is no merchant and but few artificers on the island. The proprietor has always supplied the inhabitants with such articles as they required, such as grain, linen, indigo, hemp, lint, wool, spades, fishing hooks, materials for boat building which were always settled for at accounting for the rents ...* (Fotheringhame 1804)

Whatever its merits, this system evokes questions as to how earlier, unadministered societies on Fair Isle would have fared. Vulnerability also lay with the weather. Between the mid-18th and early 19th centuries a sequence of exceptional climatic conditions caused major crop failures and loss of cattle throughout Shetland (Knox 1985, 7). Other years of famine have also been identified by O'Dell (1939, 17). At times such as those the requirement to seek supplies from elsewhere was not simply desirable, but an issue of straightforward survival. In the era of the lairds there at least existed an administrative framework, however crude, by which these requirements might be identified. There might also have been some moral obligation on the lairds' part to see that those same requirements should somehow be met, although to some this might be seen as more properly the business of the Church. The laird system also brought Fair Isle firmly within the network of other social and administrative changes, particularly those of an unwelcome fiscal nature. One such imposition, albeit minor, emerges from a late 19th century account by a visitor who landed unexpectedly at the north end of Fair Isle and was immediately mistaken for the 'much dreaded and daily-expected official, known all over Shetland, and even in this remote isle, as the Dog-tax man'.

> *I took care to undeceive them, having no desire that the memory of my visit should serve as a tomb stone to mark the time when many aged, infirm and ill-favoured members of the canine race departed this life in a precipitate manner by being thrown over the cliffs nearest their respective homes; for such, I believe, is the doom awaiting them when that gentleman shall arrive.* (Reid 1869, 49)

In the assumed absence of a formal relationship with an owner in the period from prehistory through to the end of the Middle Ages, particularly under the udal system, the inhabitants were entirely dependent on their own resources, and on their own ability to supplement those resources from outside. Population was undoubtedly a key part in the subsistence equation: the number of inhabitants needed to be sufficiently great to act as a workable community in terms of age and gender, and in terms of carrying out necessary communal tasks; it also needed to be sufficiently small in order to prevent the island's resources from being exhausted, and to be able to weather years of dearth or famine. Each generation would have its own idea of this optimum size, a size which could (and did) increase under the different social and administrative circumstances of historical ownership. Before that time, given a relatively consistent subsistence economy, it may be possible to point to the Armada population as representing an optimum figure not only for the Middle Ages, but also for the Norse period and possibly before.

In this respect the Armada account is of further interest. From the point of view of subsistence it suggests that neither cows nor sheep seem to have been maintained for their carcass value:

> *Their food is mostly fish, without bread, except it be a little of barley, baked in cakes: their fires are fed with such fuel as they have in the island, which they simply take out of the earth; they call it turba. They have cattle of a sort, enough for them; they seldom eat meat: cows, sheep, swine: the cows are the most profitable (milk and butter): they use the sheep's wool for their clothes.* (Ker 1920, 172)

The *First Statistical Account* noted the presence of some 200 head of 'black cattle' on the island (*OSA* XIX, 436), but this number had been more than halved by the time of Fotheringhame's 1804 survey. In both records the primary function of the cow is unspecified. Since then its contribution to local subsistence appears to have lessened considerably and in O'Dell's 1940 study of the island's land use the cow is unmentioned as an economic resource. The Armada reference to the importance of milk and butter, and to the absence of regular meat eating is a curious one, especially considering the potential difficulties of outwintering. Although the text might be interpreted as reflecting some reluctance on the part of the islanders to admit to eating much meat (and hence to avoid sharing their supplies with the Spaniards), it might equally be viewed as indicating an emphasis on dairying.

An interpretation along these lines has been postulated elsewhere by Bigelow on the basis of excavated faunal remains from Sandwick, Mainland Shetland (Bigelow 1987, 33; 1992, 19). There, cattle bones dated between the 12th and late 14th/early 15th centuries contained a preponderance of young calves among the food refuse, suggesting a slaughter pattern that would have produced high milk yields at the expense of meat production. Bigelow suggests that an explanation for this bias might lie in the introduction of formal taxations, both secular and ecclesiastical, which, being payable in both butter and wool, would inevitably effect changes in methods of animal husbandry. The argument might be taken to explain the transition to 'longhouses' in the later Norse period by which milk yields could be increased by maintaining cattle within a warmer environment. There is also ethnographic evidence for byres being substantially occupied by milking cows in post-medieval times (*ibid*), although there is little positive support for this on Fair Isle. The anonymous Armada writer may, indirectly, have identified the effects of this system and in doing so indicates the extent to which the island's subsistence economy might be affected by external influence, although within the tolerance limits imposed by the environment and the size of the island. The later decline of the cow may, perhaps, indicate not so much a change in land use and husbandry as a response to changes in external influences and management.

The position of the sheep in this situation is somewhat ambiguous. The *First Statistical Account* numbers the island's flock at 400 and comments on the excellence of both wool and mutton (*OSA* XIX, 436), a fact also supported shortly afterwards by Fotheringhame:

> *The number of sheep at present on the island does not exceed 400 of which about 100 belongs to the proprietor. It is certainly fit to pasture double that number. The wool is of a very superior quality and is usually manufactured into stockings and gloves which are sold to the shipping. The mutton is also much superior in flavour to the produce of Orkney.* (Fotheringhame 1804)

This reliance on sheep persists through into the 20th century, for both meat and wool. It is unclear why the Armada account should specify a lack of meat (mutton) in the diet, unless this too indicates a level of dairy intensification. Unfortunately, so few sites from the Middle Ages and later have been excavated that the practice of ewe-milking is currently insupportable by archaeological means. Ethnographic study, however, has been more rewarding: Baldwin, for example, has identified the practice on Faroe until well into the 18th century, and has pointed to the associated use of stone dykes and pens both there and on Foula (1978, 117). Elsewhere, ewe-milking was carried out in Iceland through into this century where it was seen as an essential element of seasonal subsistence activity (Bergsåker 1978, 86). A ewe produces as much as 40-90 litres of milk per season thus providing much needed butter and cheese which were both nourishing and storable (Adalsteinsson 1991). The practice has been seen as being directly linked to a native Scandinavian economy which required all round yields from sheep which remained permanently outside. Outwintering also negated the necessity of an autumn slaughter but ran the risk of producing over-high yields of wool (Small 1968a, 146). One episode in the *Faereyinga Saga* describes how the stores were full of wool waiting to be sold (Halldórsson 1987, Ch 44).

Ewe-milking might therefore be seen as a distinguishing feature between traditional and modern methods of sheep husbandry (Bergsåker 1978, 88). Are we therefore to consider that the Armada description, in the case of sheep, has identified part of a persisting native Scandinavian economy – an economy which apparently no longer existed by the time of the *First Statistical Account* and whose demise might be put down to administrative changes brought about by the feu duties imposed in Shetland in the 1560s? Whatever occurred around that time, the parts played by both sheep and cattle in the island's economy may have become realigned as a result.

Reference to sheep on Fair Isle is particularised usually with respect to Sheep Rock, a tall, precipitous land mass separated from the main island by a chasm some 100m deep on the eastern side of the island. One 18th century report described it as 'stupendous and magnificent' and containing grass of a type which produced sheep 'as remarkable for the excellence of their wool, as for the value of their carcasses' (*OSA* XIX, 434). Access was almost sheer and the sheep were physically carried to the grass-covered summit by means of a precipitous path. Scott was certainly aware of the method:

> *As it is covered with herbage on the top, though a literal precipice all round, the natives contrive to ascend the rock by a place which would make a goat dizzy, and then drag the sheep up by ropes, though they sometimes carry a sheep up on their shoulders.* (Laughlan 1982, 50)

Once there the sheep were left to their own devices until such time as they were considered adequately well-fed for collection and slaughter, a fact which is undeniably associated with meat value rather than for milk or wool, and which is graphically emphasised in Sibbald's early 17th century description:

> *... it hath excellent grass for sheep, and the Sheep there are admirably fat; they use no dogs to take them, but men on foot catch them without difficulty, for being chased but once around the Rock they fall of their own accord, which if they do not the Shepherd concludes them not fat enough for slaughter.* (Monteith 1845, 50)

Sheep in Shetland have traditionally been left to graze uninterrupted on the hill land where shepherding was to some extent carried out not by man but by the skua. Several accounts (eg Low 1774, 54-8; Drosier 1831) relate how the skua would drive away the preying eagle and effectively safeguard the lambs from their major source of danger. Shielings, which would have provided seasonal accommodation for shepherds to watch over the sheep on the summer pastures, are unevidenced on the Fair Isle moorland. The island is probably too small, although its size might not preclude less durable shelters. In other parts of the North Atlantic the shieling was a traditional element of the Norse landscape and research has shown them to have been both common and of varied design prior to the 12th and 13th century (Mahler 1991; Sveinbjarnardóttir 1991).

Complete freedom of movement and outwintering are probably factors which may have led Shetland sheep to have evolved into a characteristic species not dissimilar to that of the feral Soay species of St Kilda (see chapter 2). Scott saw fit to describe them as 'miserable looking hairy-legged creatures' (Laughlan 1982, 28) and was not alone in finding their appearance (and colour) unusual. The introduction of new stock 'south country sheep' (probably cheviots) contained within the Buness peninsula in the mid-19th century was probably an attempt on behalf of the proprietor to move the island's sheep husbandry away from its traditional Scandinavian roots. There is some general ethnographic evidence for the nature of these roots, particularly on Foula where sheep identification markings and rounding up methods reflect original Norse influences (Baldwin 1978, 99). On Fair Isle, sheep markings have been discussed briefly by Eunson (1976, 36f) but other aspects are formally unrecorded. Hibbert's account of sheep husbandry in Shetland generally gives some indication of these traditions in the early 19th century, although his view of a Scottish influence is probably over-estimated:

> *The sheep are allowed to run wild among the hills, herding and housing being almost wholly unknown in Shetland. There is an old law, that was probably introduced by the Scotch settlers ordering that every scathold have a sufficient herd, and that builling, punding and herding, be used in a lawful way, before, or a little after, sun setting; and that none scare, hound, or break up their neighbours' punds and buills, under the penalty of ten pounds Scots, besides damages; but the regulation has not, for a long time, been enforced .... The time of marking and rueing is still publically proclaimed, and on the day fixed, all the men of a district turn out, and drive their common flock, without any preparation of washing, into rude enclosures, named punds or crues.* (Hibbert 1822, 436-9)

The use of punds or small enclosures is well-attested elsewhere and provides a facility for counting, marking and shearing at specified times of the year. On Iceland this gathering and sorting of the hill sheep required communal effort and took place on a massive scale involving thousands of animals (Adalsteinnsson 1991, 291). On Foula, rounding up (*kros*) for these purposes still occurs on several occasions during the year using enclosures (*fanks*) in established positions; on each occasion the sheep are rounded up by herding in a predesigned geographical manner (Baldwin 1978, figs 10.8 and 10.9). Similar methods apply on Fair Isle by which the stock is driven systematically from the extremes of the island to a common point adjacent to the hill dyke (fig 10.2). There is, however, a tradition of three older enclosures, one of which lies on Buness, presumably constructed for the cheviot flock, and is still mostly standing (*729*). The others are said to have been near the Funniquoy mills and at the south-east side of Ulishield, although in neither case were any remains recorded during the survey. It is unclear why they were required in those locations, and to what particular herding process they belonged. To these might be added other known

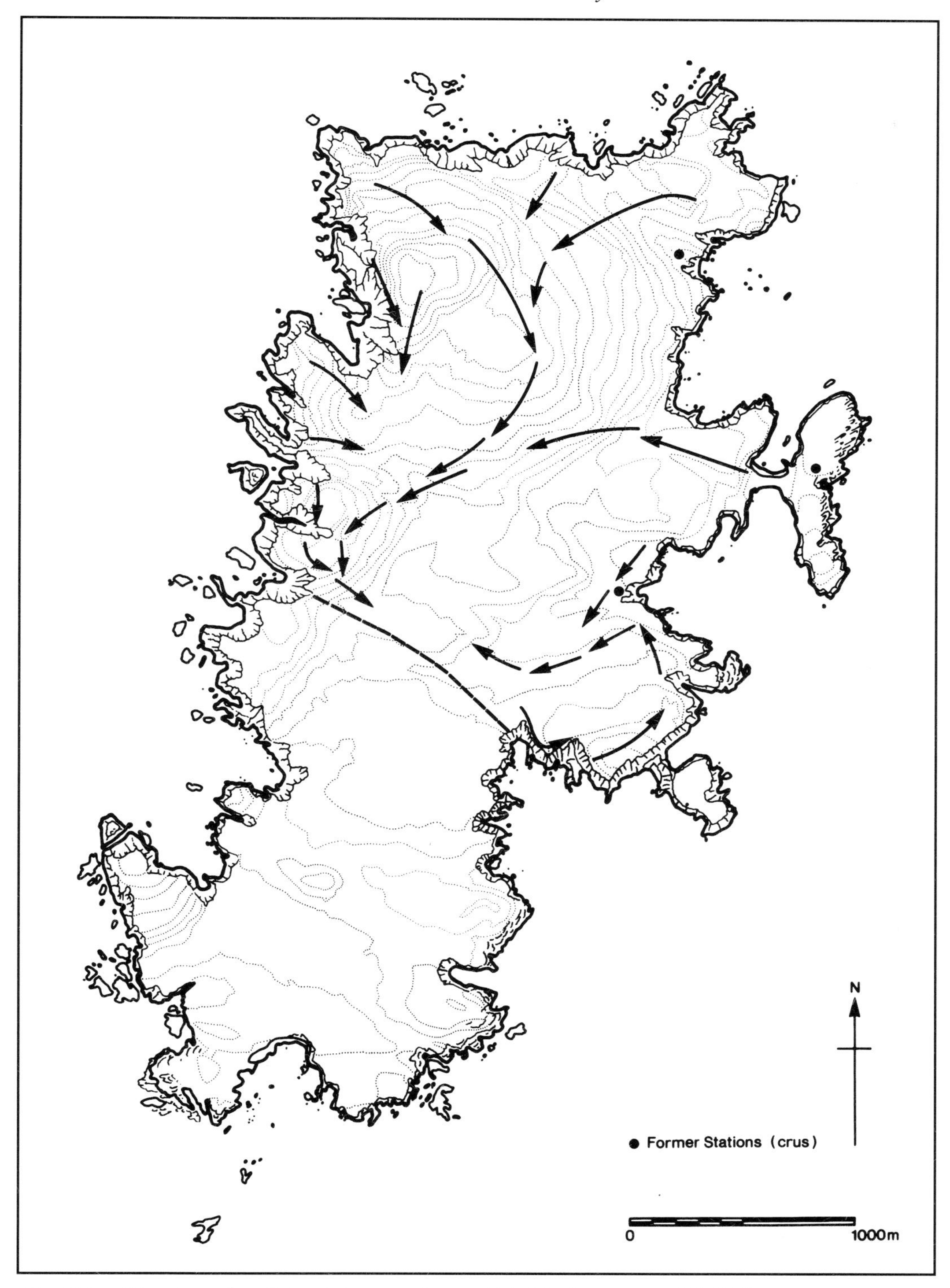

Fig 10.2 Directions of traditional sheep herding on Fair Isle, by courtesy of Neil Thomson.

enclosures defined by boundary features, arguably prehistoric in origin, which isolate headlands and, in one instance, outlie a promontory fort (see chapter 7). Do these also belong to rounding and penning methods? If so, what system of stock rearing or movement is being indicated? Taken together they suggest, in common with other implicit changes in animal husbandry, that the island's perceived subsistence economy was neither as simple nor as inflexible as is often assumed.

Fish

The growth, development and varying fortunes of the fishing industry in Shetland has been the subject of much exhaustive research and study. Relevant comment includes work by O'Dell (1939), Smith (1973), and Irvine and Morrison (1987), and need not be pursued here other than to provide a summary contextual background. Fishing on a commercial as opposed to a localised subsistence level was already being carried out in the Shetland and Fair Isle waters during the early part of the 17th century, predominantly by Dutch and German fishermen. Their fleets seem to have been well-organised and their effects on local economies significant. The period is hence historically well-documented but tends to gloss over the traditional, less vibrant fishing that existed before and during the development of these markets. This occurred throughout the islands, but appears to have persisted longest in South Mainland and in Fair Isle where the style of local boats (below) may reflect a similar degree of conservatism. The earliest detailed account of Fair Isle's fishermen derives from Kay in the later 17th century:

> *But the chiefest income of this isle is Fishes whereof they have great plenty, viz. Killing, Ling, Skate, Turbot, Seath, Sea dogs (here called Hoes), and Podlocks (here Pitlocks) which last three are very beneficial by reason of the Oyl which they make of their livers. Of the Fishes which they take (such as are for their own use) some they eat fresh, some they hang in skeos till they be sour and these they call blown fishes. Such as they design for Merchant-ware, some they salt, some they hang fresh in skeos till they be perfectly dry and these they call Stock fishes, whereof they have great plenty here.* (Bruce 1908, 51)

This system was probably little changed from Armada times when the anonymous sailor, surprised that the cattle on Fair Isle were rarely eaten, observed that the population were 'savage people whose usual food is fish'. However, the use of skeos – loosely built stone structures inside which fish were hung for wind drying (ie 'blown fishes') receives no mention in the Armada account, although later corruption of the incident by Sibbald and others allege that these were deliberately weakened in order to collapse on the sheltering foreigners. Skeos are marked in two places above the *Wick* area on Thomas' map of 1839 (plate 9.1) and are copied by Heddle (1879), at the east on the cliffs of Meoness, and at the west above the nausts by the kirk. Both sitings are slightly unexpected: the former in that the cliffs, although relatively low (*c* 40 feet), are not easily reached from the shore; and the latter in that the skeos are depicted nearer to the opposite coastline of Hesti Geo than to the coastline of the main harbourage. It is possible that the latter can be attributed to the proximity of landing at Hesti Geo as his map suggests, or even to the suitability of a windy environment, rather than to any (unusual) inaccuracy or licence on Thomas' part. The modern map of recorded place-names identifies a skeo location much closer to both the kirk and the adjacent boat nausts, but it also confirms the sitings above Meoness. It additionally identifies two further skeo names on the Buness peninsula, one at the north and one at the south.

Skeo construction required a supply of suitable stones, an open windy position, and reasonable proximity to a landing ground. All four sites satisfy these criteria, particularly the two at Buness where natural stone is readily available, but the choice of the awkward cliff site at Meoness suggests that existing stone structures or features may also have been commandeered. In general, skeos seem to have been more common in Shetland than in Orkney, possibly owing to their usefulness for fish drying. They were also known for drying or keeping cheese, meat and butter, their presence being attested by theft cases from as early as the 1600s (Fenton 1978, 438). Apart from Sibbald's dubious account of the Armada incident on Fair Isle, the earliest record derives from the pen of Kay who also attributed general baldness among men on the island as deriving from 'the distillations of the Fishes which hang above their heads as they enter the Skeos' (Bruce 1908, 53) – a wholly improbable explanation, but no worse than that of the islanders who ascribed the cause to 'excessive toiling in rowing through impetuous tides'. Before Kay's time the evidence of skeos as such is only indirect but, like that of mills, yoals and boat nausts, is seemingly the product of a longer-standing, Scandinavian-derived tradition. Fenton points to a Norwegian dialectal form *skjaa*, drying house or shed, and also to Icelandic *skjá*, shelter (1978, 160) as further affirmation of a likely Scandinavian origin.

The use of skeos or similar features has a wider context within the Atlantic islands, particularly in Faroe where Williamson's neglected ethnographic study of the 1940s has identified the same tradition. The *hjallar* or small outhouses that he describes provide an identical function to that of the skeo, although in Faroe they were made of upright wooden laths, 'spaced a little apart, so that the wind can blow through the hut' (1970, 29). On Nólsoy, one of the remoter islands, he recorded a particularly fine group sited specifically to obtain the greatest benefit from the salt winds (*ibid*, 299f). His drawings depict small rectangular buildings with pitched roofs clad in turf. The long sides were formed using vertical slats, but the ends were of stone. Research into the origins of these and similar structures in Faroe has not been entirely fruitful, Thorsteinsson's useful summary of the evidence pointing to a range of types (one being specifically for fish), but these appear to be of post-medieval date (1982,

158). He suggests, however, that some of the later stone-built types may have been developed from versions of earlier stave-built forms. Similar drystone features occur in profusion on St Kilda where recent survey has identified well over 1000 examples. These *cleitean* were also used for storage of harvested crops and even turf; they tended to be part-corbelled with turf-capped roofs and were often located on hillsides to benefit from updraughts (RCAHMS 1988, 28f).

The use of timber in a building of this type is unlikely on Fair Isle, although timber versions are recorded elsewhere in Shetland – in Delting, for example, where wooden 'kists' featured in a theft case in the early 17th century (Fenton 1978, 160). In that instance the theft was not of cheese or of meat, but of socks. A wooden outhouse also seems to feature as a place of theft in *Njal's Saga* where Oktel Skarfsson's storehouse is deprived of its butter and cheese during one of the feuds (Magnusson and Pálsson 1960, Ch 48). The building is described almost in terms of a shed, but was said to adjoin the kitchen; its burning down implies wooden, or part-wooden construction. This type of domestic arrangement, although admittedly in stone, was recorded by Fenton at a farm in Dunrossness built in the early part of the 19th century. One of the outbuildings, roughly square and set at only a slight distance from the main unit, is clearly defined as a skeo (Fenton 1978, 134f). The alleged events in *Njal's Saga* are of the late 10th century; it says much for the usefulness of the skeo tradition and the relatively unchanged nature of subsistence economy if it can still be identified 1000 years later.

Unfortunately, excavation of Norse settlements throughout the Atlantic islands has traditionally (and understandably) concentrated on central farmstead units, with particular regard to their layout and evolution. Outbuildings have been given less attention even when they occur as an obvious component of a nucleated complex, for example throughout the phases at Jarlshof. Furthermore, the interpretation of a skeo or similar building is best made from its superstructure, not from its foundation; this is a major shortcoming in attempting to identify continuity of tradition by purely archaeological means.

During the 19th century a decline in usefulness had probably reduced most skeos in Shetland to rubble, but at their peak they were undoubtedly a familiar element of the landscape. Eunson's compilation of terminology and definitions local to Fair Isle not only recalls the presence of former skeos, but also shows the extent to which they could be identified with individuals; names such as 'Jamie Irvine's skjo' or 'Wast Willie's skjo', now no longer remembered, attest to their former ubiquity (1976, 16).

Survey work on the island failed to record any real trace of likely skeos on the west side of the South Harbour, perhaps not surprisingly given their loose structure, ease of dismantling and proximity to crofting. Two possible sites, a length of walling and an area of flattened stones (*19* and *20*) may conceivably be relevant. By contrast, the Meoness area was more forthcoming; no fewer than three possible sites were identified, a low-lying area near to the nausts noted by Thomas (*401* and *414*), a cliff edge location (*399*) also noted by Thomas, and an open area on the cliff top itself (*394-397*). The first of these was represented by L-shaped walling with much associated rubble and an adjacent turf foundation, and has the tradition of once being fishing-related. The second lay directly above a natural arch – at precisely the point indicated by Thomas – and took the form of an eroded section of cliff edge which produced both stonework and coarse pottery. If this was indeed a traditional skeo site as is implied, then the presence of coarse pottery may indicate a much earlier date of origin than is usually believed.

The third covered a larger area and included three separate lengths of walling (sheep shelters), a cairn and an expanse of stones measuring some 10 x 10m. This last site which may have included a fish drying area (see below) is of particular interest, partly in view of the possibility of collapsed or reused skeos (a U-shaped length of walling some 9 x 4m may conceivably have been developed from a skeo), but also in view of the extent of loose rubble available which may have made the location attractive in the first place (plate 10.1). There was, however, no obvious evidence for any earlier monument from which this material might have been derived, nor, for that matter, is the site identified by either Thomas or Heddle.

On Buness, loose stone, quarries and collapsed walling make the interpretation of possible skeo sites extremely difficult, although some features on the north side are plausible. These include the remains of a cist-like feature with a part-kerbed outline

Plate 10.1 Area of possible fish drying and skeos (394-7) on Meoness at the S of the island.

measuring *c* 2.5 x 1.5m (*741*), a similarly defined, but circular stone feature of approximate diameter 5m (*732*), and a cairn-like feature measuring *c* 4 x 4m (*729c*). Any or all of these may represent skeo bases, the original design being unknown, although some may have been bee-hived for ease of stone roofing. The two main requirements were loose construction to allow for through-draught, and height to allow access. Larger stone spreads such as one measuring *c* 8 x 5m (*728*) on the north headland might therefore also be relevant. The same problem arises on the south part of Buness where a series of stone-built features and spreads (*735*) present equally ambiguous evidence.

Boats

The Shetlanders were major exploiters of the sea. While there is little evidence of their involvement in anything other than white fishing, there is much to support a parallel economy based on the supply of provisions (including wind-dried fish), and indeed the growth of Lerwick to some extent reflects success in this quarter. Other saleable commodities included cloth, feathers, butter and live fowl, all of which were available on Fair Isle. There is proof, too, of the renting of land for booths from where foreign merchants might legally trade. One of these booths, according to Kay, was established at the south end of Fair Isle in the 17th century (probably in the vicinity of the modern 'Puffin' which is denoted as 'warehouse' on Thomas' map) and belonged to a Hamburg merchant (Bruce 1908, 49). This siting no doubt reflects both the proximity of local habitations and the harbourage, optimising on both resources. Island trade with passing ships which is more attested in the next century almost certainly occurred throughout this period.

By the early 18th century the Dutch and German fleets were in decline due to a variety of political and economic factors. Shetland's economic fortunes, riding on the demands of merchant lairds, required a new stimulus; this was effectively to be found in the expansion of local fishing and in the opening of new white fish markets in the continent and as far afield as Spain. The period is one of social and economic transformation which is encapsulated in Gifford's contemporary account (1786), and which may also be reflected in the production of kelp on the island by the end of the 18th century (*OSA* XIX, 437; Fotheringhame 1804). There is, however, no clear indication as from where the kelp was harvested, processed or shipped out. The South Harbour is the obvious contender but no kelping pits or similar features were identified in the archaeological survey.

By the time of the *Second Statistical Account* this period of change, exacerbated by a run of bad harvests, had already been identified: the Minister of Northmaven wrote that 'to the year 1740, the fishing was not distant from the shore above 8 or 10 miles, carried out in 4-oared boats with few lines, so that the quantity caught was few, compared to the numbers now ... about 1740 the boats increased much in number, which induced them to seek further out to sea.' (*OSA* XIX, 465). A more florid account of the Fair Isle population by the Rev. Mill also suggests a parallel expansion into deeper waters:

> *Their boats, which are 14 in number, lie on the S W shore, under the little town of Gelah, from which they go with only two or three men in them, who fit in the middle of the boat, and, with an oar in each hand, row over immense billows, in a short time, to a great distance. In these pitiful skiffs, in which a landman would scarcely trust his life across a river, they fly to the fishing ground, almost out of sight of the island, where they catch plenty of fine cod, ling, tusk, skate, halibut, mackerel, cyth, and other fish of inferior quality.* (*OSA* XIX, 437)

The preparation of fish by curing and drying, either for home or 'export' consumption, was both laborious and time-consuming and appears to have followed a tradition of considerable antiquity. It required, as a matter of priority, an open expanse of cobbles or stones on which the fish could be laid or stacked as part of the drying process. A suitable beach area might suffice, but on Fair Isle such drying areas had to be created artificially. Two have been identified: at the south-west side of Kirki Geo (*9*) and on the cliffs above Meoness (*396*). The former is relatively well-attested, including a photographic record taken around 1900 (plate 10.2), and survives as an

Plate 10.2 Fish drying area at south of Fair Isle c *1900. Copyright Shetland Museum.*

area of shingle measuring approximately 30 x 5m adjacent to six(?) eroded nausts. The other, which measures approximately 10 x 10m, is more ambiguous and may include the remains of other enclosures as well as skeos. Its position would have offered some difficulty for transporting fish from the harbour. Elsewhere in Shetland archaeological attention has yet to be turned to these features which might easily be misconstrued as scree or raised beaches.

The actual process of curing and drying has been detailed at length by Hibbert, although it is not clear whether his account is first-hand or taken from earlier sources. The degree of detail is such that it has the tenor of an eye-witness account. The description pertains to Hillswick on Mainland Shetland, but the processes are in common:

> *When a boat comes on shore, the ling, cod and tusk that have been taken at the Haaf, are in a gutted state, and with their heads taken off, delivered by weight to the factor. A splitter, as he is called, then, with a large knife, cuts a fish open from the head to the tail, and takes out half the backbone next to the head; he now hands it over to the washer, who, with a heath brush, and the assistance of the sea water, clears away every particle of blood. When all the fish are in this way split and washed, they are allowed to drain; after which comes the salter, who places at the bottom of a large wooden vat a stratum of salt, and over it one of fish with the skin side undermost, until the chest is filled with alternating layers, and above all are laid heavy stones to keep the fish under the pickle. After remaining in the vat some days, they are taken out, well washed and brushed in a direction from the shoulder to the tail, and put up in small heaps called clamps, in order to allow the water to drain off. The fish are next spread out with the skin-side undermost, and exposed to the action of the sun, on a beach composed of round stones, where they are again clamped, and thus alternately spread out, turned and disposed into piles of a gradually increasing size, until dry. They are afterwards built into a large stack named a steeple; and, for the sake of equal pressure, the steeple is again taken down and rebuilt, by which means the fish that were the uppermost in one steeple, are the undermost in another. When the drying or pining as it is called, has been completed, which is indicated by a white efflorescence appearing on the surface, named the bloom, the fish are transported to a dry cellar lined with wood, and there piled up closely, or shipped off immediately to a market.* (Hibbert 1822, 519)

Preparation on such a commercial scale would have been neither necessary nor desirable on Fair Isle. The external market was limited and unpredictable and could be satisfied as easily with other items of home produce less dangerously acquired. Although trade from small boats took place in a fairly consistent way with places such as Stronsay to the south, it could hardly be described as regular, and in any event could be equally profitable with passing ships many of which, weather permitting, came close by the island for that very purpose. Janet Schaw's diary of 1774 describes the nature of the transactions when the islands' boats came out, ostensibly, she assumed, for the provision of fish:

> *This fleet, however, brought us no provisions, but were loaded with the Island manufactures: such as knit caps, mittens, stockings, and the softest cloth I ever saw made of wool. They informed us that the people we saw making to the town were gone for provisions, with which they would load their boats and be with us presently, that the best hen and duck was sold at four pence, a goose for sixpence, Chickens in proportion, eggs eighteen for a penny and plenty of cabbage to boot. This was a most agreeable account ...* (Schaw 1939, 40)

Unlike Janet Schaw, most other visitors to the island were more interested in the nature of these small boats, in particular their design and construction. Scott, as usual, revelled in this type of ethnic situation, and made much of the small boat from Fair Isle that came out to greet the Lighthouse Yacht in 1814. He ridiculed it as:

> *... a strange looking thing without an entire plank in it, excepting one on each side, upon the strength of which the whole depends., the rest being patched and joined. This trumpery skiff the men manage with the most astonishing dexterity and row with remarkable speed; they have two banks – that is, two rowers on each bench – and use very short paddles. The wildness of their appearance, with long elf-locks, striped worsted caps and shoes of raw hide – the fragility of their boat and their extreme curiosity about us and our cutter, give them a title to be distinguished as natives.* (Laughlan 1982, 86)

Schaw's observations were, in their own way, probably more valid, noting that they were 'light, pretty, neat Vessels, all extremely clean, and painted with various colours. They were each manned with four rowers and are long and narrow. I fancy they resemble Indian canoes, but appear extremely proper for these Seas' (1939, 39). In fact Schaw had managed to put her finger on what Scott in his pomposity had not, namely the suitability of the boat for the waters in which it was intended to be used – this was the key to the idiosyncratic and conservative design of the Fair Isle yoal. Low, too, identified a similar compatibility, but around the waters of Foula, where he observed that the dangerous tides and rousts could be navigated by 'skilful people in tolerable weather in the smallest Schetland Yawl, and that without the least danger' (1774, 95). The size of these boats is also significant, the earlier often being identified as carrying four people. Osler has produced a series of likely seating configurations for these and the later 6-oared boats (1983, fig 14) which takes into account the purposes for which they were used – in the case of Fair Isle this would include various types of fishing, minor cargo carriage and the pursuance of trade with passing ships. They might also be used for communication purposes. Scott recounted how, during the war with America, a boat from Fair Isle outstripped 'by speed of rowing' an American boat in order to warn the garrison on Mainland Shetland of the presence of a hostile vessel (Laughlan 1982, 51). In the episode of Janet Schaw's visit to Fair Isle the configuration was a memorable one in that three of the four rowers climbed aboard the steamer; the one that was left in the boat was nearly drowned when the yoal became caught under the steamer's stern and broke up (Schaw 1939, 41). Tudor, over a century later, was also careful to note the number of oarsmen – in his case three, each with two oars – as well as the rowing motion which he seems to have found unusual in that it required some 35 strokes per minute to cross swift currents (1883, 438). In the *Orkneyinga Saga*, Earl Rognvald's fishing trip was undertaken with two people in the boat, one (the Earl) rowing, and the other (the boat's owner) fishing. The passage not only relates how the fishing was undertaken at the edge of the currents, but also how the catches were traditionally shared out (Pálsson and Edwards 1978, Ch 85).

The traditional lines of the yoal almost certainly derive from boats of Viking origin. They reflect the culmination of hard-bitten experience and test in the tidal waters and currents where they were used most frequently (Morrison 1978; 1992). Although probably common throughout Shetland during the 17th century, only in Fair Isle and South Mainland (Dunrossness) did these small boats continue in use thereafter. Elsewhere the move towards deeper sea (*haaf*) fishing necessitated larger vessels of different character. During the 18th and 19th centuries Fair Isle's marine economy continued, as far as can be seen, to be locally based and survives in part in the names of local fishing marks or offshore spot bearings (Eunson 1961). Consequently, the tradition of the yoal, already perfected from centuries of fine-tuning in the same waters, also continued. This is supported in other quarters, for example the Faroese ambassador Christian Pløyen who visited Shetland in 1839 noted that the boats he saw fishing between Sumburgh and Fair Isle resembled those of Faroe (where the tradition was pure Scandinavian) and were particularly suited to coastal, edge-of-tide fishing (1894, 3).

The development, constructional character, and use of the Fair Isle yoal has been comprehensively detailed by Osler (1983, 67-78), who also emphasised the strength of Scandinavian pedigree in the overall design. However, the purity of this pedigree is open to question. On the basis of ethnographic evidence the lineage can be accepted as a straightforward insular development extending back for as much as 1000 years, but there is equally a wealth of written evidence to suggest that this may not have been the case – that the boats may have been reintroduced from Norway at a much later date. Trading connections between Shetland and the Bergen area show an increasing traffic of boat imports from the 16th century onwards, evidenced from both customs dues and visitors records compiled comprehensively by Thowsen (1969) and reviewed later by Osler (1983, 18f). Both Orkney and Shetland are involved, but the Shetland market emerged as the stronger with the importation of the 4-oared (inshore) type until the mid-18th century when it was joined by its larger 6-oared (deeper sea) sister. The trade eventually petered out towards the end of the 19th century. One of the most informative accounts of both boat and importation derives from the loquacious Hibbert on approaching Mainland Shetland:

> *Our proximity to land is announced, in good weather, by the appearance of numerous boats, fishing by means of hand-lines for seethe and cod. The Scandinavian character of the natives first becomes evident in the form and lightness of their boats or yawls, the planks of which are still imported from Norway, so modelled by the hands of the carpenter, that, when they arrive in Shetland, little more labour is required than to put them together. These boats are generally about eighteen feet in keel, and about six in beam; they carry six oars, and are furnished with a square sail. Their extreme buoyancy, and the ease with which they cut the waves, are the circumstances insisted upon by the fishermen, as rendering their construction particularly adapted to the stormy seas upon which they are launched. Many of the boats are, however, less in size, being adapted only for four oars.* (Hibbert 1822, 96)

The importation of 'kit' boats to which Hibbert alludes is a practice which may have persisted throughout the period of trading with Norway. Fotheringhame (1804) identifies the presence of Norwegian boats in Fair Isle in the early 19th century, although the 'kit' element is unspecified. He notes the presence of 18 boats in use, and the need for more had they been available. A general continuation of boat importation into Shetland is shown by Osler to have persisted through to the end of the 19th century (1983, 19), although there is some doubt as to whether this may have occurred on Fair Isle where different social factors applied (below). The method appears to have been sufficiently unusual to merit frequent comment, often with helpful information, for example in 1842 when the author and scientist James Wilson was passing through Lerwick and saw 'a large store full of the component parts of Norway skiffs, brought from abroad, and all numbered in such a way that they could be put into a seaworthy form in a very short period ...' (Wilson 1842, 277). The *First Statistical Account* for Unst described how these parts arrived 'ready shaped and dressed' for assembly (*OSA* XIX, 505).

While the (smaller) 4-oared yoal, being of longer tradition, was of a known and tested quantity in its behaviour, the 6-oared version was not and in certain quarters was viewed with some suspicion (Irvine and Morrison 1987, 54; Morrison 1992, 130f). It was therefore useful that the boats should arrive in broken-down form; this gave the opportunity for dismantling and modification at the end of each season –

an activity which reflected not only the seaman's distrust of the untried but also his respect for the time-honoured experience that was required to make a boat safe in local waters. This fact perhaps more than any other points to the indigenous character of the 4-oared yoal, or at least to a long-standing, specifically Shetland version of a Norwegian prototype. Either way the Viking influence is undeniable. Tudor, writing in 1883, to some extent reinforces Fair Isle's status as somehow being a relict area in this sense. He commented that the Fair Isle boats were 'peculiar to the island' and pointed out that in Low's time (late 18th century) the types were common throughout Shetland (1883, 438).

It is perhaps also significant that during the period of importation of 'kit' boats, some Fair Isle vessels were made on the island from local materials, including driftwood. Social organisation of the island, demanding a mixed economy of crofting, fishing and trade, is unlikely to have included a full-time boat builder. This is certainly supported by Osler's interpretation of 19th century fishing from the island when saithe fishing was at its peak and the demand for boats was greatest (1983, 69). It is conceivable, therefore, that the local Fair Isle design may to some extent have survived independently of later Norwegian influences. The most satisfactory interpretation also probably belongs to Osler who explains the tradition on the 'founder-effect' principle, namely that unchanged environmental and economic factors necessitated the retention of a vessel type with largely unchanged characteristics (1983, 108). If the basic nature of the marine subsistence economy on Fair Isle was largely unaltered between Viking times and the present day (despite the influences of German merchants), then this suggests much for the pedigree of the boats which carried it out.

Boat nausts

One of the few physical traces of boats in antiquity is that of the naust – the boat-shaped hollow deliberately fashioned at the coastal edge to provide safer storage for the boat against wind and tide. Easier to construct than a boathouse, especially if a natural hollow could be suitably modified, nausts provided a cheap and efficient method of protection. The basis of design was to shelter the sides of the hull from the wind which was often powerful enough to lift unprotected boats from the ground and break them in pieces (Sibbald 1711, 13). The boat became effectively camouflaged within the landscape either by being smoothed into the ground surface or, less frequently, by the construction of a small stone revetment (eg Osler 1983, fig 4). Either way the result was a shape which by necessity closely resembled the size and shape of the vessel for which it was designed. Stone linings or a stone component in the turf sides were also relatively commonplace; these had the advantage of providing durability to a feature that was otherwise vulnerable to erosion.

The origin of the naust can be traced back to Viking times (ON *naustr*), but it is unclear as to whether any discrimination between early and later types is feasible. None of the Fair Isle examples described below were constructed within living memory, and the only fact that can be argued with any certainty is that all of them have outlived the vessels for which they were originally intended. Elsewhere, a number of nausts were constructed in the 18th and 19th centuries as a result of Norwegian influences in Shetland, but other examples, notably in Orkney where this later Norse influence was less pronounced, may belong to the primary Viking/Norse culture from which the tradition originally sprang. Using examples in Westray, Lamb has suggested that the shape of many nausts may relate to boats of Scandinavian *genre* rather than to boats of the Scottish east coast type prominent during the end of last century during the height of the fishing industry (1983, 9). He also points to place-name evidence to support the view of long-standing boating traditions in certain locations. Ironically, within the context of a traditional maritime culture, nausts represent the only tangible surviving element.

Boat nausts are now recognised as relatively common coastal features in those parts of Orkney and Shetland where detailed sites and monuments work has taken place. Nevertheless, they still remain a curiously undervalued resource despite their density (Lamb 1983) and their hopeless vulnerability to coastal erosion, sea level changes and, more recently, landfill. They have not been subject, for example, to the detailed examination afforded to similar monuments in Norway where large numbers are also found. Examples in the Northern Isles are consequently not well-understood either in terms of date, construction, relation to settlement or even function. Several have been recorded and surveyed in the Scapa Flow region (eg Hunter *et al* 1982), and Osler has identified a number of likely stations in the South Mainland of Shetland (1983, fig 6). These Shetland examples represent well-attested, large sites. Detailed coastal survey would no doubt increase this number significantly.

Investigation at an appropriate level has been subsequently carried out on Westray, Orkney, where Bowman (1990) has suggested criteria for distinguishing between early and later nausts and has proposed a model for decay and abandonment processes. At Hurnips Point, Deerness, excavation and survey of a group of post-medieval nausts has given some insight into the unexpectedly complex nature of construction, and has demonstrated the difficulties of dating using typological and topographical factors (Hunter 1992). The same site also emphasised the importance of ancillary features, for example the presence of tall marker stones located up to 50m below the naust itself and covered during high water. Likely slipways and associated submerged stone jetties formed from natural bedrock outcrops may equally attest to earlier usage, readapted at a later period. To date only one recognisably early site has been excavated, a structure at Westness, Rousay (Kaland 1973; 1993), although this was structurally distinctive and would appear atypical.

In coastal Norway, from where the tradition may have been derived, nausts also hold a dominant place in the landscape, but their position within Norwegian maritime culture has been more generally explored, initially by Rolfsen (1974) and more recently by Myhre (1985). The nausts surveyed in Norway appear to show a much greater range of size than those in Orkney and Shetland, some measuring up to 30m in length, but many also compare favourably in size with those recorded by Lamb and others. Rolfsen's work has shown that the naust (defined as the *nausttoft* – an area which embraced the naust itself together with other associated elements), far from being merely a boat shelter, might also fulfil other functions – a point taken up by Myhre with regard to implications for social organisation and administration. Excavations in Norway have since illustrated the artefactual richness of these sites and their constructional techniques, together with the relevance of associated features which include both slipway (*båtopptrekk*) and landing place (*båtstø*). Their distance from the sea has also been used as an indicator of water level changes. Much still awaits enquiry along Scottish coastlines.

Fair Isle itself contains four sets of nausts, although in all the accounts and descriptions the nausts are not mentioned *per se*, reference sometimes being implicit. Nor are nausts mentioned as such in any Shetland parish in the *First Statistical Account.* Even in Northmaven where the writer describes in detail many suitable harbourages and boat stations, the presence of nausts, boathouses or shelters passes unrecorded (*OSA* XIX, 456-8). On Fair Isle all four naust sets lie at the south end of the island in the South Harbour or Wick area, their location to some extent reflecting the odd conventions on a 1750 sketch of the island probably attributable to Mackenzie (Anon 1750). The sketch, which shows a distorted landmass, clearly identifies the South Harbour. The conventions, which each consist of three vertical lines, are drawn against the shore line and correlate well with three of the four naust sets identified by survey. The most impressive (and probably the latest – *228*) lies on the west side of the bay at Kirki Geo and probably contains at least 16 individual boat stations set at two levels, a lower (summer) tier and an upper (winter) tier, representing year-round harbourage (plate 10.3 and fig 10.3). There is no doubt that the eight in the upper tier, designed for longer-term protection during the winter months, were the more carefully constructed with evidence for stone revetting and stone linings in almost all examples.

Of these eight, six were unequivocal (*b-g*) measuring between 5-7m in length and between 2-2.5m at maximum width. The maximum depth of cut lay between 0.5-0.7m. All conformed to this consistent pattern and may have been constructed according to a model. The depth of cut suggested that much of the upper part of the hull would have been protected. All six had pointed rather than rounded ends and in each case the profile narrowed towards the sea edge; all could be described as 'boat-shaped', were generally uneroded and quite distinct from the scooped hollows found

Plate 10.3 Boat nausts 228, from the east.

elsewhere. They had been built as much as excavated, the use of stone lining and walling was especially evident in (*c*), and their design contoured to a degree which suggested that the boat might have to be lifted in rather than dragged.

Five of the nausts in the upper tier (*c-g*) each appeared to have a matched summer naust immediately below (*i-m* respectively). These summer nausts were less substantial in all respects, typically 4-5m long and 1.5-2m at maximum width. Naust (*m*) was exceptional but may have been eroded to a greater extent. The construction and design suggested that a lesser degree of protection was required and was afforded to the lower part of the hull and bows only.

Two additional upper nausts may be represented by (*a*) and (*h*), the former being badly eroded at the seaward edge. The latter may have acted as a type of slipway, being approximately 13m in length, somewhat wider than the others at 4m, and less boat-shaped, although the landward end was deliberately pointed. The profile of this had been confused by rubble infilling. To the south of this, three additional nausts (*n-p*) lay at a lower level but without obvious higher tier companions. They were of inconsistent length although with a common width of around 2m, and may represent later additions – a fact dubiously supported by the presence of a boat in one

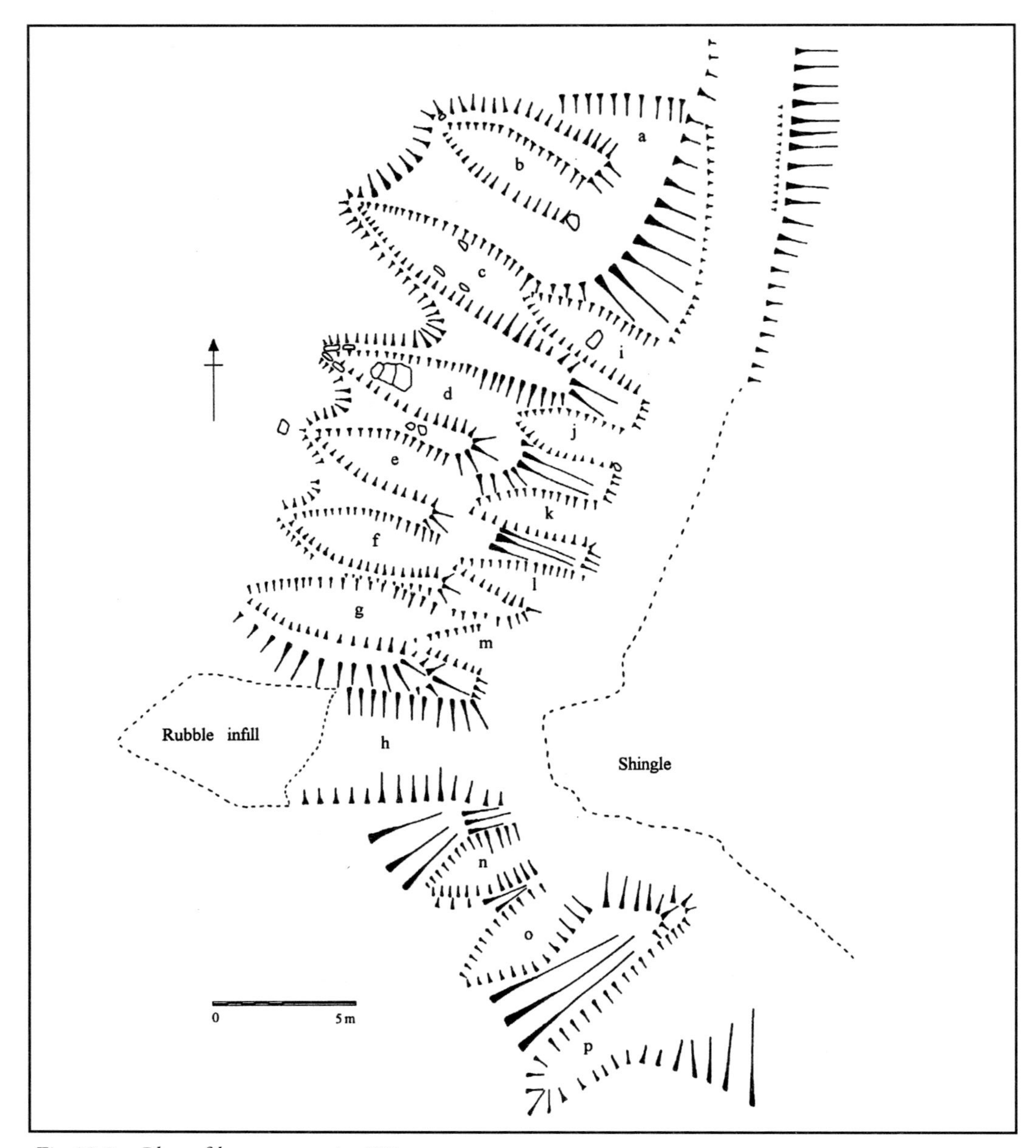

Fig 10.3 Plan of boat nausts site 228.

at the time of survey. The overview, however, points to the five pairs of nausts as being the principal (and probably earliest) of the group, constructed as a single phase of activity to a specific plan. This may have occurred with the move to increased fishing activity in the 19th century.

Earlier nausts are almost certainly represented by the sets on the north side of the bay (*429* and *430*, fig 10.4), located some 90m apart and containing approximately four and eight units respectively, although both sets were severely eroded and difficult to measure. The *First Statistical Account* is precise in its mention of 14 boats lying 'on the south-west shore, under the little town of Gelah' (*OSA* XIX, 437) – a location which might be identified particularly with one of the sets (*430*) at Leestat, although both might be equally relevant. The Leestat croft name is no longer used, but is recorded as a place-name at the head of the bay.

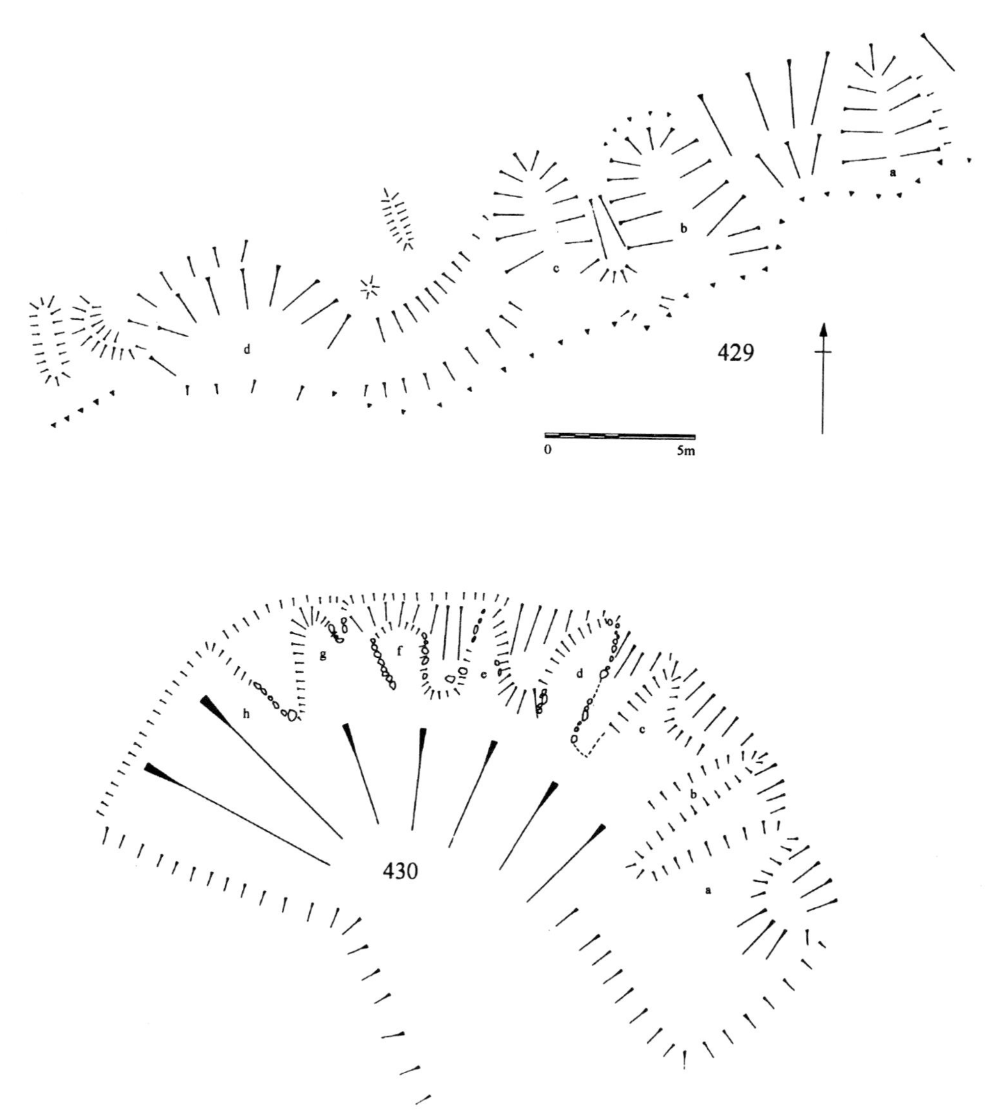

Fig 10.4 Plan of boat nausts sites 429 and 430.

In the western of the two groups (*429*), only one of the four (*a*) was seen as representing a summer naust by virtue of its low-lying position and generally smaller form. The other three, being higher up, were by implication winter versions, although one of these (*d*) was almost completely destroyed and seemed to lack the appropriate profile. All three were of rounded rather than pointed profile; (*b*) and (*c*) also had maximum surviving widths of between 2.5-3.5m. The depth, in the case of (*c*) at 1.25m, was significantly greater than in any other example on the island and could conceivably be viewed as indicating a different type of boat. All four seemed to have been made by hollowing rather than by building; nor was there any evidence of stonework.

By contrast the other group (*430*) contained greater evidence of stonework (five of the eight examples), but by virtue of being stone-defined rather than stone-built. On the basis of their position, all eight examples might be seen as winter nausts – an interpretation perhaps supported by their depth of cut which ranged from 0.75-1m. Erosion had been severe, but the maximum widths were consistently between 1.5-2m, and the lengths around 3-4.5m. Naust (*b*) was exceptional, being long and narrow (approximately 6 x 1.5m), and the group additionally contained a mixture of pointed- and round-ended types. Nor was there much evidence of boat-shaped profiles to the cuttings themselves, naust (*f*) for example gave the impression of being designed for something quite different. A considered overview, even taking into account the levels of erosion at the head of this bay, might justifiably interpret these nausts as having housed boats of different types.

The final set of nausts (*9*) lay at the south-west side of Kirki Geo in an area of attested fishing activity which included a stone drying area, and adjacent to the likely site of the Hamburg booth mentioned by Kay and others. Six nausts are probably represented, some using lengths of stone facings. All are severely eroded but exhibit estimated profiles between 5-12.5m in length and 1.5-4.5m maximum width. Where the depth of cut was possible to measure, the range was between only 0.5-0.6m. Despite the levels of erosion it might be possible to argue for different boat forms represented, but this is only conjecture. Once again, all the examples in this naust set exhibited rounded landward ends. The fact that all are relatively distant from the water and would require vessels to be dragged up from the shore argues the case for winter protection.

Whatever difficulties occur in attempting to interpret the date and significance of these features, these are overshadowed by their obvious vulnerability to erosion, distortion and coastal change generally. Ostensibly, all four sets are modern – that is to say *in use* from the 18th century onwards, or perhaps from a little earlier – and even here the levels of damage are significant. On this evidence the chances of identifying earlier boat shelters would be negligible, but it has to be remembered that on Fair Isle both landing locations and suitable naust sites are strictly limited. The sites discussed are almost certainly reused although the degree of continuity represented is open to speculation. Erosion may have obliterated earlier examples, but there is no record of the extent of coastal change at this part of the island over the centuries, nor for that matter is it possible to make even a calculated guess.

Three of the four sets are probably sufficiently damaged to be used only as indicators that the practice of naust construction occurred; in fact they may be completely destroyed in a matter of decades, these pages being their only record. The remaining group, the first discussed here (*228*), is by contrast a classic example of the tradition and is probably unrivalled elsewhere in the Northern Isles. It reflects a Norse custom, naturally adapted to a comparable climate and shoreline to that of the Scandinavian homeland and, together with the boat itself, provides one of the few tangible links with the Viking maritime world.

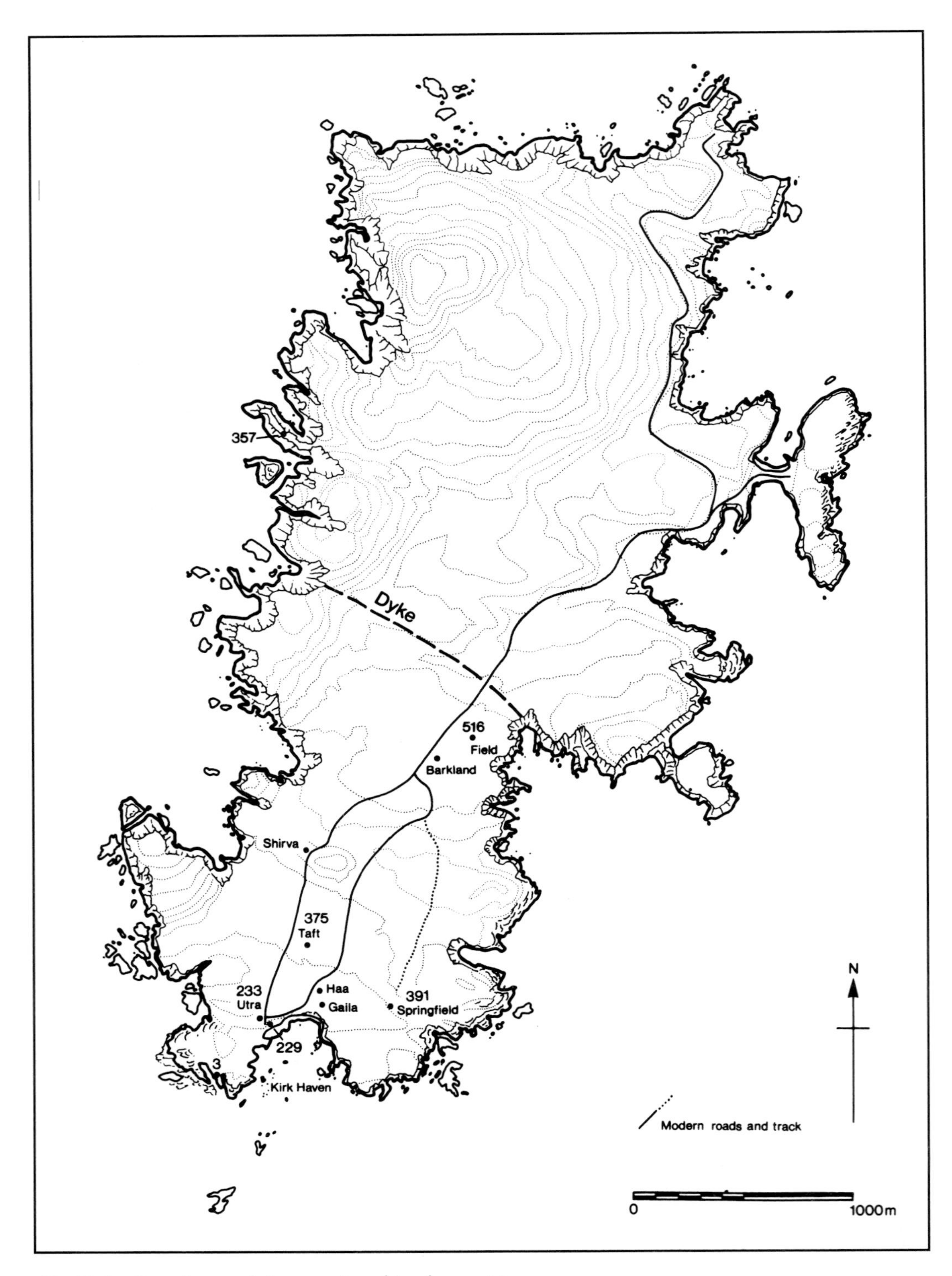

Fig 11.1 Locations and sites mentioned in chapter 11.

11

Post-Medieval Society

IN post-medieval times the land and sea continued to provide the islanders with basic sustenance. This was derived only by hard work in a harsh environment, and was often spread across too large a population. Fair Isle's economy, such as it was, remained driven by a combination of intertwined variables: the benevolence of the landowner; the frequency and availability of trade from passing shipping; and the unpredictable co-operation of Mother Nature. Subsistence surplus provided a buffer against poor winters or could be used for exchange, but the concept of either wealth or plenty was alien and belonged to a different social class in a clearly defined social structure. The Fair Isle population was predominantly a peasant community and was viewed as such by passing visitors, who were usually quick to note matters of poor sanitation in the dwellings or matters of moral laxity amongst their inhabitants. The descriptions, although often biased and selective, show a population living and working according to long-standing customs, never far from poverty.

Dwellings

The dwellings and dwelling foundations already discussed and illustrated (chapter 9) belong to a type common throughout the north of Scotland, generally taking the form of a narrow rectangle with a series of internal walls set across the long axis. This overall shape has usually been viewed as belonging to a distinctive Norse tradition based on the form defined as the 'longhouse', although this view is neither supported by the continuity of standing remains nor by geographical distribution. In the case of the former, surviving buildings elsewhere in the Northern Isles rarely tend to pre-date the 1800s, and in any event have normally been reduced from dwelling to storage or agricultural function within their relatively short life span, as time and need required (Hunter *et al* 1982). This makes it harder for the evolution of the true longhouse – the sheltering of humans and cattle under the same roof – to be physically identified. By the early part of the 19th century the longhouse format was still flourishing in Shetland as Scott's description of a Fair Isle dwelling bears witness. He points to common access for animals and humans, but was possibly too disgusted by the squalor to be specific as to the precise nature of the accommodation:

> *Visit the capital town, a wretched assemblage of the basest huts, dirty without and still dirtier within; pigs, fowls, cows, men, women and children all living promiscuously under the same roof and in the same room – the brood sow making (among the more opulent) a distinguished inhabitant of the mansion.*

> *The compost, a liquid mass of utter abomination, is kept in a square pond of seven feet deep; when I censured it, they allowed it might be dangerous to the bairns; but they appeared unconscious of any other objection.* (Laughlan 1982, 52)

The 'capital town' to which Scott refers is presumably that of Gaila which lay close to *The Haa* where he was a guest; this seems also to have been the 'largest village' where Mill found shelter in the mid-18th century, having walked almost the length of the island to find habitation from his landing point at the North Haven (Goudie 1889, 11). Slightly later is the account of a medical visitor to Shetland, Dr Mitchell, whose description was deemed an appropriate appendix for a late 19th century report on lunacy in Shetland. Mitchell also seems to focus on matters of filth, in this case more helpfully, in that the nature of shared accommodation is implicit:

> *Drainage is wholly unattended to, and the dunghill is invariably found at the very door. As the house is entered, the visitor first comes upon that part allotted to the cattle, which in summer are out night and day, but in winter are chiefly within doors. Their dung is frequently allowed to accumulate about them; and I was told that this part of the house is sometimes used by the family in winter as a privy. Passing through the byre, the human habitation is reached. The separation between it and the part for the cattle is ingeniously effected by an arrangement of the furniture, the bed chiefly serving for this purpose. The floor is of clay, and the fire is nearly always in the middle of it ...* (BPP 1872, 237)

The opening is reminiscent of MacKenzie's ministry in St Kilda, of which he noted '... at times a visit to a parishioner was quite an adventure. Inside the door you had to climb over the manure ...' (Mackenzie 1911, 20). Hibbert's description, less than a decade after Scott's visit, is a much clearer although more general observation on Shetland dwellings; he identifies not only the shared accommodation but also the common door:

> *The byre or cow house generally adjoins the dwelling, and is frequently entered by a common door that introduces the stranger first to the cattle, and afterwards to the apartment devoted to the use of the family. In most of the Shetland habitations, a partition of turf runs across the room which is occasionally carried up to the height of the house, being intended as well for the purpose of storing up victuals as for a separate dormitory.* (Hibbert 1822, 115)

There is, however, a note to the effect that the longhouse was slowly being replaced by 'detached cow houses' (*ibid*, 116), an observation also noted by Fenton in Orkney (1978, 121), although when Reid visited Shetland in the 1860s he observed that the cottages were 'somewhat antiquated, have the byre and the dwelling under one roof, and a door common to both' (1869, 51). Even then the practice is unlikely to have been unusual. It is known to have persisted into the 20th century in certain remoter parts of Scotland as a remnant of a tradition much more widely carried out than one based solely within areas of Norse contact (Fenton 1982, 232). Other potential influences behind its emergence might accordingly include those of the Celtic west, or those generated in Scotland itself. Moreover, the beginnings of the tradition appear to lie within the later Norse period, rather than with earlier Viking settlement. This is evident, for example, at Jarlshof (Shetland) and Pool (Orkney). It suggests that the impetus was economic rather than cultural – a factor which may be linked with the various demands of medieval taxation (Bigelow 1987; see also chapter 10). Ironically then, in a post-medieval agricultural tradition steeped in Norse terminology and methods, the character of the basic element of settlement, the farmstead itself, may owe its origins to completely different cultural forces. While certain elements in its construction, such as the use of turf and stone, roofing materials, even double-skin walling, may have their origins ascribed to Viking times (see Fenton 1985, 95), the beginnings of the longhouse itself may need to be sought elsewhere.

The gap of some six centuries between the first archaeological appearance of the longhouse and its eventual emergence in textual sources is one in which the tradition is assumed to have persisted. More often this persistence is interpreted on the basis of absence of specific mention of byres in formal documentation rather than by the analysis of standing buildings, although a few chronologically intermediate examples are known (Fenton 1978, 121). The analogy is with mills and boats where similar problems of continuity occur. There is, however, a difference: in the later Norse period the longhouse typifies (as far as can be seen) the standard farmstead layout and accommodation. By the 19th century it was synonymous with peasant culture and the lowest levels of rural society. As one travelling cleric observed in 1807, 'the lower ranks inhabited houses in common with their cattle' (Hall 1807, 526).

On Fair Isle several of the foundation remains identified, many of which might be ascribed to the 19th century or a little earlier, show an internal division into three units, presumably the kitchen, the bedroom and the barn/byre. In none of these cases was it possible to detect whether through-access was possible from the living area to the non-living area, or indeed whether the divisions were necessarily load-bearing. The length also ranged from approximately 15 to 20m (excluding likely corn driers at the ends) suggesting that there was no fixed constructional format. Only in the case of Gaila is the arrangement more complex, as may befit its postulated status. The two-unit dwellings (eg those around Shirva) are arguably later and on morphological grounds probably belong to the later 19th century (see Fenton 1978, 163); they lie separated from any byre or agricultural building.

A survey of the Barkland croft on Fair Isle carried out in 1962 (reproduced in Fenton 1978, fig 48) shows the use of internal partitions at that time, although it is not clear how these might manifest themselves, if at all, as grass-covered foundations. In most instances, however, probing of the foundation lines suggested a stone component. Even on Fair Isle the use of timber for partitioning and other features may have been more common than realised. At Springfield (now restored) the original building was entirely wood-lined; additionally, one of its doors was derived from a shipwreck (Fenton 1978, 172). The Barkland illustration is also of interest in that it depicts the barn end of the building as being a clear abutment to an original dwelling form. It was, additionally, the first dwelling on the island to have flagstone roofing (*ibid*, 181); this may in part be due to the fact that it was built by a Westrayman, the system being more common in Orkney (and geologically more appropriate) than in Shetland.

Fair Isle's location was one which made it particularly vulnerable to the transmission of ideas and changes of this nature from two directions. In a sense it lay in a buffer zone between Scottish influences from the south and Scandinavian influences, via Mainland Shetland, from the north. The presence of horizontal water mills is a case in point (see chapter 12). A measure of the effects of these influences emerge with Sibbald's 17th century observation that Dunrossness was inhabited mostly by 'strangers from Scotland' (Monteith 1845, 14), and by the presence of circular corn driers – a characteristic Orkney form as opposed to the square Shetland type – on the present Fair Isle landscape. The survey recorded two corn driers by elevation and ground plan, at Springfield (*391*; plate 11.1) and at Utra (*233*, fig 11.2) ahead of restoration. Both exhibited opposing doors suitable for winnowing. Other standing forms were noted at Taft, Shirva and Barkland, and several sets of foundation remains would also appear to have contained corn drier terminals. They all conform to what might be loosely described as being of 'Orkney' type and have numerous parallels in both Orkney and Shetland. Rectangular types are rarer, earlier and, unlike the circular version which was usually constructed against the end of a building, could appear internally. Of the foundations recorded only one (*375*, see chapter 9, fig 9.5) may show an appropriate small rectangular feature within the north-east corner, although the sub-circular shape at the other end of the building suggests otherwise.

Constructionally, however, it is unlikely that local materials might have changed significantly since earlier times, utilising the 'rough, unhewn stone' which Sibbald noted in Shetland buildings (Monteith 1845, 14). Hibbert believed this type of construction to be an aspect of their 'Scandinavian character', describing the oldest Shetland dwellings as being built of rude stone with a 'cement of clay', or being more coarsely formed with 'stones and clods' (1822, 114). A parallel observation was made by the Duchess of Bedford in her first visit to Fair Isle in 1909; many of the 'huts'

Plate 11.1 *Remains of the corn drier at Springfield (391).*

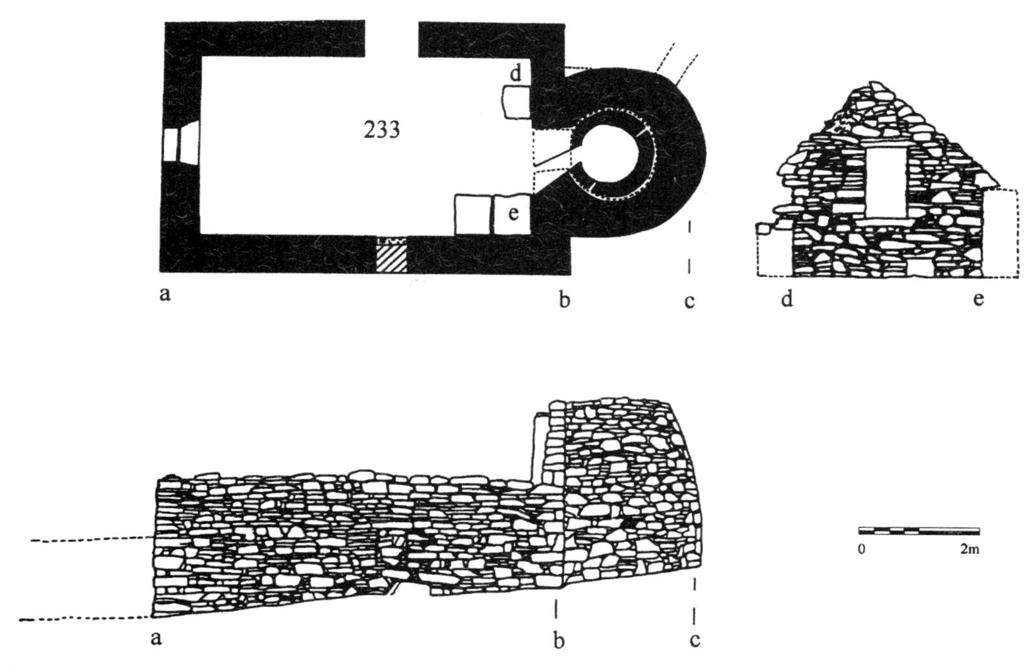

Fig 11.2 *Plan of corn drier at Utra (formerly Melville House; 233).*

she saw were 'of the usual wretched type that one meets with in the Outer Hebrides', but there was also 'a good sprinkling of stone houses' among them (Bedford 1968, 45).

A main focus of the Shetland dwelling was its central fire; 'poor houses with peat fires on the floor' were still being recorded in 1939, although by that time most fires had been moved to the end wall utilising a chimney (O'Dell 1939, 149). However, central fires may have been sufficiently unusual outside northern Scotland to have provoked comment even in the early 17th century:

> *... their h[ou]ses are all built under gr[ou]nd, having the roof onely above which is coevered with hather; and in the middle there is a barrell or such like thinge to lett forth the smoke the hearth lijnge in the midst of the roome bought which thay have broad benches to lie on ...* (cited in MacGillivray 1953)

The observation of benches is a direct reminder of Norse times, although the concept of being built 'under gr[ou]nd' is curious. Reference is known of some buildings being constructed against hillsides with a back wall of earth as late as the 19th century; these are recorded as servants quarters (Fenton 1982, 235), although the method probably derives from earlier times. The remains of a similar example on Fair Isle, adjacent to Field, measures almost 4 x 4m (*516*) and now contains a fireplace with lintel and chimney; the lowest courses of stones rest on excavated bedrock with the maximum height between floor and top of cut being approximately 1.75m.

The fireplace, its nature and position, is a continual source of comment. Hibbert implicitly ascribed its central position as a characteristic of peasant society and includes a gloomy view of living conditions, particularly with regards to windows, light and ventilation:

> *In most Shetland cottages the fireplace is in the middle of the room, and the smoke ascends through a large aperture in the roof, after the usual manner of the hovels of the Scottish Highlands. Windows are become much more general than they were some years ago; for, among some of the oldest habitations, no other light is received other than through the aperture which allows an egress to the smoke.* (Hibbert 1822, 115)

Some 40 years later the situation appears to be little changed. Reid's description is more vivid than most and confirms the nature of animals and humans sharing the same accommodation, with some added information regarding furniture:

> *The cottages ... being but rarely supplied with anything in the shape of a window, they are necessarily very dark. The fire is always to be found in the centre of the floor, and near it is the seat of honour, an armchair with a tall*

> *back of plaited straw, on which you are invited to sit down. The pig probably then fraternises with you, and rubs his scaly bulk against you familiarly, with a good-natured grunt of satisfaction. In one corner of the room are one or two calves; and in a used up keyshie, hung on the wall, nestles a sagacious old hen, with a flourishing brood of chickens. The furniture consists of the usual compliment of trunks, viz; one for each member of the family, one for meal, and another for the milk and butter; as well as box beds, a small table, and a miscellaneous array of stools and chairs.* (Reid 1869, 51)

The nature of box beds also seems to have been a focus of some descriptive interest, if not universal ridicule, by southern visitors. Hibbert described them as consisting of 'a few coarse blankets or straw' located in 'any convenient angle' (1822, 115), while another visitor referred to them as a 'violation of the plainest law of nature' and one which was aggravated by having the beds 'arranged in tiers, one above the other, in ship fashion, with the apertures of access reduced to the smallest possible size ...' (BPP 1972, 237). The most vivid account, however, belongs with a group of travellers from the south who stayed in Papa Stour in 1832; the account is of as much interest for its reflection of social behaviour as for its glimpse of living standards:

> *... after a good deal of poking about, we roused a servant girl who slept in some kitchens separate from the house, and turning her out of her bed, Edward and I proceeded to occupy it, William preferring a chair by the fire. [The bed] ... was nothing but a wooden cupboard with straw in it, divided into an upper and lower apartment, the former we occupied, and the latter was in use for an old ewe and a half grown lamb of delicate habits, which bounced and bleated and sucked and scrambled so that it was long before we could close our eyes, and when we did, it seemed as if swarms of fleas had been anticipating the opportunity of a debauch ...* (Atkinson 1832)

Such views as these identify living conditions in the islands in the earlier part of the 19th century. Hibbert seems to have realised that many of the contemporary practices and methods were slowly being changed or replaced. He perhaps also recognised an ethnographic value in what he was witnessing. Perhaps the detail of his descriptions was intentionally also a record. The changes, however, were slower than he anticipated, but while O'Dell still found plenty of scope for record in *The Historical Geography of the Shetland Islands* in 1939, Fenton was harder pushed to find similar evidence for *The Northern Isles* in 1978. Both recognised that major changes had happened. Hibbert also recognised that major changes were happening in his own day. In a sense he also laments the passing of an era:

> *... the antiquary will often be chagrined in observing such provoking modern improvements as slate roofs, regular windows, and detached cow houses, all of*

> *which have been introduced into the country by that foe to archaeological sources of pleasure – a sense and desire of increased comfort.* (Hibbert 1822, 116)

Inhabitants

Descriptions and changes of equal moment, but which normally lie beyond the scope of archaeology, are those which pertain to the inhabitants themselves, their dress, habits and attitudes. Understandably, few earlier visitors to the island, having once described the buildings, seemed to want to enter inside. The Duchess of Bedford observed one mealtime in which food was piled up centrally and the family helped themselves with their fingers (Bedford 1968, 51). This 'repulsive sight' is reflected in Scott's description of similar eating activities. Here, however, the house pig and the woman of the family are confused:

> *I cannot wonder they want a meal, for assuredly they waste it! A great bowie or wooden vessel of porridge is made in the morning; a child comes and sups a few spoonfulls; then Mrs Sow takes her share; then the rest of the children or the parents – and all at pleasure; then come the poultry when the mess is more cool; the rest is flung upon the dunghill – and the goodwife wonders and complains when she wants meal in winter! They are a long-lived race, notwithstanding utter and conceivable dirt and sluttery ...* (Laughlan 1982, 52)

It was an observation of habits more broadly based than those within the dwelling itself that led the Duchess of Bedford to realise that the women on the island tended to be more actively involved in everyday activities, including those in the field, than the menfolk (Bedford 1968, 45). Fotheringhame noted too that the arable land was chiefly laboured by the women. Her criticism that the men spent most of the day idly looking for driftwood is probably not wholly justified, although it has much in common with accounts of other islands at that time, notably St Kilda where most of the heavy labour was also carried out by the women. The phenomenon was new to the Duchess on her first visit to the island in 1909; it impressed her sufficiently for her to mention it more than once in her diary:

> *By bedtime I feel I have earned my rest as most of the male inhabitants of Fair Isle who, with the exception of a little desultory harvesting, are still extensively engaged during the day parading the hilltops and cliffs with their hands in their pockets in search of driftwood, which seldom arrives, and when it does is piled round their gardens apparently exclusively for ornament.* (Bedford 1968, 47)

There is an ironic contrast between this early 20th century view of social attitudes and those given by the *First Statistical Account* more than a century earlier; there the inhabitants are described as 'sober, prudent and industrious', and the men are singled out as 'remarkable for their strength and vigour' (*OSA* XIX, 438). The description smacks of being conventionalised and, in keeping with several other stock passages in the texts, it tends to appear as the stylised view of how an island society ought to be rather than how it actually was. The view, for example, of the womenfolk being noted for their 'sweetness and modesty' is not one which can be accepted on the basis of Scott's slightly later comments. Curiously, the words 'sober' and 'industrious' also appear in the *Second Statistical Account* (*NSA* XV, 9). Bedford's criticisms also derive some support from a late 19th century account which compares the inhabitants of Fair Isle and Foula. Comparison between the two similar island-based communities was not uncommon, partly because the two were temporarily part of the same parish (below). Tudor recounts a clearly ill-informed comparison which assumed that the Fair Isle inhabitants ought to have been darker skinned than those on Foula in view of the prolonged visit of the Armada sailors (1883, 513). A later account, although not without bias, seems more positively founded:

> *... and it is a curious fact, that during the last seven years there has been no marriage in the island [Foula], nor illegitimate children; – in this respect affording an extraordinary contrast to the state of Fair Isle. Nor does the contrast end there. In Fair Isle the natives are in general half-starved and ill-clad, seem squalid and unhealthy; and have a look of savage apathy. In Foula the reverse is the case .... It seems difficult to account for the difference between the inhabitants of two small islands so near, and in every respect so similarly situate. The difficulty entirely ceases, however, when it is known that the Fair Islanders live principally by smuggling, and the Foulaese by fishing ...* (Vetch 1882)

Even by this time Fair Isle still retained its museological identity, although perhaps the enigma of the island and its inhabitants had lost something of its elusive charm. Janet Schaw's diary, a work broadly contemporary with the *First Statistical Account*, goes some way to show how noticeable this earlier identity may have been. Her visit was brief, but her descriptions were perceptive:

> *They are entirely different from the inhabitants of Scotland in general, and even from those of the islands that lay next to them; they are of a middling stature, strong built and straight, their complexions uncommonly fair, their skins remarkably smooth, their features high, aquiline noses and small eyes. Their hair is not red but real yellow, and the older ones wore it long on the bottom of the chin which is very peaked. They wore red caps lined with skin and jackets on the same with a paulice of coarse cloth and boots of undressed skin, with the rough side outermost, over which were trousers made of cloth. They are very active and their figures tho' uncouth, are by no means disagreeable.* (Schaw 1939, 39)

Some half a century later Hibbert presented his own view of Shetland fishermen. More basic in tenor, the description is complementary to that of Schaw's, although lack of common points and time difference prevent any Fair Isle idiosyncrasies from being emphasised. Interestingly, Shetland fishermen in general, let alone those of Fair Isle in particular, were still considered distinctive to the outside world and merited their own level of museological interest.

> *The boat-dress of the fishermen is in many respects striking. A worsted cover from the head, similar in form to the common English or Scotch nightcap, is dyed with so many colours, that its bold tints are recognised at a considerable distance, like the stripes of a signal flag. The boatmen are also invested, as with a coat of mail, by a surtout of tanned sheep skin, which covers their arms, and descends from below their chin to their knees; whilst, like an apron or kilt, it overlaps their woolen femoralia; – for with the latter article, it is needless to observe, the Shetlander is better provided than the Gaelic Highlander .... A nobleman, who visited Shetland a few years ago, was, indeed, so struck with the fishing garb of the natives of the place that he took away with him a perfect specimen of the same, for the special purpose of assigning to it a place in his museum, at no remote distance from kindred illustrations of the habits of the Esquimaux or of the New Zealanders.* (Hibbert 1822, 96)

On land, according to Hibbert, the characteristics of Shetland dress were less pronounced, at least as far as men were concerned, although the development of *rivlins* may be peculiar to communities heavily committed to a pastoral economy. The badge denoting family headship appears unrecorded elsewhere. However, as far as the women were concerned, Hibbert was not of the opinion that either they or their dress merited description:

> *The dress of the Shetland peasants differs little from that of the inhabitants of the sea-coast of Scotland. To men whose chief occupation is fishing, the common sailor's jacket is a favourite attire. The red cap, which is a distinctive badge of the master of a family, merits particular attention. It is made of worsted, somewhat resembling in form a common double night cap, but much larger, and gradually tapering to a point, whilst it hangs down the back, after the fashion of the head-dress of a German hussar. It is also dyed with numerous colours. Frequently men wear on their feet rivlins, which are a sort of sandal, made of untanned seal skin, being worn with the hair side outwards and laced on the foot with strings or thongs of leather. Their lightness is particularly adapted for tramping with velocity over the soft heaths or scattholds of the country. The dress of the women merits little attention ...* (Hibbert 1822, 119)

By contrast, women appear in Pløyen's description written around 1839, but bear the same brunt of his bigotry as Shetland peat cutting, sheep neglect and the drinking habits of the Shetland male. The last of these Pløyen saw as being 'a remnant of the barbarian customs of former ages' (Pløyen 1894, 17); not surprisingly, he found little merit among the women either:

> *The dress of the women is as hideous as possible. They all wear nightcaps, which ought to be white, a gown of coloured cotton, which flutters so readily that another indispensible garment is clearly seen beneath it, and a large tartan shawl. With this costume, which has a half stylish cut, they have dirty bare legs and often a basket of peats on their backs. I once met a girl who, thus attired, held an umbrella over herself, and drove a cow on the high road; it seemed to me as if she wished to make herself ridiculous ...* (Pløyen 1894, 197)

Religion

In the Northern Isles of the 18th and 19th centuries social behaviour and morality, not to mention levels of education, were considered to reflect the presence and influence of the Church and its teachings. Fair Isle's geographical position caused some difficulty in this respect in that the inhabitants received the benefits, somewhat irregularly, of a peripatetic ministry controlled from outside the island. This provided a service in the form of baptisms and marriages which were saved up for each visit. It was also the occasion for extended preaching, for checking on the levels of education, and for the public admonishment of any sinners. The system was, at best, a clumsy compromise, but was of long standing and can be extended back to pre-Armada times to the time when the Church on Shetland was administered from Orkney:

> *... the inhabitants of [Shetland] are half-naked and destitute of riches, and support themselves by the eggs of birds and fish; they delight in peace and justice, and have never heard the name of riches and luxury; they live in extreme want and in the perpetual darkness of winter, yet almost all of them by an incredible felicity of nature, reach the summit of old age. Priests come across to them from the Orkneys, baptize the children born during the former year, and celebrate the sacred solemnities, and then, after having purified the caves and huts of the inhabitants by aspersion with holy water, and having received their tithes in hard fish, the priests abundantly enriched, return to the Orkneys.* (Jovius 1548)

The account may be taken from an earlier source and although it contains elements of descriptive licence, it is unlikely that the movement of priests was an invention. Nor is there any strong evidence to suggest that Fair Isle is the place in question, although a subsistence economy based on bird eggs and fish would tend to point to an island like Fair Isle or Foula. As a matter of additional interest, there is an element of correlation in the longevity of the inhabitants; the *First Statistical Account* comments specifically on the same phenomenon (*OSA* XIX, 436).

The mission of clerics out of Orkney rather than elsewhere in Shetland raises questions regarding the structure of church organisation at this time and the development of Christianity in the area as a whole. It is unfortunate that the earliest Christian missions to the north, presumably emanating directly or indirectly from Iona from the 6th and 7th centuries, receive only vague historical mention. Nor has archaeology been able to add much in the way of support for their movements. Monasticism based on the Celtic model almost certainly provided the vehicle for transmission in the later Iron Age, and a number of likely monastic sites have been postulated throughout Shetland (Lamb 1973), although none of these have been excavated or securely dated (see chapter 7). Together with Orkney, indications of early Christianity in Shetland rest with the indirect evidence of carved stones, for example the Papil stone, and artefacts of purported Christian significance. None of these suggest a date much before the end of the 7th century and are as likely to be expressions of Christian contact as much as of a Christian presence. More convincing is the distribution of 'Papa' names within the Northern Isles and the Hebrides; these might be viewed as housing small missionary centres of *papar* (priests) in the primary pre-Norse conversion of the islands (MacDonald 1977).

The monastic network which these names may partially reflect involved small eremitic communities based in locations which on the one hand were sufficiently remote to preserve the required setting for austerity and devotion, such as small islands or promontories, but on the other hand were sufficiently near lay populations to enable missionary work to be performed. In theory it is unlikely that Fair Isle could have satisfied either of these requirements, the island was probably too small to have offered the appropriate degree of isolation from its inhabitants, and too remote from larger areas of population to act as a functioning Christian centre. However, the presence of a sheer promontory site at Burrista (*357*) on the north-west of the island is topographically appropriate for a small eremitic cell, as well as exhibiting minor earthworks which may indicate structural remains. The topographical characteristics of this and other sites (*3* and *229*) which may have fulfilled a similar role are discussed in detail in chapter 4. Burrista is geographically the furthest accessible promontory away from the population centre at the south of the island. As such it has much to commend itself for monastic occupation.

The progress and spread of Christianity was, in the first instance, severely impeded by the Scandinavian colonisation. The degree of destruction to which local Christianity was subjected is likely to have been substantial, as the burial of the St Ninian's Isle treasure quite clearly demonstrates, but there is a suggestion, too, that some ecclesiastical communities may have survived both raids and settlement (Crawford 1987, 166). The resurgence of Christianity in the later Norse period is one in which the emergence of chapels and the presence of the scattald – a taxable land unit which later evolved as an area of commonage – appear to be linked. Shetland as a whole contained around 200 scattalds (one of which was represented by the hill land on Fair Isle) and in some parts, for example on Fetlar, there is an exact correlation between scattalds and known chapel sites (Crawford 1987, fig 68).

Research has also suggested that the scattald itself may pre-date the period of Scandinavian intervention and may belong instead to an earlier phase of territoriality (Smith 1984, 104) – a concept which may also have implications for the dating of those dykes which respect the same division. The arrangement is one in which chapels may be disposed according to a pattern of secular organisation. They emerge, as is widely held (eg Cant 1975, 9), at the behest of local worthies in order to facilitate worship within their own lands. It might indicate, in addition, the transference of cult sites into Christian use. This type of secular autonomy ended with Episcopal control, initially in Orkney at the instigation of Earl Thorfinn in the early 11th century, variously under the sees of Hamburg-Bremen, York, Lund, and finally, in the mid-12th century, Trondheim. The effect on Shetland appears to have been similar to that on Orkney where the districts ultimately developed into full parishes, composed of scattalds and using scattald boundaries.

In the late Middle Ages Shetland contained some 30 head churches with presumed jurisdiction over smaller chapels. The post-Reformation organisation of these was complex and has been discussed in detail elsewhere (Donaldson 1984). However, it is unclear whether one such building was located on Fair Isle. Reference to 'St Peter's Stouk' on the island (Cant 1975, 20 and 43) probably indicates a small land holding from which ecclesiastical rent was due, although it may possibly have had an associated chapel or altar (Cowan and Easson 1976, 219f). The location is not now known. Nor is it clear whether the presence of a building is implied in post-Reformation times when, in 1575, Laurence Sinclair is listed as being the first reader at Fair Isle and Cross Kirk, Dunrossness (Scott 1928, 282) – a 'makeshift' system which seems to have come to an end in the course of a few years (Goudie 1904, 67). The title is one which implies the handling of mission and pastoral work on the island rather than more formal liturgical functions which were conducted on a peripatetic basis by an ordained minister. Sibbald is explicit in the presence of a church on the island in the 17th century, describing it as being 'more regular, and more orderly frequented, than will be easily believed: they always have a Reader who every Sabbath reads the Sacred Scriptures ...'; he additionally comments on the relative infrequency of fornication (Monteith 1845, 52). Kay, writing in 1680, describes 'a little church' which may indicate its survival to that time (Bruce 1908, 56), but at the beginning of the 18th century Brand cites three churches in

Dunrossness: Cross Kirk (at Dunrossness itself), Sandwick and Fair Isle (1701, 83); these appear to be distinct from the numerous small chapels, many of which were ruinous, which Brand also observed throughout the islands. He cited no fewer than 24 chapels in Unst alone, marvelling at the size of the stones in their construction. He attributed the carriage of these stones to 'superstitious zealots in times of Popery' (1701, 181).

The church to which Brand and most later commentators alluded was undoubtedly the building, demolished earlier this century, at Kirk Haven, whose presence is recorded in an early photograph taken around 1900 (plate 11.2) and whose lowest courses now provide part of the modern graveyard enclosure. An appeal for a new church had already been set up as early as 1891 in the *Shetland Times*. It was, according to the report, 'at least half a century since a new church was actually required' (March 21st, 2) and appears to have been necessary on structural grounds. The photograph, although worn, shows a rectangular single-storey structure of 18th century character; the construction is of stone but the roof appears to be slated. By the time of the photograph it had undergone numerous repairs and renovations to the extent that many of the original features and materials other than the basic shape may have changed. The point is made by Fotheringhame who, about one century

Plate 11.2 Photograph of kirk on Fair Isle taken around 1900. The building was demolished earlier this century. By kind permission of Ann Sinclair.

before the photograph was taken, described it as 'almost an entire ruin' lacking a roof and with the seats covered in mould. As a matter of comparison, in the early 1700s the ordination of the Sandwick minister took place in the kirkyard for want of a building (Scott 1928, 282), suggesting perhaps that there too the medieval structure was approaching the end of its useful life. This is also apparent from Hibbert's melodramatic lament for the church at Quendale which had formerly been 'one of the neatest religious edifices in the country' and which was subsequently replaced by a new parish church:

> *The ravages of the blowing sand had then commenced, and whenever the wind came from the sea, the sand was dislodged, and an inundation took place, presenting in miniature the appearance of an Arabian desert ... clouds of drifted particles that obscured the horizon, through which horsemen and footmen were dimly descried at a distance, like the ghosts of Ossian through the dun clouds of rocky Morven ... [grains of sand] easily insinuated themselves through the minutest crannies, and were diffused over all the pews. At length the walls were no longer able to resist the causes, which, in removing the sand to a distance, undermined their foundations; melancholy exposures, at the same time, took place of the bodies of the recent dead, the remembrance of which is still perpetuated by numerous skulls and other relics of mortality ...* (Hibbert 1822, 112)

An earlier church may have lain beneath the Kirk Haven site, a possibility strengthened by both conventional and geophysical survey which have identified the presence of earlier boundary features surviving on the western side, together with a series of associated anomalies between the boundary and the present graveyard wall (*229*, figs 11.3 and 11.4). Exploratory excavation along the adjacent coastline has additionally produced midden and coarse pottery, the latter indicating a dating range considerably in excess of the period represented by the 18th century foundation alone (N Fojut, pers comm). This could point either to the site of St Peter's Chapel or, conversely, to an intermediate foundation pre-dating that of the 18th century. Also to be considered within this equation is the field name 'Kirkalees' to the north of Shirva and the tradition of burial in that vicinity. As a further possible site for any chapel dedicated to St Peter, this lies north of the four main settlement nuclei and at some distance from the main population centre. Its position adjacent to Shirva (assuming the dwelling site to have been contemporaneous) may indicate some particular, if unidentified, association.

The issue is one which also has a burial implication. One of Fair Isle's archaeological problems is the whereabouts of its dead, not only for prehistoric and medieval populations, but also for those of more modern times. The issue is by no means unique to Fair Isle, and although it poses well-known problems of

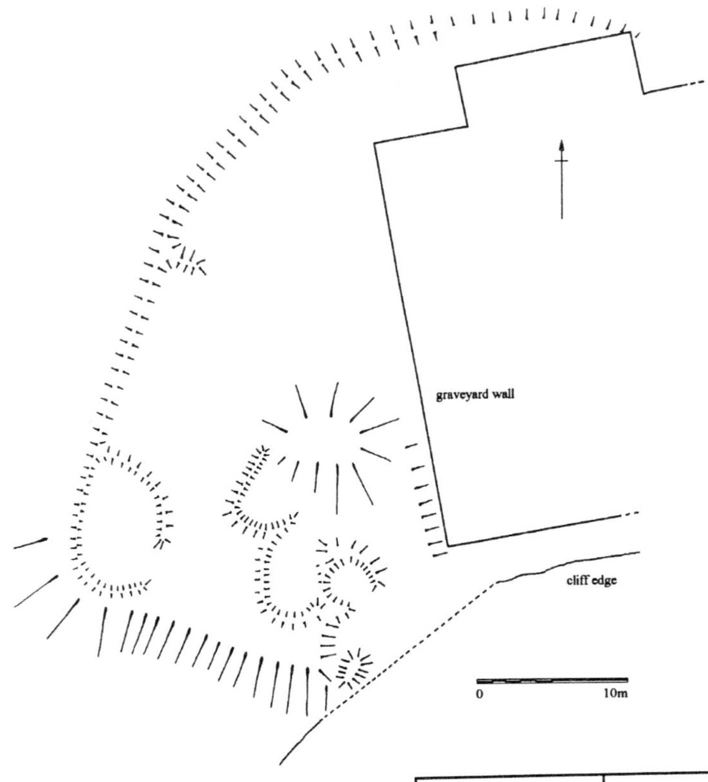

Fig 11.3 Survey plan of area around site of former kirk on Fair Isle showing possible boundary and other features.

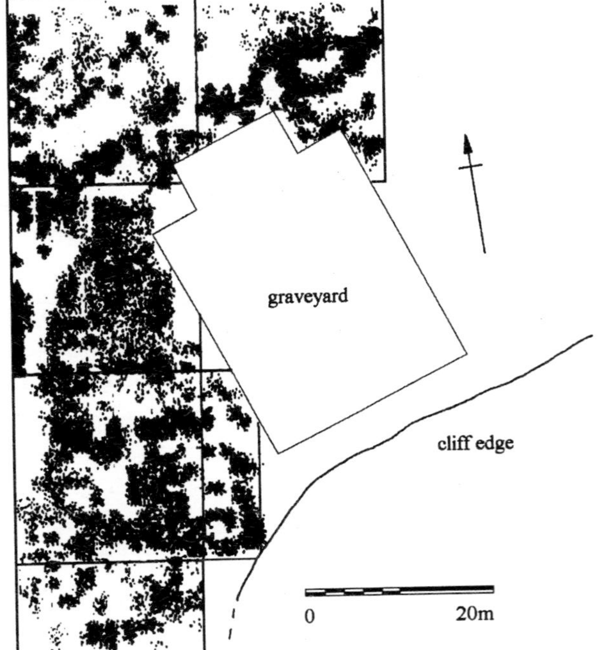

Fig 11.4 Dot density plan of fluxgate gradiometer survey around former kirk site (see also fig 11.3).

interpretation, for example within the Norse period, it rarely receives attention in periods such as the 18th and 19th centuries when the population (and hence burial) figures are known to be at their peak. The geology of the island is unsuited to deep or successive burials, nor is the present graveyard at Kirk Haven sufficiently raised to indicate the accumulation of humic soils which continuous use would generate. On a visit in 1911 the Duchess of Bedford made a fortuitous observation which might go some way to resolve the problem in more recent times:

> *I sought consolation by standing under the shelter of the old disused chapel which borders the little graveyard, where Fair Islanders take their last long rest .... But if it were me, I should not like several Fair Islanders piled on the top, with only a thin layer of turf between, which is the usual method of burial in these outlying islands.* (Bedford 1968, 52)

Elsewhere in Shetland similar problems may also have existed. Graveyards were notoriously ill-kept; Tudor particularly commented on the neat state of the Foula burial ground in comparison to the 'boneyards' he had encountered elsewhere throughout Orkney and Shetland (1883, 524).

The church at Kirk Haven is the one at which visiting ministers presumably officiated during their irregular seasonal visits. For most of Fair Isle's historical life responsibility for this lay with the minister of Dunrossness in whose parish the island officially stood, and from where, in the early 17th century, the minister was said to spend six weeks annually (Monteith 1845, 52). For reasons which appear to have been largely misguided Fair Isle, Foula and the Skerries were combined under the charge of a single ministry under an itinerant missionary arrangement from Nesting around 1730, but by 1794 this had proved to be wholly unworkable, the charge was abolished and Fair Isle reverted again to the parish of Dunrossness (Scott 1928, 285). According to Gifford, writing around 1733, the unfortunate incumbent of this three-island parish resided on Fair Isle where there was a small church, but received only a relatively small stipend 'considering his travel and dangerous passage' (1786, 17).

John Mill became minister of Dunrossness in 1743 and travelled intermittently from Dunrossness to Fair Isle until his death in 1803. The diary of his activities, edited by Goudie nearly a century later, spans a period of ministry from his first visit in 1753 until his final voyage as an octogenarian. His initial visit was undertaken in order to administer the sacrament but also involved preaching almost daily for three weeks (Goudie 1889, 11). Successive visits are more amply documented, for example in 1779 he 'rebuked two couples for ante-nuptial fornication, publickly' as well as wedding two other pairs, baptising five children and taking to task several others for 'Sabbath profanation' (Goudie 1889, 57). In 1793 the level of responsibilities are defined further. He 'examined the Society's School, and all the young people of the Isle upon the questions in the Assemblie's Catechism, baptized nine children, ordained four Elders, rebuk'd and dismissed two delinquents, preached two Sabbaths before and after noon, and distributed what was collected in that time among the poor of Fair Isle' (Goudie 1889, 141). For at least part of his ministry a precentor may have been appointed from among the islanders in order to arrange worship on a weekly basis in his absence (Ballantyne 1993, 15).

Reports of the infrequency of visits by Mill and his successors are relatively commonplace but usually fail to take into account the difficulty not only of travelling to Fair Isle, but also of getting back again. The hapless Catholic priest, George Griffin, who wrote to his Bishop regarding the difficulties in reaching the island had been sold a story by Orkneymen that when a minister was required the islanders conveyed him to the island, but that he was required to make his own way home again (Dilworth 1988, 120). Two Congregationalist preachers in 1799 were told that the islanders had not heard a sermon for six years (Anon 1799), and Bishop John Geddes who visited Orkney in 1790 and saw Fair Isle in the distance was told that a minister from Shetland visited the island once every three or four years but that until lately no sermon had been preached there for the last eleven (Anderson 1955, 142). By the time of Scott's visit in 1814 this situation was partly remedied in that the minister's visit was annual. For the remainder of the year the scriptures would be read by the schoolteacher, although during the period leading up to Scott's time the schoolteacher's persistent inebriation had prevented this duty from being performed (Laughlan 1982, 53).

Much of the information derived from these descriptions and accounts do little more than provide colour to a historical sketch, often with a high degree of personal or religious bias. The effects of religious teachings and attitudes other than for burial or for church building are only of passing archaeological interest or concern. There is, however, a relevance with respect to any inhibitions or restraints imposed by religious authority on the livelihood of the inhabitants, particularly in environments where the subsistence economy was finely balanced. A case in point is the 'Sabbath profanation' to which Mill referred which might develop from the tortuous balance between religious obedience and subsistence necessity. One such example was recorded by a visitor to Unst in the early 1800s when, on a Sunday, some 200 whales, 'huge monsters tumbling and snorting', swam into the bay at Uyea. Being the sabbath, the Shetlanders moved their boats down to the beach but were restrained from launching them until midnight when the sabbath had passed.

> *And a few minutes before that hour came, the cunning whales as though aware that their day of rest was likewise past, moved slowly out of the Sound, and made for the open sea.* (Atkinson 1832)

12

Water Milling on Fair Isle

IN the 18th and 19th centuries the Fair Isle population was aided in its subsistence routine by a small group of water mills located on the east side of the island at Funniquoy, fed by the Burn of Gilsetter. The harnessing of natural water power as an energy resource holds an absorbing position in the history of technology; in corn milling, as here, the water-driven quern followed the saddle and rotary quern as a next step in the evolution of a basic subsistence activity – drudgery and tedium providing the stimuli for crude mechanical innovation. The Fair Isle mills belong to a common basic milling tradition which originated among the Mediterranean peasant cultures of the classical world and which followed, without major change in character, a curious geographical route during the next two millennia. Even by the time of its gradual abandonment in late 19th and early 20th century Shetland, where the small crofting communities provided a comparable economic environment to that of the Mediterranean, both structure and mechanics seemed little altered from their original counterparts.

Background

In view of the conservatism of milling tradition and the varying interpretations which attempt to explain its geographical spread, the background merits some discussion in order to place the Fair Isle mills in context. A Greek epigram widely attributed to one Antipater of Thessalonika in the 2nd century BC suggests that water milling had a novelty value at that time, the passage frequently being cited as evidence for a Mediterranean origin (eg Bennett and Elton 1899, 6). The relevance here is less for this geographical focus than for the type of mill apparently represented. Mills belonged to two mechanical types: those with the vertical water wheel – the types which feature in the rural imagery of medieval England – and those less well-known which possessed a horizontal wheel. In the former, the water course either drove the paddles from the base of the wheel (*undershot*) or, less commonly, was engineered to fall against the paddles at the top of the wheel (*overshot*). Both these vertical variants required substantial water pressure and were suited to milling on a large or commercial scale, a factor which had profound sociological implications within feudal populations.

In the horizontal wheeled type, however, the water flow was diverted, often by means of moveable timber lades, down against angled paddles to turn the wheel in a horizontal plane. In both mill types the movement of the wheel caused the millstone to turn, but in the case of the horizontal wheel the gearing and general mechanics were much simpler and the overall device much smaller.

The various histories of milling are not in dispute over a general Mediterranean origin for the use of water power (eg Bloch 1967, 138), but debate still continues regarding the relative antiquity of the two different mechanical types. The issue is clouded in that these differences almost certainly reflect topographical and social factors (below), although the distribution only partly indicates this.

The distribution of the horizontal mill is relatively clear and can be traced from the Greek area of the Mediterranean (hence the definition 'Greek' mill) into parts of eastern Europe and also via central Asia into Nepal and parts of China. Later, and possibly due to Roman influences, it spread into coastal parts of Spain and France appearing ultimately in Ireland, the Northern and Western Isles of Scotland (including Fair Isle), and parts of Scandinavia. The Nordic distribution is less easy to evaluate either directionally or chronologically and the mill type is confusingly termed 'Norse' by some writers on the basis of its likely northern movement under Norse influence (eg Goudie 1886, 294). Other writers, however, have maintained that horizontal milling was not properly established in Scandinavia until as late as the 14th century and stress the need for alternative hypotheses (Bennett and Elton 1899, 138).

A description of the vertical type first appears in *De Architectura*, a 1st century AD text by Vitruvius (hence 'Vitruvian' mill), and the origins are traditionally ascribed to Roman times. The distribution complements that of the horizontal form although there is also a strong case argued for its role as a replacement in certain areas where the horizontal mill failed to survive the medieval period (Bennett and Elton 1899, 10).

The horizontal mill was the simpler form and certainly the easier to construct. It possessed a simplicity of design, 'the sort of contraption which might be discovered by anyone with some ingenuity but no mechanical knowledge' (Gauldie 1981, 116), in which one revolution of the wheel entailed a single revolution of the millstone located directly overhead. The nature of its moving parts combined with rude materials of construction gave it a crude appeal with 'all the attraction of clockwork, meccano and steam engines' (Rahtz 1981, 1), while its noisy operation evoked the popular name 'click' mill.

Its historical popularity seems to have been unquestionable. Travellers' accounts from the Middle Ages and post-medieval era in Greece, the Holy Land and other parts of Europe attest to the strength of its ongoing tradition (Bennett and Elton 1899, 10). In late 19th century Shetland the introduction (and imposition) of the Scottish vertical mill was lamented by Goudie because it belonged to 'a race and era altogether different in character' (1886, 280), a notion supported on Faroe where specific horizontal examples could be traced back for over 250 years (Williamson

1946, 85-90). More recent observations in Romania, where almost 900 examples were recorded in 1957 (Irimie and Bucur 1971, 427), and also in Crete (Rahtz 1981, 8-13) have demonstrated not only the stubbornness of this tradition but also the potential value of an ethnographic record.

Horizontal mills – mechanics and operation

The greatest weight of information deriving from post-medieval examples in Shetland undoubtedly arises from Goudie's late 19th century investigations of extant examples and from his compilation of records. These were culled from the *Tours* and *Descriptions* of informed visitors which litter the documentation of the Northern Isles in the 18th and 19th centuries. His description of a typical example (1886, 267-279) divides the building and its fittings under three headings: the structure; the prime mover (water flow and wheel); and the grinding apparatus respectively. It seems appropriate to follow a similar order for discussion here.

Post-medieval types show that in the Northern Isles the horizontal mill was normally of compact size, typically between 3.5-5.5m long and 3-4m wide (Fenton 1978, 403), and consisted of two compartments, an upper and a lower, set within thick rough stone walls and roofed with turf over tie beams (fig 12.1). Landt, writing in the early 19th century, described Faroese types as having roofs 'supported by four pillars – sometimes built of stone mixed with mud' (1810, 293), a crudeness paralleled in Shetland where a typical contemporary example was 'a low shed of unhewn stones stretching across a diminutive streamlet' (Hibbert 1822, 19). Hibbert made a valuable comparison with water mills in England and, perhaps more importantly, with those in Scotland (presumably vertical types), noting that by comparison the grinding machinery in the Shetland mills seemed 'destined for a race of pygmies' (*ibid*). In Shetland the upper chamber might be built on solid ground as well as over the lower chamber, depending on the land fall, giving a substantially greater floor area. The lower contained the wheel and axle system (*tirl*) and acted as a channel for the water while the upper contained the millstones and the (?raised) working floor.

A single revolution of the millwheel effected a single revolution of the millstone, mounted directly above on a small iron bar (*sile*) attached to a common axle which was often bedded in a metal socket or suitably worked stone located in the stream bed. One popular innovation was to mount the lower end of the axle through a moveable length of timber (*sole tree*) which could then be raised or lowered by means of a vertical timber (*lightening tree*) located through the floor of the upper chamber. Grain could be fed to the stone from a hopper suspended from the rafters and agitated by the crude device of a stick with one end connected to the hopper and the other dragging loose on the millstone. One early 19th century visitor to Shetland

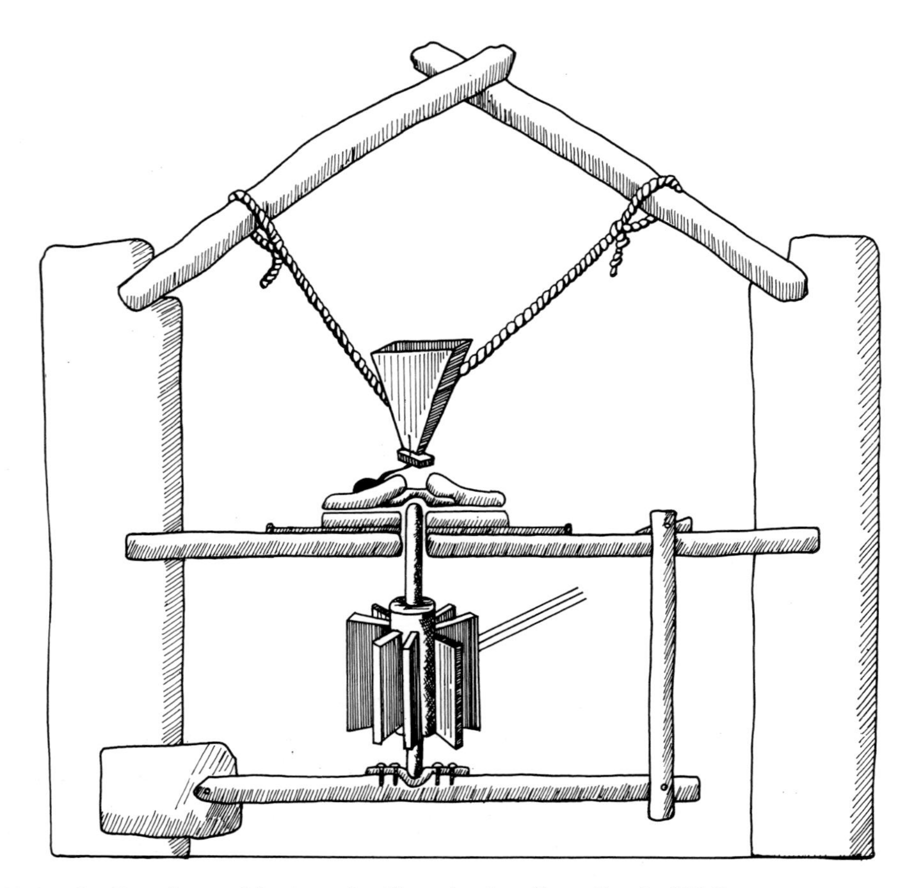

Fig 12.1 Outline of general horizontal mill mechanism (from Goudie 1886).

commented specifically on this seemingly clumsy and insecure arrangement, making the point that the clumsiness and insecurity of the device was, in fact, essential for its proper functioning:

> *... the motion ... ingeniously obtained by selecting the most unsubstantial parts of the roof to attach the supporting strings to; so that the tremulous of the whole edifice from the passage of the water below, so far from being an undesirable symptom of instability and decay, is indispensibly necessary.* (Atkinson 1832)

A number of regional differences have been observed for the workings in the upper chamber, for example with the Faroese types (Williamson 1946, 85), but the overall principles and mechanics as portrayed by Goudie (1886, fig 2) are held in common. The terminology and technical jargon have also been the subject of study and appropriate comparable listings made in relevant north European languages (eg Curwen 1944, 141; Rahtz and Bullough 1977, 31-7).

Effective operation required a supply of water which was both consistent in flow and sufficiently strong to turn the wheel, both factors being evident from archaeological as well as from ethnographic examples. At the Saxon horizontal mill at Tamworth, for example, Rahtz identified the remains of a large clay-bonded wooden millpool providing for water retention (Rahtz and Meeson 1992, 22), while a Late Iron Age form from Denmark with a similar reservoir arrangement used heather as a sealant (Steensberg 1952, 53). The use of troughs, lades, even hollowed-out tree trunks and damming seems to have been relatively common and is particularly evident in Ireland where timber remains are best preserved. The extent of the Fair Isle damming system illustrates the importance of a wide catchment area necessary for a head of water suitable for the functioning of a number of mills working simultaneously (fig 12.2). The evidence at Old Windsor, the only Saxon site excavated other than Tamworth and by all accounts a high status complex (Hope-Taylor 1958), probably illustrates an extreme scale of operations. There the horizontal mill replaced a sophisticated vertical form based around a triple-wheeled system fed from a great ditch over 20 feet wide and a three-quarters of a mile long. Its horizontal successor apparently followed this original route although with a narrower width, attesting to the potential magnitude of even this primitive mill type.

The need for a fairly fast stream may to some extent have limited the suitability of the horizontal mill in Orkney where the topography lacks the severity of Shetland. This problem could partly be overcome by the use of reservoirs and dams as evident near the restored mill at Dounby, Orkney (Cruden 1947), and from excavation of examples in Denmark where an equally unsuitable terrain is common (Steensberg 1952, 33). Recent excavations at Orphir, Orkney, have uncovered the remains of an important mill of the later Norse period (Batey 1992), and here too the nature of the landscape must have necessitated reservoir collection. Examples recovered from excavations in Ireland, at Morett, Co. Laois (Lucas 1953, 16) illustrate similar modifications.

Increased pressure could be produced by narrowing the water channel to the wheel (Avitsur 1971, 391) or, according to an example from 17th century Jutland, by the judicious positioning of a large stone (Steensberg 1952, 29). Alternatively, in most cases the system could be 'turned off' simply by redirecting the flow of water away from the wheel. The force of the stream would undoubtedly have been greater during the winter months and there is strong evidence, for example from Rousay, Orkney, to suggest that winter milling, depending on the availability of grain, might even be preferable (Fenton 1978, 396). Indeed, on Fair Isle Eunson makes it quite clear that the functioning of the water mills was a winter phenomenon (1976, 18). Goudie, in citing Gibson's *Camden,* makes a similar point by describing a mill in the Isle of Man which had insufficient water as being a 'cheap sort of mill, which as it cost very little, is no great loss though it stands six months in the year' (Goudie 1886, 288). In

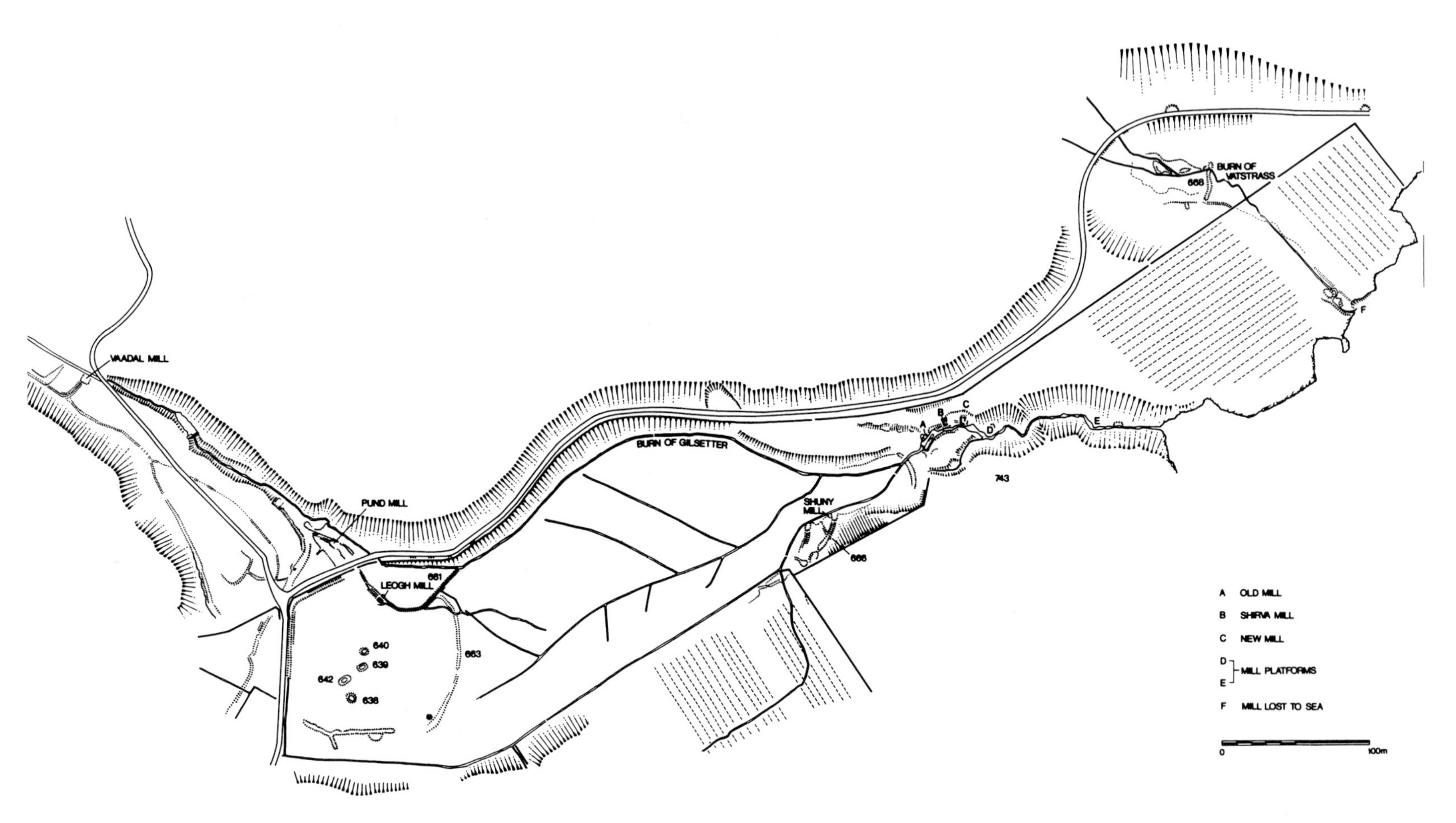

Fig 12.2 General location of milling sites in the Funniquoy area, including water coursing systems. Based on original survey by the Royal Commission.

addition, the very nature and scale of the horizontal-wheeled operation lends itself to problems of freezing, flooding or drying up during the respective seasonal extremes.

The most incontrovertible evidence for horizontal milling is the recovery of the wheel or tirl itself. The most complete archaeological example hails from Moycraig, Co. Antrim, which shows facilities for 19 individual paddles or feathers with 10 still 'perfect' (MacAdam 1856, 6), while the Tamworth wheel consisted of the shaft only showing recesses for at least 12 paddles (Rahtz and Meeson 1992, fig 95). The paddle itself is of some interest given that in later examples there appears to be a regional distinction between those with a flat surface and those which are curved. The former appear to follow a distribution in Scotland, Faroe and Norway while the latter appear more specifically in Ireland and S Europe (Lucas 1955, 109; Reynolds 1970, 61). The evidence consists of an awkward mixture of archaeological and ethnographic information but is, nevertheless, difficult to dismiss. A single paddle recovered from Tamworth belongs to the southern group, being curved on one face (Rahtz and Meeson 1992, 100-103), the cup-like form enabling the water to act by weight as well as by pressure. Curved paddles, however, required a more laborious or elaborate method of fixing to the shaft, sometimes by the preparation of curved recesses.

Water direction was more important to the flat northern types and this could be achieved either by setting the paddles at an angle or by ensuring that the water fell on the paddles from a specific direction, usually by means of a moveable lade. This presumably depended on local factors, for example in Faroe Williamson noted two mills, one with eight paddles fixed vertically (1946, 84) and the other with twelve paddles set at a slight angle (*ibid*, 86). Observations by Knox, writing in the early part of this century, described two of the last horizontal mills working in Ireland in Co. Mayo and pointed out that in one case the paddles were circumscribed by a thin iron hoop while in the other they were kept in position by a system of iron stays (1907, 268). It was, apparently, not unusual for paddles to become loose, 'fly out and float down the stream'.

Millstones, as well as being good archaeological survivors, hold an important place in milling studies in view of the complexities of geology, manufacturing and trade. At Tamworth, for example, 20 individual millstones were estimated from the *c* 200 pieces recorded and it was possible to demonstrate that while most were locally produced from North Midlands gritstone some were imported from the Rhineland (Wright 1992). The diameter of the Tamworth stones varied between *c* 0.6-0.7m, slightly smaller than the later Shetland examples cited by Fenton as being between *c* 0.75-0.9m (1978, 402). Diameter is a potentially significant dimension; the *First Statistical Account* for Unst indicated that the diameter of the tirl was always equal to that of the millstone (*OSA* XIX, 508). On Skye in the 19th century millstones were produced from the granophyre found on the island of Raasay, from where they were also traded to the adjacent Mainland (Nicolson 1930, 398). The majority of the stones used in southern Shetland, however, probably derive from Colsay which contained the most suitable geological deposits, although according to one entry in the *First Statistical Account* their ultimate appearance on Shetland was only 'at the expense of laborious transport and much inconvenience' (*OSA* XIX, 193f).

Distribution and social implications

The advantages of the horizontal mill were the simplicity of design (and hence its simplicity of construction and operation) and its ability to function on a narrow stream with a minimum of water. Seen essentially as 'an element of peasant culture' (Curwen 1944, 143), its historical and ethnographic associations lie with individual household units or small groups of such where it provides small-scale milling rather than the larger scale commercial production with which the vertical wheeled forms became associated. In as much as the evidence shows, these mills were built and used by individuals or small groups of individuals sharing by rotation. The type of subsistence economy represented was both domestic and independent and therefore clearly at variance with any centralised control or authority.

The obliteration of 'the little Norse mill' in England is traditionally seen as a consequence of changes in social organisation (Bennett and Elton 1899, 12), but within more peripheral areas the horizontal mill either persisted or became reintroduced, the latter seeming more likely on present evidence. Goudie's description of late 19th century Shetland bears witness to their density in the post-medieval landscape, one standing 'near every homestead ... turning its tiny axle ... either alone or as one of a series, corresponding as the case may be to the extent and requirements of the more or less sparsely peopled district around' (1886, 257). A similarly dense picture has been produced for other island areas such as Colonsay and Oronsay (Bennett and Elton 1889, 16) or the Faroes (Williamson 1946, 83).

The pedigree, however, is less easy to evaluate, partly because of sketchy documentation and partly through possible replacement of horizontal mills by vertical types. Recent research in Ireland has pointed towards the two types co-existing as early as the 7th century (Rynne 1989). While the endpoints of the horizontal tradition are identifiable, especially in the post-medieval records and landscapes of Shetland, the intervening centuries are poorly recorded, or more strictly fail to provide the technological information that would be of most value. Illustrative material is at a premium from before the 12th century and surviving medieval representations have been found to be exclusively of the vertical type (Rahtz 1981, 3). Even in Shetland the earliest illustration of a horizontal mill belongs to the late 18th century.

Much now relies on excavation work, and this has been particularly fruitful in Ireland (Baillie 1980) in establishing a 7th-10th century constructional period for the horizontal type giving the important implication of a pre-Norse introduction – an idea long considered but unproven (Curwen 1944, 144). Although only nominally supporting the earlier view that the horizontal mill was brought to Ireland during Roman times (Bennett and Elton 1899, 81), these dates seriously question the traditional concept of a direct Viking influence (eg MacAdam 1856, 10). On this basis the presence of the horizontal mill on Shetland might be seen as deriving from Ireland on transmission route to Scandinavia, and not *vice versa.*

Excavation elsewhere in Britain has produced a horizontal example at Tamworth from a similar period and another seemingly replacing a vertical type at Old Windsor, Berkshire (Hope-Taylor 1958, 183), both possibly reflecting the 'exceptional resources and technological leadership' available to important royal estates (Rahtz and Bullough 1977, 27). These stand as exceptional examples within an interpreted tradition which assumes the vertical mill introduced by the Romans to be the standard English type, although some historians take the view of a more substantive later impetus at the hands of monastic orders (Lucas 1953, 3). The Domesday evidence of the 11th century identifies some 5600 mills, with the greatest concentrations lying in central and eastern England (Hodgen 1939, 267). All are thought to be of the vertical type although none have been subject to excavation. Research undertaken into 16th century (vertical) mills in England produced a tally of around 2700 examples (Jones 1971), attesting to the persisting importance of centralised milling facilities.

Centralised milling was an important element of the English feudal system and one which necessitated the presence of large-scale processing and, normally, a resident miller. His reputation as an evil, thieving figure and an 'agent of manorial exploitation' (Bloch 1967, 140) became legendary, literature from Chaucer onwards seeing him as a stock character of greed and treachery. Horizontal mills were unsuitable for large-scale processing not only through size and efficiency, but also because their localised use was directly at odds with the concept of centralised manorial authority. There appear to be no records attesting either to their destruction or replacement and the question regarding their pre-Conquest distribution (or even presence) must remain open.

History has placed greater emphasis on the sociological impact and oppression caused by the more fundamental change from handquerns to water power, a development which evoked violent confrontation best exampled in the early 13th century among the monks of Jumiéges, Normandy, with the compulsory breaking of handmills (Bloch 1967, 154). Bloch's detailed study of these events chronicles the uneasy evolution of water milling in medieval Europe (1967, 150-160) and additionally illustrates legal problems concerning water and water coursing which also seem to have been relevant to the early horizontal mill in Ireland (Lucas 1953, 32). Milling effectively became a feudal monopoly, although this occurs somewhat later and in a more diluted way in Orkney and Shetland under the lairds.

For this reason, no doubt, these legal issues seem less pronounced in Scottish studies (eg MacAdam 1856, 7), although a number of problems have been collated from the Northern Isles particularly by Clouston (1925a and b) and by Fenton (1978, 396-410), including evidence of attempts to enforce regulations banning handquerns. Reference is also made to 'multures' – payments made by individual farms allowing the right to use specific mills. Clouston's analysis of the relevant documentation for this period implicitly suggests the presence of earlier 'click' mills and the conditions required for those who built their own. This highlights a fundamental problem of the study, namely the extent of any continuity in the horizontal mill tradition between the time of its early introduction into Britain, as dated in Ireland (Baillie 1980, 62) and Tamworth (Rahtz and Meeson 1992, 9), and its observed use and decline in the late 18th and 19th centuries.

Between those early centuries and the post-medieval period evidence for the horizontal mill is unforthcoming, partly because the sparse documentary record pertains exclusively to the vertical wheeled mills and partly because archaeological research designs have never seen the issue as being one of great priority. The result is therefore an apparent re-emergence of the horizontal mill around the 18th and 19th centuries in those areas such as Shetland where landscape and society were again more conducive to the nature of its operation. Whether it persisted quietly throughout the intervening years remains a matter for speculation, its presence being by inference rather than by positive identification and record. A re-invention or re-introduction is difficult to envisage, although in the case of Shetland the latter is plausible by analogy with boat-building. Continued post-medieval trade with Norway resulted in the reintroduction of Norse boat-building techniques and styles into Shetland, thus re-establishing a tradition initially set in Viking times (Osler 1983, 18). On this basis there is surely no reason why the horizontal mill should not have followed similar routes.

British and Irish examples

Physical evidence of the earliest horizontal type is best seen from Ireland, where a combination of land surface changes and waterlogging provide ideal conditions for preservation. The archaeological circumstances, however, have not always been similarly ideal, many occurring during drainage operations. The recorded finds tend to comprise of scattered assemblages of blades, oak beams and identifiable components of water coursing systems such as at Ballykilleen, Co. Offaly (Lucas 1955). MacAdam's pioneering study of Irish mills (1856), even by the mid-19th century, had plenty of material to work from, notably the remains of a wheel and shaft from a bog at Moycraig, Co. Antrim. He describes this as being 'the most perfect specimen yet found in Ireland' (1856, 6), implying the presence of other examples known at the time.

Discoveries in the 19th century are otherwise well-documented (Bennett and Elton 1899, 13-15), including a framework and water coursing at Ballymartin, Kilkenny, a trough/lade system at Bantry and other generalised material remains. Lucas' reconstruction of the Morett, Co. Laois, example (1953, fig 4) shows what is presumably a representative version although with a somewhat elaborate water system, while a further form at Killogrone, Co. Kerry (1953, fig 2) appears to be exceptional. The great advantage of these early Irish mills is in demonstrating variation around a common theme, the variation normally being attributable to landfall, constructional materials or local need.

Irish literature contains a relatively plentiful supply of useful references, initially discussed by MacAdam (1856) and later pursued in a paper devoted to horizontal mills in Ireland by Lucas (1953), which included sources of both a historical and miraculous nature from the early Christian period (also Bennett and Elton 1899, 87f). Lucas' list of sites has since been revised, although using slightly different criteria (Wikander 1986, 154), and Baillie's list of 12 dated sites (1980) has now been increased to over 20 (Baillie, pers comm), attesting not only to the wealth of material available but also to the growing role of these remains in Irish oak chronologies. Unfortunately, even today, the remains are not necessarily recovered in the most ideal circumstances, for example the remains at Drumard, Co. Derry (Baillie 1975, 28). However, partial recovery there and elsewhere has been sufficient for dating purposes and the major contribution of Irish mill studies lies in this quarter.

In Shetland itself, despite at least one late medieval reference and a number of place-names such as *Kwenitaps* (mill-foundations) and *Queenigeo* (mill-geo) which may point to a long tradition of this type of milling (B Smith, pers comm), the surviving remains appear to be those of the post-medieval era. Few of these have been investigated in any detail and the extent of their antiquity or even their tradition is left open. Pioneering work by Gilbert Goudie (1886) not only considered the Shetland horizontal mill within a wider northern European context, but also involved the physical restoration of mill remains at Troswick at the Loch of Clumlie, one of a line of eight mills and sluices (reproduced in Fenton 1978, fig 199). A simple but valuable observation by Low in the later 18th century (1774, 74) describes the Shetland mill as being 'little better than a handmill or quern' and is one of the earliest reliable illustrated accounts. A further useful description of the mills belongs to Scott who, in his novel *The Pirate* published in 1822, wrote that Shetland inhabitants were 'obliged to have at least 50 in each parish, each trundling away upon its paltry millstone, under the thatch of a roof no bigger than a bee-skep'. Even allowing for literary licence the description emphasises both number and size, two factors echoed elsewhere in travellers' descriptions.

Scott visited Shetland in 1814. The observations in his diary represent one of the more detailed early accounts of horizontal millworking in Shetland and merits quotation here:

> *The wheel is horizontal with the cogs turning diagonally to the water; the beam stands upright and is inserted in a stone quern of the old-fashioned construction. This simple machine is enclosed in a hovel about the size of a pig-sty – and there is the mill! There are about 500 such mills in Shetland, each incapable of grinding more than a sack at a time.* (Laughlan 1982, 29)

Even by the later part of that century and probably at the peak of mill usage in Shetland, little had changed. One description denoted horizontal mills as being:

> *... built like all other structures, of stone or turf, the only abundant and ever-present material of construction thatched with peats, or strips of turf, weighted with stones for securing against storms. No portion of the material is purchased, except as a single clasp of iron which is fixed in the running shoe. Five or six families co-operate in the building of a mill ...* (Evershed 1974, 197)

Such economy of construction was an important point in their favour throughout the various areas of distribution. Those in the Western Isles, for example, were seen as being particularly basic, one visitor pointing out that 'it would not be easy to construct the horizontal mill on cheaper terms' (MacCulloch 1819, 30). Available local materials were invariably relied upon, even to the extent of utilising a whale vertebra as a tirl (now in the Lerwick museum) in the Shetland mill at Stromfirth.

At about this time the Ordnance Survey map shows six mills on Fair Isle and 11 on Foula (Shaw 1984, fig 2) with 36 in Dunrossness, the closest part of Mainland Shetland (Goudie 1886, 281). The density can perhaps best be envisaged from the 24 mills within the six square miles of Papa Stour (Fenton 1978, 408), and the frequently cited entry in the *First Statistical Account* for Aithsting and Sandsting (*OSA* XIX, 587) which refers to 50 water mills in the parish and 'handquerns without number'. In the Western Isles, too, the (earlier) first edition maps show a considerable spread with some 150 located along the north-west coastline (Shaw 1984, fig 3) although it is unclear how many of these were of the horizontal type. On Mull only three of the eight noted by Goudie were horizontal (1886, 285), whereas MacAdam's earlier comment that the Lewis mills were 'probably the greatest curiosity a stranger can meet with on the island' (1856, 13) leaves little doubt that these were predominantly horizontal examples. In Faroe nine mills were noted by an observer visiting the islands in 1781-2 (Svabo 1924) who also commented on the location of three mill ruins. Williamson's study of these interprets a likely Shetland influence in their construction – an influence he rather unconvincingly ascribes to boats calling at Shetland en route between Bergen and Torshavn (1946, 84).

By contrast with other islands and island groups, Orkney shows a different picture. Around AD 1600 some 50 mills are identifiable within the Orkney group (Fenton 1978, 398) although it is unclear as to the types represented. Using evidence from later 15th and early 16th century rentals Fenton has interpreted the presence of both types (1978, 397), although by the beginning of the 17th century almost all the horizontal mills had presumably disappeared from the landscape with the introduction of various oppressive measures. Lord Robert Stewart's imposed system by which farms were limited to a specific mill created a structure within which the small horizontal type was both ineffective and politically dangerous. The history of the surviving larger 'feudal' mills and the monopolies they enjoyed has been detailed at length by Clouston (1925b). He too finds evidence that in some remote or inaccessible Orkney districts the older forms still existed (1925a, 50). The only functioning horizontal mill which survives in Orkney, now in state guardianship, was constructed near Dounby between 1822-4, remarkably late considering the demise of other smaller mills in the Orkney islands. Shortage of flour in two world wars gave simple mills of this type a new importance (Fenton 1978, 408), but their usefulness was otherwise superseded.

Away from the islands in mainland Scotland the horizontal mill made little impact or left little evidence. The *First Statistical Account* entry for a lowland parish in Ayrshire describes horizontal mills (inferred) as 'miserable machines, at which much time was consumed and the grain horribly abused' (*OSA* VI), while an entry for Reay, Caithness and Sutherland, describes the type as a 'highland' mill (*OSA* VII, 576). In that area Goudie noted the use of a system of fixing four wooden beams at right angles along the sides of the lower chamber to form a square frame (1886, 283); this makes an interesting analogy with preserved waterlogged timbers from early Irish sites. Absence of suitable timber on Shetland may explain why this particular feature seems not to occur outside the mainland; it might also go some way to explain why the wheels and paddles of the mainland examples were also substantially larger. Their occurrence is recorded in other parts of Scotland but, unlike those in the islands, they were more vulnerable to post-medieval political and agricultural changes, the last functioning example being identified in Kinlochbervie in 1864 (Gauldie 1981, 115).

Fair Isle mills

The mill systems on Fair Isle appear to have no precise dating record, but by analogy belong to the later 18th or 19th centuries. Their use and importance within the community is still remembered (Eunson 1976) and their distribution seems to have been more widespread than the landscape suggests, being largely concealed by the re-routing and re-cutting of original stream lines. Unconfirmed sites are traditionally located at the south-west of the island along the burn at Hesti Geo and also in the curious ditched area to the east of Quoy. The burn of Vatstrass which runs below Eas Brecks on the east side of the island shows damming immediately east of the sharp curve in the road, but no standing remains or even earthworks survive in the immediate vicinity. Exploratory excavations further downstream on a low, suitably located mound demonstrated nothing other than the extent of ditch re-cutting over the years. Local evidence now suggests that the mill (or mills) for which the dam was built has since fallen from the cliff into the sea.

However, the main concentration of physical and documented remains lies to the top of a steep gully at Funniquoy on the Burn of Gilsetter and provides the focus for a system of dams, channels and mills spread across an area almost 1km long (*743*, fig 12.2). The water catchment system was primarily dependent on the natural course of the burn, but this seems not to have been adequate for the number of mills eventually constructed. Local ditch cutting and land drainage, probably including the curious parallel markings on the Vaasetter headland (*676*), might all be seen as being directed at least in part towards the overall catchment.

Survey work carried out during the 1950s provided the basis for Fenton's map of this area (1978, fig 198, incorporated here into a 1989 Royal Commission plan, fig 12.2), and identified no fewer than 10 sites (seven named), of which the part-standing remains of only three are still visible (Old mill, Shirva mill and New mill) while much of the damming has been obliterated. Later surveys undertaken between 1984-1987 additionally identified a number of more minor artificial channels and low dams which were presumably integral to this overall catchment system. The main concentration of damming, however, lies near the point at which the road crosses the burn where at least three broadly concentric dams, the largest some 80m in length (*663*), indicate the scale of the requirements. It might be added that the greater part of the mill system with its associated dam and coursing facilities is best seen as the product of communal planning and effort as opposed to a piecemeal, *ad hoc* growth. Indeed Eunson specifically comments on the fact that all the mills in the system were capable of running simultaneously (1976, 18).

This same central area also houses two earthwork features traditionally associated with mill sites, Pund mill to the north, located on the main natural stream (*285*), and Leogh mill lying some 80m to the south-east along an excavated channel (*660*), both being fed from a small dammed reservoir. Neither exhibit upstanding remains although their general forms and earthwork characteristics are readily identifiable. Pund mill (fig 12.3) lies in a carefully constructed hollow and survives as a stone foundation *c* 4 x 3m with the water channelled to one side, while the slightly larger form of Leogh mill (fig 12.3) is of similar proportions but constructed astride, rather

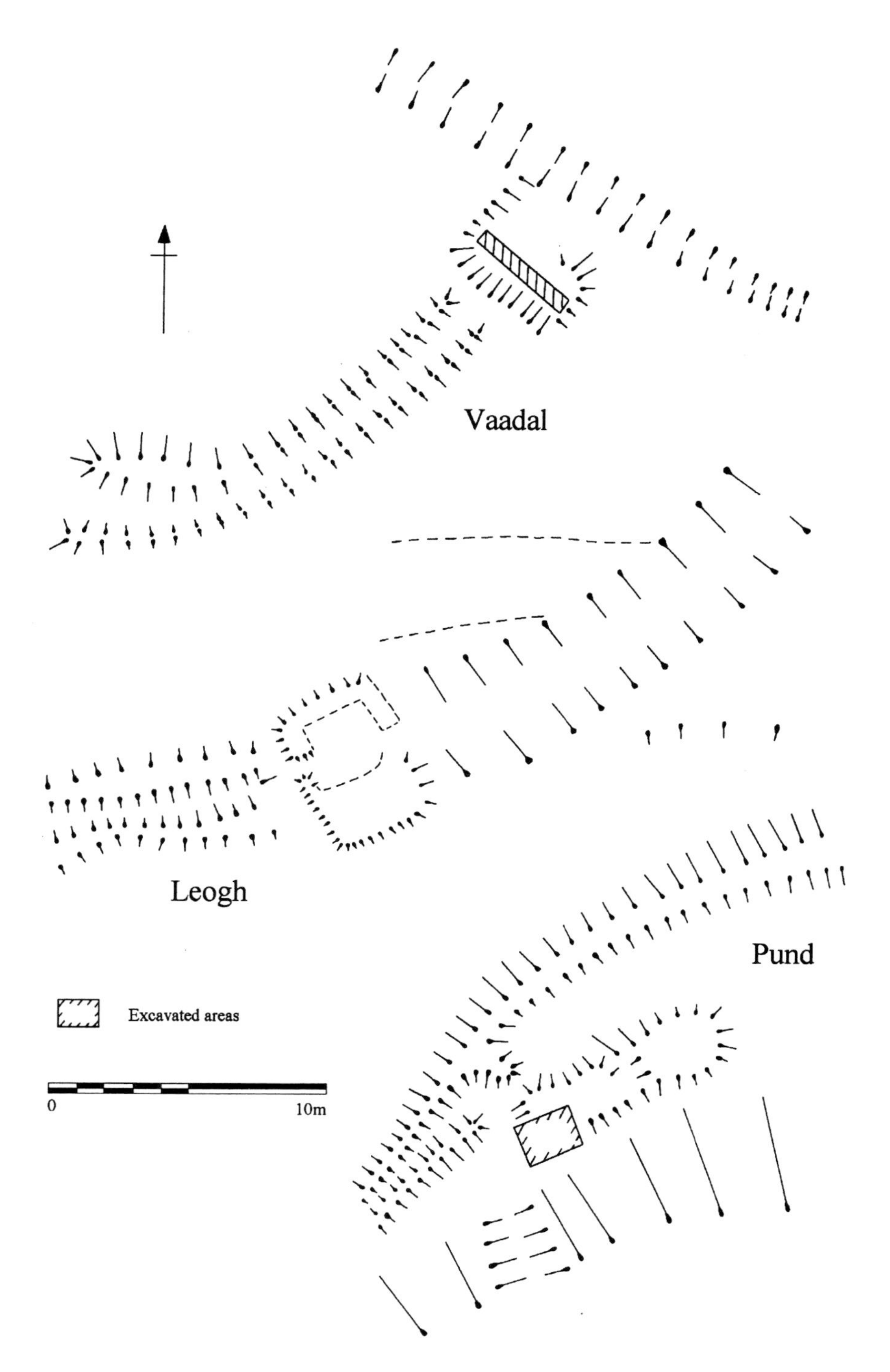

Fig 12.3 Survey plans of surviving elements of Pund, Leogh and Vaadal mills.

than along the stream. A small test excavation at Pund mill confirmed the presence of a compacted rubble base. Elsewhere in the immediate vicinity, particularly to the south and west, the earthworks suggest that other mills may also have existed but have since been destroyed by ditch cutting and road construction.

It was, however, possible to identify the location of Vaadal mill, the most westerly example known and of which an early photograph survives. This had presumably been robbed for road and bridge construction but the lade route was still visible to the south of the modern ditch course. An exploratory trench 5 x 0.5m (fig 12.3) was fortunate in identifying not only the surviving spread of rubble remains but also the *in situ* presence of part of the collapsed tirl base.

The remaining named mill on this part of the early survey, Shuny mill, lay some 300m east of Pund mill but could only be interpreted from a lade route (*666*), the building itself presumably being used in the construction of the nearby stone dyke. Trial excavation failed to locate anything other than a rubble spread and disturbed levels containing both 19th century and prehistoric pottery.

The full force of both land drainage and burn are now combined into a single natural channel (formerly two separate channels) at the head of a steep gully at Funniquoy some 200m from outflow into the sea. At that point the construction of a substantial revetted dam controls the flow down to three stone-built mill foundations identifiable as (from west to east) Old mill, Shirva mill and New mill. Old mill survives only as partial foundation coursing and was not investigated further here, but Shirva mill and New mill show greater evidence of superstructure (plate 12.1), particularly New mill where revetting against the stream is still well-preserved. All three lie on the north bank of the stream, each being powered indirectly through a lade system.

According to the early survey two additional mills had been sited further downstream, and exploratory work was undertaken in the steep-sided valley below New mill in order to verify these locations. The first was interpreted from a spread of earthfast stones and associated rubble located immediately to the east of the confluence of the two water courses in the burn. Few surface stones were visible but a small plantation in the valley bottom had been lined with large stones, presumably by robbing some adjacent structure. An area of some $8m^2$ was opened around the edge of the plantation in the area of surface rubble and this revealed the remains of a packed rubble foundation defined by an edge of larger stones (plate 12.2). A return was evident although little else of the platform had survived, many elements being obscured by hillwash and silted deposits. A mill platform was considered a reasonable interpretation although some doubt is expressed as to how the lade system might have operated in view of the need to generate a fast stream at that point. The most obvious solution would have required the construction of a moveable lade leading directly from the base of the waterfall below New mill.

Plate 12.1 General view of the Funniquoy mill system with New mill located in the centre. Excavations for documented mill below New mill are evident in the foreground at the base of the waterfall.

Plate 12.2 Detail of foundation platform for mill at base of waterfall.

The most easterly mill in the Funniquoy system was hardest to identify. The location shown on the early plan seemed least likely in terms of both accessibility and water flow but, given the erosion and changing contour of the valley, was not altogether implausible. No other location seemed to offer possibilities, although a small plateau site on the north bank of the burn some 70m downstream from the main complex was sectioned as being potentially significant. No evidence was found and the location finally selected lay at a sharp turn in the burn some 20m further downstream, approximately 50m before outflow at the cliff edge.

The site consisted of a small outcrop protruding through the turf at a particularly precipitous point in the valley, with an overhanging cliff some 30m high to the south and a steep slope offering difficult access from the north. The narrowness of the stream at this point would have made damming a relatively convenient and appropriate exercise. An area of some $9m^2$ was opened to reveal a composite and seemingly deliberately fashioned platform of natural bedrock *in situ*, eroded stone and conglomerate boulders covering a broad area approximately 3 x 2.5m. The collection and arrangement was not one that could be attributed to natural phenomena in that place and a mill foundation, although unevidenced further, seems a reasonable interpretation at this stage. Little in the way of form was evident, although at least one possible return could be inferred suggesting a small platform 2m broad with the longer axis spanning the stream.

Although there were some slight undulations in the vicinity, a general lack of tumble and structural evidence was a cause for some concern, the concept of robbing in this particular location being unlikely. Examination of the visible burn section did, however, show evidence of grass-grown tumble which was not present elsewhere along the burn. Although no artefacts were recovered the site is one which reflects man's activity and, if not a mill, is otherwise difficult to explain.

Excavations at Shirva and New mills

The standing remains of Shirva and New mills compare favourably in state of preservation with other ruined mills elsewhere in Shetland, for example the series of foundations fed from the Loch of Clumlie in Dunrossness. Only those restored forms preserved as working museums in both Orkney and Shetland offer substantially more complete superstructure and workings. It is, nevertheless, sad to record the extent to which even these two Fair Isle mills had become dilapidated from their condition in a photograph of 1934 (plate 12.3; compare plate 12.1). In form they must be considered reasonably typical Shetland examples. Both show a construction of double-faced, but irregular, coursed walling with typical external dimensions of *c* 5 x 3.5m, and both have their long axes positioned across the diverted stream with water entering the lower chamber through an opening in the long wall.

Opportunity to excavate and consider the workings in more detail arose in 1989 ahead of a restoration programme planned by the National Trust for Scotland. As a result of this it became possible to locate a series of trenches and sections (fig 12.4) with a view to elucidate certain aspects of the overall system.

The water course leading to Shirva mill was identified as a cut gully of maximum depth *c* 0.6m below the present turf line (trench A, section 1, fig 12.5). The fill indicated that levelling had been achieved by the careful positioning of flat cap-like stones upon which the wooden trough was presumably set. No timbers or traces of timber were found although these had survived comparatively well in trench B where the lade led directly into the mill itself by means of a wooden trough.

The trough survived as base slats, nails and side pieces to a total width of *c* 0.45m and was held in place by side stones wedged into the channel between the cut sides and the trough itself (section 2, fig 12.5). Levelling was carried out by the use of packing stones wedged underneath the trough ensuring that the water fell at a suitable angle and speed. This construction ended some 0.85m from the outer face of the mill wall although timberwork was still evident over the remaining distance. The plans of trench B illustrate the survival of these timbers after the clearance of

Plate 12.3 Photograph of New mill and Shirva mill taken around 1934. Copyright Shetland Museum.

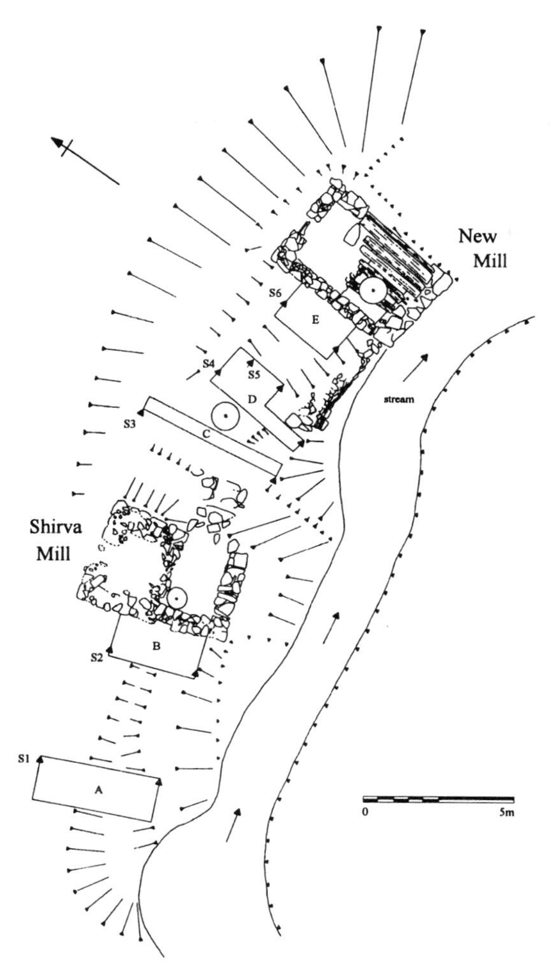

Fig 12.4 Detailed plans of Shirva and New mills showing location of excavation trenches and sections.

superficial deposits (fig 12.5, top) and after removal of rubble packing (fig 12.5, bottom) respectively. However, at the point where the construction appeared to end, the lines of supporting stones were replaced by fragments of a wooden mechanical device suggesting the position of some facility such as a gate or sluice, or more likely a directional mechanism enabling the water to be deflected to or from the wheel. It was at this point that the fall increased significantly into the mill itself.

Trenches D and E identified a similar water course system leading into New mill, trench D showing the presence of a wooden slatted lade (section 5, fig 12.6). As at Shirva this had been supported by packed rubble to give the appropriate falling height but, unlike Shirva, appeared to utilise clay packing as an upper levelling bed.

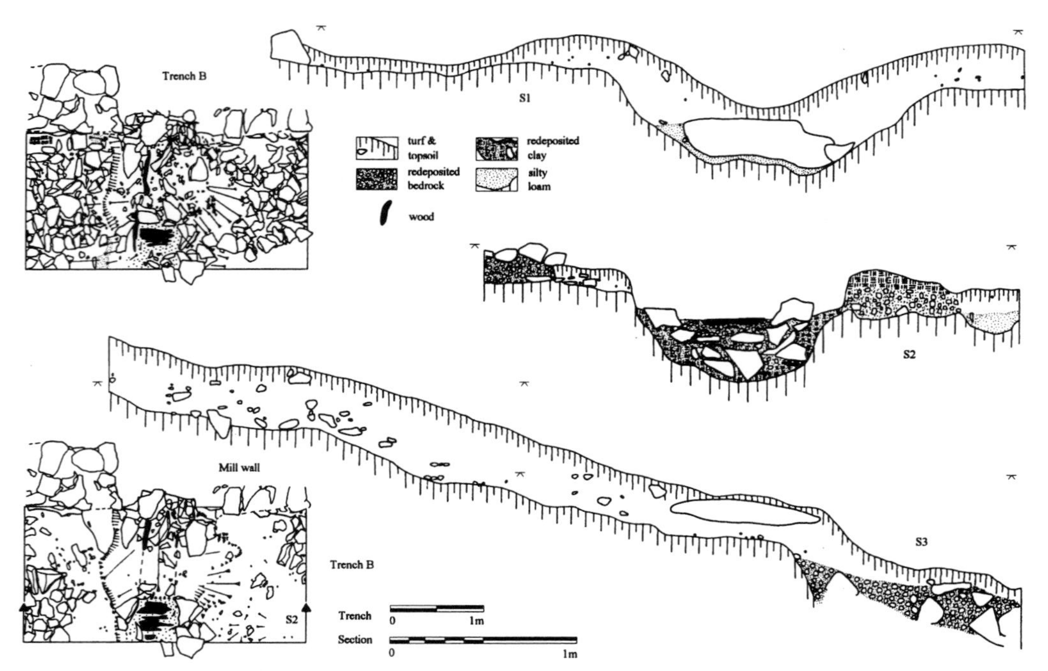

Fig 12.5 Excavation plans and sections at Shirva mill.

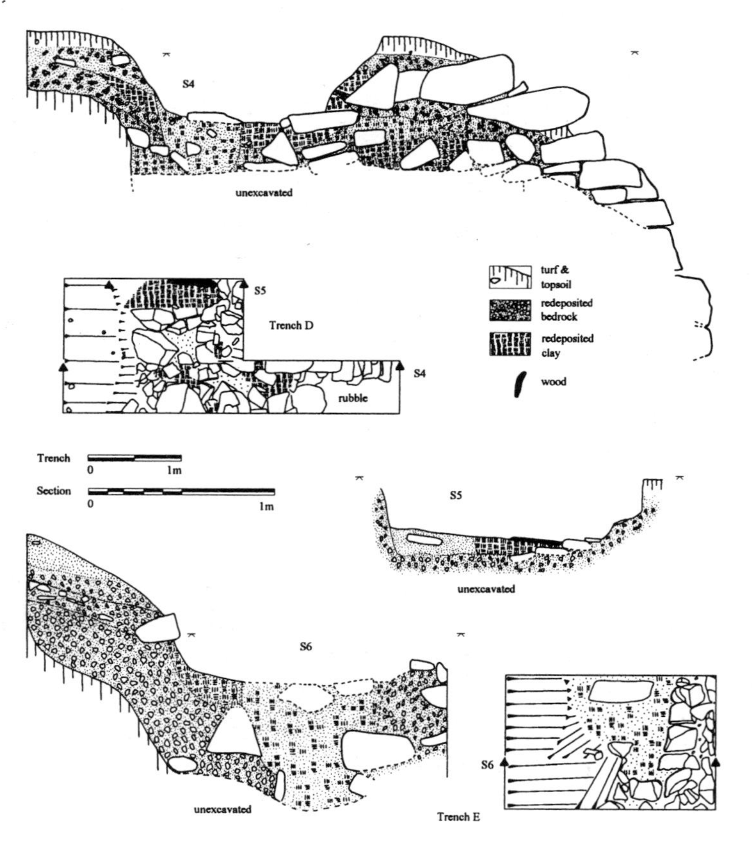

Fig 12.6 Excavation plans and sections at New mill.

Investigation of the water channelling indicated that the supply was derived from the outlet of Shirva mill and not directly from the natural burn. The possibility that a water course had been engineered to the north of Shirva making the system completely independent was discounted on the findings from trench C (section 3, fig 12.5) located between the two mills.

The lade system at New mill utilised the natural bedrock on the north side, but to the south was revetted to a height of *c* 2m from the natural stream bed (plate 12.4). This revetting was coarsely faced on the burn side and was composed mostly of rubble including the stones supporting the lade itself. Excavation showed that this revetting had been undertaken fairly crudely (hence the need for clay bedding and levelling), although this belies the generally smooth superficial outer appearance of the revetted bank. The fill was not bottomed in either trenches D or E (sections 4 and 6, fig 12.6), the depths involved giving some indication of the magnitude of the artificial embankment.

Trench E was located at the point at which the water entered the long wall of the mill, the difference in fall height from trench D being quite considerable in view of the relatively short horizontal distance involved. At a point little over 1m from the mill wall, marked by a stone, the course took an increased fall down a steeper

Plate 12.4 New mill showing revetted side and location of excavation trenches.

gradient and into the mill itself to where the tirl was located. The tirl was offset from the centre of the lower chamber in order to allow the water to meet the paddles squarely and maximise the power available. A similar setting was assumed at Shirva mill although no axle or pivot was evident. The tirl at New mill, however, was still *in situ* even to the extent of retaining a millstone located directly above on a rotting log floor. The tirl itself showed angled recesses for 12 paddles (plate 12.5) although none had survived.

Plate 12.5 The New mill tirl showing angled recesses for 12 paddles.

Although no traces of the wooden lade had been preserved, its route was clearly evident from the line of levelling within the revetting. Again, as in trench D, the course utilised the natural bank to the north and the crude build-up of rubble to the south although the latter was partially faced on the inside in the area immediately adjacent to the mill wall (plate 12.6). In both trenches D and E redeposited natural (red clay and yellow degraded bedrock) was reused in the backfilling and lade support system, particularly at the natural bank side (section 6, fig 12.6).

The building of New mill required great effort, the present topography being almost entirely artificial. The need for a new mill must have been considerable and its construction says much for a stubborn retention of traditional design irrespective of terrain and the difficulty of transporting building materials. The natural slope effectively ends at the east end of Shirva mill where the setting of a series of crudely formed stone steps allowed the stream to flow down into its course without undue erosion of the mill footings. The eventual functioning of New mill required the stream to pass above these steps presumably by means of wooden troughs; Shirva mill therefore had the unusual distinction of having both an output and input lade system. The operation of New mill, sited some 10m away, relied heavily on the efficiency of these lades.

Plate 12.6 New mill showing opening for lade carrying water through to the tirl.

Internally both mills appeared to conform to a common arrangement whereby the inner area was divided into two roughly equal parts, one wooden where the milling took place directly above the water course and tirl, and the other earthen on the flat landward side of the stream. There was no evidence of internal partitioning, nor indeed of any mechanical devices such as the *sole* or *lightening* timbers, and access was in both cases by an opening in the short north wall. The roofs, according to photographic evidence, were pitched and thatched or turf-covered. Old timbers, probably from ships, were almost certainly utilised in their construction and indeed are still to be seen in the floors and lintels of the milling chamber at New mill.

The adherence both to simplicity and to economy of materials is self-evident and the retention of tradition, given the known prototypes from Ireland, is unquestionable. Less clear, and the equally unquestionable subject of future enquiry, is the problem as to whether this tradition is inherent or one which was reintroduced.

13

Overview

RELIANCE on the immediate resources of land and sea is a characteristic hallmark of Fair Isle settlement over the last 4000 years. Equally characteristic is the level of resourcefulness that self-sufficiency often requires and which manifests itself in an adherence to tried and tested traditions. The degree to which this occurs in modern times with respect to mills and boats was presumably even more pronounced in prehistory. Mankind's impact on Fair Isle appears to have been much less emphatic than Fair Isle's influence on those who tried to settle there. It seems more a case of the island's position, resources and climate conditioning the nature of settlement and subsistence economy irrespective of any cultural differences imposed. Some flexibility to animal husbandry or cultivation systems was possible, but wholesale change was out of the question, even on the climatic fringes of the North Atlantic zone. But despite these limitations, and despite the unashamed hardship suffered by its inhabitants even with the relatively sophisticated comforts of the 18th and 19th centuries, the island appears always to have been well-populated. Whether this was by necessity or by choice is another matter, and the absence of much detailed survey elsewhere is also unhelpful. For example, in earlier prehistoric times (Neolithic/Early Bronze Age) the island shows some eight or nine possible settlement foci (fig 6.1); these would, assuming contemporaneity, illustrate an unparalleled density to which might be added a number of 'lost' sites located on more favourable land in the south. They exhibit a consistent topographical factor in that the majority lie within sheltered valley locations; furthermore, the association of some with burial sites may indicate a degree of territoriality of a type similar, although not identical, to that postulated by Renfrew on Rousay, Orkney (1976, fig 4).

Burials pose a particular problem on Fair Isle throughout all periods of occupation. Apart from one or two possible sites, none of the stock monument types known from either Orkney or Shetland are evident. The superficial excavation of one cairn (erroneously described as a house site from field survey) demonstrates the difficulties that the local geology poses to tomb building; it also shows the dangers of applying morphological criteria derived from other areas where better quality building materials were available. A number of sites are also undoubtedly obscured by blanket peat within the moorland areas. There are, however, no traditional centres where early burials may have occurred, although the field known as *Kirkalees* located towards the centre of the island may merit further investigation.

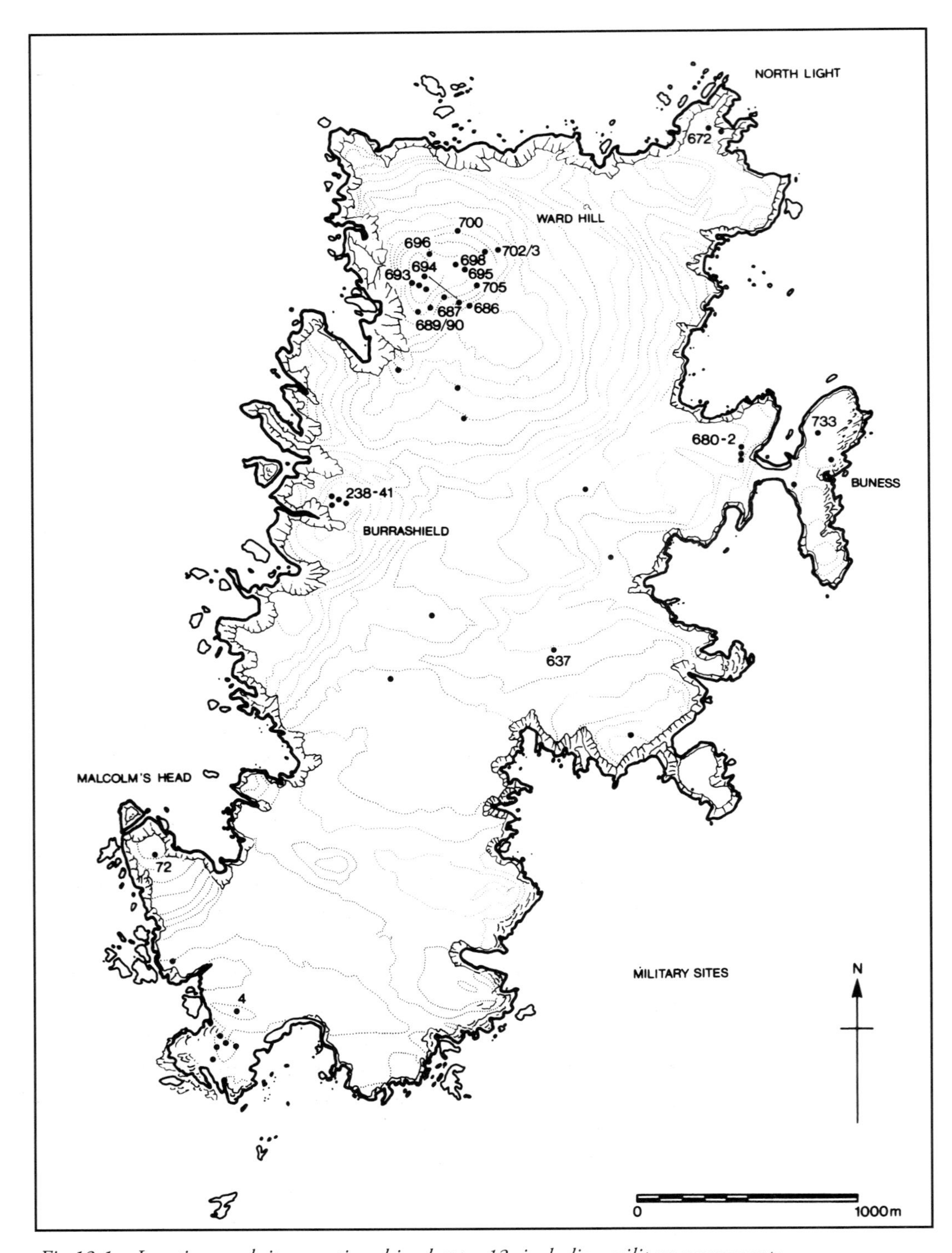

Fig 13.1 Locations and sites mentioned in chapter 13, including military monuments.

One of the advantages of detailed survey of this kind within a fixed area is in being able to identify problems of interpretation and to produce modelling for research purposes. Specific areas of enquiry include testing the veracity of both inferred settlement locations and burial sites, as well as testing the viability of the burnt mound as being a monument diagnostic of settlement foci. Burnt mounds, in view of their survival in both moorland and cultivated land, take on a special role in this study. They appear to lie peripherally to the main settlement foci, possibly relating to different influences or indeed to a later date. The part-excavation of one example reaffirms the effectiveness of magnetometry in their identification. Their function still remains unclear although excavation continues to show the presence of a focal pit, in this case earth-cut rather than lined as a result of the geology. It seems reasonably clear, too, that the larger mounds may be little more than the composite product of smaller mounds and indicate places of more persistent activity either through site importance, or through the greater availability of suitable stone. The largest example, which lies near the croft of Pund, also appears to have been instrumental in the line of one of the great *feelie* dykes which either ran to it as though integral, or ran around it as Thomas' 1839 map depicts. Either way this mound was seen as an important landscape monument.

Dykes and boundaries cause a number of problems of interpretation for which the rough typology based on constructional techniques (see chapter 4) is little more than a suggestion for their solution. Some boundary lengths are clearly late and have tunship associations, but others appear to play no part in the known or inferred post-medieval economy and are, by definition, earlier. It is difficult to see how they might be better explained other than as part-enclosures, land divisions and field boundaries. Their greater understanding might benefit from prospection through the blanket peat which appears to conceal much of their respective lengths, or from extending the model to Shetland and viewing the surviving surface traces across a greater geographical area. In fact, since the outset of the survey, Fair Isle has emerged more and more as a microcosm of Shetland itself where subsequent research designs might now utilise this survey data as a basis for analogy and further investigation. Remarkably, the great *feelie* dyke and its parallels elsewhere are undated. While their modern land division role is clear enough, their original function and the purpose which underlies their communal construction may have been substantially different. Furthermore, as Fair Isle shows, the present dyke may have had precursors.

The survey also shows that settlement patterning on the island exhibits no distinct differences from patterning phenomena identified elsewhere by archaeological means – namely that the moorland and marginal land provide the greatest resource for relict landscapes as well as for some individual monuments. In the south of the island the modern fence boundary provides an emphatic delineation between archaeological survival and archaeological loss, even with respect to the differential survival of post-medieval field systems. However, in later prehistory, and in common with most other parts of Shetland for which models are now well-established, settlement foci no longer occur on higher ground and are lost within areas of modern cultivation on lower ground. Archaeologists now reluctantly acknowledge this hiatus in landscape chronology. Site locations only emerge later, and indirectly, in the form of names containing Scandinavian elements.

The movement of settlement in the Late Bronze Age down to lower slopes was a slow climate-driven process which resulted in the saturation of the fertile south part of the island. Many of the settlement locations favoured today were probably occupied by that time and many others might be identified from pointers in the form of upstanding stone remains, typically sheep shelters, sporadic lengths of stone walling and planticrues. Such is the sparsity of usable stone that the material from many of these features was quarried from earlier foundations. In some cases this reuse is blatantly demonstrable. These modern stone constructions can be used to identify the general locations of earlier stone monuments – monuments of unknown date and character whose only known attribute is that of pre-dating the post-medieval landscape. As a result Iron Age Fair Isle can only be viewed wistfully. There appears to have been no broch, for example, although this may in part be excused by the geology. However, the occurrence of an earlier promontory fort at the Landberg – a strategic and dramatic site – and the later material of the 7th and 8th centuries AD at the south end of the island point towards some continuity of settlement during this period. The site at the south end may even have Christian connotations in this period, as may the promontory located at Burrista on the west side of the island.

The next set of landscape controls appears with place-names containing Scandinavian elements: those which identify major topographical features may represent landmark characteristics visible from the sea and date to the earliest phases of Scandinavian shipping movement; and those with attested habitative elements may relate more directly to evolved internal settlement. In some ways settlement evolution in the early Middle Ages can be best interpreted by working backwards from the modern place-name distribution, and in the case of Fair Isle this has a valuable aid in the form of the *First Statistical Account* which provides an important interim statement by identifying the main settlement foci in the late 18th century. On an island of strictly limited resources and land where the same habitation positions are likely to have been retained over the longer term, this is especially valuable. As a result, the (deserted) site of Gaila emerges as a key location; it holds a classic position on the best land, adjacent to the best harbourage, and is of known status within an area of recorded intensive activity and place-name concentration. The Gaila site is a clear candidate for more detailed examination (including exploratory excavation) as is the present croft site of Busta to the east which, on the basis of place-name modelling, also seems to be of relatively early date in the

Scandinavian settlement sequence. These two sites, together with Shirva and Leogh, constitute the earliest recorded settlement foci in the southern part of the island. They presumably also reflect the choicest habitation sites with respect to land and are likely to be of earlier settlement origins than the Norse period alone.

As in other parts of the Northern Isles, determination of the settlement character throughout the Middle Ages is a matter of attempting to project elements of the Norse landscape forward in time while simultaneously extrapolating backwards from post-medieval times, such being the paucity of surviving physical evidence. Fair Isle, however, has the advantages of a small number of useful texts which were recorded during this 'missing' period, of which the Armada account is particularly noteworthy in being specific to the island. Other early examples include that of Kay (1680) who presents much evidence on resources and subsistence, and that of Sibbald (1633) who covers a broader geographical area but whose works were ultimately published by Monteith in 1845. Certainly the later part of the period can be viewed with greater accuracy by utilising many of the later texts belonging to *Tours* and *Descriptions* logged by travellers and visitors in the 18th and 19th centuries. Most texts either mention the island in diarist form or provide general descriptions of Orkney or Shetland in which Fair Isle receives passing mention. Collectively they portray a colourful but primitive island society, in fact a society which even by the 19th century still retained much of its prehistoric subsistence base. Bias in these accounts is rife, but the inexplicit details of houses, farming and fishing do much to illustrate the common threads which can be argued to link together the differing periods of occupation. Some accounts are quite astute socially (eg Scott); others are more concerned with anthropology (eg Schaw), with mechanical attention to detail (eg Hibbert), or with the natural world (eg Low). But perhaps of greatest *historical* (as opposed to social) value are the factual accounts such as factor's reports, or coverage in the pages of the *Shetland Times.*

Sadly, there seem to be no similar eye-witness accounts to describe the military activities of the 20th century. In fact, even today, there are few on the island able to recall the events of 1939-1945 despite the extensive military remains that still litter the landscape, especially in the area around Ward Hill. Remarkably, it seems that nothing has been written on this period other than texts pertaining to more general aspects of conflict. Nor indeed do there appear to be any records available for study. This is all the more surprising considering that Fair Isle's maritime location has always been a point of strategic interest for military as well as for navigational purposes. Both reflect the importance of a geographical position within the North Atlantic, a factor first recorded in the Norse sagas (chapter 8) when the island was used as a beacon point for communication between Orkney and Shetland. The beacon was located on Ward Hill, the highest point on the island (217m), and was later followed in the 18th century by a Napoleonic look-out tower on a lower summit known as Malcolm's Head (107m) further to the south. The ruined trunk of this still stands (*72*), showing an original construction *c* 5 x 5m with substantial quoin stones. The south wall survives to a height of some 2.2m, although the other walls have been reduced to somewhat less. The advantage over Ward Hill, which may in part have compensated for the lower height, lies in the better visibility over shipping moving east/west between Orkney and Fair Isle; Ward Hill is also frequently cloud- or mist-covered and its height advantage lost.

The importance of height, although in this case not of visibility, was causal in the establishment of a radar station on the summit of Ward Hill during the Second World War. Of some 40 likely military sites of this period on the island, well over half focus around the Ward Hill area (fig 13.1). Smaller concentrations lie on Burrashield further to the south, as well as near the North Light, in the Buness area where a number of military structures have since been utilised, and also in the south-west corner of the island. The monuments consist of structures (some still roofed), earthworks and lesser features. Together they emphasise the high degree of preservation afforded to even obsolete 20th century remains. Although part of this preservation results from the predominant use of concrete in building construction, it can also be attributed to the marginal or moorland locations where casual robbing or erosion is minimised. The Ward Hill area is a classic case in point, housing a complex of structures and remains which functioned for the garrisoning and service of a radar station on the summit. Apart from some peat cutting and grazing on the upper slopes the area now plays no part in the modern economy of the island, and the remains are therefore undisturbed and to some extent fossilised. The radar station itself, sadly, has been reduced to rubble in an attempt to re-establish the natural skyline. It survives only as an area of *c* 80 x 60m of concrete fragments, brickwork and twisted iron (*694*) covering at least three concrete foundations. Two small flat-roofed structures lie adjacent, but off the skyline. The summit was serviced by a narrow gauge track and winch on the south-east side (*695*) which was presumably for carriage of constructional and supply materials.

Approximately 175m down from the summit near the base of the track stand the remains of at least six nucleated flat-roofed structures (*686*, plate 13.1), ranging in size between 4 x 3m and 7 x 5m, built using pebble concrete. Other buildings in the immediate vicinity are represented by sets of concrete foundations; all lie in a relatively sheltered part of the hillside hidden from view from the lower slopes. On the higher slopes to the north-east, but still below the skyline, are two structures with gabled roofs (*702* and *703*, plate 13.2). On the south side a set of concrete platforms (*689* and *690*) appear to belong to Nissen-type huts; one still contains a stove *in situ*. A further concrete platform (*687*), measuring some 35 x 4m, may represent the base of some form of tank or reservoir and lies, appropriately, below a natural spring. The focal radar station was 'protected' by a series of dug-outs or temporary gun

Plate 13.1 Military structures (site 686) towards the base of Ward Hill.

Plate 13.2 Military structure (site 703) on Ward Hill.

emplacements to the north (*696*), east (*698* and *705*) and to the west (*693*). In each case the diameter ranges between 5 to 7m with banking against the downward slope. The whole area also contains a number of minor cairn or cairn bases, some of which may have acted as mast or post supports. A line of these runs up the hill on the north-east side to a further possible, but eroded, dug-out location (*700*).

Along the cliffs south of Ward Hill, located at the summit of Burrashield which is the second highest point on the island (150m), stands a smaller nucleus of monuments which may also have held a specific function. The group consists of four main elements (*238-241*): an earthen enclosure measuring some 11 x 5m and containing remains of concrete posts; two smaller enclosures; and a dug-out banked against the seaward side. All four possess commanding views on all but the north (Ward Hill) side.

Another cluster of remains occurs in the vicinity of the North Light, although it is not wholly clear whether these are military- or lighthouse-related. All but one are cairns which appear to have served as mast bases. The exception is a small uncoursed rubble building measuring some 6 x 3m located within a steep hollow (*672*). An equally unusual rubble structure occurs on Buness (*733*) but without obvious military association. There is, however, some surveillance afforded to the North Haven and to the Buness harbour approaches by a pair of banked dug-outs and associated concrete foundations (*680-682*) located on the cliffs overlooking the tombolo. It seems probable that these performed some defensive function. There are no comparable features at the South Harbour in the south-west of the island, although this might be explained by greater subsequent activity and land use. Possible monuments, like those at the North Light, might also be associated with lighthouse activity although one (*4*) may conceivably represent a gun emplacement.

Elsewhere on the island, apart from putative mast supports and minor concrete features, the military evidence is to some extent random in the form of bomb craters. At least five of these were recorded, the majority lying towards the centre of the island in the moorland approaches to Ward Hill. A further monument, also in this category and perhaps the best known military remain on the island, takes the form of the tailplane of a German Heinkel (*637*) which crash-landed during a reconnaissance mission in 1941. This part of the wreckage lies in a ditch near the Burn of Gilsetter south-west of the mill complex. Other fragmented parts still litter the surrounding fields. Although little more than 50 years old it provides remarkable physical testimony to the breadth of Fair Isle's archaeological resource, and a fitting conclusion to a study spanning over 4000 years of island life.

Fair Isle Inventory of Sites

Site 1 HZ 19846 69821
Bomb crater of diameter *c* 8m filled and now levelled with rubble to present turf line.

Site 2 HZ 1983 6979
Field system covering *c* 500 sq m.

Site 3 HZ 19860 69677
Low sub-circular earthwork of diameter *c* 7.5m on promontory. Maximum surviving height of bank *c* 0.2m. Two arms at E and W effectively isolate end of promontory. Possible continuation *c* 80m NE to S of site 9. Possible boundary feature.

Site 4 HZ 19895 69824
Flat iron ring of diameter *c* 1m and thickness *c* 0.2m. Filled with concrete in centre. Gun emplacement on high ground?

Site 5 HZ 19884 69851
Remains of iron post set in concrete surviving to height of *c* 0.3m and of diameter *c* 0.8m. Mast position on high ground.

Site 6 HZ 19917 69803
Small cairn of diameter *c* 2m and maximum surviving height *c* 0.3m. Partially turf-covered.

Site 7 HZ 1997 6980
Field system covering *c* 4500 sq m.

Site 8 HZ 19960 69660
Shallow remains of quarry working. Depression *c* 16 x 12m now partially flooded.

Site 9 HZ 19971 69730
Remains of maximum of 6 boat nausts on E coast relating to earlier fishing industry. From N to S:

- **a.** 5 x 1.5m, *c* 0.5m maximum depth, shallow rounded profile.
- **b.** 7 x 2m, *c* 0.5m maximum depth, shallow rounded profile. Evidence of stone facings in S wall.
- **c.** 9 x 4.5m, *c* 0.6m maximum depth, flat bottomed. Evidence of stone facings in N wall and less clearly in S wall. Separated from naust (d) by earthen bank *c* 3m wide, stone faced on either side and supporting winch.
- **d.** Badly eroded, maximum length *c* 12.5m, maximum width *c* 3m, maximum depth *c* 0.6m.
- **e.** Difficult to interpret, sharing common wall with (d) estimated at *c* 12 x 2.5m, varying depth *c* 0.5m.
- **f.** Possible naust represented by surviving large stones. Maximum length *c* 11 m and width *c* 2.5m.
- **g.** Approximately 12m N of nausts, area of shingle artificially laid *c* 30 x 5m (long axis N/S) for fish drying.

Site 10 HZ 19933 69853
Quarry working *c* 12 x 10m. Maximum depth of cutting *c* 4m. Waterfilled.

Site 11 HZ 19893 69901
Crude length of walling across inlet. Length *c* 37m, maximum height at seaward side *c* 2m. Flush with ground surface at landward side. Uneven with maximum width *c* 2m. Constructed of large boulders roughly faced on seaward side with smaller rubble at top. Presumably formed as sea barrier.

Site 12 HZ 19887 69911
Semi-concealed concrete base on foundation *c* 2 x 2m. Considerable soil/turf cover. Military (?) and related to site 11?

Site 13 HZ 1992 6992
Field system covering *c* 870 sq m.

Site 14 HZ 1994 6987
Field system covering *c* 1620 sq m.

Site 15 HZ 1998 6988
Field system covering *c* 870 sq m.

Site 16 HZ 19966 69897
Eroded earthen enclosure against rock outcrop *c* 8 x 4m externally. Maximum height of bank *c* 0.2m at short ends. Some stones, timber and ironwork evident internally.

Site 17 HZ 20035 69884
Rectangular earthen enclosure *c* 13 x 7m, maximum surviving height *c* 0.7m. Stones evident within earthen walls. Probable turf-covered rubble in centre. Presumably structural.

Site 18 HZ 19936 69974
Wooden flagpole, formerly used for signalling to vessels. Two posts (square-sectioned) each *c* 3m in height set in concrete pad with flagpole pivoted in between at top. Flagpole *c* 8m high. Approximately 3m to NW sub-circular area of flat stones of diameter *c* 3m with bronze rivet attached to centre stone. Possible conductor or former radio mast. Iron ring to S.

Site 19 HZ 19962 69994
Walling *c* 3m in length, *c* 1m wide standing to maximum height of *c* 1m. Large stones well-set in lower courses, smaller rubble used in upper courses. No obvious function or association. May relate to adjacent drain/pipe line to NE.

Site 20 HZ 19849 70007
Flattened area of headland *c* 3.5 x 2.5m showing spread of small stones.

Site 21 HZ 1992 7006
Field system covering *c* 4500 sq m.

Site 22 HZ 19976 70034
Quarry working against bedrock *c* 15 x 5m. Maximum depth of cut *c* 1m. Now waterfilled.

Site 23 HZ 19985 69989
Quarry working against bedrock *c* 12 x 6m. Maximum depth of cut *c* 4m.

Site 24 HZ 20012 69975
Quarry cutting against bedrock *c* 14 x 6m maximum. Maximum depth of cut *c* 2.5m.

Site 25 HZ 2004 7005
Field system covering *c* 6000 sq m.

Site 26 HZ 1989 7010
Field system covering *c* 3300 sq m.

Site 27 HZ 1990 7013
Field system covering *c* 500 sq m.

Site 28 HZ 19840 70137
Crude stone wall or boundary *c* 70m in length. Maximum height *c* 0.7-0.8m, maximum width *c* 1m. Constructed of large stones with little evidence of facings. Considerable rubble and tumble in vicinity. Overlies field system (site 26).

Site 29 HZ 19857 70124
Sub-circular mound of diameter *c* 4m and maximum surviving height *c* 0.5m. Long axis NW/SE with highest point at SE. Central denuded depression *c* 2 x 1m and *c* 0.2m deep. Some stones in mound bulk. Local information denotes earlier windmill in general area.

Site 30 HZ 19891 70177
Possible buried foundation lines identified on E/W axis for *c* 21m with possible return at W for further 6m. Feature appears to turn N at E end, also for *c* 6m. Surviving width *c* 1m and height *c* 0.3-0.5m. Some small stones protruding. Visible best with low sun.

Site 31 HZ 20000 70127
Two possible structural foundations:

a. To W structural form *c* 15 x 7.5m with long axis orientated N/S. Walls *c* 1 m wide and of maximum height *c* 0.3m. Internal division creating separate 'rooms' to N and S.

b. To E partial form visible for length of *c* 12m with returns. Walls *c* 1m wide and of maximum height *c* 0.3m.

Site 32 HZ 19800 70240
Wall foundation or boundary identified for *c* 25m. Maximum width *c* 1m and maximum surviving height *c* 0.3m. Constructed of earth, turf and stones. Long axis orientated N/S.

Site 33 HZ 19804 70337
H-shaped sheep shelter. Arms set out at slight angles each *c* 5m long. Bar *c* 7m long. Height *c* 1m and width *c* 0.4m. Walling faced both sides with even coursing. W arms slightly

lower and of poorer construction. House bricks and concrete evident among stonework.

Site 34 HZ 19780 70360
Possible enclosure *c* 45 x 17.5m, almost plateau-like in form. Long axis orientated E/W. Maximum height *c* 0.5m at E. Possible trackway and field systems associated. Visible best with low sun.

Site 35 HZ 1985 7038
Field system covering *c* 2500 sq m.

Site 36 HZ 1993 7024
Field system covering *c* 3500 sq m.

Site 37 HZ 19959 70267
Stone-capped bridge covered with earth and turf. Trackway width *c* 2m. Capping stones supported by crude coursing *c* 0.4m apart.

Site 38 HZ 1999 7020
Field system covering *c* 1250 sq m.

Site 39 HZ 2012 7023
Field system covering *c* 1870 sq m.

Site 40 HZ 2011 7018
Field system covering *c* 370 sq m.

Site 41 HZ 2010 7036
Field system covering *c* 8750 sq m.

Site 42 HZ 2014 7040
Field system covering *c* 10720 sq m.

Site 43 HZ 19956 70358
Stone-capped bridge covered with earth and turf. Trackway width *c* 2m. Capping stones supported by crude coursing *c* 0.4m apart.

Site 44 HZ 19934 70226
Location of well according to OS. Identified but feature sealed by wooden slats *c* 0.5 x 0.5m.

Site 45 HZ 19880 70422
H-shaped sheep shelter situated on large natural (?) mound. Arms each *c* 6m in length, *c* 1m high and *c* 0.3-0.4m wide. Bar *c* 7m in length with long axis orientated E/W. Similar width but slightly higher at *c* 1.5m and constructed of more substantial stones.

Site 46 HZ 19900 70492
Stone wall *c* 14m in length surviving to height of *c* 1.2m. Maximum width *c* 0.3m. Some large stones at base, particularly at E end in buttressing capacity. Smaller stones at top. Faced both sides.

Site 47 HZ 1995 7045
Field system covering *c* 10,500 sq m.

Site 48 HZ 19916 70540
T-shaped sheep shelter. Bar *c* 6m long, arm *c* 3m long positioned off-centre to bar and with large stones acting in buttressing capacity at E end. Both *c* 1m high and *c* 0.3-0.4m wide. Faced both sides.

Site 49 HZ 1982 7042
Field system covering *c* 3750 sq m.

Site 50 HZ 19784 70426
L-shaped sheep shelter, N/S length *c* 7m, E/W length *c* 8m. Angle for shelter at SW. Maximum height *c* 1m and maximum width *c* 0.4m. Some substantial stones at W end. Slightly dilapidated at S. Faced both sides.

Site 51 HZ 2000 7055
Field system covering *c* 2620 sq m.

Site 52 HZ 2005 7053
Field system covering *c* 5250 sq m.

Site 53 HZ 2009 7050
Field system covering *c* 1000 sq m.

Site 54 HZ 2012 7048
Field system covering *c* 3750 sq m.

Site 55 HZ 2020 7045
Field system covering *c* 4200 sq m.

Site 56 HZ 20206 70493
P-shaped sheep shelter butted against existing length of field wall. Maximum dimensions *c* 9 x 3m, *c* 1.5m in height, and *c* 0.5m in width. Area enclosed *c* 4 x 3m. Unroofed. Substantially built with larger stones in lower regions and acting in buttressing capacity at E end of long wall. Outside to S and W evidence of possible lagging and revetting. Situated on natural (?) mound.

Site 57 HZ 19865 69845
Circular depression surrounded by low bank on headland. External diameter *c* 5.5m, internal diameter *c* 3.2m lined with undressed

stones. Bank broken at W by two large stones and projecting iron bar *c* 0.9m in length. Military?

Site 58 HZ 2000 7040
Field system covering *c* 6750 sq m.

Site 59 HZ 1986 7041
Field system covering *c* 870 sq m.

Site 60 HZ 1990 7045
Field system covering *c* 1750 sq m.

Site 61 HZ 1994 7052
Field system covering *c* 1750 sq m.

Site 62 HZ 1998 7057
Field system covering *c* 2620 sq m.

Site 63 HZ 2010 7053
Field system covering *c* 500 sq m.

Site 64 HZ 2020 7042
Field system covering *c* 1000 sq m.

Site 65 HZ 1992 7042
Area of ploughed-out burnt mound according to local information. Recorded as being of diameter *c* 2m. Possibly a cairn.

Site 66 HZ 2004 7062
Field system covering *c* 4500 sq m.

Site 67 HZ 2010 7059
Field system covering *c* 1300 sq m.

Site 68 HZ 2013 7059
Field system covering *c* 870 sq m.

Site 69 HZ 2015 7054
Field system covering *c* 4650 sq m.

Site 70 HZ 19790 70188
Small concrete jetty in cliff cleft approached by badly eroded flight of concrete steps. Jetty *c* 3 x 3m with iron ring at seaward end. Narrow inlet. Jetty seemingly unused.

Site 71 HZ 19590 70651
Field boundary across Malcolm's Head. Approximately 100m in length from cliff to cliff, *c* 2m in width and with maximum surviving height of *c* 0.6m. Partial section exposed showing line of single large stones on S side with the remaining composition of earth and turf. Approximately 40m from S end junction of further boundary running NE for *c* 70m to cliff. Less substantial in form *c* 1.5m wide and surviving to maximum height of *c* 0.2m.

Site 72 HZ 19588 70715
Remains of Napoleonic Tower on Malcolm's Head. Originally square (?) *c* 5 x 5m with S, E and W walls still standing to *c* 2.2m, 1.5m and 1.2m respectively. S wall contains opening *c* 1m wide with later (now tumbled) blocking. N wall no longer extant. Construction of mortared stone using substantial quoins. Rubble and concrete throughout surrounding area.

Site 73 HZ 19970 70639
Rough walling *c* 4m in length, *c* 0.7m in height and *c* 0.5m wide. Small stone construction without obvious facings. Probably used as sheep shelter.

Site 74 HZ 20430 71210
Wall composed of large stones *c* 4m in surviving length. Maximum surviving height *c* 1.3m and width *c* 0.7m. Large stones used to buttress E end. Adjacent to W, mound *c* 6 x 4m and *c* 1m in height appears to contain part-rubble fill and may represent possible structural foundation. Standing wall presumably sheep shelter.

Site 75 HZ 20325 71279
Obtuse angled wall in corner of field partially constructed over rock outcrop. Total length *c* 7m. Maximum surviving height *c* 1.5m and width *c* 0.4m. Large stones at base and over outcrop. Presumably sheep shelter.

Site 76 HZ 20344 71268
Curved field boundary identified for *c* 45m. Maximum surviving height *c* 0.5m and width *c* 1.5m. Three large stones projecting at intervals, largest *c* 0.5m tall. Boundary cut through by later field system (site 148).

Site 77 HZ 20380 71592
Dilapidated crub *c* 4 x 4m. Maximum surviving height *c* 1.4m and width *c* 0.4m. Constructed with larger stones at base. NE corner and part of W wall collapsed. Possible T-shaped arm projecting from N side represented by interpreted rubble base.

Site 78 HZ 20434 71628
Possible structural foundation *c* 5 x 4m with long axis orientated E/W represented by large stones marking line of walling. Largest stone *c* 0.6 x 0.6 x 0.6m. Two large stones in interior. Surrounded by slight bank *c* 1m wide.

Site 79 HZ 20455 71637
Possible structural foundation defined by stones and rubble visible through turf. Estimated dimensions *c* 6 x 5m with long axis orientated E/W. W wall defined by bank *c* 1m wide and *c* 0.3m in height. Largest stones at S and E sides.

Site 80 HZ 19670 70195
Earthen mound of diameter *c* 8.5m at base of Malcolm's Head. Maximum height *c* 0.5m with possible depression *c* 1 x 1m in centre. Single stone protruding at SE corner. Possibly military.

Site 81 HZ 1990 7034
Field system covering *c* 7500 sq m.

Site 82 HZ 1998 7032
Field system covering *c* 3500 sq m.

Site 83 HZ 20227 70707
Two probable structural forms. To N foundation remains covering area *c* 20 x 5m showing partial house form to W represented by double bank each *c* 0.4m in width and of maximum surviving height *c* 0.3m. Irregular banking of similar dimensions at E. To S turf-covered mound *c* 15 x 12m slightly depressed at centre and with maximum height of *c* 1.5m. Small structural foundations *c* 2.5 x 2.5m at W of mound defined by low bank *c* 0.4m wide and *c* 0.3m in height. Whole area contains surface undulations and features.

Site 84 HZ 20206 70700
Two probable structural forms. To E structure *c* 13 x 3.5m represented by single banking at NW and SW and by double banking at NE and SE. Banking *c* 0.3m wide with maximum surviving height *c* 0.3m. Interior subdivided into three roughly equal areas. To W partial structure *c* 6 x 4.5m defined by double banking to NE and single banking to SE and SW all *c* 0.3m wide and with maximum surviving height of *c* 0.3m. Whole area contains surface undulations and features.

Site 85 HZ 20204 70795
Mound of diameter *c* 15m and maximum height of *c* 1m. Possibly natural but contains partial perimeter of large stones. Cut through by field system (site 119).

Site 86 HZ 20242 70910
U-shaped embankment covering area *c* 3 x 3m with open end facing E. Banking composed of earth and turf *c* 0.7m wide and surviving to height of *c* 0.5m. Slight depression in centre. Possible relationship to unusual curved field system (site 130) adjacent to W. Interpreted as possibly structural.

Site 87 HZ 20357 70767
Structural foundation *c* 24 x 5m with long axis orientated *c* N/S. Turf-covered walls *c* 1.5m wide surviving to maximum height of *c* 0.7m. Interior subdivided into three separate areas. Stone evident in wall lines.

Site 88 HZ 20348 70770
Walling line of length *c* 14m orientated E/W. At E butted against site 87. Further *c* 9m of rubble foundation at W end. Height *c* 1.5m, width at top *c* 0.3m and at base *c* 0.6m. Rough facings.

Site 89 HZ 20440 70881
Structural foundation *c* 12 x 5m with long axis orientated *c* N/S. Part-standing walling at S end of height *c* 1.2m showing (blocked) opening. Drystone construction butting against remains of small enclosure built in similar manner. Remainder of structure defined by irregular low mound of maximum height *c* 0.5m.

Site 90 HZ 20308 70880
'Standing stone'. Length *c* 1.5m, height *c* 1m, maximum width *c* 0.4m. Long axis orientated approximately N/S. Leans at slight angle at turn of field ditch in small pool. Possible result of quarrying which seems to have occurred in rock face to N. Now focal point for traditional carving of initials.

Site 91 HZ 2045 7105
Disturbed and undulating area *c* 30 x 20m

with particular peak at W. Local information suggests structural remains. Partially cut by field system (site 137).

Site 92 HZ 20545 71018
Base of clearance cairn *c* 3 x 2.5m composed of small stones and rubble. Now flattened to maximum surviving height of *c* 0.2m.

Site 93 HZ 20606 71099
Clearance cairn *c* 6 x 3m, partially turf-covered but exposed at top showing small rubble. Maximum surviving height *c* 0.7m.

Site 94 HZ 20698 71038
Probable boundary line curving for *c* 45m from W to N adjacent to modern building. Maximum width *c* 1.5m and height *c* 0.5m. Minor quarrying adjacent.

Site 95 HZ 20535 71194
Circular well-defined area of stones of diameter *c* 1.5m cleanly cut within turf. Some evidence of perimeter stones. Surface flush with turf. Depth at least *c* 0.2m.

Site 96 HZ 20465 71239
Line of walling *c* 5m in length, *c* 0.7m wide and of maximum surviving height *c* 1m. Probably former boundary feature followed by modern fence line. Large stones at base with smaller rubble and concrete higher up. Buried stones to E suggest original continuation.

Site 97 HZ 1996 7013
Field system covering *c* 1870 sq m.

Site 98 HZ 2008 7008
Field system covering *c* 500 sq m.

Site 99 HZ 1993 7018
Field system covering *c* 1750 sq m.

Site 100 HZ 2006 7016
Field system covering *c* 1250 sq m.

Site 101 HZ 2008 7012
Field system covering *c* 250 sq m.

Site 102 HZ 2010 7013
Field system covering *c* 350 sq m.

Site 103 HZ 1991 7021
Field system covering *c* 850 sq m.

Site 104 HZ 1999 7025
Field system covering *c* 1370 sq m.

Site 105 HZ 2006 7021
Field system covering *c* 2970 sq m.

Site 106 HZ 20087 70060
Possible structural platform *c* 7 x 4m with long axis orientated E/W. Service trench cut through centre with stones excavated. Visible only as turf-covered platform. Local information records earlier structure.

Site 107 HZ 2007 7079
Field system covering *c* 2250 sq m.

Site 108 HZ 2001 7077
Field system covering *c* 2000 sq m.

Site 109 HZ 2008 7070
Field system covering *c* 3500 sq m.

Site 110 HZ 2003 7067
Field system covering *c* 750 sq m.

Site 111 HZ 2014 7071
Field system covering *c* 3500 sq m.

Site 112 HZ 2013 7065
Field system covering *c* 870 sq m.

Site 113 HZ 2019 7066
Field system covering *c* 1750 sq m.

Site 114 HZ 2023 7061
Field system covering *c* 1000 sq m.

Site 115 HZ 2005 7074
Field system covering *c* 320 sq m.

Site 116 HZ 2009 7088
Field system covering *c* 1250 sq m.

Site 117 HZ 2016 7091
Field system covering *c* 8870 sq m.

Site 118 HZ 2014 7083
Field system covering *c* 2500 sq m.

Site 119 HZ 2022 7078
Field system covering *c* 5400 sq m.

Site 120 HZ 2033 7074
Field system covering *c* 2250 sq m.

Site 121 HZ 2018 7087
Field system covering *c* 2370 sq m.

Site 122 HZ 2021 7085
Field system covering *c* 150 sq m.

Site 123 HZ 2025 7084
Field system covering *c* 1400 sq m.

Site 124 HZ 2030 7081
Field system covering *c* 650 sq m.

Site 125 HZ 2033 7084
Field system covering *c* 1000 sq m.

Site 126 HZ 2034 7086
Field system covering *c* 1120 sq m.

Site 127 HZ 2038 7090
Field system covering *c* 1750 sq m.

Site 128 HZ 2035 7088
Field system covering *c* 1600 sq m.

Site 129 HZ 2028 7088
Field system covering *c* 950 sq m.

Site 130 HZ 2023 7089
Field system covering *c* 170 sq m.

Site 131 HZ 2022 7096
Field system covering *c* 1500 sq m.

Site 132 HZ 2030 7074
Local information records area of burials and excavation of 'headstones'. Strong tradition of former burials in this general area.

Site 133 HZ 20248 70730
Irregular mound *c* 8 x 8m with maximum surviving height of *c* 1.5m. Some denudation. Local information reports cause as being earlier copper prospecting.

Site 134 HZ 20082 70810
Edge of possible burnt mound exposed *c* 1 x 1.5m during construction of enclosed reservoir. Small burnt stones evident.

Site 135 HZ 2036 7104
Field system covering *c* 30,000 sq m.

Site 136 HZ 2044 7097
Field system covering *c* 10,000 sq m.

Site 137 HZ 2045 7103
Field system covering *c* 500 sq m.

Site 138 HZ 2052 7100
Field system covering *c* 700 sq m.

Site 139 HZ 2051 7103
Field system covering *c* 100 sq m.

Site 140 HZ 2049 7114
Field system covering *c* 11,000 sq m.

Site 141 HZ 2058 7111
Field system covering *c* 5700 sq m.

Site 142 HZ 2066 7110
Field system covering *c* 2400 sq m.

Site 143 HZ 2072 7107
Field system covering *c* 3750 sq m.

Site 144 HZ 2059 7102
Field system covering *c* 7650 sq m.

Site 145 HZ 2052 7098
Field system covering *c* 150 sq m.

Site 146 HZ 2049 7122
Field system covering *c* 2800 sq m.

Site 147 HZ 2043 7123
Field system covering *c* 1370 sq m.

Site 148 HZ 2038 7123
Field system covering *c* 8100 sq m.

Site 149 HZ 2035 7128
Field system covering *c* 400 sq m.

Site 150 HZ 2036 7118
Field system covering *c* 3250 sq m.

Site 151 HZ 2034 7118
Field system covering *c* 500 sq m.

Site 152 HZ 2034 71178
Irregular earthwork *c* 4 x 3m, externally defined by possible walling *c* 1m wide and of maximum surviving height *c* 0.4m. Long axis orientated approximately E/W with possible opening at E adjacent to large stone. Probably structural.

Site 153 HZ 20262 71210
Quarry working *c* 10 x 5m with maximum depth of cut *c* 1m. Probably caused by copper prospecting.

Site 154 HZ 20290 71233
Quarry working *c* 6 x 4m with maximum depth of cut *c* 1m. Probably caused by copper prospecting.

Site 155 HZ 2029 7105
General area of disturbance *c* 30 x 10m with long axis orientated approximately N/S. Turf-covered, no obvious form but recorded locally as former settlement site.

Site 156 HZ 20797 71186
General area of disturbance *c* 30 x 30m with numerous undulations, protruding stones and patch of bog ore. Only partially encroached on by field systems. Possibly structural.

Site 157 HZ 20828 71225
Clearance cairn of diameter *c* 1m and of maximum surviving height *c* 0.4m. Partly denuded.

Site 158 HZ 20717 71176
Clearance cairn *c* 3 x 2m and of maximum surviving height *c* 0.6m. Located in centre of field and composed of both large and small stones.

Site 159 HZ 20644 71255
Dilapidated dwelling *c* 6 x 3.5m in centre of field without obvious trackway. Long axis N/S. Maximum height (S wall) *c* 2m and width *c* 0.6m. Flat drystone construction at base with rubble (rebuild) in upper regions to create sheep shelter. Opening in E wall *c* 0.7m wide and butted junction on W side *c* 0.5m from NW corner. Tumble and rubble in immediate vicinity.

Site 160 HZ 20642 71269
Low mound *c* 12 x 2m and maximum height *c* 0.5m. Long axis orientated approximately E/W. According to denuded surface composition appears to be of bog ore.

Site 161 HZ 20464 71245
Irregular turf-covered mound *c* 8.5 x 5m with stones protruding through SW side. Long axis orientated E/W. Partly embanked against natural slope but with maximum height of *c* 1m. Possible wall-like feature around N side. Probably structural.

Site 162 HZ 20475 71288
Crub *c* 4 x 4m on high ground. Maximum surviving height *c* 1m. Rough rubble walling set on large foundation stones *c* 1m in width. Entrance (secondary sheep shelter use?) located along W side of N wall.

Site 163 HZ 20386 71285
Cruciform-shaped walling with main length of *c* 8m curving from S to NE. Cross-wall located at midpoint and constructed for *c* 2m either side. Maximum surviving height *c* 1.3m with width at base *c* 1m and at top *c* 0.5m. S, E and W ends buttressed with large stones. General rubble construction throughout. Situated along line of earlier field boundary. Presumably functions as sheep shelter.

Site 164 HZ 20403 71360
T-shaped length of walling. Main length *c* 6m orientated E/W with arm *c* 5m in length at E end. Maximum surviving height *c* 1.7m. Ends of arm buttressed with large stones, unsuccessfully at N end. Smaller rubble in upper regions. Maximum base thickness *c* 1m narrowing to *c* 0.5m at top. Main length constructed using larger stones than arm and is conceivably primary. Presumably functions as sheep shelter.

Site 165 HZ 20437 71415
Walling *c* 8m in length with abutment. Orientated E/W with *c* 2m of tumble to E. Flush with modern fence and may represent earlier boundary. Maximum surviving height *c* 1.3m. Width at base *c* 1m and at top *c* 0.6m. Larger stones at base with buttressing at S. Presumably now used as sheep shelter.

Site 166 HZ 20570 71338
Stone-capped bridge *c* 2m wide. Capping stones supported by crude coursing *c* 0.5m apart.

Site 167 HZ 20822 71288
Crub (in use) *c* 5.5 x 3.5m. Long axis orientated N/S. Even walling of maximum height *c* 1m, base width *c* 1m and width at top *c* 0.6m. Probably derived from earlier structural form (see site 168). Larger stones at base. Smaller rubble in upper regions.

Site 168 HZ 2082 7129
Raised platform *c* 25 x 18m with long axis approximately E/W supporting site 167. Maximum height *c* 0.5m. Well-defined E

perimeter (wall foundation?). Number of small stones protruding through turf, particularly at E. Probably structural.

Site 169 HZ 20818 71330
Remains of two structural forms in marginal uncultivated land:

a. At W, sub-rectangular *c* 6 x 5m defined by low earthen bank *c* 1-2m wide and of maximum height *c* 0.2m. Appears to be of turf composition.

b. At E, open-sided *c* 3.5 x 3.5m defined by low earthen bank *c* 1m wide and of maximum height *c* 0.2m. Open side faces E. Appears to be of turf composition.

Site 170 HZ 20477 71389
Clearance cairn *c* 5 x 2m on slight mound at edge of field. Located on flat unrigged area of land *c* 8 x 5m. Rubble composition now spread.

Site 171 HZ 20452 71474
Crub or former structure *c* 5 x 4m with long axis orientated *c* E/W. Maximum height of walling *c* 1.5m, maximum base width *c* 1m narrowing to *c* 0.6m at top. NW corner and part of S wall collapsed. Constructed using larger stones at base. Walling possibly too high for crub. No internal evidence.

Site 172 HZ 20444 71427
Area *c* 20 x 20m of irregular undulations. Clearance (?) cairn in centre *c* 2 x 1m and surviving to height of *c* 0.4m. Evidence of possible stonework at W end and possible field boundaries at W and curving in from SW.

Site 173 HZ 20420 71561
Field boundary running *c* E/W for *c* 35m then due N adjacent to modern fence. Varied in form but of maximum width *c* 0.75m and maximum surviving height *c* 1m in northward part. General composition of earth and turf but large stones evident at E.

Site 174 HZ 20575 71656
Area *c* 50 x 50m containing number of quarry workings. Largest *c* 10 x 4m, smallest *c* 2 x 2m. Maximum depth *c* 1.5m with some containing large stones, others now waterfilled.

Site 175 HZ 20544 71586
Three parallel lengths of walling with long axes *c* N/S. Lengths from E to W *c* 5m, 5m and 4.5m. N ends show evidence of tumble. All three appear to have been rebuilt over large stones embedded in ground. Maximum surviving height *c* 1.7m with maximum base width *c* 1.2m narrowing to *c* 0.5m at top. Evidence of likely return connecting all three walls at N end. Centre wall also has return at S end identified for *c* 0.7m. Possible original structural entity *c* 11.5 x 5m externally subsequently used as sheep shelter (?). Concrete-lined well adjacent to SE and numerous ground undulations in immediate vicinity. Field boundary (site 224) located *c* 20m S of S end of walls.

Site 176 HZ 20544 71600
L-shaped walling approximately on compass axes with sheltered corner facing NE. Length *c* 3m, maximum surviving height *c* 1.2m. Constructed with large stones at base and smaller rubble elsewhere. Base width *c* 1m narrowing to *c* 0.5m at top. Probable sheep shelter.

Site 177 HZ 20651 71516
Quarry or possible military shelter. Roughly S-shaped, *c* 15 x 4m. Maximum depth *c* 1m with upcast creating type of embankment on long sides. Concrete and iron remains internally.

Site 178 HZ 20714 71489
Flat grassy platform *c* 9 x 8m respected by field systems. Maximum height *c* 0.3m. Probing suggests area of stone under turf. Possibly structural or eroded burnt mound.

Site 179 HZ 20702 71470
Flat grassy platform *c* 3 x 3m respected by field systems. Maximum height *c* 0.3m. Probing suggests area of stone under turf. Possibly structural or eroded burnt mound.

Site 180 HZ 20705 71588
L-shaped dilapidated walling *c* 5 x 2m with long axis orientated N/S. Maximum height *c* 0.7m and maximum width *c* 1m. Constructed using larger stones at base. A number of small

quarry-like workings in the vicinity, typically *c* 4 x 3m and *c* 0.5m deep, may be associated.

Site 181 HZ 20812 71630
Grassy platform *c* 11 x 6m. Maximum height *c* 0.4m. Probing suggests area of stone under turf. Possibly structural.

Site 182 HZ 20875 71546
Flattened remains of ploughed-out burnt mound covering area *c* 10 x 8m and consisting of small burnt stones.

Site 183 HZ 20856 71555
Flattened remains of ploughed-out burnt mound covering area *c* 5 x 5m and consisting of small burnt stones.

Site 184 HZ 2035 7131
Field system covering *c* 2700 sq m.

Site 185 HZ 2049 7125
Field system covering *c* 2000 sq m.

Site 186 HZ 2048 7132
Field system covering *c* 5500 sq m.

Site 187 HZ 2049 7137
Field system covering *c* 5000 sq m.

Site 188 HZ 2060 7126
Field system covering *c* 16,200 sq m.

Site 189 HZ 2073 7119
Field system covering *c* 21,870 sq m.

Site 190 HZ 2079 7126
Field system covering *c* 2450 sq m.

Site 191 HZ 2079 7136
Field system covering *c* 4750 sq m.

Site 192 HZ 2070 7138
Field system covering *c* 2270 sq m.

Site 193 HZ 2069 7132
Field system covering *c* 3400 sq m.

Site 194 HZ 2067 7136
Field system covering *c* 2100 sq m.

Site 195 HZ 2064 7133
Field system covering *c* 2000 sq m.

Site 196 HZ 2060 7137
Field system covering *c* 6370 sq m.

Site 197 HZ 2062 7143
Field system covering *c* 3750 sq m.

Site 198 HZ 2052 7141
Field system covering *c* 2870 sq m.

Site 199 HZ 2052 7155
Field system covering *c* 10,620 sq m.

Site 200 HZ 2050 7150
Field system covering *c* 2500 sq m.

Site 201 HZ 2035 7146
Field system covering *c* 3000 sq m.

Site 202 HZ 2049 7172
Field system covering *c* 200 sq m.

Site 203 HZ 2048 7160
Field system covering *c* 500 sq m.

Site 204 HZ 2060 7152
Field system covering *c* 2500 sq m.

Site 205 HZ 2072 7150
Field system covering *c* 6300 sq m.

Site 206 HZ 2082 7153
Field system covering *c* 7500 sq m.

Site 207 HZ 2093 7143
Field system covering *c* 13,250 sq m.

Site 208 HZ 2092 7135
Field system covering *c* 1000 sq m.

Site 209 HZ 2082 7161
Field system covering *c* 15,500 sq m.

Site 210 HZ 2075 7159
Field system covering *c* 2250 sq m.

Site 211 from HZ 21022 71417 to HZ 21005 71517
Possible major dyke, now eroded, of maximum surviving height *c* 0.2m and width *c* 5m. Identified for *c* 80m and observed less clearly for further *c* 20m to NW. Cut by road at SE. Now flattened but seemingly respected by field systems. Visible best in low sun.

Site 212 HZ 21194 71699
Earthwork probably representing field boundary or (more likely according to local information) associated with damming of mill. Identified for *c* 55m running due N

before curving W before mill. Maximum height *c* 1.2m. Width at base *c* 1.2m, width at top *c* 0.6m.

Site 213 HZ 2039 7187
Area of quarry working *c* 50 x 40m on hillside containing numerous small excavations, typically *c* 5 x 3m and of maximum depth *c* 1m.

Site 214 from HZ 20165 71455 to HZ 20300 71477
Field boundary identified for *c* 120m. Maximum surviving height *c* 0.3m and maximum width *c* 0.7m. Curves from cliff towards grassland but lost at critical point near modern field system. Visible best in low sun.

Site 215 HZ 20390 71374
Possible structural complex *c* 6 x 4m defined by earthen bank of maximum surviving height *c* 0.6m and width *c* 0.5-1m. Bank continues for further *c* 18m running SE. Several stones in interior including three orthostats, maximum height *c* 0.6m. Probable hut circle. Approximately 5m to W rectangular platform *c* 7 x 3.5m composed of small stones with tumble around exterior. Larger stones around perimeter of both features.

Site 216 HZ 20508 71570
Mound *c* 5 x 3m with long axis orientated E/W. Maximum surviving height *c* 0.6m at S side. Ditch cut through N side. Probing suggests stone composition. Possible burnt mound.

Site 217 HZ 2104 7146
Field system covering *c* 1225 sq m.

Site 218 HZ 2099 7151
Field system covering *c* 250 sq m.

Site 219 HZ 2117 7164
Field system covering *c* 7500 sq m.

Site 220 HZ 2057 7155
Field system covering *c* 875 sq m.

Site 221 HZ 2043 7159
Field system covering *c* 175 sq m.

Site 222 HZ 2046 7160
Field system covering *c* 500 sq m.

Site 223 HZ 20478 71612
Field boundary identified for *c* 80m on irregular course. Maximum surviving height *c* 1m and width *c* 0.7m. Composition of earth and turf.

Site 224 HZ 20584 71560
Junction of two field boundaries. To N identified for *c* 20m, irregular, of maximum surviving height *c* 0.4m and width *c* 0.5m. To S identified for *c* 70m, maximum surviving height *c* 0.5m and width *c* 1m.

Site 225 from HZ 20360 71940 (NW) to HZ 2066 7165 (SE)
Major boundary dyke identified for *c* 240m with traces observable for further *c* 170m running approximately NW/SE. Maximum height at NW *c* 2m and width *c* 8m with rounded profile. Height decreases consistently towards SE and flattens into landscape at HZ 2066 7165. Detected running towards burnt mound (site 230). Considerable rabbit activity shows evidence of earthen composition. Local information suggests feature partly ploughed out in living memory.

Site 226 from HZ 20394 71950 (W) to HZ 21260 71310 (E)
Major boundary dyke identified for *c* 950m running approximately E/W, with less apparent length of *c* 130m westwards of road at Vaasetter. Cut by road but continues through to coast. Varies in profile according to land use with maximum height at W of *c* 2m and width *c* 8m with flattened area at top *c* 2-3m wide. Appears to have been constructed against natural slope and along geological fault line. Followed by substantial stone wall constructed immediately to N which now separates cultivated from non-cultivated land on the island. Considerable rabbit activity shows evidence of earthen composition.

Site 227 HZ 2020 7101
Field system covering *c* 700 sq m.

Site 228 HZ 2005 6985
At least 16 boat nausts in two tiers. Top tier from N to S:

a. Putative. Maximum surviving length *c*

5m and width *c* 2.5m. Evidence of stone revetting.

b. Maximum surviving length *c* 5m and width *c* 2m. Maximum depth of cut *c* 0.5m. Evidence of stone revetting.

c. Maximum surviving length *c* 7m and width *c* 2.5m. Maximum depth of cut *c* 0.7m. Evidence of stone revetting and floor.

d. Maximum surviving length *c* 7m and width *c* 2m. Maximum depth of cut *c* 0.6m. Evidence of stone revetting and floor.

e. Maximum surviving length *c* 5m and width *c* 2m. Maximum depth of cut *c* 0.5m. Evidence of stone revetting.

f. Maximum surviving length *c* 5m and width *c* 2m. Maximum depth of cut *c* 0.7m. Evidence of stone revetting.

g. Maximum surviving length *c* 7m and width *c* 2m. Contains modern boat.

h. Maximum surviving length *c* 13m and width *c* 4m. Possible former slipway now partly infilled with rubble.

Lower tier from N to S:

i. Maximum surviving length *c* 5m and width *c* 2m.

j. Maximum surviving length *c* 4m and width *c* 1.5m. Evidence of stone revetting.

k. Maximum surviving length *c* 5m and width *c* 1.5m.

l. Maximum surviving length *c* 4m and width *c* 1.5m. Evidence of stone revetting.

m. Maximum surviving length *c* 2m and width *c* 2m. Evidence of stone revetting.

n. Maximum surviving length *c* 4m and width *c* 2m. Contains modern boat.

o. Maximum surviving length *c* 5m and width *c* 2m.

p. Maximum surviving length *c* 9m and width *c* 2m.

Approximately 10m E of (p) stone-built jetty *c* 7m in length, *c* 1m wide and *c* 0.6m deep.

Site 229 HZ 2007 6990

Possible chapel or monastic site located to W and SW of cemetery. Identified by curving bank identified for *c* 40m with maximum height of *c* 0.3m and width *c* 1.5m. Bank appears to enclose a number of cell-like features although some of these may represent modern disturbance. Landscape features also reflected in fluxgate gradiometer survey. Current cemetery located on site of earlier church and general area appears to be of traditional ecclesiastical antiquity (RCAHMS 1946 no. 1203).

Site 230 HZ 20700 71610

Burnt mound (or possibly two burnt mounds) quarried at centre. Total dimensions *c* 17 x 9m with maximum surviving height *c* 1.5m. Composition of small burnt stones. Individual dimensions, to N *c* 8.5 x 7.5m and to S *c* 9 x 8m. Royal Commission *Inventory* (RCAHMS 1946 no. 1200) denotes site as representing two mounds although it seems equally likely that present form is result of quarrying from the centre of a single large mound.

Site 231 HZ 20748 71550

Burnt mound quarried in centre by ditch. Overall dimensions *c* 30 x 20m with maximum surviving height of *c* 3.7m. Now irregular in form as a result of disturbances but quarried profiles indicate a composition of small burnt stones. Probably one of the largest examples in Shetland. Quarrying previously noted in Royal Commission *Inventory* (RCAHMS 1946 no. 1196).

Site 232 HZ 20782 71555

Burnt mound adjacent to site 231. Irregularly shaped as a result of quarrying. General dimensions *c* 19 x 13m with maximum surviving height of *c* 1.9m. Quarried area indicates composition of small burnt stones. Noted briefly in Royal Commission *Inventory* (RCAHMS 1946 no. 1196).

Site 233 HZ 20042 69968

Structure with integral corn drier. Structure rectangular *c* 6.7 x 4m. Maximum diameter of drier *c* 1.6m at *c* 0.75m from floor level. Partial evidence of flagged flooring and some rebuilding.

Site 234 HZ 2031 7095

Field system covering *c* 6750 sq m.

Site 235 HZ 20818 72373
Mound *c* 3.5 x 3m with long axis orientated approximately NE/SW. Maximum surviving height *c* 1m. Slightly denuded at NE end. Little evidence of fill, possibly clearance cairn.

Site 236 HZ 20672 72452 (NW) to 20804 72381 (SE)
Linear earthwork running approximately NW/SE along gully, identifiable clearly for *c* 60m. Site 235 appears to mark lower terminal. Partially denuded and eroded with maximum surviving height *c* 0.3m and width *c* 1m. Composition of earth, turf and some large stones.

Site 237 HZ 20323 72427 (N) to 20345 72380 (S)
Linear earthwork identified for *c* 50m curving in S-shape from cliff to cliff across headland. Maximum surviving height *c* 0.3m and width *c* 1.5m. Composition mainly of large stones with an earth and turf fill.

Site 238 HZ 20416 72359
Earthen enclosure *c* 11 x 5m with long axis orientated approximately N/S. Commanding position overlooking Atlantic. Maximum surviving height of bank *c* 0.4m and width *c* 2m. Remains of three concrete post supports on inside of W bank. General denudation in vicinity, particularly at W. Presumed military.

Site 239 HZ 20392 72400
Narrow dug-out *c* 3.0 x 0.5m possibly related to site 238. Maximum surviving depth *c* 0.4m. Sea-facing edge protected by low bank of turf and stones (upcast) *c* 0.5m. wide. Some erosion on landward side.

Site 240 HZ 20458 72362
Flattened area *c* 8 x 4m with stones from the interior bedrock used to create low peripheral rubble walling of maximum surviving height *c* 0.3m and width *c* 1.5m. Inside concrete square *c* 1.3 x 1.3m containing iron bedding presumably to support mast or aerial. Probably related to site 238 and presumed military.

Site 241 HZ 20505 72349
Enclosure *c* 4.5 x 3m created against hillside with long axis orientated approximately E/W. W bank represented by exposed bedrock to height of *c* 1.5m, other walls of maximum surviving height *c* 1.5m and width 3m composed of rough stones. Little overgrowth or lichen. Interior suggests possible original turf wall base to which stonework may be secondary. Possibly military.

Site 242 HZ 20482 72213 (NW) to 20699 72161 (SE)
Linear earthwork running approximately NW/SE along gully, identifiable clearly for *c* 240m from low ground to cliff edge. Maximum surviving height *c* 0.5m (upstanding stone) and width *c* 1.5m. Variable composition but mostly of large stones (some semi-orthostatic) with an earth and turf fill.

Site 243 HZ 20685 72139
Four minor quarry workings cut into E-facing hillside. From N to S:

- **a.** *c* 2.5 x 2m, maximum depth of cut *c* 1.5m.
- **b.** *c* 3 x 3m, maximum depth of cut *c* 1.5m (reference point).
- **c.** *c* 3 x 2.5m, maximum depth of cut *c* 1.3m.
- **d.** *c* 2 x 1.5m, maximum depth of cut *c* 1m.

Other minor cuttings in the locality.

Site 244 HZ 20957 71677
Sub-rectangular well *c* 1.5 x 1m. Roughly stone-lined along NW side as far as could be seen. Maximum depth *c* 0.7m.

Site 245 HZ 20806 71787
Bomb crater of diameter *c* 7m. Funnel-shaped in profile with maximum centre depth of *c* 1.5m. Lined with outwashed gravel, mostly from rabbit activity.

Site 246 HZ 20868 72006 (NE) to 20806 71975 (SW)
Curving linear earthwork identified for *c* 60m running approximately NE/SW with the NE end destroyed by modern airstrip. Identified as part of dam and sluice system for former reservoir. Sluice located *c* 50m from SW end where bank survives to maximum height of *c* 1.5m and width *c* 8m. Peters into landscape at SW end with final width of *c* 1m. Composition of earth and turf. Sluice stone-

lined of width *c* 1m with some timber work and capping stones across stone linings. Gap *c* 2m wide *c* 10m SW of sluice now infilled with large stones, possibly representing relief channel.

Site 247 HZ 20653 71942
Putative quarrying in hillside *c* 17 x 4m. Maximum depth of cut *c* 1.5m. Exposed bedrock and loose stones in vicinity.

Site 248 HZ 20753 72066
Burnt mound of amorphous shape partially destroyed by quarrying. Main surviving bulk oval in form *c* 16 x 7m with long axis orientated approximately N/S. Maximum surviving height *c* 2m. Quarried slightly at E and centre to depth of *c* 1m. Curving arm of mound runs SE for *c* 14m with maximum width of *c* 3.5m. Small burnt mound to S (site 351) may originally have been part of the same feature giving mound diameter of *c* 25m prior to quarrying. RCAHMS 1946 no. 1199.

Site 249 HZ 20694 72052
Rectangular earthen enclosure *c* 3.5 x 3m internally. Long axis orientated approximately E/W. Maximum surviving height of bank *c* 0.3m and width *c* 0.75m. Composed of large stones with earth and turf fill. Possible entrance in E bank. S and W banks badly eroded. Curving outer bank at SE and S sides of estimated length *c* 10m, maximum surviving height *c* 0.2m and width 0.5m.

Site 250 HZ 20711 72085
Sub-rectangular earthen enclosure *c* 5 x 2m internally. Long axis orientated approximately NW/SE. Banking (where visible) of maximum surviving height *c* 0.3m and width *c* 1m. Badly eroded but steep bank immediately to SE suggests deliberate terracing.

Site 251 HZ 20724 72110
Rectangular earthen enclosure *c* 8 x 2.5m internally. Long axis orientated approximately NW/SE. Maximum surviving height of bank *c* 0.4m and width *c* 1m. Composition of earth and turf. Possible 'partition' bank *c* 1m wide across centre dividing enclosure into roughly two equal parts. Division seems deliberate terracing effect with NW part of enclosure located on higher ground. Possible entrance at SW.

Site 252 HZ 20746 72129
Amorphous earthen enclosure estimated at *c* 3.5 x 2.5m internally. Long axis orientated approximately NW/SE. Maximum surviving height of bank *c* 0.5m and width *c* 1m. Composition of earth, turf and some large stones. Constructed on pronounced terrace (?) slope. Possible further form to S identified as low curved banking *c* 5m in length of maximum surviving height *c* 0.2m and width *c* 1m.

Site 253 HZ 20736 72141
Amorphous earthen enclosure *c* 6 x 4.5m internally. Long axis orientated approximately NW/SE. Maximum surviving height of bank *c* 0.2m and width *c* 1.5m. Composition of earth, turf and large stones. Visible best at long sides. Appears to be terraced into hillside and revetted by earthen bank to SE. Some outlying tumble (?) to NE with possible evidence of outer banking.

Site 254 HZ 20767 72154
Rectangular earthen enclosure *c* 3.5 x 2.5m internally. Long axis orientated approximately NW/SE. Maximum surviving height of bank *c* 0.3m and width *c* 1m. Composition of earth and turf. Possible entrance at S corner.

Site 255 HZ 20769 72181
Interpreted rectangular earthen enclosure *c* 4.5 x 3m internally. Long axis orientated approximately NW/SE. Maximum surviving height of bank *c* 0.3m and width *c* 1.5m. Composition mostly of earth and turf but rabbit action at W shows possible stone coursing along inner face. NE and SE banks only partially evident with possible entrance through latter.

Site 256 HZ 20787 72216
Interpreted rectangular earthen enclosure *c* 4 x 2.5m internally. Long axis orientated approximately NW/SE. Maximum surviving height of bank *c* 0.3m and width *c* 1.5m. Composition of earth and turf. Possible entrance in NW side. No banking evident at SE side. Appears to be terraced into hillside and revetted by earthen bank to SE.

Site 257 HZ 20792 72228
Rectangular stone enclosure *c* 5.5 x 4m internally. Long axis orientated approximately NW/SE. SW wall composed of only a few large stones but other three walls suggest collapsed construction. Some evidence of facing stones on NW outer face. Largest stones located at corners, typically *c* 0.75 x 0.5m and *c* 0.75m in height. No obvious entrance.

Site 258 HZ 20798 72236
Amorphous rectangular earthen enclosure *c* 9 x 3.5m internally, roughly divided into two parts. Long axis orientated approximately NW/SE. Earlier (?) part *c* 4 x 3.5m lying to SE and later (?) addition *c* 3 x 3.5m to NW. Banking incomplete particularly at junction of forms and at SE end. Maximum surviving height of bank *c* 0.3m and width *c* 1.5m. Composition of earth and turf. Possible entrance at SE. Terraced effect with NW part lying on slightly higher but levelled ground. To N, *c* 2m from NW corner, further possible enclosure form interpreted as *c* 4 x 2m.

Site 259 HZ 20789 72253
Interpreted rectangular earthen enclosure *c* 4 x 3m. Long axis orientated approximately NW/SE. Maximum surviving height of bank *c* 0.3m and width *c* 1.5m. Composition of earth and turf with some evidence of large basal stones on inner face. Constructed in terraced fashion with steep earthen bank to SE.

Site 260 HZ 20802 72254
Rectangular stone enclosure *c* 5 x 2.5m internally. Long axis orientated approximately NW/SE. Defined by single line of stones and some external tumble particularly to NW. Largest stones located at corners, typically *c* 0.5 x 0.5m and 0.75m in height. No obvious entrance.

Site 261 HZ 20813 72243
Amorphous earthen enclosure *c* 5 x 2.5m internally. Long axis orientated approximately NW/SE. Maximum surviving height of bank *c* 0.3m and width *c* 2m. Composition of earth and turf. Possible entrance to NW but considerable erosion at that end of enclosure.

Site 262 HZ 20803 72264
Complex of earthen banking forming overall enclosure *c* 10 x 6.5m internally. Long axis orientated approximately NW/SE. Consists of possibly 4 internal units of *c* 2 x 2m (NW), *c* 4 x 2m (NE), *c* 3 x 2.5m (SW) and *c* 3.5 x 2m (SE). Only one of these (at SE) has banking on four sides and possible entrance. Other three all open ended and U-shaped in form. Possible central passageway running approximately NE/SW allowing access to all three. Maximum surviving height of bank *c* 0.4m and width *c* 1.5m. Composition of earth and turf. No stones visible. Some erosion at NW.

Site 263 HZ 20811 72292
Rectangular earthen enclosure *c* 4 x 2.5m internally. Long axis orientated approximately E/W. Maximum surviving height of bank *c* 0.4m and width *c* 1m. Composition of earth and turf. E end partly eroded, but possible evidence of entrance at SE corner.

Site 264 HZ 20820 72284
Interpreted rectangular earthen enclosure *c* 4.5 x 3m internally. Long axis orientated approximately NW/SE. Maximum surviving height of bank *c* 0.5m and width *c* 1m. Composition of earth and turf. SE end barely visible through erosion. Outer banking located *c* 4m to NE running parallel to NE bank of enclosure. Identified for *c* 9m with slight returns to SW at either end. Maximum surviving height *c* 0.3m and width *c* 1m. Composition of earth and turf.

Site 265 HZ 20825 722977
Amorphous rectangular (?) earthen enclosure *c* 6 x 4m internally. Long axis orientated approximately NW/SE. Maximum surviving height of bank *c* 0.5m and width *c* 1m. Composition of earth and turf with some evidence of large stones in NW bank. Only sporadic identification of banking. None visible at SE end.

Site 266 HZ 20813 72307
Interpreted rectangular earthen enclosure *c* 4 x 2.5m internally. Long axis orientated approximately NW/SE. Maximum surviving height of bank *c* 0.3m and width *c* 1.5m.

Composition of earth and turf but with large stones located at NE and SE corners. Overall outline barely visible.

Site 267 HZ 20810 72323
Rectangular earthen enclosure *c* 4 x 3m internally. Long axis orientated approximately NW/SE. Maximum surviving height of bank *c* 0.3m and width *c* 1m. Composition predominantly of earth and turf but with some large stones located along SE side.

Site 268 HZ 20832 72317
Interpreted low enclosure *c* 7 x 3m internally. Long axis orientated approximately NW/SE. Divided by terracing into two parts; to NW *c* 2.5 x 2m and to SE *c* 4 x 3m. NW part identified as slight depression with small stone setting *c* 0.75 x 0.5m at NE end. Visible banking of maximum surviving height *c* 0.3m and width *c* 1.5m. Composition of earth and turf with some stones evident. SE part identified as deliberate plateau with sporadic evidence of stonework around perimeter.

Site 269 HZ 20817 72331
Amorphous sub-rectangular earthen enclosure *c* 5 x 4m internally. Long axis orientated approximately NW/SE. Maximum surviving height of bank *c* 0.3m and width *c* 1.5m. Composition of earth and turf with some stones. Only the two long sides easily visible with the short sides badly eroded. Evidence of slight low mound towards centre. Additional feature consisting of small patch of green containing some tumble (?) located 2m E of NE corner.

Site 270 HZ 21029 72276
Cairn of base dimensions *c* 1 x 0.75m and surviving height *c* 0.5m. Possible erosion. No obviously significant topographical position. Probably modern.

Site 271 HZ 20980 72273
Cairn of base dimensions *c* 2 x 1.5m and of surviving height *c* 0.3m. Base only but easily visible on small patch of green amid heather. Lichen-covered. No obviously significant topographical position.

Site 272 HZ 20566 72639
Remains of stone-built structure *c* 7 x 3.5m internally in final form. Long axis orientated approximately NE/SW. Original form heel-shaped with maximum internal dimensions *c* 4 x 3.5m and constructed of massive orthostats to typical height of *c* 0.8m surviving on NW side in double-faced construction. Other walls now largely rubble and tumble to width of *c* 0.75m on SE side and *c* 1.5m around orthostats on NW side. Likely entrance to SW. Secondary phase identified as SW projection of existing form and rough straightening of NW walling to produce broadly rectangular shape. Extension evident best at SE with orthostat walling *c* 1m wide. Only sporadic stonework to NW. OS card, antiquity no. HZ 27 SW (M) 2.

Site 273 HZ 20486 73030 (NE) to 20343 72974 (SW)
Linear feature identified for *c* 200m winding from cliff to cliff across headland. Constructed as series of large stones surviving at irregular intervals in curving line. Some evidence of turf and earth construction between. Maximum height of stones *c* 0.4m.

Site 274 HZ 20778 73008
Foundations and lower walling of square structure *c* 4 x 4m located on high ground. Walling standing to maximum height of *c* 1m. Constructed of concrete rubble on concrete floor and surrounded by rubble and turf heaped against outer walling. Entrance at W side. Some concrete revetting to W and S faces. Some possibility that site may have been positioned on existing earthen mound. Presumably military.

Site 275 HZ 21146 72348
Bomb crater of diameter *c* 5m. Funnel-shaped in profile with maximum centre depth *c* 1.5m.

Site 276 HZ 21245 73117
Cairn of base diameter *c* 1m and surviving height *c* 0.6m. Loosely laid stones without lichen cover. No obviously significant topographical position.

Site 277 HZ 21423 73044
Cairn of base diameter *c* 1.5m and surviving height *c* 0.6m. Loosely laid stones without

lichen cover. Larger stones at base. No obviously significant topographical position.

Site 278 HZ 21284 72945
Cairn of base diameter *c* 1.5m and surviving height *c* 0.8m. Base of turf and small stones with larger lichen-covered stones above. Prominent location in landscape.

Site 279 HZ 21062 72771
Corner of stone-built structure (recorded by OS as cairn). L-shaped with sheltered corner facing E. W wall *c* 1.5m in length and N wall *c* 1.3m in length. Maximum surviving height *c* 1.3m. Substantial foundations for N wall but less substantial in W wall. No obvious facings. Some evidence to suggest that N wall could be projected westwards. Possibly an original cairn reused to create a structure. Local information suggests military use.

Site 280 HZ 20946 72741
Cairn, probably clearance, of base area *c* 2 x 1m in patch of green amid heather. Only few stones surviving to maximum height of *c* 0.1m.

Site 281 HZ 21033 72840
Square rubble concrete shaft 1.3 x 1.3m. External height *c* 0.6m and internal depth *c* 1.4m with remains of iron pipe at centre. Each corner adjacent to concrete block *c* 0.75 x 0.75m and height *c* 0.3m as bedding for iron support. Remains of concrete and iron tank *c* 4m adjacent to S. Local information suggests water tower, probably military.

Site 282 HZ 21049 71873
Linear earthwork identified for *c* 30m running from N to W and presumably related to former mill system. Feature comprises of channel with bank on either side surviving to height of *c* 0.75m. Maximum width from outer edges of banks *c* 2.5m. Width of channel varies between *c* 1m (W end) and *c* 0.3m (N end). Cut by stream and road at N end.

Site 283 HZ 20945 71685
Cairn of base dimensions *c* 0.5 x 0.5m and surviving height *c* 0.3m. Composition of small lichen-covered stones. Fairly insignificant but located in prominent position and visible from a long distance.

Site 284 HZ 21184 71774
Linear earthwork identified for *c* 18m and presumably related to former mill system. Maximum surviving height *c* 0.75m and width *c* 1m. Composition of earth, turf and some stones.

Site 285 HZ 2124 7181
Complex of banks and ditches associated with former mill system. Main ditch identified for *c* 45m between road junction and bird trap. Maximum width *c* 3m and depth *c* 1.25m. Bird trap also marks junction with series of smaller banks and ditches covering total area of *c* 25 x 20m. Inside bird trap evidence of possible platform and race (Pund Mill).

Site 286 HZ 21231 71937
Cairn of base diameter *c* 1m and surviving height *c* 0.4m. Composition of fairly large stones but without lichen cover. No obviously significant topographical position.

Site 287 HZ 21223 71958
Cairn of base diameter *c* 0.5m and surviving height *c* 0.2m. Composition of small lichen-covered stones. Clearly evident on patch of green amid heather.

Site 288 HZ 21296 71984
Area of stones and turf of diameter *c* 3.5m. No obvious alignment or arrangement of stones but some turf overgrowth. Clear landscape anomaly. Slight depression adjacent to W.

Site 289 HZ 21528 71985
Possible base of former cairn of diameter *c* 1.75m. Evidence of turf and small stone base although no cairn stones surviving. Prominent position on landscape.

Site 290 HZ 21700 72058
Putative bomb crater adjacent to road. Diameter of main crater *c* 4m with funnel-shaped profile of maximum centre depth *c* 1m. Slight extrusion to E.

Site 291 HZ 21589 72272
Sub-circular earthwork feature of estimated diameter *c* 9m. Appears to consist of earthen bank of maximum surviving height *c* 1.25m (including probable revetting) and width *c* 2m. Composition of earth and turf but rabbit

activity also suggests significant stonework in foundations. Depression in centre to depth of *c* 0.5m. Banking only partially evident and eroded at N and S sides.

Site 292 HZ 21845 72379 (NE) to 21788 72319 (SW)
Stone alignment identified for *c* 100m curving from NE to SW. Ten stones recorded, others interpreted from surviving sockets. Minimum spaced distance approximately 5m. Largest stone *c* 1.0 x 0.5m and height *c* 0.5m.

Site 293 HZ 21782 72338 (NW) to 21790 72295 (SE)
Stone alignment identified for *c* 130m curving from NW to SE. Twelve stones recorded, others interpreted from surviving sockets. No regular spacing apparent. Typical size *c* 0.5 x 0.4m and height *c* 0.5m. One stone shows putative cup mark.

Site 294 HZ 21819 72308
Partially concealed area of stones (*c* 3 x 3m) amid heather. Defined by rough bank with stone base enclosing possible low orthostats. Maximum surviving height of bank *c* 0.4m.

Site 295 HZ 21725 72510
Burnt mound *c* 8.5m in diameter and maximum height *c* 1.5m. Centre quarried to diameter of *c* 3.5m and depth *c* 1m. As result of quarrying highest point located to the N side. Burnt stones exposed in S face. RCAHMS 1946 no. 1198, OS card, antiquity no. HZ 27 SW 3, B.

Site 296 HZ 21807 72577
Burnt mound suffering from considerable quarrying. Estimated original diameter *c* 13m and surviving height *c* 1.5m. Erosion most severe at NW, SE and at centre to depth of *c* 1m. Quarrying in E face across area of *c* 5 x 4m shows exposed burnt stones. Site 337 probably part of original feature. RCAHMS 1946 no. 1198. OS card, antiquity no. HZ 27 SW 3, A.

Site 297 HZ 21417 72268
Burnt mound *c* 12 x 10m with long axis orientated approximately NE/SW. Maximum height *c* 2m. Some erosion or quarrying at NW and SW. Heather-covered against predominantly grassy landscape. Some burnt stones visible in N face.

Site 298 HZ 21449 72232
Mound *c* 3.5m in diameter and of maximum height *c* 1m. Probing and rabbit action suggest stone fill but no evidence of burnt stones.

Site 299 HZ 21431 72281 (N) to 21425 72265 (S)
Stone alignment identified for *c* 18m curving from N to S. Five stones recorded together with one socket. Stones typically *c* 0.7 x 0.5m and height *c* 0.5m. Possibly related to site 300 below.

Site 300 HZ 21440 72313 (N) to 21435 72294 (S)
Irregular stone alignment identified for *c* 20m curving broadly from N to S. Five stones recorded typically *c* 0.6 x 0.5m and height *c* 0.5m. Lies on similar course to site 299 and possibly related. Ditch cutting offers useful section and shows deeper set stones with turf backing.

Site 301 HZ 21503 72356
Crub *c* 5 x 5m and standing to maximum height of *c* 1.5m at corners. Uncoursed, unfaced rubble walls with substantial foundation stones along W wall, centre of N wall and at corners. S wall dilapidated, now providing entrance. Thick organic soil in interior covered with tumble and collapse.

Site 302 HZ 21466 72378
Crub *c* 5.5 x 4.5m with long axis orientated approximately NW/SE. Now deliberately collapsed and flattened at top to height of *c* 0.6m to provide painted airstrip marker. Substantial foundation stones at base and at corners.

Site 303 HZ 21409 72385
Remains of sub-circular earthen enclosure of estimated diameter *c* 11m. No banking evident at SE side. Maximum surviving height *c* 0.7m and width *c* 2.5m. Bank ends peter out into moorland. Modern drain cut through centre but reveals no useful information.

Site 304 HZ 21417 72295
Putative stone alignment identified for *c* 7m running approximately NW/SE. Probing suggests continuation for *c* 10m to SE. Five stones visible along total length, typically *c* 0.5 x 0.5m and height *c* 0.4m. Stones set within earthen embankment of maximum surviving height *c* 0.3m and width *c* 1.5m.

Site 305 HZ 21411 72301
Foundations for putative crub/structure estimated at *c* 6 x 6m. Sporadic stones without clear alignments. Probing suggests further buried tumble in vicinity. No outline plan possible.

Site 306 HZ 21406 72307
Foundations for putative crub/structure estimated at *c* 5 x 5m. Sporadic stones but some evidence for position of walling lines. Large stones, typically *c* 1.0 x 0.6m and height *c* 0.6m. General tumble in vicinity.

Site 307 HZ 21394 72346
Crub *c* 4.75 x 4.75m and standing to consistent height of *c* 1.5m. Uncoursed, unfaced rubble walls with substantial foundation stones along all walls and at corners. Largest stone in NW corner *c* 1.0 x 0.6m and height *c* 0.6m. Thick organic soil in interior. Well-preserved example and still in use.

Site 308 HZ 21384 72355
Tumbled crub *c* 4.5 x 4.5m. Maximum height of collapsed walling *c* 0.7m. Rubble composed mostly of substantial stones with some examples *in situ* at foundation level and at E corner. Evidence of thick organic soil in interior. Low mounds located adjacent to NE and NW walls each *c* 4.5m in length and of maximum surviving height *c* 0.8m and width *c* 2m. Both lie parallel to respective walls with composition of earth and turf.

Site 309 HZ 21428 72373
Crub *c* 5 x 4.75m and standing to maximum height of *c* 1.3m. Long axis orientated approximately NW/SE. Uncoursed, unfaced rubble walls with substantial foundation stones, particularly in S wall and at corners. Some thick organic soil in interior. Some collapse of N wall. Low grassy bank around perimeter. Maximum surviving height of bank 0.3m and width *c* 2m. Composition predominantly of earth.

Site 310 HZ 21409 72381
Crub *c* 5.5 x 5m and standing to maximum height of *c* 1.2m. Long axis orientated approximately NE/SW. Uncoursed, unfaced rubble walls with substantial foundation stones in SE wall and at corners. E corner appears slightly rounded. All but SE wall surrounded by low grassy bank. Maximum surviving height *c* 0.7m and width *c* 3m. Composition of earth and turf.

Site 311 HZ 21425 72378
Square earthen enclosure *c* 6 x 6m internally. Maximum surviving height *c* 0.6m and width *c* 1.5m. NE bank only partially evident. SE bank appears to curve inwards slightly. Composition of earth and turf.

Site 312 HZ 21414 72390 (E) to 21408 72390 (W)
Stone alignment identified for *c* 20m curving from E to W, Four stones visible, largest *c* 0.8 x 0.75m and height *c* 0.5m.

Site 313 HZ 21410 72434 (NE) to 21313 72365 (SW)
Stone alignment identified for *c* 55m running approximately NE/SW. Five stones visible although four other examples might be included taking into account possible N projection of feature for further 60m. Largest stone *c* 1.0 x 0.9m and height *c* 0.5m.

Site 314 HZ 21297 72472
Burnt mound *c* 13 x 5m with long axis orientated approximately NW/SE. Maximum height *c* 1.5m at NW end. Some quarrying evident at NW and towards centre. Rabbit activity indicates burnt stone fill.

Site 315 HZ 21336 72502 (NE) to 21324 72487 (SW)
Putative earthen embankment identified for *c* 30m curving approximately NE/SW. Maximum width *c* 1m, height difficult to interpret as a result of terracing effect on lower side of embankment. Composition of earth,

turf and small stones. Possibly related to site 316 below.

Site 316 HZ 21317 72532 (NW) to 21331 72516 (SE)
Putative earthen embankment identified for *c* 20m curving approximately NW/SE. Flattened in places but maximum surviving height *c* 0.3m and width *c* 1m. Composition of earth, turf and small stones. Possibly related to site 315 above.

Site 317 HZ 21520 72377
Putative bomb crater *c* 6 x 4.5m. Funnel-shaped profile with maximum centre depth of *c* 1.2m.

Site 318 HZ 21601 72544
Remains of circular (?) earthen enclosure of internal diameter *c* 5m. Maximum surviving height *c* 0.6m and width *c* 1.5m. S part of bank indistinct. Composition of earth and turf. Centre waterlogged.

Site 319 HZ 21627 72542
Sub-circular earthen enclosure of internal diameter *c* 3.5m. Maximum surviving height of bank *c* 0.4m and width *c* 1.5m. Possible entrance at NW. Composition of earth and turf.

Site 320 HZ 21648 72568
Irregular mound of diameter *c* 3m and height *c* 1m. Probing suggests stones within fill.

Site 321 HZ 21658 72576 (NW) to 21704 72557 (SE)
Linear earthwork identified for *c* 50m running across valley approximately NW/SE. Maximum surviving height *c* 0.8m and width *c* 2m although irregular in form, particularly towards centre. Composition of earth, turf and some stone.

Site 322 HZ 21686 72557 (NE) to 21665 72539 (SW)
Linear earthwork identified for *c* 30m running along valley bottom approximately NE/SW. Maximum surviving height *c* 0.4m and width *c* 2m. Composition of earth, turf and some stone. Dominant feature in boggy area. NE end adjoins site 321 above.

Site 323 HZ 21692 72527
Partial remains of circular (?) earthen enclosure of internal diameter *c* 7m. SW part indistinct and maximum surviving height of bank *c* 0.6m and width *c* 3m. N part of bank robbed showing fill of earth, turf and stones. Large stones evident here probably secondary. Interior contains two roughly parallel stone lines of estimated length *c* 5m set *c* 4m apart running approximately NE/SW. NW example indicates roughly faced foundation course. Interpreted as secondary feature.

Site 324 HZ 21697 72542
Sub-rectangular earthen enclosure *c* 4 x 4m internally. Long axis orientated approximately NW/SE. Maximum surviving height of bank *c* 0.3m and width *c* 1m. Composition of earth and turf. Bank indistinct at NW and SE ends. Low mound of diameter *c* 2m and height *c* 0.3m identified *c* 3m from S corner. Probing indicates stone fill.

Site 325 HZ 21706 72551
Mound of diameter *c* 2.5m and height *c* 0.4m. Probing indicates stone fill.

Site 326 HZ 21687 72590
T-shaped earthwork. Leg of 'T' identified for *c* 10m running approximately NW/SE. Maximum surviving height *c* 0.4m and width *c* 1m. Arm of 'T' identified as deliberate terracing of hillside to depth of *c* 0.5m creating lower flatter area to SE.

Site 327 HZ 21704 72576
Mound of diameter *c* 6m and height *c* 1m set amid boggy ground. Probing suggests fill of stones. Curving earthen bank adjoins mound at NE side running northwards for *c* 6m. Maximum surviving height of bank *c* 0.3m and width *c* 1.5m. Composition of earth, turf and stones.

Site 328 HZ 21727 72559 (NW) to 21736 72552 (SE)
Linear earthwork identified for *c* 12m running approximately NW/SE. Maximum surviving height *c* 1m and width *c* 1.2m. Composition of earth, turf and some stones. Steeper slope to NE as part of terracing effect. Adjoins similar feature from site 333.

Site 329 HZ 21681 72623
Stone foundation remains of structure *c* 4 x 3.5m internally. Long axis orientated approximately NE/SW. Evidence of walling *c* 1m wide with part use of orthostats.
Substantial foundation stones especially on W side. Considerable tumble and collapse at N and S sides. Possible entrance at NE. Located in sheltered gully and known locally as the 'Ferny Cup'.

Site 330 HZ 21712 72593 (NE) to 21705 72588 (SW)
Linear earthwork identified for *c* 20m turning from NE to SW. Maximum surviving height *c* 0.3m and width *c* 1.5m. Composition of earth and turf.

Site 331 HZ 21714 72615 (NW) to 21717 72610 (SE)
Linear earthwork identified for *c* 15m running approximately NW/SE. Maximum surviving height *c* 0.3m and width *c* 2m. Composition of earth and turf.

Site 332 HZ 21697 72616 (NW) to 21701 72609 (SE)
Linear earthwork identified for *c* 7m running approximately NW/SE. Maximum surviving height *c* 0.5m and width *c* 1.5m. Evidence of large stones in composition. SE end marked by large stone.

Site 333 HZ 21734 72585
Structural enclosure of internal diameter *c* 6m (c 10.5m externally). Maximum surviving height *c* 1m and width *c* 1.5m. Entrance *c* 0.75m wide at SE. Evidence of stone revetting around inner edge of enclosure including stone-lined pit *c* 1 x 1m and depth *c* 0.5m at SW. Several large stones (*in situ* ?) in interior presumably representing part of original internal arrangements. Entrance, flanked by stones *c* 0.4m in height, leads to adjacent mound of diameter *c* 5m and height *c* 0.6m across stone passageway. Mound appears to contain some burnt stones and midden. Feature joined by three linear earthworks, each effectively terracing the surrounding land into level areas:

a. From the N of the enclosure curving slightly E for *c* 45m to join junction of sites 334 and 336. Lower land lies to NE to a maximum depth of *c* 1m.
b. From the SE of the enclosure running for *c* 16m. Lower land lies to SE to a maximum depth of *c* 0.4m.
c. From the S of the enclosure curving slightly SW for *c* 16m to join site 328. Lower land lies to SE to a maximum depth of *c* 0.4m.

OS card, antiquity no. HZ 27 SW 3, C.

Site 334 HZ 21754 72627 (NW) to 21870 72595 (SE)
Linear earthwork identified for *c* 35m running approximately NW/SE. Maximum surviving height *c* 0.3m and width *c* 1.5m. Slightly lower land level on NE side. Erosion from sheep track shows composition of earth, turf and stones. Adjoins N earthwork of site 333 at NW end.

Site 335 HZ 21768 72637 (NW) to 21792 72612 (SE)
Linear feature identified for *c* 32m running approximately NW/SE and parallel to site 334 above. Maximum surviving height *c* 0.4m and width *c* 2m. Slight curve at SE end. Composition of earth, turf and stone. SE end appears to adjoin earthwork relating to site 342 and NW end adjoins site 336.

Site 336 HZ 21792 72661 (NE end)
Linear feature identified for *c* 50m running approximately NE/SW. Survey point at NE end. Effectively a deliberate terracing of hillside to create lower flat land to SE. Maximum depth to SE *c* 0.7m. Arguably a continuation of the N earthwork of site 333. Adjoins the NW ends of sites 334 and 335.

Site 337 HZ 21805 72587
Burnt mound *c* 7 x 3m and height *c* 0.7m. Long axis orientated approximately E/W. Some minor quarrying towards W end. Composition of burnt stones. Probably part of larger burnt mound site 296 lying to S and joined by narrow bank *c* 4m in length also containing stony fill.

Site 338 HZ 21802 72655
Cairn of base diameter *c* 3.5m and maximum surviving height *c* 0.3m. Turf-covered but

denuded at E showing stone composition. Together with sites 339-341 may represent a rough linear feature.

Site 339 HZ 21806 72652
Cairn base of diameter *c* 1.5m and maximum surviving height *c* 0.3m. Base composition of small stones and turf. Together with sites 338 and 340-341 may represent a rough linear feature.

Site 340 HZ 21815 72654
Cairn of base dimensions *c* 4 x 3m with long axis orientated approximately E/W. Maximum surviving height *c* 0.3m. Denuded at centre showing composition of smaller stones. Together with sites 338-339 and 341 may represent a rough linear feature.

Site 341 HZ 21818 72658
Mound *c* 4.5 x 4m with long axis orientated approximately N/S. Maximum surviving height *c* 0.5m. Probing suggest part stone composition. Together with sites 338-340 may represent a rough linear feature.

Site 342 HZ 21817 72617
Structural enclosure in rough figure-of-eight shape with long axis orientated approximately E/W. Composed of sub-circular bank to W of internal diameter *c* 5m and sub-circular bank to E of internal diameter *c* 3.5m. Open ends of banks conjoin at centre of feature giving mutual access *c* 1.5m wide and a total internal length of *c* 11m (externally *c* 17m). Maximum surviving height of banks *c* 0.7m and width *c* 2m. Composition of earth, turf and stone, but rabbit activity at SW indicates more substantial stone foundations. Some stonework also evident at NE. Probable entrance *c* 1m wide at centre of N side. Feature joined by two linear earthworks:

- **a.** From N identified for *c* 10m running due N towards site 340. Effectively terraces land levels with lower level lying to E to maximum depth of *c* 0.4m.
- **b.** From NW part identified for *c* 16m curving SW to join (?) SE end of site 335. Earthwork of maximum surviving height *c* 0.3m and width predominantly *c* 1m. Composition of earth and turf.

OS card, antiquity no. HZ 27 SW 3, D.

Site 343 HZ 21802 72695
Mound of diameter *c* 5.5m and maximum surviving height *c* 0.6m. Sheep track erosion in centre and rabbit activity both indicate presence of stonework including one orthostat. Composition otherwise unclear. Irregular, barely discernible feature.

Site 344 HZ 21917 72885
Sub-circular earthen enclosure of diameter *c* 4m internally. Maximum surviving height of bank *c* 0.3m and width *c* 1.5m. Composition of earth and turf. Evidence of stones set in interior. Possible entrance to E.

Site 345 HZ 21749 72847
Sub-circular earthen enclosure of diameter *c* 2m internally. Maximum surviving height of bank *c* 0.3m and width *c* 1.5m. Composition of earth and turf. Stones evident set against inner edge. Possible entrance located at E side. Large stone recorded *c* 4m E of entrance.

Site 346 HZ 21772 72826
Grassy area *c* 1.5 x 1m amid heather containing upright stone of height *c* 0.3m. Probing suggests additional stones in alignment.

Site 347 HZ 22131 72418
Cairn of base dimensions *c* 2 x 2m and height *c* 0.3m. Composition of small stones. Located on high ground.

Site 348 HZ 22066 72411
Mound *c* 5 x 4m with long axis orientated approximately E/W and maximum surviving height *c* 0.5m. Slight depression in S face. Composition of earth and turf and some stones.

Site 349 HZ 20544 72711 (N) to 20537 72687 (S)
Linear earthwork identified for *c* 20m running approximately N/S. Maximum surviving height *c* 0.4m and width *c* 0.5m. Composed of earth and turf with some small stones protruding.

Site 350 HZ 21427 72198
Rectangular earthen enclosure *c* 5.5 x 4.4m with long axis orientated approximately N/S. Maximum surviving height of bank *c* 0.3m

and width *c* 1m. Composition of earth, turf and some stones. Form generally indistinct.

Site 351 HZ 20753 72065
Irregular burnt mound *c* 5.5 x 2m with long axis orientated approximately NW/SE. Maximum surviving height *c* 0.4m. Probably a part of burnt mound site 248 isolated after quarrying.

Site 352 HZ 21055 71868 (NW) to 21165 71740 (SE)
Ditch or drain identified for *c* 200m curving approximately NW/SE. Maximum width *c* 4m (towards SE) and maximum depth of cut *c* 1.5m. Generally flat-bottomed profile. Assumed to relate to former reservoir and mill system.

Site 353 HZ 22116 72410 (NE) to 22043 72297 (SW)
Stone alignment identified for *c* 150m curving approximately NE/SW. Seven stones only recorded, but each clearly visible on landscape. Largest *c* 0.5 x 0.5m and *c* 0.5m in height.

Site 354 HZ 21732 72605 (NE) to 21718 72585 (SW)
Group of five large stones set in general NE/SW orientation. No specific alignment but all stand out clearly on landscape. Largest *c* 0.75 x 0.5m and *c* 0.5m in height.

Site 355 HZ 20388 71969 (NW) to 21039 71625 (SE) to 21210 71751 (NE)
Wall (hill dyke) running from NW to SE for *c* 720m and then turning to NE for *c* 230m. NW length of thickness *c* 0.6-0.7m and height of *c* 1.75m. Construction of densely packed stones in upper regions and more substantial stones at base. NE length of thickness *c* 0.5m and height *c* 1.35m. Loosely packed stone construction with few large stones at base. Wall separates moorland region from grassland region.

Site 356 HZ 20910 71944 (NW) to 21037 71889 (SE)
Bank and ditch system identified for *c* 150m curving approximately NW/SE. Outer bank of maximum surviving height *c* 0.5m and width *c* 1m. Composition of upcast earth, turf and stone. Width of ditch *c* 3m at NW narrowing to *c* 0.75m at SE. Maximum depth from top of banking *c* 1m. Presumed to relate to former reservoir and mill system.

Site 357 HZ 20260 72635
Possible promontory fort or stack settlement located on peninsula. Access gained by narrow precipitous track over natural arch (reference point). Five features identifiable:

- **a.** Partial sub-rectangular earthen enclosure *c* 6.5 x 5m with long axis orientated approximately NW/SE. Banking of maximum surviving height *c* 0.3m and thickness varying from 0.5-1.5m. No evidence of stone in composition.
- **b.** Sub-circular earthen enclosure of internal diameter *c* 2.75m located adjacent to SE of (a). Banking of maximum surviving height *c* 0.3m and thickness *c* 1.5m. Opening *c* 2m wide at NW.
- **c.** Remains of wall foundation identified for *c* 3.5m and consisting of two close-set lines of small stones of maximum total width *c* 0.5m. Located adjacent to access point and unlikely to represent substantial feature.
- **d.** Mound of diameter *c* 3.5m and maximum surviving height *c* 0.5m located adjacent to SW corner of (a). Quarried (?) at NE side. No evidence of burnt stones.
- **e.** Mound of diameter of *c* 2m and maximum surviving height *c* 0.3m located immediately to E of (d).

Site 358 HZ 2170 7240 (area)
General location of discovery of flint core. OS card, antiquity no. HZ 27 SW (2), Shetland Museum Acc. no. ARC 65750.

Site 359 HZ 20178 70248
Mound of diameter *c* 5m and maximum surviving height *c* 0.4m. Amorphous form. Cut by rig lines to S and W.

Site 360 HZ 20274 70168
Walling of length *c* 3m abutting field dyke. Maximum surviving height *c* 0.75m and width *c* 0.7m. Uncoursed rubble construction with large stones at base and chamfered end. Presumably pre-dates field dyke.

Site 361 HZ 20340 70200
Quarry working *c* 9 x 8m to S of kirk. Maximum surviving depth of cut *c* 1m. Partially infilled with rubble.

Site 362 HZ 20249 70278
Former corn drier of height *c* 2.75m. Convex in form with base diameter of *c* 2.6m and top diameter of *c* 1.8m. Original drystone construction now cemented.

Site 363 HZ 20342 70292
Stone-lined spring or well *c* 0.75 x 0.75m. Lined to depth of *c* 0.75m. Open to S feeding into small ditch.

Site 364 HZ 20306 70301
Walling of length *c* 3m running to stone enclosure. Maximum surviving height *c* 1.25m and width *c* 0.7m. Rubble construction with largest stones at base and at chamfered end. W face runs through enclosure wall with possible blocked entrance to E.

Site 365 HZ 20386 70176
Quarry working of diameter *c* 12m to S of kirk. Maximum surviving depth of cut *c* 2.5m. Now turf-covered.

Site 366 HZ 20420 70120
Walling of length *c* 17m running approximately E/W with short returns to S at each end. E return *c* 6m in length and W return *c* 4m in length. Maximum surviving height *c* 1.25m and width *c* 1m. Uncoursed rubble construction with largest stones at base.

Site 367 HZ 20363 70083
Former walling line of length *c* 40m running approximately N/S. Identified by depression of width *c* 0.6m containing embedded and scattered stones. Wall line shown on OS map.

Site 368 HZ 20350 70070
Walling of length *c* 9m running approximately NW/SE. Return at NW for *c* 3.5m and at SE for *c* 4.5m. Maximum surviving height *c* 1.5m and width *c* 1m. Uncoursed rubble construction with largest stones at base, ends and corners. Badly dilapidated at SE end.

Site 369 HZ 20248 70110
Irregular cairn *c* 4 x 3m and maximum surviving height *c* 0.4m. Fill of small stones identified by probing. Probably clearance.

Site 370 HZ 20300 70164 (NW) to 20318 70126 (SE)
Wall foundation of large stones and tumble identified for *c* 24m running approximately NW/SE, parallel to rig lines. Maximum surviving height *c* 0.3m and width *c* 1.5m. Slight ditch to SW. Wall survives within field dyke to N showing triangular profile with pair of large stones at base. Original height *c* 1.5m.

Site 371 HZ 20288 70156
Spring or well *c* 0.75 x 0.75m covered by wooden lid. Stone-lined to depth of *c* 0.5m with rough coursing. Stands proud to *c* 0.3m opening to S.

Site 372 HZ 20185 70029
L-shaped walling of main length (N/S) *c* 13.5m and shorter length of *c* 7.5m (E/W) forming sheltered corner to NW. Small eastern adjunct of *c* 1.5m at S end of main length. Maximum surviving height *c* 1m and width *c* 0.8m. Uncoursed rubble construction with largest stones at base and chamfered ends.

Site 373 HZ 20148 70046
Walling of length *c* 4m butting against outcrop. Maximum surviving height *c* 1m and width *c* 1m. Uncoursed rubble construction with largest stones at base.

Site 374 HZ 20278 20244
Mound of diameter *c* 4m and maximum surviving height *c* 0.4m. Probing suggests stone fill. Probably clearance.

Site 375 HZ 20291 70282
Structural foundation internally *c* 25 x 5m with long axis orientated approximately E/W. Footings of maximum surviving height *c* 0.3m and width *c* 2m. W end narrower and slightly rounded. Internal area divided into four roughly equal parts by cross-walls. Notable depression *c* 2 x 2m in NE corner. Structure cut by cable line running approximately NW/SE.

Site 376 HZ 20302 70000
Walling of length *c* 3.5m and maximum surviving height *c* 0.6m. Probably double-faced but only NE side visible. Coursed.

Site 377 HZ 20258 70078
L-shaped walling of main length *c* 14m running approximately NW/SE with shorter length *c* 10m forming sheltered corner to NE. Maximum surviving height *c* 1.2m and width *c* 0.7m. Uncoursed rubble construction with largest stones at base, ends and corner. Now partially obscured but recorded on OS map.

Site 378 HZ 20114 69970
Amorphous mound interpreted as *c* 13 x 4m with long axis orientated approximately NW/SE. Maximum surviving height *c* 0.4m. Probing suggests some stone in fill.

Site 379 HZ 20098 69989
Mound of diameter *c* 2m and maximum surviving height *c* 0.3m. Immediate vicinity shows numerous undulations formed by outcrops but fill here appears contrastingly soft by probing.

Site 380 HZ 20267 70468
Cairn base *c* 2 x 1.5m at head of ditch. Little turf cover. Composition of small stones. Probably clearance from ditch cutting.

Site 381 HZ 20231 70477
U-shaped walling of overall dimensions *c* 2.3 x 2m formed by single line of facing stones. Maximum surviving height of stones *c* 0.6m and width *c* 0.5m. Probably former spring or well outlet.

Site 382 HZ 20495 70620
Probable former crub represented by two parallel walls aligned approximately E/W adjacent to field dyke. Both appear to pre-date construction of dyke. N wall of length *c* 4.5m and S wall *c* 4m. Slight robbing at W end suggests original larger form. Maximum surviving height *c* 1m and width *c* 0.75m. Slight linear mound at W side may represent lost wall. Badly dilapidated.

Site 383 HZ 20780 70488
Amorphous cairn *c* 4 x 3.5m and maximum surviving height *c* 0.75m. Some turf over base stones.

Site 384 HZ 20717 70526
Rectangular cairn *c* 5.5 x 1.5m with long axis orientated approximately N/S. Cover of small stones with larger stones buried under turf. Unusual shape but location at edge of field suggests clearance function.

Site 385 HZ 20513 70493
Walling of length *c* 3m and maximum height *c* 0.75m revealed from ditch cutting. Width *c* 0.7m with coursed facings on N side. Probable return to S represented by low bank with evidence of rubble fill. Feature recorded on OS map.

Site 386 HZ 20622 70432
Quarry working *c* 6 x 2m with open face to E. Maximum depth of cut *c* 1m. Turf-covered on inside.

Site 387 HZ 20468 70488
Well *c* 1 x 1m opening to S with stone linings on other three sides. Height at back *c* 1m. Cast-iron base.

Site 388 HZ 20475 70478
Remains of stone-lined corn drier *c* 1.5m wide and *c* 0.3m in height. Evidence of other stone wall footings in vicinity.

Site 389 HZ 20445 70322
Quarry working *c* 11 x 8m with open face to W. Maximum depth of cut *c* 2m.

Site 390 HZ 20448 70340
Cairn of diameter *c* 3m and height *c* 0.75m composed of small and medium sub-angular stones. Probably clearance.

Site 391 HZ 20694 69987
Corn drier at Springfield. Convex in form, with maximum height *c* 2.2m, base diameter *c* 2m and top diameter *c* 1.6m. Drystone construction with small opening *c* 0.4 x 0.4m to N. Maximum internal diameter *c* 1.5m measured approximately 0.5m above external ground surface. Maximum wall thickness *c* 0.5m. Drier butted against rectangular building *c* 6 x 2.75m internally and wall thickness *c* 0.6m. Maximum surviving height of walling *c* 1.5m with NE gable end standing to approximate original roof height of *c* 3m. Access through to drier via opening *c* 1.25m high and 0.6m wide in gable end.

Site 392 HZ 20797 69809
Walling of length *c* 4m curving from N to SW. Maximum surviving height *c* 0.9m and width *c* 0.7m. Three large stones at N end. Remainder of wall composed of small uncoursed rubble.

Site 393 HZ 20726 69667
Cross-shaped walling of main length (E/W) *c* 4.5m and shorter length (N/S) of *c* 4m. Maximum surviving height *c* 1m and width *c* 0.5m. Two main sheltered corners to NE and NW. Uncoursed rubble construction with largest stones at base and ends. Tradition of local quarrying in vicinity.

Site 394 HZ 20545 69662
Walling of length *c* 10m running approximately E/W. Maximum surviving height *c* 0.75m and width *c* 0.5m. N face slightly battered and S face revetted with general rubble.

Site 395 HZ 20540 69660
Sub-circular depression of diameter *c* 3m and maximum depth *c* 0.3m. Located adjacent to site 394 and probably related.

Site 396 HZ 20525 69652
Walling of length *c* 7m running approximately NE/SW. Maximum surviving height *c* 0.75m and width *c* 0.6m. Battered on W side and revetted on E with general rubble. Feature appears to relate to area of deliberate stone cover *c* 10 x 10m immediately adjacent to SE. Possible fish-drying area. Cairn of diameter *c* 2m and height *c* 0.5m located *c* 5m to SW of wall.

Site 397 HZ 20510 69645
U-shaped walling of overall dimensions *c* 9 x 4m. Maximum surviving height *c* 1.2m and width *c* 0.7m. Some large stones at base.

Site 398 HZ 20504 69808
Rectangular cairn *c* 4 x 1.5m with long axis orientated approximately E/W. Maximum surviving height *c* 0.6m. Some large stones at E and W ends and others embedded along edges. Clearance function possibly secondary.

Site 399 HZ 20408 69772
Eroded cliff-top section of length *c* 10m and maximum depth *c* 0.4m. Darker soil and minor stonework evident. Coarse pottery recovered. Some undulations in vicinity.

Site 400 HZ 20525 69923
Cairn base of diameter *c* 1.5m and maximum surviving height *c* 0.2m. Composed of turf-covered, small sub-angular stones.

Site 401 HZ 20350 69910
L-shaped walling of main length (NW/SE) *c* 7.5m and other length (NE/SW) *c* 3m sheltering N corner. Maximum surviving height *c* 1.1m and width *c* 1m. Uncoursed rubble construction with largest stones at base and corners. Some rough facing evident on W (sea) side. Considerable rubble on landward side of wall, presumably derived from clearance activity.

Site 402 HZ 20468 69855
Cairn base of diameter *c* 2m and maximum surviving height *c* 0.2m. Composition of small, sub-angular stones. Presumably clearance.

Site 403 HZ 20624 69885
Cairn base of diameter *c* 2m and maximum surviving height *c* 0.3m. Composition of small sub-angular stones. Presumably clearance.

Site 404 HZ 20688 69868
Cairn base *c* 2 x 1m with long axis orientated approximately N/S. Maximum surviving height *c* 0.2m. Composition of small sub-angular stones. Probably clearance.

Site 405 HZ 20600 70003
Cairn base of diameter *c* 2m and maximum surviving height *c* 0.3m. Probably robbed at centre. Composition of small sub-angular stones. Presumably clearance.

Site 406 HZ 20496 70068
Cutting *c* 5 x 4m with long axis orientated approximately E/W opening S to 'Pig Street'. Infilled with small angular stones to depth of *c* 0.5m below ground surface. Depth of stone fill *c* 0.5m. Function unclear.

Site 407 HZ 2031 7002
Structural complex covering area of *c* 50 x 30m to S of 'Pig Street'. Main structure *c* 25 x

4.5m internally with long axis orientated approximately E/W. W gable end surviving to height of *c* 1.75m showing faced, drystone construction and quoining. Return on long walls also surviving for *c* 4m at N and for *c* 2m at S. Remainder of structure identified by turf-covered wall footings of maximum surviving height *c* 0.3m and width *c* 0.75m. Main structure subdivided into three units, each of approximate internal length *c* 7m. Adjoining structural unit *c* 9 x 4.5m internally located at NE end of N wall of main form. Similar foundation remains with internal subdivision giving unit at N of length *c* 4.5m and at S of 3m.

Other, more amorphous foundations identified to NE of complex. Whole area established on revetted stone bank *c* 0.75m high and incorporating probable water coursing.

Site 408 HZ 20377 70744
Burnt mound, partly eroded at E, with estimated original diameter of *c* 12m. Maximum surviving height *c* 0.75m with some flattening and denudation at top showing composition of small burnt stones.

Site 409 HZ 20425 70809
Spring or well *c* 0.75 x 0.75m formed by upright slabs and covered by perforated stone. Opens to SE. Flagged base *c* 1m below top of feature.

Site 410 HZ 20510 70700
Burnt mound, broadly circular with diameter of *c* 11m and slight extension to S. Maximum surviving height *c* 1.5m with some denudation and flattening at top showing composition of small burnt stones. RCAHMS 1946 no. 1202; OS card, antiquity no. HZ 27 SW 10.

Site 411 HZ 20515 70692
Crub *c* 5 x 4.5m externally with long axis orientated approximately NE/SW. Walls of maximum surviving height *c* 0.9m and width *c* 0.6m. Uncoursed rubble construction with largest stones at base and corners. Some dilapidation in NW corner. Interior surface slightly lower than field level.

Site 412 HZ 20533 70658
Mound *c* 6 x 3m with long axis orientated approximately N/S. Maximum surviving height *c* 0.3m. No stones evident by probing. Distinct feature in locality.

Site 413 HZ 20532 70645
Mound of diameter *c* 5m and maximum surviving height *c* 0.3m. No stones evident from probing. Distinct feature in locality.

Site 414 HZ 20352 69928
Earthen enclosure *c* 5.5 x 5.5m. Maximum surviving height of banking *c* 0.2m and width *c* 0.5m. Local tradition suggests fish-drying area.

Site 415 HZ 20615 70315
Evidence of wall foundation identified for *c* 20m from rubble spread. Wall shown on OS map.

Site 416 HZ 20829 69982
Quarry working *c* 2 x 2.5m opening to S. Maximum depth of cut *c* 1m.

Site 417 HZ 20815 69988
Quarry working *c* 4 x 3m opening to S. Maximum depth of cut *c* 1m. Minor adjunct to N.

Site 418 HZ 20778 70092
T-shaped walling of main length *c* 13m running approximately N/S and shorter length of *c* 6m running approximately E/W. Maximum surviving height *c* 1.3m and width *c* 0.7m. Uncoursed rubble construction with largest stones at base and ends. Roughly faced on all sides. Crude cairn at N end, presumably where collapse has been supplemented by clearance debris.

Site 419 HZ 20714 70182 (centre)
Linear feature identified for *c* 40m running from N to NW and into crub (site 420). Interpreted as wall foundation from probing and from large stones located on alignment and in S wall of crub. Foundation of maximum surviving height *c* 0.2m and width *c* 1m. Wall shown on OS map.

Site 420 HZ 20674 70206
Crub of maximum dimensions *c* 7 x 3.5m with long axis orientated approximately E/W

and angled W wall. S wall originally part of field dyke (site 419). Maximum surviving height *c* 1m and width *c* 0.5m. Uncoursed rubble construction with largest stones at base, ends and along S side.

Site 421 HZ 20670 70218
Sub-rectangular cairn base *c* 8 x 2m with long axis orientated approximately E/W. Maximum surviving height *c* 0.3m located at W.

Site 422 HZ 20654 70222
Wall foundation identified for *c* 22m running approximately E/W. Maximum surviving height *c* 0.2m and width *c* 0.5m. Stony fill evidenced from probing. Appears to act as division in field system.

Site 423 HZ 20744 70248
Rectangular enclosure *c* 17 x 15.5m with long axis orientated approximately E/W. Indistinct on S side. Maximum surviving height of banking *c* 0.3m and width *c* 1m. Some stone in composition. Presumed wall base. Other undulations in vicinity.

Site 424 HZ 20795 70365
Former corn drier of convex form and maximum surviving height *c* 2.6m. Diameter at base *c* 2m but top damaged. Drystone construction with possible former opening facing SE now blocked inside. Building to which butted now blocked off and partly infilled with rubble.

Site 425 HZ 20704 70812
Crub of maximum dimensions *c* 5 x 5m. Walls of maximum surviving height *c* 1.1m and width *c* 0.7m. Uncoursed rubble construction with largest stones at base and corners. Slightly dilapidated. Slight mound or bank of width *c* 4m adjacent to SW.

Site 426 HZ 20623 70830
Cairn base *c* 5 x 2m with long axis orientated approximately N/S. Maximum surviving height *c* 0.2m. Composition of small sub-angular stones.

Site 427 HZ 20505 70869
Crub of maximum dimensions *c* 4 x 3m with long axis orientated approximately N/S. Walls of maximum surviving height *c* 1.2m and width *c* 0.5m. Uncoursed rubble construction with largest stones at base and corners. Probably recently built or repaired. In use.

Site 428 HZ 20524 70840
Site of burnt mound recorded on OS map. Only natural outcrop identified at this location. RCAHMS 1946 no. 1201; OS card, antiquity no. HZ 27 SW 9.

Site 429 HZ 2020 6996
Series of four boat nausts, all eroded at sea edge to S. From E to W:

a. Surviving length *c* 3.5m, maximum width *c* 2.5m and depth of cut *c* 0.8m. Summer naust.
b. Surviving length *c* 4.5m, maximum width *c* 3.5m and depth of cut *c* 0.75m. Winter naust.
c. Surviving length *c* 5m, maximum width *c* 2.5m and depth of cut *c* 1.25m. Winter naust.
d. Surviving length *c* 2.5m, maximum width *c* 4.5m and depth of cut *c* 1.5m. Winter naust with rounded rather than pointed end.

Site 430 HZ 2029 6997
Series of eight boat nausts, all eroded at sea edge to S. From E to W:

a. Surviving length *c* 4m, maximum width *c* 2m and depth of cut *c* 1m. Winter naust.
b. Surviving length *c* 6m, maximum width *c* 1.5m and depth of cut *c* 1m. Winter naust.
c. Surviving length *c* 3.5m, maximum width *c* 1.5m and depth of cut *c* 0.75m. Winter naust.
d. Surviving length *c* 4.6m, maximum width *c* 2m and depth of cut *c* 1m. Winter naust, stone-lined on both sides.
e. Surviving length *c* 3m, maximum width *c* 1.5m and depth of cut *c* 0.75m. Winter naust, stone-lined on both sides.
f. Surviving length *c* 3m, maximum width *c* 1.5m and depth of cut *c* 0.75m. Winter naust, stone-lined on both sides.
g. Surviving length *c* 3.5m, maximum width *c* 1.5m and depth of cut *c* 0.75m. Winter naust, stone-lined at E only.
h. Surviving length *c* 4m and maximum

depth of cut *c* 0.75m. Winter naust, stone-lined at E only.

Site 431 HZ 2029 7067

Remains of at least seven structural foundations bounded by modern roadway at W and by former trackway to E. Standing walling in vicinity recorded as being of modern construction.

- **a.** Sub-rectangular foundation *c* 10 x 4.5m internally with long axis orientated approximately E/W. Footings of maximum surviving height *c* 0.3m and width *c* 1m. Subdivided internally to give E room of length *c* 5.75m and W room of length *c* 3.5m.
- **b.** End of structure of internal width *c* 3.5m and long axis orientated approximately E/W. Footings of maximum surviving height *c* 0.3m and width *c* 1m.
- **c.** End of structure interpreted from footings of total length *c* 6m. Maximum surviving height *c* 0.3m and width *c* 1m.
- **d.** Sub-rectangular foundation *c* 11 x 4m internally with long axis orientated approximately NE/SW. Footings of maximum surviving height *c* 0.3m and width *c* 1m. Subdivided internally to give NE room of length *c* 3.5m and SW room of length *c* 6.5m.
- **e.** End of structure of internal width *c* 5m. Maximum surviving height of footings *c* 0.3m and width *c* 0.5m.
- **f.** Sub-rectangular foundation *c* 15 x 4.5m internally with long axis orientated approximately NW/SE. Footings of maximum surviving height *c* 0.3m and width *c* 1m. Subdivided internally to give NW room of length *c* 3.5m and SE room of length *c* 3.5m.
- **g.** Probable corner of structure interpreted from footings of total length *c* 6m, maximum surviving height *c* 0.3m and width *c* 0.5m.

Site 432 HZ 20850 71146

Corn drier of convex form and maximum surviving height *c* 3.5m. Diameter at base *c* 3m and at top *c* 1.7m. Drystone construction, butted against E wall of building.

Site 433 HZ 20831 71098

Area *c* 6 x 6m containing five large stones. Other outliers to NE. Type of stones similar to those recorded from base of crubs, typically *c* 1 x 0.3 x 0.2m. Cairn of diameter *c* 1m and maximum surviving height *c* 0.2m located *c* 12m to SE.

Site 434 HZ 20914 71100

Cairn base of diameter *c* 2m and maximum surviving height *c* 0.2m. Composition of sub-angular stones of various sizes. Probably result of clearance of well/spring immediately to N. Well/spring *c* 2 x 1m with stone capping and supports.

Site 435 HZ 20921 71060 (N) to 20896 71014 (S)

Linear earthwork identified for *c* 40m running approximately N/S. Maximum surviving height *c* 0.2m and width *c* 1.2m. Some stones evident in composition. May adjoin site 436.

Site 436 HZ 20874 70976 (NE) to 20858 70952 (SW)

Linear earthwork identified for *c* 13m running approximately NE/SW. Maximum surviving height *c* 0.2m and width *c* 1.2m. Some stones evident in composition. May adjoin site 435.

Site 437 HZ 20934 71042

L-shaped walling of main length *c* 7m (N/S) and minor length *c* 2m (E/W) with sheltered corner at NE. Further rubble evident on alignment to N. Maximum surviving height *c* 1m and width *c* 0.7m. Uncoursed rubble construction with largest stones at base and ends. Main length may originally have been component of field dyke.

Site 438 HZ 21060 70966 (E) to 21000 71004 (W)

Linear earthwork identified for *c* 73m running approximately E/W. Maximum surviving height *c* 0.3m and width *c* 1m. Composition of earth, turf and some stone. Appears not to be component of existing fence line.

Site 439 HZ 20934 71002

Rectangular cairn *c* 4 x 2m with long axis

orientated approximately E/W. Maximum surviving height *c* 0.3m. Composition of small sub-angular stones with larger stones embedded around perimeter. Clearance cairn but with former structural origins.

Site 440 HZ 20875 70909
Amorphous mound of diameter *c* 6m and maximum surviving height *c* 0.5m. Located on edge of cultivated ground. Now turf-covered. Probably clearance cairn.

Site 441 HZ 20829 70816
Quarry working *c* 9 x 9m opening to SW. Maximum depth of cut *c* 1.7m.

Site 442 HZ 20816 70844
Quarry working *c* 11 x 7m opening to E. Maximum depth of cut *c* 1.75m. Shallower extension to NE *c* 10 x 4m with maximum depth of cut *c* 0.5m.

Site 443 HZ 20994 70950
Walling arrangement based on T-shaped unit. Main length *c* 12m running approximately N/S with E/W adjunct of length *c* 8m. Sheltered SW corner enclosed by later walling to form unit *c* 5 x 4m. Maximum surviving height of walling *c* 1.4m and width *c* 0.7m. Uncoursed rubble construction with largest stones at base and chamfered ends. Later enclosure notably of poorer construction. Main N/S length probably primary. Now levelled at top with larger stones.

Site 444 HZ 20940 70870
Sub-rectangular foundation *c* 10 x 2.5m internally with long axis orientated approximately N/S. Footings of maximum surviving height *c* 0.4m and width *c* 1m with evidence of coursed stone construction. Subdivided giving two internal rooms of length *c* 5m (at N) and *c* 3.5m (at S). N end showing curved projection characteristic of a corn drier.

Structure appears to represent part of enclosed area *c* 21 x 16m with long axis orientated approximately N/S. Remainder of boundary denoted by linear feature of maximum surviving height *c* 0.4m and width *c* 1m with stone fill. Presumably wall base. Structure located at SW corner. Enclosure roughly bisected by remains of standing wall of length *c* 12m running due E from interpreted corn drier.

Site 445 HZ 20940 70855
Rectangular structural foundation *c* 11 x 3m internally with long axis orientated approximately E/W. Footings of maximum surviving height *c* 0.4m and width *c* 1m with evidence of coursed stone construction. Possible partition, now rubble covered, creating subdivision into two rooms; at E of length *c* 4.5m and at W of length *c* 5.5m. Further structural unit *c* 3.5 x 3.5m butted to W end and aligned to S wall of main structure. Footings of maximum surviving height *c* 0.3m and width *c* 0.5m with evidence of coursed stone construction.

Site 446 HZ 20926 70820
Area of rubble or tumble *c* 4 x 4m showing remains of walling at E. Walling of length *c* 2m, maximum surviving height *c* 0.6m and width *c* 0.6m. Possible location of former crub.

Site 447 HZ 20916 70786
T-shaped walling with main length *c* 14m running approximately N/S and cross-wall of *c* 13.5m running approximately E/W. Large stones mostly at chamfered ends and with few at base. Different construction to most features of this type. Reasonably faced, unlike the majority of similar wall types identified.

Site 448 HZ 20914 70728
Putative burnt mound evident from turf erosion in peat-cutting area. Exposed area of small burnt stones *c* 2 x 1m suggests part of larger monument.

Site 449 HZ 20916 70682
L-shaped walling of main length (N/S) *c* 4m and shorter length (E/W) *c* 3m with sheltered corner at NW. Maximum surviving height *c* 1.1m and width *c* 0.8m. Uncoursed rubble construction with largest stones at base, ends and corner. Some evidence of rebuilding.

Site 450 HZ 21006 70682 (NE) to 20941 70652 (SW)
Linear earthwork identified for *c* 32m running approximately from NE to SW.

Maximum surviving height *c* 0.3m and width *c* 1m. Possibly continues after gap to NE. Evidence of some stone in composition.

Site 451 HZ 21019 70686
Mound *c* 4 x 2m with long axis orientated approximately NE/SW. Maximum surviving height *c* 1m. Small stones located in fill. Possible burnt mound although location suggests relationship with linear earthwork site 450.

Site 452 HZ 21034 70698
Mound of diameter *c* 3m and maximum surviving height *c* 0.4m. No stones evident from probing. Located on alignment with sites 450, 451 and 453.

Site 453 HZ 21044 70704
Mound of diameter *c* 4m and maximum surviving height *c* 0.5m. No stones evident from probing. Located on alignment with sites 450-452. Other smaller, more amorphous mounds in vicinity.

Site 454 HZ 21061 70712 (NE) to 21052 70683(S)
Linear earthwork identified for *c* 20m curving from NE to S. Amorphous in form but of maximum surviving height *c* 0.2m and width *c* 1.5m. Possibly related to site 455.

Site 455 HZ 21049 70679 (NE) to 21044 70642 (SW)
Linear earthwork identified for *c* 20m curving from NE to SW. Amorphous in form but of maximum surviving height *c* 0.2m and width *c* 1.5m. Evidence of some stone in composition. Possibly related to site 454.

Site 456 HZ 21034 70662
Earthen enclosure *c* 4 x 4m internally. Maximum surviving height of banking *c* 0.2m and width *c* 1.5m. Slight depression at centre and possible entrance at NE. Some stone in composition.

Site 457 HZ 21009 70666
Sub-rectangular earthen enclosure of surviving form *c* 6 x 3.5m internally with long axis orientated approximately E/W. Maximum surviving height of banking *c* 0.3m and width *c* 1.5m. Some stone in composition. Likely internal division giving rooms at E and W.

Site 458 HZ 20726 70650
U-shaped earthen enclosure *c* 6 x 5.5m with open end to E. Maximum surviving height of banking *c* 0.3m and width *c* 1.5m. Composition of earth, turf and some stone.

Site 459 HZ 20709 70658
Broadly W-shaped earthen enclosure *c* 10 x 6.5m with open ends to N. Maximum surviving height of banking *c* 0.3m and width *c* 2m. Composition of earth, turf and some stone.

Site 460 HZ 20705 70668
Amorphous platform of general diameter *c* 9m containing roughly rectangular sunken area *c* 7 x 4m at centre. At least two smaller depressions also visible.

Site 461 HZ 20696 70683
Putative earthen enclosure. Location only. Maximum surviving height of banking *c* 0.2m.

Site 462 HZ 20693 70694
Putative earthen enclosure. Location only. Maximum surviving height of banking *c* 0.2m.

Site 463 HZ 20713 70671
Putative earthen enclosure. Location only. Maximum surviving height of banking *c* 0.2m.

Site 464 HZ 20708 70632
Sub-circular earthen enclosure of internal diameter *c* 4.5m. Maximum surviving height at banking *c* 0.3m and width *c* 1.5m. Composition of earth, turf and some stone.

Site 465 HZ 20704 70621
Sub-rectangular earthen enclosure *c* 4 x 2.5m internally with long axis orientated approximately NE/SW. Maximum surviving height of banking *c* 0.3m and width *c* 2m. Composition of earth, turf and some stone.

Site 466 HZ 20690 70621
Amorphous earthen enclosure of estimated internal diameter *c* 3m. Maximum surviving height of banking *c* 0.3m and width *c* 2m (at

NE). Composition of earth, turf and some stone.

Site 467 HZ 20692 70605
Sub-circular earthen enclosure of estimated internal diameter of *c* 2.5m. Maximum surviving height of banking *c* 0.4m and width *c* 2.5m. Composition of earth, turf and some stone.

Site 468 HZ 20672 70640
Remains of rectangular earthen enclosure estimated at *c* 9 x 3m internally with long axis orientated approximately NW/SE. Maximum surviving height of banking *c* 0.4m and width *c* 2m. Composition of earth, turf and some stone. Subdivided to give area of length *c* 4m to NW and of at least *c* 3.5m to SE.

Site 469 HZ 20676 70653
Square earthen enclosure *c* 5.5 x 5.5m internally. Maximum surviving height of banking *c* 0.4m and width *c* 1.5m. Composition of earth, turf and some stone. Eroded or open side to SE. Some undulations to NE and SE.

Site 470 HZ 20673 70607
Putative earthen enclosure. Location only. Maximum surviving height of banking *c* 0.2m.

Site 471 HZ 20646 70609
Sub-rectangular earthen enclosure *c* 4.5 x 4m internally with long axis orientated *c* N/S. Maximum surviving height of banking *c* 0.3m and width *c* 0.75m. Composition of earth, turf and some stone. Subdivided internally to give area of width *c* 2.5m to E and *c* 1.5m to W. Slight projection to S of feature for *c* 2.5m.

Site 472 HZ 20647 70593
Crub *c* 5 x 5m externally. Walls of maximum surviving height *c* 1.1m and width *c* 0.6m. Uncoursed rubble construction with largest stones at base and corners. Grassy banks to S and W, but less distinct to N and E. In use.

Site 473 HZ 20623 70598
Crub *c* 4.5 x 4.5m externally. Walls of maximum surviving height *c* 1m and width *c* 0.7m. Uncoursed rubble construction with largest stones at base and corners. Grassy banks evident, particularly to S. In use.

Site 474 HZ 20616 70625
Crub *c* 4.5 x 4.5m externally. Walls of maximum surviving height *c* 1. 1m and width *c* 0.6m. Uncoursed rubble construction with largest stones at base and corners. Possibly of fairly recent date. In use.

Site 475 HZ 20607 70630
Putative earthen enclosure. Location only. Maximum surviving height of banking *c* 0.2m.

Site 476 HZ 20598 70622
Putative earthen enclosure. Location only. Maximum surviving height of banking *c* 0.2m.

Site 477 HZ 20599 70631
Putative earthen enclosure. Location only. Maximum surviving height of banking *c* 0.2m.

Site 478 HZ 20610 70618
Putative earthen enclosure. Location only. Maximum surviving height of banking *c* 0.2m.

Site 479 HZ 20622 70629
Putative earthen enclosure. Location only. Maximum surviving height of banking *c* 0.2m.

Site 480 HZ 20614 70607
Putative earthen enclosure. Location only. Maximum surviving height of banking *c* 0.2m.

Site 481 HZ 20635 70595
Putative earthen enclosure. Location only. Maximum surviving height of banking *c* 0.2m.

Site 482 HZ 20684 70569
Remains of sub-circular earthen enclosure of diameter *c* 4m. Banking of maximum surviving height *c* 0.3m and width *c* 1.5m. Composition of earth, turf and some stone. Largely lost at E and W.

Site 483 HZ 20694 70579
Sub-rectangular earthen enclosure *c* 3 x 2.5m internally. Banking of maximum surviving

height *c* 0.4m and width *c* 3m. Notably uneven thickness. Composition of earth, turf and some stone.

Site 484 HZ 20722 70589
Cairn base of diameter *c* 1m and maximum surviving height *c* 0.2m. Composition of angular stones.

Site 485 HZ 20736 70591
Sub-rectangular earthen enclosure *c* 7.4 x 5m internally with long axis orientated approximately N/S. Banking to W and S only with possible erosion/robbing at N and E. Maximum surviving height *c* 0.3m and width *c* 2m. Composition of earth, turf and some stone. Roughly square foundation platform *c* 2.5 x 2.5m within containing low banking of height *c* 0.2m and width *c* 1.5m.

Site 486 HZ 20757 70565
Sub-circular earthen enclosure of internal diameter *c* 1.5m. Banking of maximum surviving height *c* 0.2m and width *c* 1.5m. Composition of earth, turf and some stone. Evidence of linear earthwork of length *c* 10m and maximum width *c* 3m located *c* 3m to E.

Site 487 HZ 20727 70538
Putative earthen enclosure. Location only. Maximum surviving height of banking *c* 0.2m.

Site 488 HZ 20766 70512
Putative earthen enclosure. Location only. Maximum surviving height of banking *c* 0.2m.

Site 489 HZ 20801 70495
Putative earthen enclosure. Location only. Maximum surviving height of banking *c* 0.2m.

Site 490 HZ 20790 70530
Crub *c* 6 x 5m externally with long axis orientated approximately N/S. Walls of maximum surviving height *c* 1.4m and width *c* 0.7m. Uncoursed rubble construction with largest stones at base and corners, notably at SW where the walls overlap in unusual manner. Grassy mounds located immediately to S and E.

Site 491 HZ 20852 70389
Burnt mound, broadly circular, of diameter *c* 15m but with slight extension of *c* 6m to SE. Maximum surviving height *c* 1.2m (at N side), but with excavated depression at centre to depth of *c* 0.5m showing composition of burnt stones. Two associated (?) minor burnt mounds immediately to S and SE of diameters *c* 7m and *c* 6m respectively. Each of maximum surviving height *c* 0.5m. RCAHMS 1946 no. 1197; OS card, antiquity no. HZ 27 SW 5. Recorded location of a cist-like construction and a number of stone implements.

Site 492 HZ 21000 70373 (E) to 20982 70376 (W)
Linear earthwork identified for *c* 24m running approximately E/W. Maximum surviving height *c* 0.5m although feature flattens to W. Maximum width *c* 2m. Denudation shows fill of earth and small stones.

Site 493 HZ 20139 70413
Rectangular earthen enclosure *c* 5.5 x 3m internally with long axis orientated approximately NW/SE. Banking of maximum surviving height *c* 0.3m and width *c* 1.5m. Composition of earth, turf and some stone.

Site 494 HZ 21045 70393 (N) to 21048 70377 (S)
Linear earthwork identified for *c* 15m running approximately N/S. Maximum surviving height *c* 0.4m and width *c* 1.5m. Appears to run across natural gully. Composition of earth, turf and some stone.

Site 495 HZ 21051 70400
Cairn base of diameter *c* 3m and maximum surviving height *c* 0.3m. Erosion shows fill of small sub-angular stones. Possible clearance cairn but no field systems evident.

Site 496 HZ 21114 70485
U-shaped earthen enclosure *c* 7 x 5m internally with open end to SE. Banking of maximum surviving height *c* 0.4m and width *c* 1.5m. Composition of earth, turf and some stone.

Site 497 HZ 21119 70490
U-shaped earthen enclosure *c* 4.5 x 2m internally with open end to SE. Banking of maximum surviving height *c* 0.4m and width *c* 1.5m. Composition of earth, turf and some stone.

Site 498 HZ 21125 70496
U-shaped earthen enclosure *c* 5 x 2m internally with open end to SE. Banking of maximum surviving height *c* 0.3m and width *c* 1m. Composition of earth, turf and some stone.

Site 499 HZ 21006 70483
Quarry working *c* 16 x 14m and maximum depth of cut estimated at *c* 2.5m. Now waterfilled. Sources suggest workings related to construction of kirk.

Site 500 HZ 21005 70451
Linear earthwork identified for *c* 8m running approximately NE/SW. Maximum surviving height *c* 0.4m and width *c* 2m. Stony fill exposed in places.

Site 501 HZ 21003 70442
Grassy platform *c* 4 x 3m terraced into hillside overlooking valley. Slight banking of maximum surviving height *c* 0.3m on S edge.

Site 502 HZ 21002 70436
Grassy platform *c* 5 x 5m terraced into hillside overlooking valley. Slight banking of maximum surviving height *c* 0.3m on S edge.

Site 503 HZ 20993 70443
Grassy platform *c* 5 x 5m terraced into hillside overlooking valley. Slight banking of maximum surviving height *c* 0. 3m on S edge.

Site 504 HZ 20998 70457
Cairn base of diameter *c* 3.5m and maximum surviving height *c* 0.4m. Exposed to S showing small sub-angular stones. Possibly part of boundary system.

Site 505 HZ 20984 70472 (NE) to 20947 70437 (SW)
Linear feature composed of earthen embankment and cairns identified for *c* 60m curving approximately NE/SW. Earthen embankment located at SW end for distance of *c* 20m. Maximum surviving height *c* 0.4m and width *c* 2m. Composition of earth, turf and stone. At NE end appears to terminate at cairn of diameter *c* 3m and maximum surviving height *c* 0.4m. Three additional cairns located on same NE alignment of diameters (from SW to NE) *c* 3m, 1.5m and 3m respectively. Maximum surviving heights *c* 0.5m, 0.4m and 0.5m respectively.

Site 506 HZ 20967 70473
Square earthen enclosure *c* 2.5 x 2.5m internally. Banking of maximum surviving height *c* 0.2m and width *c* 1m. Composition of earth, turf and some stones.

Site 507 HZ 20996 70491
Crub *c* 6.5 x 5m externally with long axis orientated *c* NE/SW. Walls of maximum surviving height *c* 1.4m and width *c* 0.7m. Uncoursed rubble construction with largest stones at base and corners. Slight grassy mound to N.

Site 508 HZ 21018 70520
Crub *c* 5 x 5.5m externally with long axis orientated approximately NE/SW. Walls of maximum surviving height *c* 1.4m and width *c* 0.6m. NE corner curved, but without obvious reason other than relationship with existing mound *c* 2m wide at that point. Uncoursed rubble construction with largest stones at base and corners. Slight grassy mound to W.

Site 509 HZ 21000 70534 (W) to 21021 70522 (SE)
Amorphous earthen embankment identified for *c* 22m curving from W to SE. Maximum surviving height *c* 0.3m and width *c* 1.5m. Composition of earth, turf and stone.

Site 510 HZ 20985 70584
Quarry working *c* 14 x 10m. Maximum depth of cut estimated at *c* 1.5m. Now waterfilled. Sources suggest workings relate to construction of kirk.

Site 511 HZ 20922 70576
Cairn base of diameter *c* 3m and maximum surviving height *c* 0.2m. Presumably robbed but some small sub-angular stones evident in denuded area.

Site 512 HZ 20985 70480 (NE) to 20956 70423 (SW)
Linear earthwork identified for *c* 70m curving approximately NE/SW. Maximum surviving height *c* 0.4m and width *c* 2m. Composition of earth, turf and stone.

Site 513 HZ 21025 71356
Series of six stones within area *c* 5 x 2.5m probably representing some structural base. Largest stone *c* 0.7 x 0.5 x 1m. Cairn of diameter *c* 1m and maximum surviving height *c* 0.2m located *c* 5m to W. Composition of sub-angular stones of various sizes. Additional cairn of diameter *c* 1.5m, maximum surviving height *c* 0.2m and similar fill located *c* 7m further to SW.

Site 514 HZ 21102 71366
Crub *c* 5 x 5m externally. Walls of maximum surviving height *c* 1.2m and width *c* 0.7m. N/S wall continues to N for additional 2m. Uncoursed rubble construction with largest stones at base, corners and within northern projection.

Site 515 HZ 21076 71197
Rectangular earthen enclosure *c* 6 x 3.5m internally with long axis orientated approximately E/W. Banking of maximum surviving height *c* 0.3m and width *c* 2m. S side mostly lost. Composition of earth, turf and some stone.

Site 516 HZ 21024 71209
Surviving W end of structure formerly terraced into hillside. Surviving dimensions *c* 4 x 3.75m with long axis orientated approximately E/W. Semi-subterranean construction of mortared, coursed stones with lowest levels resting on bedrock. Maximum depth from present turf level to floor *c* 1.75m. Fireplace of width *c* 0.6m in centre of W wall with stone lintel and chimney.

Site 517 HZ 20929 71208
Amorphous circular earthen enclosure of diameter *c* 10m. Banking of maximum surviving height *c* 0.3m and width *c* 2m. Composition of earth and turf.

Site 518 HZ 20487 70119
Well, represented by iron outlet of diameter *c* 0.7m surmounted by circular slatted wooden cover. Known locally as 'The Minister's Well'.

Site 519 HZ 20336 70684
Quarry working of diameter *c* 5m. Maximum depth of cut *c* 1.5m although tradition of local copper working would suggest greater depth.

Site 520 HZ 2117 7007
Located site of wreck *El Gran Grifon* recorded lost in 1588. 0S card, antiquity no. HZ 27 3W (M); Martin 1972.

Field Systems
The following sites (521-627) represent the field system units identified during the 1986 survey. Each unit is numbered below together with a general (ie 8-figure) grid reference taken at an approximate centre point and an estimated, rounded area.

Site 521 HZ 2015 6995, *c* 500 sq m.

Site 522 HZ 2011 7003, *c* 3000 sq m.

Site 523 HZ 2021 7002, *c* 2500 sq m.

Site 524 HZ 2018 7005, *c* 500 sq m.

Site 525 HZ 2013 7011, *c* 3100 sq m.

Site 526 HZ 2016 7014, *c* 1700 sq m.

Site 527 HZ 2014 7017, *c* 400 sq m.

Site 528 HZ 2015 7022, *c* 500 sq m.

Site 529 HZ 2017 7022, *c* 2500 sq m.

Site 530 HZ 2026 7020, *c* 1000 sq m.

Site 531 HZ 2032 7016, *c* 1500 sq m.

Site 532 HZ 2025 7033, *c* 5600 sq m.

Site 533 HZ 2032 7034, *c* 600 sq m.

Site 534 HZ 2036 7031, *c* 4200 sq m.

Site 535 HZ 2040 7027, *c* 2600 sq m.

Site 536 HZ 2041 7023, *c* 1000 sq m.

Site 537 HZ 2040 7016, *c* 1300 sq m.

Site 538 HZ 2045 7025, *c* 2600 sq m.

Site 539 HZ 2054 7026, *c* 400 sq m.

Site 540 HZ 2057 7026, *c* 3000 sq m.

Site 541 HZ 2065 7025, *c* 5000 sq m.

Site 542 HZ 2066 7018, *c* 2600 sq m.

Site 543 HZ 2062 7021, *c* 600 sq m.

Site 544 HZ 2059 7015, *c* 5000 sq m.

Site 545 HZ 2053 7018, *c* 900 sq m.

Site 546 HZ 2047 7018, *c* 1800 sq m.
Site 547 HZ 2047 7022, *c* 400 sq m.
Site 548 HZ 2051 7200, *c* 300 sq m.
Site 549 HZ 2051 7018, *c* 700 sq m.
Site 550 HZ 2042 7014, *c* 600 sq m.
Site 551 HZ 2039 7008, *c* 8200 sq m.
Site 552 HZ 2051 7010, *c* 300 sq m.
Site 553 HZ 2051 7008, *c* 500 sq m.
Site 554 HZ 2055 7005, *c* 1300 sq m.
Site 555 HZ 2062 7003, *c* 2000 sq m.
Site 556 HZ 2077 7014, *c* 1600 sq m.
Site 557 HZ 2042 7003, *c* 900 sq m.
Site 558 HZ 2050 7003, *c* 2400 sq m.
Site 559 HZ 2053 7003, *c* 700 sq m.
Site 560 HZ 2058 7004, *c* 500 sq m.
Site 561 HZ 2043 6999, *c* 1900 sq m.
Site 562 HZ 2035 6997, *c* 4800 sq m.
Site 563 HZ 2042 6996, *c* 2700 sq m.
Site 564 HZ 2048 6998, *c* 1200 sq m.
Site 565 HZ 2041 6988, *c* 4600 sq m.
Site 566 HZ 2053 6995, *c* 750 sq m.
Site 567 HZ 2049 6994, *c* 1500 sq m.
Site 568 HZ 2059 6990, *c* 1900 sq m.
Site 569 HZ 2050 6985, *c* 18,000 sq m.
Site 570 HZ 2076 6987, *c* 2000 sq m.
Site 571 HZ 2070 6979, *c* 15,500 sq m.
Site 572 HZ 2065 6988, *c* 2500 sq m.
Site 573 HZ 2066 6994, *c* 1200 sq m.
Site 574 HZ 2035 7044, *c* 22,500 sq m.
Site 575 HZ 2027 7038, *c* 2100 sq m.
Site 576 HZ 2033 7037, *c* 1800 sq m.
Site 577 HZ 2037 7037, *c* 900 sq m.
Site 578 HZ 2040 7037, *c* 700 sq m.
Site 579 HZ 2050 7033, *c* 2000 sq m.
Site 580 HZ 2055 7035, *c* 4500 sq m.
Site 581 HZ 2069 7031, *c* 10,000 sq m.
Site 582 HZ 2072 7035, *c* 1900 sq m.
Site 583 HZ 2075 7043, *c* 15,000 sq m.
Site 584 HZ 2069 7044, *c* 2000 sq m.
Site 585 HZ 2066 7047, *c* 5000 sq m.
Site 586 HZ 2066 7043, *c* 500 sq m.
Site 587 HZ 2065 7047, *c* 700 sq m.
Site 588 HZ 2050 7053, *c* 500 sq m.
Site 589 HZ 2065 7056, *c* 300 sq m.
Site 590 HZ 2055 7060, *c* 2000 sq m.
Site 591 HZ 2053 7057, *c* 600 sq m.
Site 592 HZ 2055 7068, *c* 1200 sq m.
Site 593 HZ 2045 7075, *c* 5000 sq m.
Site 594 HZ 2041 7077, *c* 600 sq m.
Site 595 HZ 2051 7067, *c* 3500 sq m.
Site 596 HZ 2045 7080, *c* 600 sq m.
Site 597 HZ 2051 7091, *c* 800 sq m.
Site 598 HZ 2056 7089, *c* 6000 sq m.
Site 599 HZ 2056 7080, *c* 2400 sq m.
Site 600 HZ 2061 7081, *c* 1800 sq m.
Site 601 HZ 2065 7085, *c* 9000 sq m.
Site 602 HZ 2074 7089, *c* 6900 sq m.
Site 603 HZ 2081 7088, *c* 1500 sq m.
Site 604 HZ 2072 7073, *c* 3800 sq m.
Site 605 HZ 2077 7074, *c* 1300 sq m.
Site 606 HZ 2079 7077, *c* 300 sq m.
Site 607 HZ 2077 7079, *c* 300 sq m.
Site 608 HZ 2075 7078, *c* 600 sq m.
Site 609 HZ 2076 7077, *c* 200 sq m.
Site 610 HZ 2093 7065, *c* 65,600 sq m.
Site 611 HZ 2105 7079, *c* 1000 sq m.
Site 612 HZ 2097 7082, *c* 65,000 sq m.
Site 613 HZ 2103 7090, *c* 7500 sq m.
Site 614 HZ 2088 7099, *c* 62,400 sq m.
Site 615 HZ 2082 7103, *c* 4000 sq m.
Site 616 HZ 2091 7105, *c* 6400 sq m.
Site 617 HZ 2092 7110, *c* 65,600 sq m.
Site 618 HZ 2098 7104, *c* 63,000 sq m.
Site 619 HZ 2105 7101, *c* 66,000 sq m.
Site 620 HZ 2110 7110, *c* 2000 sq m.
Site 621 HZ 2111 7116, *c* 7200 sq m.
Site 622 HZ 2113 7123, *c* 1900 sq m.
Site 623 HZ 2117 7122, *c* 6300 sq m.
Site 624 HZ 2099 7130, *c* 1300 sq m.
Site 625 HZ 2103 7126, *c* 600 sq m.

Site 626 HZ 2105 7130, *c* 4500 sq m.

Site 627 HZ 2113 7143, *c* 400 sq m.

Site 628 HZ 21425 71404
Dilapidated crub *c* 7 x 5m of uneven width with long axis orientated approximately N/S. Maximum surviving height *c* 0.6m along E wall. Possible entrance *c* 0.5m wide at centre of N wall. Uncoursed rubble construction with largest stones at base and corners. Base width *c* 0.7m. Considerable tumble in vicinity to S.

Site 629 HZ 21416 71410
Area of stones *c* 7 x 7m including 5 stones in apparent alignment. At N, cairn of diameter *c* 3m and maximum surviving height *c* 0.7m composed of large rounded stones. Considerable undulation in vicinity.

Site 630 HZ 21386 71386
Area *c* 20 x 20m containing 8 large stones, typically 1.0 x 0.5 x 0.5m. No obvious alignment but anomalous feature in vicinity.

Site 631 HZ 21383 71406
Area *c* 4 x 3m containing possible stone alignments; one (4 stones) running approximately N/S, the other (5 stones) running approximately E/W and joining at right angle. Stones typically 0.7 x 0.5 x 0.4m. Possible crub foundations.

Site 632 HZ 21516 71530
Burnt mound originally *c* 11 x 10m with long axis orientated approximately N/S. Now quarried at SE and at top showing composition of small burnt stones. Maximum surviving height *c* 1m.

Site 633 HZ 21507 71546
Burnt mound originally *c* 8 x 5m with long axis orientated approximately E/W. Now quarried at W face giving concave slope and showing composition of small burnt stones. Maximum surviving height *c* 1m.

Site 634 HZ 21542 71651
Cairn base of diameter *c* 0.7m and height *c* 0.2m. Mostly turf-covered.

Site 635 HZ 21616 71578
Crub (?) *c* 5.5 x 4m with long axis orientated approximately E/W and maximum surviving height *c* 1m at E end. Uncoursed rubble construction with largest stones at base and corners. General dilapidation but wall width at base *c* 0.7m. Grassy mounds immediately adjacent to N and W, each of width *c* 2m and height *c* 0.4m.

Site 636 HZ 21599 71616
Burnt mound of diameter *c* 9m and maximum surviving height on hillside *c* 1.2m. Turf-covered but some evidence of small burnt stones on surface.

Site 637 HZ 21377 71698
Part of tailplane of Heinkel aircraft recorded as having crash-landed in 1941. Tailwing *c* 4m long on fuselage *c* 4m long. Parts of engine and mountings *c* 60m to SE. Other debris identified throughout adjacent fields.

Site 638 HZ 21266 71704
Burnt mound of diameter *c* 9m and maximum surviving height *c* 1.5m. Quarried at centre to fairly uniform depth of *c* 0.5m showing composition of small burnt stones. RCAHMS 1946 no. 1195. OS card, antiquity no. HZ 27 SW 7,1.

Site 639 HZ 21272 71720
Earthen enclosure *c* 5.5 x 4m internally with long axis orientated approximately N/W. Maximum surviving height of banking *c* 0.3m and width *c* 2m. Composition of earth, turf and some stone.

Site 640 HZ 21276 71730
Earthen enclosure *c* 4.5 x 4.5m internally. Maximum surviving height of banking *c* 0.3m and width *c* 2m. Composition of earth, turf and some stone.

Site 641 HZ 21321 71703
Mound of diameter *c* 7m presumably formed as part of adjacent ditch upcast. Maximum surviving height *c* 1.5m from ditch base. Turf-covered but rabbit activity shows possible stonework. Recorded location of fragment of worked steatite. OS card, antiquity no. HZ 27 SW 7, 2 (denoted as mill).

Site 642 HZ 21262 71717
Earthen enclosure *c* 5 x 4m internally with long axis orientated approximately N/S.

Maximum surviving height of banking *c* 0.3m and width *c* 2m. Composition of earth, turf and some stone. Open end at N.

Site 643 HZ 21701 71590
Amorphous mound *c* 7 x 4m with long axis orientated approximately E/W and maximum surviving height *c* 0.5m. Probing indicates some stone in composition. Possible surface quarrying in vicinity. Possible upcast mound?

Site 644 HZ 21670 71523
Possible spring or well, *c* 0.6 x 0.6m, with large stones set at S and W standing *c* 0.4m above ground surface. Submerged stones at N and E.

Site 645 HZ 21679 71471
Possible earthen enclosure of diameter *c* 8m defined by low bank. Maximum surviving height of bank *c* 0.3m and thickness *c* 2m. Possible square depression *c* 4 x 4m evident inside perhaps representing former crub site with external banking.

Site 646 HZ 21639 71448
Cairn base of diameter *c* 0.75m and maximum surviving height *c* 0.2m. Both large and small stones evident.

Site 647 HZ 21778 71424
Dilapidated crub *c* 5.5 x 4.75m with long axis orientated approximately E/W. Maximum surviving height *c* 1.2m along W wall. Uncoursed rubble construction with largest stones at NE and SW corners. Wall thickness estimated at *c* 0.5m. Slight grassy mounds identified on all four sides, typically of maximum surviving height *c* 0.3m and width *c* 2m.

Site 648 HZ 21762 71356
Stone setting *c* 6.5 x 3.5m with long axis orientated approximately E/W. Stones typically 0.6 x 0.5 x 0.2m set at irregular intervals defining rectangular area, although less clear at SE. Largest stone (*c* 1.5 x 0.7 x 0.6m) with flat top located alongside.

Site 649 HZ 21598 71376
Minor quarry working *c* 4 x 2.5m with long axis orientated approximately E/W and maximum depth of cut *c* 0.5m. Some loose stone to W and other smaller workings *c* 10m to SW.

Site 650 HZ 21594 71399
Stone setting interpreted as *c* 5 x 5m and defined by sporadic stone alignment particularly at N and E. Stones typically *c* 0.3 x 0.2 x 0.2m. Slight grassy mounds identified on all four sides, typically of maximum surviving height *c* 0.3m and width *c* 2m. Probably former crub site.

Site 651 HZ 21568 71411
Stone setting interpreted as *c* 3.5 x 3m with long axis orientated approximately N/S. Arrangement defined by residual internal raised turf platform against which stones appeared to have been set. Surviving stones evident at SW corner and along E side. Slight grassy mounds adjacent to SW and E. Probably former crub site.

Sub-circular enclosure of diameter *c* 10m identified *c* 5m to NE. Feature appears to contain turf plateau *c* 6 x 5m which may represent further crub area. Single stone located at NE corner. Enclosure banking of height *c* 0.3m and width *c* 2m. Probably former crub site.

Site 652 HZ 21544 71464
Dilapidated crub *c* 5.5 x 5.5m and maximum surviving height *c* 1.3m at SE corner. Only SE wall standing to any extent. W wall robbed? Tumble to width of *c* 1.5m with estimated wall thickness at base of *c* 0.8m. Uncoursed rubble construction with largest stones at base, including bedrock *c* 2 x 1m providing footing for NW corner. Grassy banks evident especially to S and W, typically of maximum surviving height *c* 0.3m and width *c* 2m.

Site 653 HZ 21552 71491 (NE) to 21511 71457 (SW)
Wall foundations, presumably originally connected over length of *c* 55m, identified at two points at NE and SW. At NE point, base line of packed stones of length *c* 4m, width *c* 0.3m and height *c* 0.2m. Similar but larger stones over length of *c* 4.5m at SW point. Wall offset from standing stone wall and presumably represents former boundary feature.

Site 654 HZ 21448 71342
Walling of length *c* 14m and running approximately NW/SE with maximum surviving height of *c* 1.2m. Uncoursed rubble construction with base width *c* 0.8m tapering to *c* 0.6m at top. Some large stones at base. Partial dilapidation in places.

Site 655 HZ 21383 71340 (NE) to 21342 71302 (SW)
Linear feature identified for *c* 56m running approximately NE/SW. Maximum surviving height *c* 1m and width *c* 3m. Composition of earth, turf and stone. Appears to represent upcast from adjacent ditch to E, but also underlies line of stone wall to N. Ditch may be secondary effect of creating linear feature which clearly pre-dates wall.

Site 656 HZ 21603 71170 (NW) to 21703 71096 (SE)
Linear feature curving from NW to SE for *c* 150m along cliff edge. Stone-built, surviving to general height of *c* 0.4m and width *c* 0.5m. Now mostly tumble of angular stones. Recorded locally as the 'Pony Dyke'.

Site 657 HZ 21770 71164
Cairn or setting of diameter *c* 2.5m located on high ground. Defined by ring of set stones typically *c* 0.3 x 0.2m flush with ground surface. Central depression of diameter *c* 0.3m possibly for pole or mast?

Site 658 HZ 21998 71483
Interpreted stone setting in sub-circular form of estimated diameter *c* 15m located on sheltered plateau. E end of feature presumably lost through coastal and surface erosion. SW side formed against natural bedrock. Defined by set stones, typically *c* 0.4 x 0.3 x 0.2m. Possible internal setting *c* 4 x 2m located against SE side.

Site 659 HZ 21385 71686
Walling of length *c* 14m running approximately NW/SE. Tumbled and uneven, of maximum surviving height *c* 0.5m and width *c* 0.5-2m. Shows original extent of walling to run down to mill ditches.

Site 660 HZ 21278 71771
Area of upcast and disturbance *c* 5 x 4m at head of ditch and presumed site of former Leogh Mill. Upcast in form of U-shaped mound of maximum surviving height *c* 1m composed of earth, turf and deliberate stonework probably representing mill dam.

Site 661 HZ 21264 71787 (NW) to 21326 71797 (NE)
Ditch system, presumably associated with mill (site 660), identified for *c* 85m running approximately from NW to NE. Ditch *c* 1m wide with upcast banks of maximum surviving height *c* 0.5m and width *c* 1.5m. Ditch line includes site 660.

Site 662 HZ 21291 71741 (NE) to 21288 71717 (S)
Earthwork identified for *c* 25m running from approximately NE to S and presumably associated with mill systems. Maximum surviving height *c* 0.4m and width *c* 2m, tapering at ends. No indications of associated ditch. Composition predominantly of earth and turf.

Site 663 HZ 21317 71779 (NW) to 21324 71699 (S)
Earthwork identified for *c* 80m running from approximately NW to S and presumably associated with mill systems. Terminates at NW at site 661 and at S at site 641. Maximum surviving height *c* 0.3m and width *c* 2m. Composition predominantly of earth and turf.

Site 664 HZ 21541 71829
Earthwork of length *c* 20m adjacent to ditch and presumably related to mill systems. Maximum surviving height from ground to E *c* 0.3m, from depression to W *c* 0.7m. Curved feature with composition of earth, turf and some stone.

Site 665 HZ 21549 71837
L-shaped length of walling of maximum surviving height *c* 0.3m and width *c* 0.6m. Appears to be *c* 6m continuation of adjacent large E/W wall with return of *c* 5m to S. Presumably shows original extent to walling to run down to (and along?) mill ditches.

Site 666 HZ 21570 71878 (N) to 21564 71840 (S)
Earthwork identified for *c* 30m curving from N and S. Maximum surviving height *c* 0.5m and width *c* 1m. Composition of earth, turf and some stone. Other minor cutting and undulations identified immediately adjacent to W and presumably associated with mill systems. Probable site of former Shuny Mill.

Site 667 HZ 21848 72109
Possible burnt mound of diameter *c* 7m and maximum surviving height *c* 0.7m. Heather-covered but probing suggests stone fill. Some evidence of burnt stones in denuded areas.

Site 668 HZ 21795 72137
Curved earthwork identified for *c* 24m running from approximately N to SW. Maximum surviving height *c* 1m and width *c* 3m. Composition of earth, turf and stone. Crosses stream and presumably relates to mill system.

Site 669 HZ 21784 71360
Amorphous mound of diameter *c* 5.5m and maximum surviving height *c* 0.5m. Rabbit activity at centre and at N suggests presence of stonework within composition. Possible settlement site.

Site 670 HZ 22211 74124
Circular stone setting of diameter *c* 3.5m consisting of inner and outer ring of stones, typically *c* 0.3 x 0.2m, flush with turf. Probable base point for mast or pole.

Site 671 HZ 22226 74054
Circular stone setting of diameter *c* 2.5m with stones typically 0.5m wide flush with turf. Concrete block *c* 0.4 x 0.4m containing metal pin located at approximate centre. Probable aerial or mast support.

Site 672 HZ 22203 74044
Building remains *c* 6 x 3m externally with long axis orientated approximately N/S. Uncoursed rubble walling of maximum height *c* 1.5m. Width of walling *c* 0.3m at top but *c* 1m at collapsed base. Structural division located *c* 2.5m from N end of E wall suggesting that NE corner was later addition. Paved entrance *c* 0.5m wide located at NW corner. Construction includes brick and concrete but evidence for stone footings set inside long walls suggests earlier foundation. Undulation identified immediately to W. Feature located in hollow and hidden from view.

Site 673 HZ 22473 73740
Mound of diameter *c* 5.5m and maximum surviving height *c* 0.4m containing two probable cists at NE and SW sides respectively. Cist at NE *c* 1 x 0.6m with long axis orientated approximately NW/SE and orthostats at short ends. Cist at SW *c* 1 x 0.6m with long axis orientated approximately NW/SE and orthostat located along SW side. Mound composition of earth, turf and some stone. Possible burials?

Site 674 HZ 22109 73620
Series of cultivation beds covering area of *c* 250 sq m. 32 individual beds identified within sheltered gully. Anomalous cultivated patch in moorland area.

Site 675 HZ 21773 73881 (NW) to 22033 73680 (road) to HZ 22092 73622 (SE) to 22060 73508 (S)
Linear feature identified over distance of *c* 400m running from NW to SE across road (*c* 300m) and then S to stream (*c* 100m). Appears to have been formed by alignment of stones set at no particular interval and originally infilled with earth, turf and smaller stones. Some large stones typically *c* 0.8 x 0.6 x 0.2m although most examples smaller. Some significant gaps in line but also some well-preserved lengths, notably E of small loch at NW end. Typical width *c* 1.5m. Length running to S shows more complete turf cover and is presumably more indicative of original form. No evidence of associated ditch to indicate provenance of infill material.
Feature appears to include two additional sites (sites 719 and 720), as components of original layout.

Site 676 HZ 21750 71340
Field or drainage alignment identified across area of *c* 370 x 60m and consisting of 7 parallel field/drain lines running from SE cliff

to lowland drainage ditch system. Remarkable regularity of feature suggests modern activity but local information suggests to the contrary. Interconnection of lines suggests possible catchment system for mill streams. Visible from a considerable distance. Total area covered *c* 20,400 sq m.

Site 677 HZ 21867 73629
Structural form (collapsed) *c* 7 x 4m with long axis orientated approximately E/W. General form appears to be U-shaped with open end to E. Collapsed walls of likely original width *c* 1m now tumbled to over *c* 2.5m, with maximum height of *c* 0.5m and composition of angular stones. No wall evident at W end but slight rise suggests presence of footings. Some local association with construction of adjacent modern road.

Site 678 HZ 22342 72765 (NE) to 22168 72685 (W)
Linear feature identified following cliff line over distance of *c* 205m from NE to W. Maximum surviving height *c* 0.7m and width *c* 2m. Composition of earth, turf and stone. Probably stone based but no evidence of associated ditch from which material may have been derived. Now substantially eroded in places and in danger of collapsing into sea.

Site 679 HZ 22266 72586
Cairn or cairn base of diameter *c* 2m and maximum surviving height *c* 0.2m. Bed of small angular stones partially turf-covered.

Site 680 HZ 22299 72514
Sub-circular structural form of external diameter *c* 5m. Rubble walling of maximum surviving height *c* 1m from base of hollowed interior. Walling of tumbled width *c* 1.2m. Some upcast in wall composition. Probable original entrance at E side but now infilled with stones. Located on cliff edge, probably military.

Site 681 HZ 22299 72506
Excavated depression *c* 2.5 x 2m with long axis orientated approximately NE/SW on cliff edge. Maximum depth of cut *c* 0.5m. No bank surrounding. Probably military.

Site 682 HZ 22298 72502
Excavated depression *c* 5 x 4m externally with long axis orientated approximately NE/SW on cliff edge and evidence of low banking on N and S sides. Stone revetted on inside of NE and SW banks. Width of banking *c* 0.6m and depth of excavation *c* 0.7m. Probably military.

Site 683 HZ 22264 72422
Quarry working *c* 3 x 2m with exposed face to SW. Maximum depth of cut *c* 1.5m.

Site 684 HZ 22161 72245
Quarry working *c* 8 x 6m on level ground. Maximum depth of cut *c* 1.5m. Some loose rock evident.

Site 685 HZ 21058 73101
Probable cairn base covering area *c* 3 x 3m on slight rise. Stones typically *c* 0.4 x 0.3 x 0.3m. Stoneless area of diameter *c* 1m at centre.

Site 686 HZ 2108 7326
Remains of at least 6 nucleated roofed structures associated with military activity. All constructed using pebble-concrete in bands of *c* 0.5m. From NE to SW:

- **a.** *c* 6.5 x 4m, height *c* 2.8m with flat roof.
- **b.** *c* 6.5 x 4m, height *c* 2.8m with flat roof.
- **c.** *c* 6.5 x 4m, height *c* 4m with flat roof and two windows.
- **d.** *c* 4 x 3m, height *c* 2.5m with flat roof. Adjunct to S.
- **e.** *c* 7 x 5m, height *c* 2.7m with flat roof.
- **f.** *c* 7 x 5m, height *c* 2.7m with flat roof.

All buildings appear to have tall concrete screens constructed to protect doorways. Within area of *c* 50 x 50m to SE remains of 3 further structures represented by concrete foundation platforms.

Site 687 HZ 2100 7323
Structural foundations *c* 35 x 4m with long axis orientated approximately NE/SW. Height *c* 0.5m and covered with concrete for length of 4m at NE and for 6m at SW. Remainder infilled with rubble and concrete. Possible reservoir or tank.

Site 688 HZ 20943 73285
Well or spring *c* 0.6 x 0.6m. Deliberately stone faced to N but rest of stone facing probably natural.

Site 689 HZ 20880 73243
Structural foundations *c* 3.5 x 3.5m internally with concrete block walling *c* 0.2m wide and standing to maximum height of *c* 0.6m. Nissen-type form with curved roof and inner cladding of corrugated iron.

Site 690 HZ 2082 7324
Structural foundations *c* 30 x 5m with long axis orientated approximately NW/SE consisting of two Nissen-type huts. NW example shows collapsed roof, SE example consists of rubble and concrete debris, including stove, to typical height of *c* 0.5m. Both with curved roof and inner cladding of corrugated iron. A winding kerbed path leads S to additional structural base *c* 15m to S. Structure probably not roofed.

Site 691 HZ 20861 73383
Possible cairn of diameter *c* 6m and maximum surviving height *c* 0.7m underlying concrete rubble. Composition of loose and broken stone now bonded by turf. Prominent position.

Site 692 HZ 20839 73387
Cairn or cairn base of diameter *c* 3m and maximum surviving height *c* 0.3m. Indications of set stones. Possibly a post-support feature. Prominent position.

Site 693 HZ 20830 73404
Excavated depression *c* 7 x 6m with long axis orientated approximately NE/SW and surrounded by amorphous banks created from upcast. Maximum depth of cut *c* 1m. Some evidence for concrete revetting on W side.

Site 694 HZ 2088 7341
Area *c* 80 x 60m at top of Ward Hill containing expanse of concrete rubble spread, brickwork, twisted iron and general structural debris covering remains of at least three military foundations. Deliberate destruction. At SE side winch for railway system. Approximately 30m SE terraced roofed structure *c* 2.5 x 2.5m with flat roof *c* 1m high. Further structure *c* 3.5 x 2.5m and height *c* 2.5m to flat roof located *c* 50m to N of this.

Site 695 HZ 20912 73382 (NW) to 21058 73249 (SE)
Railway track of gauge *c* 1m running for *c* 185m from top of Ward Hill down to site 686(f).

Site 696 HZ 20892 73504
Excavated feature (dug-out) probably located on cairn. External diameter *c* 7m with bank width *c* 0.5m and maximum surviving height *c* 1m. Banking composed of turf with stone facing on W side. E side appears to have lost stone facings. Access from both N and S.

Site 697 HZ 20926 73443
Probable cist *c* 2 x 1m with long axis orientated approximately N/S. Large slabbed stone on W side with four smaller examples on E side. No evidence of end stones. Some loose stone in vicinity. Possible robbing.

Site 698 HZ 20987 73395
Excavated feature (dug-out) of external diameter *c* 6m. Banking surviving to maximum height of *c* 1m and width *c* 1.5m. Composition of upcast with piled stones presumably derived from surrounding shallow ditch. Entrance probably at E facing side.

Site 699 HZ 21075 73532
Possible cairn *c* 3 x 3m identified within scree. Stones typically *c* 0.4 x 0.3 x 0.3m.

Site 700 HZ 21051 73529
Clearing *c* 3 x 2m containing shallow depression and marked by semi-circle of stones to height of *c* 0.2m and width *c* 0.5m on seaward side. Stones typically small and angular.

Site 701 HZ 21067 73539
Clearing *c* 2 x 1.5m marked by semi-circle of stones to height of *c* 0.2m and width *c* 0.5m on seaward side. Stones typically small and angular.

Site 702 HZ 20980 73445
Concrete windowless structure *c* 5 x 4m with long axis orientated approximately NW/SE and gabled roof. Height to top of wall *c* 2.5m. Large opening in SE wall.

Site 703 HZ 21200 73426
Concrete windowless structure *c* 9 x 3.5m

with long axis orientated approximately NW/SE and gabled roof. Height to top of wall *c* 2.5m. Centre length of *c* 4.5m slightly taller and wider than two ends. Doorway blocked at SE end.

Site 704 HZ 21066 73351
Cairn base of diameter *c* 1.5m and maximum surviving height *c* 0.2m. Composition of turf-covered, small angular stones.

Site 705 HZ 21078 73351
Excavated feature (dug-out) of external diameter *c* 5m with bank width of *c* 2m. Upcast bank composition of earth, turf and stone to maximum surviving height of *c* 1m from base of interior. Upcast stone used as revetting on exterior.

Site 706 HZ 21148 73457
Three small stone-sided features overlooking NE approach to Ward Hill. Each marked by semi-circle of stones enclosing diameter of *c* 2m. Stone lines each of height *c* 0.2m and width *c* 0.3m. Features located *c* 5m apart in approximate N/S alignment. Grid reference taken on centre example.

Site 707 HZ 21189 73448
Group of anomalous large stones within area *c* 5 x 3m. Stones typically *c* 0.3 x 0.3 x 0.2m. Similar group *c* 3 x 2m approximately 5m to N. Evidence of cuttings between.

Site 708 HZ 21254 73378
Cairn base of diameter *c* 2m. Turf-covered outer ring of stones typically *c* 0.3 x 0.2 x 0.2m. Stones apparently bedded.

Site 709 HZ 21354 73274
Cairn base of diameter *c* 2.5m and maximum surviving height *c* 0.2m. Base of angular and rounded stones.

Site 710 HZ 20730 73762
Area *c* 25 x 25m containing anomalous undulations and apparently set stones. Possible platform feature, but difficult to interpret. Similar feature located *c* 40m to NW.

Site 711 HZ 20972 73912 (E) to 20561 73938 (W)
Linear feature identified for *c* 480m running approximately from E to W, from cliff to cliff. Construction based on individual large stones apparently positioned at close-set intervals and infilled with earth, turf and smaller stones. Only surviving in sporadic lengths and with no indication of associated ditch to provide upcast. Maximum surviving height *c* 0.5m width *c* 2m. Feature follows no particular contour.
Square stone-sided feature *c* 2 x 2m and height *c* 0.4m located at HZ 20638 73917 as part of main feature.

Site 712 HZ 21630 73580
Cairn of diameter *c* 1m and maximum surviving height *c* 0.4m. Composed of angular stones and heather-covered at S.

Site 713 HZ 21761 73500
Cairn of diameter *c* 1.5m and maximum surviving height *c* 0.6m. Angular stones with some turf cover at base. Upper stones have recent appearance.

Site 714 HZ 21504 73783
Possible cist *c* 2 x 1.5m with long axis orientated approximately NE/SW. Defined by bedded stones, kerb-like in appearance, at long sides and at SW end. Uneven in appearance suggesting disturbance.

Site 715 HZ 21585 73824
Area of collapsed stone *c* 4 x 1.5m located in cutting with long axis orientated approximately E/W. Fill of broken bedrock and heather. Possibly connected with water coursing system.

Site 716 HZ 21671 73856 (N) to 21671 73829 (turn) to HZ 21707 73803 (SE)
Linear feature identified for *c* 70m running approximately from N to S for *c* 30m, then approximately SE for *c* 40m along stream. Construction based on individual large stones apparently positioned at close-set intervals and infilled with earth, turf and smaller stones. Surviving stones typically *c* 0.4 x 0.3 x 0.3m. Sporadic survival of feature of maximum height *c* 0.5m and width *c* 1.5m. No evidence of associated ditch from which infill material might have been derived.

Site 717 HZ 21822 73887 (NW) to 21860 73841 (SE)
Linear feature identified for *c* 60m comprising of stones bedded at intervals of *c* 2-5m and running approximately NW/SE. Stones almost flush with turf.

Site 718 HZ 21799 73807
Series of cultivation beds covering area of *c* 230 sq m. Bed widths of either *c* 2m (at SE) or *c* 1m (at NW).

Site 719 HZ 21928 73754
Sub-circular mound of maximum external diameter *c* 13.5m including uneven banking of width *c* 1.5-3m and maximum surviving height *c* 0.3m. Banking composed of earth, turf and stone. Interior consists of heaped tumble, partially turf-covered. Superficial excavation identified several large earthfast stones and chamber *c* 6 x 2m leading to SE with possible additional chamber *c* 1.1 x 1.6m to NE. Interpreted as burial mound integral to linear feature site 675.

Site 720 HZ 21986 73716
Amorphous mound of diameter *c* 9m including uneven and collapsed banking. Banking of maximum surviving height *c* 0.5m width *c* 3m and with a composition of earth, turf and stone. Heaped tumble inside and to N. Structure badly dilapidated and difficult to interpret. Mound appears to be integral to linear feature site 675 and might be interpreted as burial monument (see site 719).

Site 721 HZ 22112 73830
Cairn base or stone setting *c* 2 x 2m composed of angular stones to a maximum surviving height of *c* 0.3m. Largest stone *c* 0.5 x 0.4 x 0.3m. Possibly former flag or mast station.

Site 722 HZ 22129 73857
Cairn *c* 2 x 2m with large orthostat *c* 1m long and *c* 0.7m high; revetting stones heaped to S. Maximum surviving height of stones *c* 0.3m.

Site 723 HZ 22115 74065
Circular depression of diameter *c* 4m and maximum depth *c* 0.2m. Small cairn of diameter *c* 2m at centre possibly defined by bedded stone setting. Possibly former mast or flag station. Approximately 5m to N, 4 concrete supports with iron attachments identified.

Site 724 HZ 22155 74141
Cairn base or stone setting of diameter *c* 3m. Now partially turf-covered with possible evidence for inner stone setting. Possibly former flag or mast station.

Site 725 HZ 22753 72704
Stone setting *c* 1.5 x 1 .5m forming base of later (?) cairn. Composition of angular stones of maximum surviving height *c* 0.3m.

Site 726 HZ 22743 72706
Mound *c* 13 x 10m with long axis orientated approximately E/W and containing stone area *c* 6.5 x 5.5m defined by possible kerbing. Substantial outer stones, typically *c* 1.0 x 0.4 x 0.4m. Tumble within but evidence of two hollowed areas to centre, each of diameter *c* 1m. Feature partially turf-covered and difficult to interpret in its surviving form. Clear landscape monument surviving to height of *c* 1m above general field surface. Local tradition of burials in vicinity. OS card, antiquity no. HZ 27 SW(M) 3.

Site 727 HZ 22734 72709
Stone setting *c* 2 x 1m with long axis orientated approximately N/S and open at N end. Loose angular stones of width *c* 0.3m and maximum surviving height *c* 0.4m. Some lichen cover but otherwise of modern appearance.

Site 728 HZ 22728 72710
Amorphous area of stones *c* 8 x 5m with long axis orientated approximately N/S and of maximum surviving height *c* 0.7m. Cover of medium/large angular stones without clearly defined overall form. Considerable lichen cover. Possible product of local quarrying.

Site 729 HZ 2268 7278
Series of stone-built features or spreads:

a. Walled enclosure *c* 20 x 16m with long axis orientated approximately NE/SW. NW and NE sides comparatively well-built and faced to height of *c* 1.4m with base width *c* 0.8m tapering to *c* 0.5m at top. Other walls essentially created of rubble lines; at SE maximum surviving height *c* 0.7m and width *c* 2m, at SW maximum surviving height *c* 1m and width *c* 3m.

b. Area *c* 30 x 30m immediately E of (a) consisting of scree and rough stone and produced by both structural collapse and storm deposition.

c. Cairn *c* 4 x 4m and maximum surviving height *c* 0.6m located adjacent to NE corner of (a). Feature of modern appearance.

d. 4 cairns typically of diameter *c* 2m and maximum surviving height *c* 0.5m located *c* 15m N of NE wall of (a). Lichen-covered but modern in appearance.

e. 5 quarry workings typically of diameter *c* 4m located *c* 30m to NE of (a). Workings set in line along slope with maximum depth of cut *c* 0.5m. Local tradition indicates vicinity of slate quarrying.

f. Walling of length *c* 3m and maximum surviving height *c* 1m. and width *c* 1m located *c* 10m SW of (a).

g. Pair of orthostats set at right-angles within stone area and located *c* 16m SE of (a). Each stone of height *c* 0.3m and *c* 0.8m in length. Possible continuation of setting to E.

All features lie in vicinity of recorded quarrying for lighthouse construction.

Site 730 HZ 22679 72617

Possible structural foundation of diameter *c* 8m including banking of maximum surviving height *c* 0.4m and width *c* 1m. Bank composition of earth, turf and stone. Form unclear at E side. Interior filled with tumble including large angular stones typically *c* 0.3 x 0.3 x 0.3m. Confusing monument with possible banking extending to E. OS card, antiquity no. HZ 27 SW(M) 4.

Site 731 HZ 22654 72564

Walling of length *c* 19m, maximum surviving height *c* 0.5m and width *c* 1.5m. Presumably produced from local stone spreads. Largest stones located at base with smaller stones above. Length of *c* 6m at W end composed of smaller, less well-packed stones and probably later. Single stone *c* 1.5 x 0.5 x 0.5m at E end.

Site 732 HZ 22592 72563

Circular stone feature of diameter *c* 5m with possible kerb stones and loose stones in centre. Maximum surviving height *c* 0.4m. Lichen-covered and clearly identifiable as landscape feature.

Site 733 HZ 22636 72622

Stone-built structure *c* 3 x 2.5m with long axis orientated approximately NW/SE located against hillside. Constructed of drystone walling to height of *c* 1.2m and width *c* 0.5m. Entrance *c* 1m wide at SW. NW side provided by natural bedrock. Presumably military.

Site 734 HZ 22714 72487

Stone-built structure *c* 4 x 3m with long axis orientated approximately N/S and of maximum surviving height *c* 0.5m. N wall provided by rock face and S face open. E and W walls both *c* 1m in width. W wall more densely packed. Interior shows evidence of turf-covered stones.

Site 735 HZ 22629 72283

Series of stone-built features or spreads:

a. Cairn of diameter *c* 2m represented by ring of built stones of height *c* 0.5m and width *c* 0.5m. Feature lichen-covered but otherwise of modern appearance.

b. Area of scree and stone *c* 40 x 30m with long axis orientated approximately NE/SW. Cairn (a) located within E part of spread. Various features identifiable but mostly patches of dense stone often disposed in lines, for example at E end *c* 10 x 6m with maximum surviving height of *c* 0.5m.

Area bounded to SE by site 736.

Site 736 HZ 22639 72282 (NE) to 22612 72260 (SW)

Packed stone feature of length *c* 30m running approximately from NE to SW. Maximum surviving height *c* 0.4m and width *c* 3m. Composition of densely packed, lichen-covered stones.

Site 737 HZ 22602 72287 (NE) to 22566 72274 (SW)

Linear feature identified for *c* 40m winding approximately from NE/SW and defined by individually aligned stones set at irregular intervals. Line presumably infilled with earth, turf and smaller stones. Maximum surviving height *c* 0.4m and width *c* 1m. No evidence of associated ditch from which infill might have been derived.

Site 738 HZ 22489 72386
Circular earthen enclosure of external diameter *c* 5m. Maximum surviving height of banking *c* 0.3m and width *c* 1.5m with composition of earth and turf. Banking flat-topped. Slight rise at centre of feature with diameter *c* 0.6m. Possible flagpole or mast location.

Site 739 HZ 22108 72246
Earthen enclosure *c* 6 x 5m with long axis orientated approximately E/W. Banking of maximum surviving height *c* 0.2m and width *c* 1m. Composition of earth, turf and some stone. Feature difficult to interpret within heather landscape.

Site 740 HZ 2230 7225
Eroded promontory fort with ramparts. Promontory now severely depleted by natural agencies and covers an approximate area of *c* 430 sq m with maximum dimensions *c* 45 x 12m. Long axis orientated approximately NE/SW. Landward end of promontory contains rectangular structural base *c* 9 x 5m with long axis orientated approximately E/W. Maximum surviving height of banking *c* 0.6m and width *c* 1m with evidence of stonework in composition.

From promontory, land neck reached by descent of *c* 4m into excavated ditch. Inner bank of maximum surviving height *c* 2m and width *c* 6m. Second and third banks of similar dimensions but less substantial on W side. Outer bank slightly lower. All banks created from turfed upcast as result of intermediate ditch being quarried into bedrock. Access to promontory provided by track *c* 1m wide and now sheep-worn through defences. Surviving length of E banks *c* 13m, but W banks only *c* 6m in length. Evidence of large stones within composition.

Sub-circular enclosure of diameter *c* 8m identified adjacent to outer bank and with shallow depression of diameter *c* 4m to S. Banking of maximum surviving height *c* 0.4m and width *c* 0.4m. Feature appears to relate to low outer embankment which isolates present headland. Embankment identified for *c* 70m running approximately NW and N, and for *c* 30m running approximately NE. Maximum surviving height *c* 0.4m and width *c* 1m. Composition of earth, turf and some stone. RCAHMS 1946 no. 1194. OS card, antiquity no. HZ 27 SW 6.

Site 741 HZ 22585 72463
Cist-like feature *c* 2.5 x 1.5m with long axis orientated approximately NE/SW. Probable kerb stones located at long sides and at NE end. Clearly discernible feature in vicinity.

Site 742 HZ 2182 7240
Field system, the most northerly on the island, estimated to cover area of *c* 9000 sq m.

Site 743 HZ 2170 7197
Mill systems located in Burn of Gilsetter. 3 mill sites identified below dam bank at S end of feature. Dam of length *c* 30m to E of stream and *c* 7m to W of stream. Maximum surviving height *c* 0.5m but revetted at N to depth of *c* 1.5m. Maximum width *c* 6m tapering to *c* 2m at ends. Composition of upcast but revetted along S face with band of stone *c* 0.5m high and *c* 0.5m wide.

Approximately 15m downstream, mill race of maximum width *c* 3m leads off to W through concrete dam down to first mill site A (Old Mill) *c* 7m below. Further dry stream leads off W for *c* 5m with depth of *c* 0.3m and width of *c* 0.5m widening into pool of diameter *c* 1.5m. Mill system defined by stone foundations *c* 6 x 3m across W arm of stream. Foundations of large stones indicate general dimensions of feature. No detailed plan possible.

Approximately 9m downstream, further mill race of maximum width *c* 2.5m and depth *c* 0.5m leads off to W to next mill B (Shirva Mill) located *c* 10m downstream. Mill foundation *c* 5 x 3.5m with long axis across stream. Of uneven construction with walls typically *c* 0.5m wide. Built of drystone construction with E wall surviving to height of *c* 2.5m and *c* 0.4m at W. Constructed on bedding stones. Collapsed millstone still within structure.

Approximately 10m downstream further mill race, mostly eroded, leads to third mill C (New Mill). Upcast banks of race *c* 0.4m in height and *c* 0.5m wide. E bank revetted against stream. Mill foundation *c* 5.5m x 3.5m with long axis across stream. Terraced into hillside to W requiring stone revetting of height *c* 3m at E. Maximum surviving height of N wall *c* 4m from bedrock revetted base. Maximum surviving height of S wall *c* 2.5m. Millstone and tirl still partly surviving.

Site 744 HZ 2126 7180
General area of documented discovery of possible burnt mound. No evidence survives but records indicate 'a small mound, 8′ in diameter and 2½′ high' with a fill of small stones and earth. Mound reported to have contained two urns, one being of steatite. The larger may have contained a cremation. Adjacent to the mound are recorded a further 10 or 12 locations of possible bone ash below flat stones. Discovery made as a result of road construction during 1873/4. The most likely location appears to be the point at which the present road crosses the small stream which runs down to the mills. RCAHMS 1946 no. 1195. OS card, antiquity no. HZ 27 SW 12(1).

Site 745 HZ 2155 7165
Field system estimated to cover area of *c* 50,000 sq m.

Site 746 HZ 2130 7150
Field system estimated to cover area of *c* 25,000 sq m.

Site 747 HZ 2115 7150
Field system estimated to cover area of *c* 10,000 sq m.

Site 748 HZ 2128 7138
Field system estimated to cover area of *c* 7500 sq m.

Site 749 Not identified
Recorded mound 'near North Harbour' from which a stone cup was recovered during road construction, presumably during later 19th century. RCAHMS 1946 no. 1204. *PSAS* 17 (1882-3), 294.

Site 750 HZ 2214 7408
Dwelling houses for the North Light designed by Stevenson in 1890 and demolished during 1985. Copies of ground plans and elevations held in archive.

Bibliography

Adalsteinsson, S. 1991. Importance of sheep in early Icelandic agriculture, *Acta Archaeologica* 61, pp. 285-291.

Alcock, L. and Alcock, E. 1980. Scandinavian settlement in the Inner Hebrides: recent research on placenames and in the field, in Thoms, L.M. (ed.) *Scott. Archaeol. Forum* 10, pp. 61-73.

Anderson, A.O. 1922. *Early Sources of Scottish History*, Edinburgh.

Anderson, J. 1883. *Scotland in Pagan Times – The Iron Age*, Edinburgh.

Anderson, P. 1988. The Armada in the Northern Isles, *Northern Studies* 25, pp. 42-57.

Anderson, W.J. 1955. Ambula coram Deo: the journal of Bishop Geddes for the year 1790, *Innes Review* 6, pp. 131-143.

Anon. 1750. *The Fisheries Revived or Britain's Hidden Treasure Discovered.* Sketch map attached by 'a surveyor of note'.

Anon. 1799. Religious intelligence, *Missionary Magazine* 4, pp. 462-464.

Armit, I. (ed.). 1990. *Beyond the Brochs*, Edinburgh.

Atkinson, G. C. 1832. *An Excursion to the Shetland Isles*, Manuscript.

Avitsur, S. 1971. Watermills in Ertz, Israel and their contribution to water power technology, in Jespersen, A. (ed.), pp. 389-408.

Baillie, M.G.L. 1975. A horizontal mill of the eighth century AD at Drumard, Co. Derry, *Ulster J. Archaeol.* 38, pp. 25-32.

Baillie, M.G.L. 1980. Dendrochronology – the Irish view, *Current Archaeology* 73, pp. 61-63.

Baillie, M.G.L. 1990. Provision of dates for fulachta fiadh, in Buckley, V. (ed.), pp. 165-169.

Baldwin, J.R. 1978. Norse influences in sheep husbandry on Foula, Shetland, in Baldwin, J.R. (ed.), pp. 97-127.

Baldwin, J.R. (ed.). 1978. *Scandinavian Shetland. An Ongoing Tradition?*, Edinburgh.

Baldwin, J.R. 1983. Structure in a community: the outfield, its use and its organisation in the settlement at Gásadalur, Faeroe Islands, *Northern Studies* 20, pp. 4-37.

Baldwin, J.R. 1984. Hogin and Hametoun: thoughts on the stratification of a Foula *Tun*, in Crawford, B.E. (ed.), pp. 33-64.

Ballantyne, J. 1993. Fair Isle in the mid-18th century, *Coontin Kin*, Shetland Family History Society, Lerwick, 6, pp. 15-18.

Barber, J. 1990a, Burnt mound material on settlement sites in Scotland, in Buckley, V. (ed.), pp. 92-97.

Barber, J. 1990b, Scottish burnt mounds: variations on a theme, in Buckley, V. (ed.), pp. 98-102.

Barfield, L. and Hodder, M. 1987. Burnt mounds as saunas and the prehistory of bathing, *Antiquity* 61, pp. 370-379.

Batey, C.E. 1982. The late Norse site of Freswick, in Baldwin, J.R. (ed.), *Caithness, a Cultural Crossroads,* Scottish Society for Northern Studies, pp. 45-59.

Batey, C.E. 1987. *Freswick Links, Caithness, a re-appraisal of the late Norse site in its context,* BAR Brit. Ser. 179, Oxford.

Batey, C.E. 1992. Earl's Bu, Orphir, excavation of a Norse horizontal mill, in Morris, C.D. and Rackham, D.J. (eds.), pp. 33-42.

Batey, C.E., Jesch, J. and Morris, C.D. (eds.). 1993. *The Viking Age in Caithness, Orkney and the North Atlantic*, Edinburgh.

Bedford, J. Duke of. 1968. *The Flying Duchess, her diaries and letters*, London.

Bennett, R. and Elton, J. 1899. *A History of Corn Milling and Windmills*, Vol 2 (1975 facsimile edition, Scolar Press, Menston).

Bergsåker, J. 1978. The keeping and milking of sheep in the old subsistence economy of Scandinavia, Iceland and Northern Europe, in Baldwin, J.R. (ed.), pp. 85-96.

Berry, R.J. 1974. The Shetland fauna, its significance, or lack thereof, in Goodier, R. (ed.), pp. 151-163.

Berry, R.J. and Johnston, J.L. 1980. *The Natural History of Shetland*, London.

Berry, R.J. and Tricker, B.J.K. 1969. Competition and extinction: the mice of Foula, with notes on those of Fair Isle and St Kilda, *J. Zool.* 158, pp. 247-265.

Bigelow, G.F. 1985. Sandwick, Unst and Late Norse Shetland economy, in Smith, B. (ed.), pp. 95-127.

Bigelow, G.F. 1987. Domestic architecture in medieval Shetland, *Rev. Scott. Cult.* 3, pp. 23-38.

Bigelow, G.F. 1992. Issues and prospects in Shetland Norse archaeology, in Morris, C.D. and Rackham, D.J. (eds.), pp. 9-32.

Birse, E.L. 1974. Bioclimatic characteristics of Shetland, in Goodier, R. (ed.), pp. 24-30.

Bloch, M. 1967. *Land and Work in Medieval Europe*, London.

Bond, J.M. forthcoming. The environmental evidence, in Hunter, J.R. *et al* (eds.).

Bourne, W.R.P. and Dixon, T.J. 1974. The seabirds of Shetland, in Goodier, R. (ed.), pp. 130-144.

Bowes, H.R. (ed.). 1976. *Samuel Dunn's Shetland and Orkney Journal 1822-1825.* Privately printed.

Bowman, A. 1990. Boat naust survey on Papa Westray, Orkney, *Int. J. Nautical Archaeol.* 19, pp. 317-325.

BPP. 1872. British Parliamentary Papers. From appendix to the *Second Report of the General Board of Commissioners for Lunacy in Scotland 1860.*

Bramwell, D. 1977. Bird and vole bones from Buckquoy, Orkney, in Ritchie, A., pp. 209-211.

Bramwell, D. 1979. The bird bones, in Renfrew, C., pp. 138-143.

Brand, Rev. J. 1701. *A Brief Description of Orkney, Shetland, Pightland Firth and Caithness*, Edinburgh.

Brindley, A.L. and Lanting, J.N. 1990. The dating of fulachta fiadh, in Buckley, V. (ed.), pp. 55-56.

Bruce, J. 1908. *A Description of the County of Zetland*, Edinburgh. (See also Kay 1680)

Buchanan, G. 1827 edition. *History of Scotland*, Vol 1, Edinburgh.

Buckley, V. (ed.). 1990. *Burnt Offerings*, Dublin.

Burrows, E.M., Conway, E., Lodge, S.M. and Powell, H.T. 1954. The raising of intertidal algae zones on Fair Isle, *J. Ecol.* 42, pp. 283-288.

Buttler, S. 1989. Steatite in Norse Shetland, *Hikuin* 15, pp. 193-206.

Buttler, S. 1991. Steatite in the Norse North Atlantic, *Acta Archaeologica* 61, pp. 228-232.

Calder, C.S.T. 1962. Neolithic structures in Shetland, in Wainwright, F.T. (ed.) *The Northern Isles*, Edinburgh, pp. 26-43.

Calder, C.S.T. 1963. Cairns, neolithic houses and burnt mounds in Shetland, *Proc. Soc. Antiq. Scotl.* 96 (1962-3), pp. 37-86.

Cant, R.G. 1975. *The Medieval Churches and Chapels of Shetland,* Lerwick.

Cant. R.G. 1984. Settlement, society and church organisation in the Northern Isles, in Fenton, A. and Pálsson, H. (eds.), pp. 169-179.

Chaloner, W.G. 1972. Devonian plants from Fair Isle, Scotland, *Rev. Palaeobot. Palynol.* 14, pp. 49-61.

Charlton, E. 1832. *Journal of a visit to and residence in the Shetland Islands in 1832,* MS National Library of Scotland, Edinburgh.

Chrystall, F.H. 1994. Formation processes of anthropogenic soils on Fair Isle, unpubl. undergraduate dissertation, University of Stirling.

Clouston, J.S. 1925a. The old Orkney mills I, *Proc. Ork. Antiq. Soc.* 3 (1924-5), pp. 49-54.

Clouston, J.S. 1925b. The old Orkney mills II, *Proc. Ork. Antiq. Soc.* 3 (1924-5), pp. 65-71.

Clouston, J.S. 1932. Our ward hills and ensigns, *Proc. Ork. Antiq. Soc.* 10, pp. 33-41.

Cowan, I.B. and Eassen, D.E. 1976. *Religious Houses in Scotland,* Edinburgh.

Cracknell, S. and Smith, B. 1983. Archaeological investigations at Mavis Grind, Shetland, *Glasgow Archaeol. J.* 10, pp. 13-39.

Crawford, B.E. 1984. Papa Stour: survival, continuity and change in one Shetland island, in Fenton, A. and Pálsson, H. (eds.), pp. 40-48.

Crawford, B.E. (ed.). 1984. *Essays in Shetland History,* Lerwick.

Crawford, B.E. 1985. The Biggins, Papa Stour – a multi-disciplinary investigation, in Smith, B. (ed.), pp. 128-158.

Crawford, B.E. 1987. *Scandinavian Scotland,* Leicester.

Crawford, B.E. 1991. Excavations at the Biggins, Papa Stour, *Acta Archaeologica* 61, pp. 36-43.

Cruden, S.H. 1947. The horizontal water mill at Dounby, on the Mainland of Orkney, *Proc. Soc. Antiq. Scotl.* 81, pp. 43-47.

Curwen, E.C. 1944. The problem of early water mills, *Antiquity* 13, pp. 130-146.

Dilworth, M. 1988. An abortive missionary visit to Fair Isle in 1941, *Rev. Scott. Cult.* 4, pp. 119-123.

Donaldson, G. 1984. Some Shetland parishes at the Reformation, in Crawford, B.E. (ed.), pp. 143-160.

Dron, R.W. 1908. Iron and copper mining in Shetland, *Trans. Geol. Soc. Glasgow* 13, pp. 165-169.

Drosier, R. 1830. Account of an ornithological visit to the islands of Shetland and Orkney in the summer of 1828, *Mag. Nat. Hist.*, pp. 321-326.

Drosier, R. 1831. Account of an ornithological visit to the islands of Shetland and Orkney in the summer of 1828, *Mag. Nat. Hist.*, pp. 193-199.

Dunn, R. 1837. *The Ornithologist's Guide to the Islands of Orkney and Shetland,* London.

Eunson, J. 1961. The Fair Isle fishing marks, *Scottish Studies* 5, pp. 181-198.

Eunson, J. 1976. *Words, Phrases and Recollections from Fair Isle,* Lerwick.

Evershed, H. 1874. *The Agriculture of the Islands of Shetland,* Trans. Highland and Agricult. Soc.

Fellows-Jensen, G. 1984. Viking settlement in the Northern and Western Isles – the placename evidence as seen from Denmark and the Danelaw, in Fenton, A. and Pálsson, H. (eds.), pp. 148-168.

Fenton, A. 1978. *The Northern Isles,* Edinburgh.

Fenton, A. 1982. The longhouse in northern Scotland, in Myhre, B. *et al* (eds.), pp. 231-240.

Fenton, A. 1985. *The Shape of the Past 1, Essays in Scottish Ethnography,* Edinburgh.

Fenton, A. and Pálsson, H. (eds.). 1984. *The Northern and Western Isles in the Viking World,* Edinburgh.

Flinn, D. 1970. The glacial till of Fair Isle, Shetland, *Geol. Mag.* 107, pp. 273-276.

Flinn, D. 1974. The coastline of Shetland, in Goodier, R. (ed.), pp. 13-25.

Flinn, D. 1989. *Travellers in a Bygone Shetland: An Anthology,* Edinburgh.

Fojut, N. 1986. *A Guide to Prehistoric Shetland,* Lerwick.

Fotheringhame, P. 1804. *Report respecting the Fair Isle,* Shetland Archives, Call no. D25/5/1.

Fraser, D. 1983. *Land and Society in Neolithic Orkney,* BAR Brit. Ser. 114, Oxford.

Gauldie, E. 1981. *The Scottish Country Miller 1700-1900,* Edinburgh.

Gifford, T. 1786. *Historical Descriptions of the Zetland Islands in the Year 1733,* Edinburgh.

Gimingham, C. H. 1964. Maritime and sub-maritime communities, in Burnett, J.H. (ed.), *The Vegetation of Scotland,* pp. 67-142.

Goode, D.A. 1974. The flora and vegetation of Shetland, in Goodier, R. (ed.), pp. 50-72.

Goodier, R. (ed.). 1974. *The Natural Environment of Shetland*, Nature Conservancy Council, Edinburgh.

Goudie, G. 1886. On the horizontal water mills of Shetland, *Proc. Soc. Antiq. Scotl.* 20, pp. 257-297.

Goudie, G. 1887. The Danish claims upon Orkney and Shetland, *Proc. Soc. Antiq. Scotl.* 21, pp. 236-250.

Goudie, G. (ed.). 1889. *Diary of John Mill 1740-1803*, Scottish Historical Society, Edinburgh.

Goudie, G. 1904. *The Celtic and Scandinavian Antiquities of Shetland*, London and Edinburgh.

Graham-Campbell, J. 1976. Viking-Age silver and gold hoards from Scotland, *Proc. Soc. Antiq. Scotl.* 107 (1975-6), pp. 114-135.

Graham-Campbell, J. 1993. The northern hoards of Viking-Age Scotland, in Batey, C.E. *et al* (eds.), pp. 173-186.

Hall, J. 1807. *Travels in Scotland II*, London.

Halldórsson, O. 1987. *Faereyinga Saga*, Reykjavik.

Hamilton, J.R.C. 1956. *Excavations at Jarlshof, Shetland*, Edinburgh.

Heddle, M.F. 1879. The geognosy and mineralogy of Scotland, Mainland (Shetland), Foula, Fair Isle, *Mineralogy Mag.* 3, pp. 18-56.

Hedges, J.W. 1975. Excavation of two Orcadian burnt mounds at Liddle and Beaquoy, *Proc. Soc. Antiq. Scotl.* 106 (1974-5), pp. 39-98.

Hedges, J.W. 1984. Gordon Parry's West Burra Survey, *Glasgow Archaeol. J.* 11, pp. 41-59.

Hedges, J.W. 1985. The broch period, in Renfrew, C. (ed.), pp. 150-175.

Hedges, J.W. 1986. Bronze Age structures at Tougs, Burra Isle, Shetland, *Glasgow Archaeol. J.* 13, pp. 1-43.

Hedges, M.E. 1977. The excavation of the Knowes of Quoyscottie, Orkney: a cemetery of the first millennium BC, *Proc. Soc. Antiq. Scotl.* 108 (1976-7), pp. 130-155.

Hibbert, S. 1822. *A Description of the Shetland Islands*, Edinburgh.

Hodgen, M T. 1939. Domesday watermills, *Antiquity* 13, pp. 261-279.

Hope-Taylor, B. 1958. In Wilson, D.M. and Hurst, J.G. (eds.), Medieval Britain in 1957, *Medieval Archaeology* 2, pp. 183-185.

Hunter, J.R. 1986. *Rescue Excavations on the Brough of Birsay 1974-82*, Soc. Antiq. Scotl. Monogr. Ser. 4, Edinburgh.

Hunter, J.R. 1990. Pool, Sanday – a case study for the later Iron Age and Viking periods, in Armit, I. (ed.), pp. 175-193.

Hunter, J.R. 1991. The multi-period landscape, in Hanson, W.S. and Slater, E.A. (eds.), *Scottish Archaeology: New Perceptions*, Aberdeen, pp. 178-195.

Hunter, J.R. 1992. The survey and excavation of boat nausts at Hurnips Point, Deerness, Orkney, *Int. J. Nautical Archaeol.* 21:2, pp. 125-133.

Hunter, J.R. and Dockrill, S.J. 1990. Recent research into burnt mounds on Fair Isle, Shetland and Sanday, Orkney, in Buckley, V. (ed.), pp. 62-68.

Hunter, J.R., Dockrill, S.J., Bond, J.M. and Smith, A. forthcoming. *Archaeological Investigations on Sanday, Orkney*, Soc. Antiq. Scotl. Monogr. Ser., Edinburgh.

Hunter, J.R., Dockrill, S.J. and McKinley, J.I. 1982. *The Sites and Monuments of Fara, Orkney*, Bradford University Schools of Archaeological Sciences and Physics, Occ. Pap. 2.

Irimie, C. and Bucur, C. 1971. Typology, distribution and frequency of watermills in Romania in the first half of the twentieth century, in Jespersen, A. (ed.), pp. 421-434.

Irvine, J.J.A. and Morrison, I.A. 1987. Shetlanders and fishing: historical and geographical aspects of an evolving relationship. Part 1, *Northern Studies* 24, pp. 43-56.

Jakobsen, J. 1936. *The Place-Names of Shetland*, London.

Jensen, W. 1881. *Fair Isle. A Tale in Verse*, Kirkwall. (Trans. from the German)

Jespersen, A. (ed.). 1971. *Transactions of the Second International Symposium on Mollinology*, Denmark 1969.

Johnston, J.L. 1974. Shetland habitats, an outline ecological framework, in Goodier, R. (ed.), pp. 33-50.

Jones, A. 1991. Preliminary observations on fish remains from a late Norse settlement in Caithness, *Acta Archaeologica* 61, pp. 220-227.

Jones, D. 1971. The water-powered cornmills of England, Wales and the Isle of Man. A preliminary account of their development, in Jespersen, A. (ed.), pp. 303-354.

Jones, R.L. 1979. Vegetational studies, in Renfrew, C., pp. 21-28.

Jovius, P. 1548. *Descriptio Britanniae, Scotiae, Hyberniae et Orcadum,* Venice. (Trans. *Shetland Times* Oct 9th 1886).

Kaland, S.S.H. 1973. Westnessutgravingene på Rousay, Orknøyene, *Viking* 37, pp. 77-102.

Kaland, S.S.H. 1993. The settlement of Westness, Rousay, in Batey, C.E. *et al* (eds.), pp. 308-317.

Kay, J. 1680. *A description of the Fair Isle.* (See also Bruce 1908)

Keith-Lucas, M. 1986. Vegetational development and human impact, in Whittle, A. (ed.), pp. 92-118.

Ker, W.P. 1920. The Spanish Story of the Armada, *Scott. Hist. Rev.* 17: 67, pp. 165-176.

van Keulen, J. 1695. *Nieuwe pastaart van de Orcades Eylanden*, Amsterdam.

Knox, H.T. 1907. Notes on gig-mills and drying kilns near Ballyhaunis, Co. Mayo, *Proc. Roy. Irish Acad.* 26 (1906-7), pp. 265-273.

Knox S.A., 1985, *The Making of the Shetland Landscape*, Edinburgh.

Lamb, R.G. 1973. Coastal settlements of the North, *Scott. Archaeol. Forum* 5, Edinburgh, pp. 76-98.

Lamb, R.G. 1980a. *The Archaeological Sites and Monuments of Sanday and North Ronaldsay,* RCAHMS (archaeological sites and monuments series 11), Edinburgh.

Lamb, R.G. 1980b. *Iron Age Promontory Forts in the Northern Isles,* BAR Brit Ser. 79, Oxford.

Lamb, R.G. 1983. *The Archaeological Sites and Monuments of Papa Westray and Westray,* RCAHMS (archaeological sites and monuments series 19), Edinburgh.

Lamb, R.G. 1984. *The Archaeological Sites and Monuments of Eday and Stronsay,* RCAHMS (archaeological sites and monuments series 23), Edinburgh.

Lamb, R.G. 1985. Sumburgh: prehistory under sand, in Smith, B. (ed.), pp. 27-46.

Landt, J. 1810. *The Feroe Islands,* London. (English edition).

Larsen, A-C. 1991. Norseman's use of juniper in Viking age Faroe Islands, *Acta Archaeologica* 61, pp. 54-59.

Laughlan, W.F. (ed.). 1982. *Northern Lights.* The diary of Sir Walter Scott, Hawick.

Low, G. 1774 (1879). *A Tour through the Islands of Orkney and Shetland in 1774,* Kirkwall.

Lowe, C.E. 1990. Kebister: burnt mounds and burnt mound material, in Buckley, V. (ed.), pp. 84-86.

Lucas, A.T. 1953. The horizontal mill in Ireland, *J. Roy. Soc. Antiq. Ireland* 83, pp. 1-39.

Lucas, A.T. 1955. A horizontal mill at Ballykilleen, Co. Offaly, *J. Roy. Soc. Antiq. Ireland* 85, pp. 10-113.

MacAdam, R. 1856. Ancient water-mills, *Ulster J. Archaeol.,* pp. 6-15.

MacCulloch, J.A. 1819. *Description of the Western Isles of Scotland,* London.

MacDonald, A. 1977. On 'papar' names in N and W Scotland, *Northern Studies* 9, pp. 25-30.

MacGillivray, E. (ed.). 1953. Richard James (1592-1638). Description of Shetland, Orkney and the Highlands of Scotland. *Orkney Miscellany* I, Kirkwall, pp. 48-56.

MacGregor, L.J. 1986. Norse naming elements in Shetland and Faroe: a comparative study, *Northern Studies* 23, pp. 84-101.

McGovern, T.H., Bigelow, G., Amorosi, T. and Russell, D. 1988. Northern islands, human error, and environmental degradation: a view of social and ecological change in the medieval North Atlantic, *Human Ecology* 16:3, pp. 225-270.

Mackenzie, J.B. (ed.). 1911. *Episode in the Life of the Rev. Neil MacKenzie at St Kilda from 1829 to 1843*, Edinburgh.

Mackenzie, M. 1752. *Orcades: or a geographic and hydrographic survey of Orkney and Lewis islands*, Edinburgh.

Magnusson, M. and Pálsson, H. (trans.). 1960. *Njals Saga*, Penguin.

Mahler, D.L.D. 1991. Argisbrekka: new evidence of shielings in the Faroe Islands, *Acta Archaeologica* 61, pp. 60-72.

Martin, C.J.M. 1972. El Gran Grifon, an Armada wreck on Fair Isle, *Int. J. Nautical Archaeol.* 1, pp. 59-71.

Martin, C.J.M. 1975. *Full Fathom Five*, London.

Marwick, H. 1952. *Orkney Farm Names*, Kirkwall.

Mellars, P. 1987. *Excavations in Oronsay*, Edinburgh.

Monteith, R. 1845. *Description of the islands of Orkney and Zetland 1633*, Edinburgh. (See also Sibbald 1711)

Moore, P.D. 1975. Origin of blanket mires, *Nature* 256, pp. 277-279.

Morris, C.D. (ed.). 1989. *The Birsay Bay Project*, Vol 1, Durham.

Morris, C.D. and Rackham, D.J. 1992. Excavations at Freswick Links, Caithness 1980-82: environmental samples from the cliff-side, in Morris, C.D. and Rackham, D.J. (eds.), pp. 43-102.

Morris, C.D. and Rackham, D.J. (eds.). 1992. *Norse and Later Settlement and Subsistence in the North Atlantic*, Glasgow.

Morrison, I. 1978. Aspects of Viking small craft in the light of Shetland practice, in Baldwin, J.R. (ed.), pp. 57-75.

Morrison, I. 1981. Maritime catastrophes, their archaeological and documentary legacies: with reflections on the centenary of the Shetland fisheries disaster of 1881, *Northern Studies* 18, pp. 20-39.

Morrison, I. 1992. Traditionalism and innovation in the maritime technology of Shetland and other North Atlantic communities, in Smout, T.C. (ed.), pp. 114-136.

Muir, T.S. 1885. *Ecclesiological Notes on Some of the Islands of Scotland*, Edinburgh.

Myhre, B. 1985. Boathouses as indicators of political organisation, *Norwegian Archaeol. Rev.* 18, pp. 36-60.

Myhre, B., Stoklund, B. and Gjaerder, P. (eds.). 1982. *Vestnordisk byggeskikk gjennom to tusen år*. Arkeologisk Museum i Stavanger, Skrifter 7, Stavanger.

Mykura, W. 1972. Igneous intrusions and mineralisations in Fair Isle, Shetland Islands, *Bull. Geol. Surv. Gt. Br.* 41, pp. 33-53.

Mykura, W. 1976. *British Regional Geology. Orkney and Shetland.* HMSO, Edinburgh.

Mykura, W. and Young, B.R. 1969. Sodic scapolite (dipyre) in the Shetland Islands, *Rpt. Inst. Geol. Sci.* 69/4.

NSA. 1845. *New Statistical Account of Scotland*, Vol XV, Sutherland, Caithness, Orkney, Shetland – General Index, Edinburgh and London.

Nicolaisen, W.F.H. 1976. *Scottish Place Names*, London.

Nicolson, A. 1930. *History of Skye*, Glasgow.

Noddle, B. 1977. The animal bones from Buckquoy, Orkney, in Ritchie, A., pp. 201-209.

O'Dell, A.C. 1939. *The Historical Geography of the Shetland Islands*, Lerwick.

O'Dell, A.C. 1940. *The Land of Britain*, Vol 5, *Zetland*, Report of the Land Utilisation Survey of Great Britain, London.

O'Drisceóil, D.A. 1988. Burnt mounds: cooking or bathing?, *Antiquity* 62, pp. 671-680.

O'Kelly, M.J. 1954. Excavations and experiments in ancient Irish cooking places, *J. Roy. Soc. Antiq. Ireland* 84, pp. 105-155.

OSA. *The Statistical Account of Scotland 1791-1799*, Sir John Sinclair (ed.), Vol VI, *Ayrshire* (1983 reissue, E. P. Publications).

OSA. *The Statistical Account of Scotland 1791-1799*, Sir John Sinclair (ed.), Vol VII (original edition).

OSA. *The Statistical Account of Scotland 1791-1799*, Sir John Sinclair (ed.), Vol XIX, *Orkney and Shetland* (1978 facsimile Thomson, W.P.L. and Graham, J.J. (eds.), Wakefield).

Osler, A.G. 1975. The Fair Isle yole, *Fair Isle Bird Observatory Reports* 28, pp. 76-81.

Osler, A.G. 1983. *The Shetland Boat, South Mainland and Fair Isle*, National Maritime Museum Monograph and Reports 58.

Owen, O. 1993, Tuquoy, Westray, Orkney: a challenge for the future?, in Batey, C.E. *et al* (eds.), pp. 318-339.

Palmer, R.C. and Scott, W. 1969. *A Check-List of the Flowering Plants and Ferns of the Shetland Islands*, Scalloway and Oxford.

Pálsson, H. and Edwards, P. (trans.). 1976. *Egil's Saga*, London.

Pálsson, H. and Edwards, P. (trans.). 1978. *Orkneyinga Saga*, London.

Platt, M.I. 1956. The animal bones, in Hamilton, J.R.C., pp. 212-215.

Pløyen, C. 1894. *Reminiscences of a Voyage to Shetland, Orkney and Scotland in the Summer of 1839*, Lerwick.

Raby, J. 1824. *Letters.* Manuscript in Methodist archives, John Rylands Library, Manchester University.

Rackham, D.J., Allison, E.P., Colley, S.M., Donaldson, A.M. and Nye, S. 1989. Excavations beside the Brough Road: the biological assemblage, in Morris, C.D. (ed.), pp. 231-271.

Rackham, D.J., Bramwell, D., Donaldson, A.M., Limbrey, S., Spencer, P. and Wheeler, A. 1989. Cuttings 5 and 6: the biological assemblage and soil sampling in Morris, C.D. (ed.), pp. 99-107.

Rahtz, P.A. 1981. Medieval milling, in Crossley, D.W. (ed.), *Medieval Industry*, CBA Res. Rep. 40, London, pp. 1-15.

Rahtz, P.A. and Bullough, D. 1977. The parts of an Anglo-Saxon mill, *Anglo-Saxon England* 6, pp. 15-37.

Rahtz, P.A. and Meeson, R. 1992. *An Anglo-Saxon Watermill at Tamworth*, CBA Res. Rep. 83, London.

RCAHMS. 1946. Royal Commission on the Ancient and Historical Monuments of Scotland, *Inventory for Orkney and Shetland*, Vol 3 *Shetland*, Edinburgh.

RCAHMS. 1987. Royal Commission on the Ancient and Historical Monuments of Scotland, *East Rhins* (archaeological sites and monuments series 26), Edinburgh.

RCAHMS. 1988. Royal Commission on the Ancient and Historical Monuments of Scotland, *Buildings of St Kilda*, Edinburgh.

Reid, J.T. 1869. *Art Rambles in Shetland*, Edinburgh.

Renfrew, C. 1976. Megaliths, territories and populations, in De Laet, S.J. (ed.) *Acculturation and Continuity in Atlantic Europe*, Bruges, pp. 198-220.

Renfrew, C. 1979. *Investigations in Orkney*, London.

Renfrew, C. (ed.). 1985. *The Prehistory of Orkney*, Edinburgh.

Reynolds, J. 1970, *Windmills and Watermills*, London.

Ritchie, A. 1977. Excavation of Pictish and Viking-age farmsteads at Buckquoy, Orkney, *Proc. Soc. Antiq. Scotl.* 108 (1976-7), pp. 174-227.

Ritchie, A. 1985. Orkney in the Pictish Kingdom, in Renfrew, C. (ed.), pp. 183-204.

Ritchie, P.R. 1968. The stone-implement trade in third-millennium Scotland, in Coles, J.M. and Simpson, D.D.A. (eds.), *Studies in Ancient Europe*, Leicester, pp. 117-136.

Ritchie, P.R. 1984. Soapstone quarrying in Viking lands, in Fenton, A. and Pálsson, H. (eds.), pp. 59-84.

Rolfsen, P. 1974. *Båtnaust på Jaerkysten*, Stavanger Museum Skrifter, Stavanger.

Rowley-Conwy, P. 1983. Animal and bird bones, in Hedges. J.W., Trial excavations on

Pictish and Viking settlements at Saevar Howe, Birsay, Orkney, *Glasgow Archaeol. J.* 10, pp. 109-111.

Russell-White, C.J. 1990. Synthesis, in Buckley, V. (ed.), pp. 87-91.

Rynne, C. 1989. The introduction of the vertical watermill into Ireland: some recent archaeological evidence, *Medieval Archaeology* 33, pp. 21-31.

Schaw J. 1939. *Journal of a lady of quality; being the narrative of a journey from Scotland to the West Indies, Northern Carolina, and Portugal, in the years 1774 to 1776.* (Andrews, E.W. (ed.), Yale.)

Scott, H. (ed.). 1928. *Fasti Ecclesiae Scoticanie*, Vol VII, Edinburgh.

Seller, T.J. 1986. Animal bone material, in Hunter, J.R., pp. 208-216.

Serjeantson, D. 1988. Archaeological and ethnographic evidence for seabird exploitation in Scotland, *Archaeozoologia* II (1-2), pp. 209-224.

Shaw, J. 1984. *Water Power in Scotland 1550-1870*, Edinburgh.

Sibbald, R. 1711. *Description of the Islands of Orkney and Shetland 1633*, Edinburgh. (Reprint 1845, see Monteith)

Small, A. 1966. Excavations at Underhoull, Unst, Shetland, *Proc. Soc. Antiq. Scotl.* 98, pp. 225-248.

Small, A. 1968a. The distribution of settlement in Shetland and Faroe in Viking times, *Saga Book* 17: 2-3 (1967-8), pp. 144-155.

Small, A. 1968b. The historical geography of the Norse colonisation of the Scottish Highlands, *Norsk Geografisk Tidsskrift* 22, pp. 1-16.

Small, A. 1982. The Norse building tradition in Shetland, in Myhre, B. *et al* (eds.) pp. 241-254.

Smith, B. 1977. Local history: Shetland archives and sources of Shetland history, *History Workshop Journal* 4, pp. 203-214.

Smith, B. 1980. Stock-stove houses, *Shetland Folk Book* 7, pp. 22-27.

Smith, B. 1984. What is a skattald? in Crawford, B.E. (ed.), pp. 99-124.

Smith, B. (ed.). 1985. *Shetland Archaeology*, Lerwick.

Smith, B. 1988. Shetland in saga-time: rereading the Orkneyinga Saga. *Northern Studies* 25, pp. 21-41.

Smith, B. 1990. Shetland, Scandinavia, Scotland, 1300-1700: the changing nature of contact, in Simpson, G.G. (ed.) *Scotland and Scandinavia 800-1800*, Edinburgh, pp. 25-37.

Smith, B. 1992. Adam Smith's rents from the sea: maritime sharecropping in Shetland, in Smout, T.C. (ed.), pp. 94-113.

Smith, D.C.F. 1987. The progress of the *Orcades* survey, with biographical notes on Murdoch Mackenzie Senior (1712-1797), *Annals of Science* 44, pp. 277-288.

Smith, H.D. 1973. The development of Shetland fisheries and fishing communities, in Fricke, P.H. (ed.), *Seafarer and Community*, London, pp. 8-29.

Smout, T.C. (ed.). 1992. *Scotland and the Sea*, Edinburgh.

Spence, D.H.N. 1960. Studies in the vegetation of Shetland III. Scrub vegetation in Shetland and S. Uist, *J. Ecol.* 48, pp. 73-95.

Spence, D.H.N. 1970. Scottish serpentine vegetation, *Oikos* 21, pp. 22-31.

Spence, D.H.N. 1974. Subartic debris and scrub vegetation of Shetland, in Goodier, R. (ed.), pp. 73-88.

Steensberg, A. 1952. *Bondehuse og Vandmøller i Danmark gennem 2000 år*, Copenhagen.

Steinnes, A. 1959. The 'Huseby' system in Orkney, *Scott. Hist. Rev.* 38, pp. 36-46.

Stewart, J. 1965. Shetland farm names, in Small, A. (ed.), *The Fourth Viking Congress*, Aberdeen, pp. 247-266.

Stewart, J. 1987. *Shetland Place-Names*, Lerwick.

Stoklund, B. 1984. Building traditions in the northern world, in Fenton, A. and Pálsson, H. (eds.), pp. 96-115.

Svabo. 1924. Extracts from Mss, Jacobsen, M. (ed.), *Foroyafeðin 1781-82*, Torshavn.

Sveinbjarnardóttir, G. 1991. Shielings in Iceland. An archaeological and historical survey, *Acta Archaeologica* 61, pp. 73-96.

Thom, V.M. 1989. *Fair Isle, An Island Saga*, Edinburgh.

Thomas, G. 1839. *Chart of the Shetland Islands*, London.

Thorsteinsson, A. 1976. The testimony of ancient architecture, *Faeroe Isles Rev.* 1, pp. 12-19.

Thorsteinsson, A. 1982. Faerøske huskonstruktioner fra vikingetid til 1800-årene, in Myhre, B. *et al* (eds.), pp. 149-161.

Thowsen. A. 1969. The Norwegian exports of boats to Shetland, and its influence upon Shetland boatbuilding and usage, *Sjøfartshistorisk Arbok*, pp. 145-208.

Traill, J.W.H. 1906. Flora of Fair Isle, *Ann. Scott. Nat. Hist.*, pp. 165-170.

Tudor, J.R. 1883. *The Orkneys and Shetland: their Past and Present State*, London.

Vetch, J. 1882. Account of the island of Foula, *Mem. Wernerian. Nat. Hist. Soc.* 4, pp. 237-252.

Waterson, G. and Jones, J. 1981. *Fair Isle – A Photographic History*, Edinburgh.

Waugh, D.J. 1991. Placename evidence for Scandinavian settlement in Shetland, *Rev. Scott. Cult.* 7, pp. 15-24.

Wheeler, A. 1977. The fish bones from Buckquoy, Orkney, in Ritchie, A., pp. 211-214.

Wheeler, A. 1979. The fish bones, in Renfrew, C., pp. 144-149.

Whittle, A. (ed.). 1986. *Scord of Brouster, An Early Agricultural Settlement on Shetland*, Oxford University Committee for Archaeology Monograph 9, Oxford.

Wikander, O. 1986. Archaeological evidence for early watermills – an interim report, *History of Technology* 10, Smith, N. (ed.), pp. 151-180.

Williamson, K. 1946. The horizontal watermills of the Faeroe Islands, *Antiquity* 20, pp. 83-97.

Williamson, K. 1965. *Fair Isle and its Birds*, Edinburgh.

Williamson, K. 1970. *The Atlantic Islands*, London.

Wilson, D.M. 1973. The treasure, in Small, A., Thomas, A.C. and Wilson, D.M. (eds.), *St Ninian's Isle and its Treasure*, Aberdeen University Studies, pp. 45-158.

Wilson, J. 1842. *A Voyage Round the Coasts of Scotland and the Isles*, 2 vols, Edinburgh.

Wright, S.M. 1992. Millstones, in Rahtz, P. and Meeson, R., pp. 70-79.

INDEX

Compiled by Lesley Adkins

Page numbers in *italics* indicate a reference within a figure, plate or table.

HMSO publications are available from:

HMSO Publications Centre
(Mail, fax and telephone orders only)
PO Box 276, London, SW8 5DT
Telephone orders 071-873 9090
General enquiries 071-873 0011
(queuing system in operation for both numbers)
Fax orders 0171-873 8200

HMSO Bookshops
71 Lothian Road, Edinburgh, EH3 9AZ
0131-228 4181 Fax 0131-229 2734
49 High Holborn, London, WC1V 6HB
0171-873 0011 Fax 0171-873 8200 (counter service only)
68-69 Bell Street, Birmingham, B4 6AD
0121-236 9696 Fax 0121-236 9699
33 Wine Street, Bristol, BS1 2BQ
0121-236 9696 Fax 0121-236 9696
9-21 Princess Street, Manchester, M60 8AS
0161-834 7201 Fax 0161-833 0634
16 Arthur Street, Belfast, BT1 4GD
01232 238451 Fax 01232 235401
The HMSO Oriel Bookshop, The Friary,
Cardiff CF1 4AA
01222 395548 Fax 01222 384347

HMSO's Accredited Agents
(see Yellow Pages)

and through good booksellers

Printed and bound in Great Britain by
Butler & Tanner Ltd, Frome and London